Bob's Red Mill Baking Book

Bob's Red Mill
Baking Book

More than 400 Recipes Featuring Whole & Healthy Grains

By JOHN ETTINGER *and the*
BOB'S RED MILL FAMILY

Foreword by PETER REINHART

RUNNING PRESS
PHILADELPHIA · LONDON

9 8 7 6 5 4 3 2 1

Digit on the right indicates the number of this printing

Library of Congress Control Number: 2006921033

ISBN-13: 978-0-7624-2744-4
ISBN-10: 0-7624-2744-2

Cover design by Corinda Cook
Interior design by Susan Van Horn
Edited by Diana C. von Glahn
Typography: Fairfield and Myriad

This book may be ordered by mail from the publisher.
Please include $2.50 for postage and handling.
But try your bookstore first.

Running Press Book Publishers
125 South Twenty-Second Street
Philadelphia, Pennsylvania 19103-4399

Visit us on the web!
www.runningpresscooks.com
www.bobsredmill.com

Credits

Front cover:
Still life with many types of bread and rolls Copyright © Eising FoodPhotography / Stockfood America

Back cover:
Two Homemade Pizzas: Goat Cheese, Red Onions, Olives and Sardines and Tomato with Basil and Mozzarella Copyright © Conrad & Company Photography / Stockfood America
Garden party cake (summer berry cake, 3) Copyright © Studio Schmitz - StockFood Munich / Stockfood America
Blueberry muffins Copyright ©Brauner/GU - StockFood Munich / Stockfood America

To my wife, Charlee Lucille Coote Moore, who plucked me from the food wilderness and patiently schooled me—meal after meal—in how to traverse the path of healthy eating with whole grain foods, fruits, and vegetables. How she found and shopped in then-obscure natural food stores and made time for scratch baking and meal preparation to nurture our three boys and me remains a mystery. The fact that her ideas gave wings to a business making whole grain foods for every meal of the day—Bob's Red Mill Natural Foods—is certainly no mystery. It is a grand reality.

—Bob Moore

Few things in my life are better than cooking for a couple of young men I love, admire, and can never have too many hours with: my sons Andrew and Joseph.

Now eat boys, you look thin.

—John Ettinger

Contents

ACKNOWLEDGMENTS

This book wouldn't have been possible without a lot of friends. It's lucky that this author and Bob's Red Mill are blessed with so many.

We appreciate the recipe contestants who contributed recipes so enthusiastically, and thank Yvonne Fyan and Chelsea Lincoln for their efforts in reviewing everything. Thanks especially to Dennis Gilliam and Diana von Glahn who both championed the book from the get go, and of course to Bob, who took so much time to convey to both the author and the editor his passion for whole grains. We hope this book reflects that deep and true love of what is his life work. This book would not be here without the unwavering support of Katie Schultze, whose unrelenting confidence is appreciated beyond words. A friend in need, indeed.

Special thanks to Mary Munson for the tireless efforts and hours pouring over the drafts in excruciating detail, truly willing to help in any way to make sure recipes in this book were right. Our gratitude also goes out to the many other contributors and testers: Pauline Baughman, Jan Brazeau, Paula Creamer, Juliet Johnson, Mel Derbyshire, Matthew Cox, Nancy Garner, Rachel Frankel-Moore, Leah Hinchcliff, John Lien, Amy Loy, Jan Mancuso, Caitlin Stone, Allison Cassie, Lori Warner, and Haben Woldu.

And, oh yeah, the author has to say, thanks Mom. You always made a heckuva pie.

Foreword

I teach bread baking at the largest culinary school in the world and every time I get a new class, we talk about the history of baking and milling. I tell them that Oliver Evans is often credited with inventing automated milling sometime around 1785, but he was just a link in a long lineage of anonymous millers who advanced the process from the early days of smashing wheat kernels with a stone, then on to grinding grain between stones, one of them moving while the other remained stationary. Later civilizations harnessed the energy of animals and humans to increase productivity until water and wind mills came along to move that big turning stone. Milling is a long and noble profession, I tell my students, just as is baking.

During the past twenty years or so, artisan bakers have gotten a lot of attention during what has been called an American bread revolution, while millers have received hardly any notice, except from the grateful bakers. What the majority of modern consumers do not realize is how interdependent bakers and millers are, a symbiotic team, the millers being the anonymous, behind-the-scenes players in an intricate drama that begins in the earth and ends in a loaf, a bun, a cake, cookie, muffin, scone, and on and on.

Millers and bakers are an inseparable team who cannot really survive, nor even exist, without the other. The miller is every bit as dedicated to the subtle nuances of transforming grain into flour as the baker is to transforming flour into dough. What Oliver Evans did when he automated his mill was to begin a process that made flour so affordable most people take it for granted and have little appreciation for what it takes for a kernel to grow, be harvested, threshed, tempered, ground, bolted, packaged, and delivered to one's kitchen—all for a few pennies per pound. Who among us truly appreciates how many kernels, precious seeds of life, it takes to make a cup of flour? If we did, we would probably guard every single seed as if our life, and the world, depended on it. And it does.

Of course, we also know that innovation did not begin nor end with Oliver Evans, and that milling advanced into the modern era with all sorts of new toys: huge roller mills and synchronized blowing and sifting systems; climate controlled storage silos; and automated packaging systems all designed to process tons of wheat into flour by the hour. Bakers, too, were presented with new options to increase their productivity via rotating ovens, huge, powerful mixers, conveyer ovens, and additives to speed fermentation and oxidize the dough in the oven to create maximum volume in minimum time. As our population grew and demand for inexpensive baked goods increased, bakers became even more dependent on their mills to supply them with large quantities of quality flour at a reasonable price. And thus were the masses fed.

Toward the end of the twentieth century, the glorious technology revolution spun off its own counter reformation, the artisan movement. We saw it in micro beers, in arts and crafts, in slow food movements, and without a doubt we saw it in bread and milling. There is an implicit assumption in the concept of arti-sanship that slow is better than fast, and that hand crafted is, in some qualitative manner, superior to mass produced. This is not always objectively provable but more of a subjective intuition, emerging from a basic human need called connectivity.

I cannot speak for everyone when I say this, but I get nervous when things seem to be happening too fast, a fear that I am going to lose touch with what is real and important. A nervous little voice wells up inside me, compels me to slow down, call a time out, or just simply connect with something that grounds me in the here and now. It is a natural impulse and, as such, yearns for natural images that connect me to long-valued traditions, deeply rooted memories, and honorable ways of life. I am drawn to song, dance, festivals, wholesome food, and bread made from freshly milled flour. I imagine the miller as an artisan, tending his turning stone, making sure it does not grind too quickly lest it heat up the kernels of grain and clog. I do not want to do away with technology and big mills and big bakeries that feed the masses, but I want to know that there still exist places that are of a human scale, that grind flour for me, that bake loaves for me, that through hand crafted processes and products I can sense and feel the effort of the earth, of nature, of creation, and of human hands that nourish and sustain me. I do want good products at rea-sonable prices, but I want even more. I want these products to be transparent, to reveal through them-selves their very source, and in so doing, to connect me to it as well. By our very nature we cannot and will not abandon the old stone mill. It is an icon imbedded too deeply in our souls.

Peter Reinhart,
author of five books on bread baking,
including *Brother Juniper's Bread Book* and
The Bread Baker's Apprentice

A Letter from Bob Moore

Dear Folks,

You may be wondering, as you look at our recognizable Bob's Red Mill logo, whether or not there is, in fact, a real Bob. Well, of course I'm real. See, that's me at the top of the page! How could my wife Charlee and I have created the Red Mill in the first place if I weren't? If you're not convinced I'm real, come on down to the mill and I'll shake your hand and show you around.

Who ever heard of someone collecting grain milling machinery that was built 100 to 200 years ago, refurbishing it, setting it up in a modern sanitary environment, and then seriously going into the business of supplying natural foods to the world? Well, that's what I did! And it's been great fun, the most challenging and fulfilling thing I've ever accomplished, and it all started with my knack for tinkering.

My first love (besides my wife!) has been machinery. Even as a young lad, I loved to take things apart. From Mom's alarm clocks to Dad's cars, I "fixed" things. Charlee's passion was cooking good, wholesome food. From the moment we were married, she introduced me to health food stores where she bought the flours and cereals she used to prepare healthy meals for me, and soon, our three boys. Eventually, we put our two loves together, and in the early 70s, we created a stone-grinding flour mill and wholesale business that provides healthy, delicious foods to people around the world.

Of course, first I had to learn how to work our charming old stone mills. Through the formative years, I received a lot of help and inspiration by visiting more than fifty stone-grinding flour mills around North America and the British Isles. Some were derelict, some were museums, and several were still running. Early on, I discovered a wealth of information from old milling journals and books available at the Bancroft Library near San Francisco.

As an addendum to this story, we recently discovered a company in Denmark that has been manufacturing stone mills throughout the entire twentieth century. We not only have several of these fine machines running at Bob's Red Mill, but have sold a number of them to small bakeries around the United States. Will wonders never cease?

As you look through the recipes we've collected for you in this book, you will find use for many of the great-tasting grains we make and sell throughout the United States and Canada at many fine retail establishments. For years, our customers have brought their out-of-town relatives and guests to our picturesque and fully operating flour mill. They also send our products as gifts for special holidays and occasions. The recipients of these gifts have literally stuffed our letter files full of notes of praise and thanks for our unique, diverse, and nutritious products.

I hope you enjoy this collection of recipes from the family and friends of Bob's Red Mill, and truly enjoy whole grain goodness for every meal of the day. When you are in Portland, Oregon, come to the mill and see for yourself!

To Your Good Health,

Bob Moore

Bob Moore

Bob's Red Mill: Who Are We?

Bob's Red Mill is dedicated to the manufacturing of natural whole grain foods in a traditional and time-honored way. Despite all the sophisticated technological knowledge and advancements of recent times, no modern machinery has yet been developed that grinds whole grains into flour quite as well as the flint-hard, quartz millstones quarried in France and used by discriminating millers for hundreds of years. At Bob's, our "well-dressed" (meaning sharpened) sets of millstones turn the highest quality grains into a finer consistency, better baking bread flour than any of the hammer mills, steel roller mills, steel buhr mills, or pulverizers ever made. These slow-turning millstones grind the bran, endosperm and germ (which contain nutritious wheat germ oil) into flour in a natural way. The result is a food that's more easily assimilated, healthier, and frankly, more delicious.

At Bob's Red Mill, huge, slow turning, 100-year-old millstones naturally grind together the bran, endosperm, and germ that contains the grain's nutritious oil without overheating it. This cool stone grinding process preserves valuable nutrients that are otherwise lost in conventional high-speed, high-heat milling when the oil in the kernel is exposed to excessive temperature. The heat causes the fat from the germ to oxidize and much of the vitamins to be destroyed. Real stone grinding mixes the germ, its precious oil, and finely ground bran throughout the flour without over-processing or heating it, making for a more easily digested and healthier food.

At Bob's, we mill all common grains (and many unique grains, as well) into the healthy flours and meals (36 different baking flours alone) appearing in the recipes throughout this book, but we also blend a large array of unique cereals, pancake and waffle mixes, bread mixes, and muffin and quick bread mixes. We are continually adding to this list, making our product line of natural, organic, and gluten-free whole grain foods the most varied and complete in the industry.

Our milling staff proudly showing off the source of Bob's Red Mill's uniqueness—stone ground whole grain products.

HOW WE GOT HERE

It was Bob's wife, Charlee, who had introduced the family to wholesome natural foods. Her desire to make healthy alternatives was the start of what would become Bob's Red Mill. At the time, the Moores were living on a five-acre farm in California with their three pre-teen sons, growing their food and canning for the winter. Bob was always interested in how things work, and because of Charlee's interest in whole grains, he wanted to know how the different milling processes were done. One day, Bob came across a book that would change his life: *John Goffe's Mill*, by George Woodbury, told the story of a young man and how he restored his family's old stone grinding flour mill in Bedford, New Hampshire. After reading it, Bob knew that milling would become his life's work.

Charlee doing what she does best—looking pretty and selling whole grains.

Bob began a nationwide search for the French-quarried millstones legendary the world over, but only a few of them survived the industrial revolution. In the late 1800s, high-speed steel roller mills had ushered in a new era of mechanized manufacturing, the result of which was the creation of white flour devoid of wheat's important bran and germ. That fast-paced, high-volume process ended the need for the slow-turning stone mills that had, for centuries, supplied the world with whole grain flours. But Bob persisted, and managed to locate a set of 100-year-old millstones from an old water-powered flourmill in North Carolina. Soon after, Bob's first mill commenced grinding in Northern California. Many of Bob's most popular mixes today, like his 10-Grain Pancake Mix and Date Nut Bran Muffin Mix, were created at that time.

The above picture was taken early on when there were only eleven of us. What a wonderful thrill it has been building a successful, wholesome business from almost nothing to our present 140 employees working in a 165,000 sq. ft. facility.

After building the Northern California mill into a thriving business, Bob and Charlee sold the mill to their sons and moved to Portland, Oregon, to retire and study at a seminary. But soon after the move, the couple stumbled upon a derelict flour mill near historic Oregon City and Bob decided to come out of retirement. The couple purchased the mill and opened up their business. Their mission: grinding whole grains into flours, meals, and cereals, as well as blending whole grain mixes for sale in the greater Portland, Oregon area.

The story of Bob's Red Mill is one of continuous growth and perseverance. In 1988, the Oregon City mill was destroyed by fire. When asked by firefighters what he most wanted to save, Bob replied, "Save the mill stones." The rescue mission was successful and Bob and Charlee were able to rebuild their mill at a lakeside location in Milwaukie, Oregon using the refurbished millstones saved from the fire. Now utilizing three modern facilities totaling 165,000 square feet on six acres, with 135 employees working around the clock, Bob's Red Mill has become a multimillion-dollar business both milling and marketing whole grain natural foods throughout the USA and Canada. But despite the company's fast and tremendous growth, the product's uniqueness and quality remain the same: wholesome goodness and authentic and highly traditional milling techniques make Bob's Red Mill grains, flours, mixes and cereals simply the best.

WHOLE GRAINS: THE REAL THING

At one time, all flour was ground on large, slow-turning millstones using a process that dates back to the days of ancient Rome. References to the importance of stone mills are even in the Old Testament, where we find: "No one shall take a hand mill or upper millstone in pledge, for he will be taking a life in pledge" (Deuteronomy 24:6). Just think: every time you eat a bowl of Bob's Red Mill whole grain cereal or a slice of whole grain bread, you're eating just like the Romans did centuries ago.

A stone mill grinds slowly. When this slower method is coupled with the highest quality wheat, it requires a modest premium price to produce, but the result is worth every penny. Stone mills gradually became obsolete thanks to mechanized steel-roller mills that could grind flour faster and cheaper. Today, there are products claiming to be stone ground whole wheat, and some of these products are offered at a price close to that of high-tech, mass-produced roller milled flour. Some milling companies label their flour as stone ground when they only flush their wheat rapidly through a stone mill and finish the grind on steel rolls. Others mill only a small percentage by stone and then blend it with roller milled flour. Only the flour produced on 100% millstones can rightfully and accurately be called "100% stone ground."

Mill stones. They have occupied my life for well over thirty years. I love their slow, quiet determination to turn out wholesome whole grain flours year upon year for decades without need of replacement. This shot was taken in our mill room. We operate eight milling machines, similar to the one behind me, 24 hours a day.

At Bob's Red Mill, huge, slow turning, millstones naturally grind together the bran, endosperm, and germ that contains the grain's nutritious oil without overheating it, thereby causing the fat in the germ to oxidize and become rancid, destroying some of its nutritious value. This cool stone grinding process preserves valuable nutrients that are otherwise lost in conventional high-speed, high-heat milling. Real stone grinding mixes the germ, its precious oil, and finely ground bran throughout the flour without overprocessing it, making for a more easily digested and healthier food.

For years, Bob has traveled the country searching for abandoned mills and successfully turning up stone mills of this age-old craft.

The Famous Quarries of Le Fert-sous-Jouarre

Imagine your car breaking down and the only repair person who knew how to fix it lived more than 100 years ago. If it weren't for yellowed milling journals and turn-of-the-twentieth-century repair manuals, Bob's Red Mill would be in the same predicament. Now transport yourself to Le Fert-sous-Jouarre, France, 40 miles east of Paris. This town was famous for its quartz quarries that produced buhrs (chunks of stone) perfect for millstone production. The porosity and hardness of this stone make it perfect for millstones. Buhrs, or chunks of stone, were delivered to the rough finishing yard for trimming. The stone was shaped, fitted, glued and banded by artisans. The igneous deposits there produced stone for millstones for the world's flour mills from at least the 1400s. The quarry still supplies stone for the Skijold Mills in Denmark. Because of the superiority of these mill stones, Bob's Red Mill uses many French Buhr Millstones that were hand cut and assembled in Le Fert-sous-Jouarre in the 1870s.

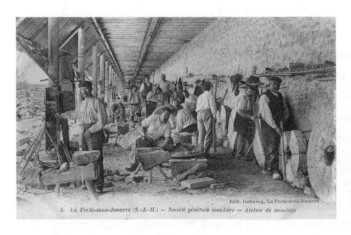

5. La Ferté-sous-Jouarre (S.-&-M.) — Société générale meulière — Atelier de montage

LA FERTÉ-sous-JOUARRE (S.-et-M.) — La générale Meullière

Bob's Red Mill Grain Primer

At Bob's Red Mill, we live, breathe, and (naturally) eat whole grains. We've made it our job and our passion to provide you with the finest grain products available anywhere, and to show you how to use and prepare them in the most delicious manner possible. When we talk about grains that are processed the old-fashioned way, we do so knowing that they comprise one of the greatest components of a healthy diet rich in vitamins, fiber, and protein, making them a perfect food.

But what, exactly, are grains? Simply, they are the seeds and fruits of cereal grasses, and the most nutritionally valuable of all foods. Cultivated for more than 10,000 years, grains comprise the most widely consumed food group the world over.

Hold a tiny grain in your hand and you'll be looking at a humble yet complex food consisting of many parts:

HULL—A grain's tough protective coating that is inedible and removed from most grains prior to grinding.

BRAN—Envelops and protects the kernel and germ during the reproductive process. The bran layer holds the moisture needed by the germ to sprout. Bran is rich in B vitamins and minerals and is one of the best and most available sources of dietary fiber. Unfortunately, it is totally milled away to make white flour.

GERM—Found at the base of the kernel. The germ contains the life force that sprouts with a new plant when the kernel of grain is sown. Germ is high in Vitamins E and B1, unsaturated fats, and protein. Bob's Red Mill is a major provider of pure wheat germ, which can be added to almost all cooking and baking as an excellent nutrition booster. You can even sprinkle it on ice cream, it tastes great!

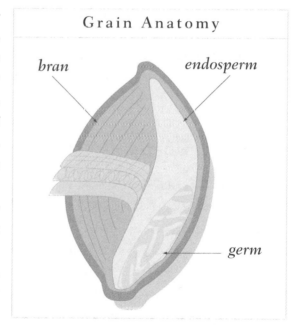

Grain Anatomy

bran   *endosperm*

germ

ENDOSPERM—The largest part of the grain kernel, consisting mostly of starch and protein. In the life cycle of wheat, the germ draws moisture from the bran layer to begin the sprouting process and draws its nutrition from the endosperm until the root grows sufficiently to bring nutrients from the soil and begin forming the mature plant. A wonderful little world all its own! Alas, this creamy white portion of the kernel is all that is left in white flour. Both the bran and the germ are milled away and replaced with a few chemical vitamins and minerals—a very sorry trade-off.

This description is similar in function to most all cereal grains from Amaranth to Wheat.

The Grind

Grains can be ground to several different consistencies, specifically for different purposes. At Bob's Red Mill, we create our products in the following grinds:

FLOUR—Grain that is slowly stone ground on buhr stones at very cool temperatures. Absolutely nothing is removed. All the bran and germ is reduced to a very fine flour consistency.

GRAHAM FLOUR—A slightly coarser whole wheat flour. Small quantities can be substituted in bread recipes for a coarser, crunchier effect.

MEAL—Grain that has been stone ground with the stones separated slightly to allow a coarser product.

FARINA—Grains carefully milled into tiny granules, free from flour.

CRACK—Grains stone ground into larger pieces, free from flour.

STEEL CUT—A whole kernel of grain (oats, barley, wheat, etc.) cut into about three pieces by passing it through two rotating steel rolls configured to cut rather than grind the grain.

ROLLED OR FLAKED—Grain that has been infused with steam and rolled flat between two smooth rolls. The moisture from the steam keeps the grain from fracturing while it is being rolled and imparts a deep and delightful toasted flavor to the rolled grain.

WORDS WE USE FOR PEOPLE AND EQUIPMENT

GRISTMILLER—An artisan trained in the stone-milling tradition who is capable of setting, adjusting and operating a sharpened set of millstones to produce flour, meal, farina, and cracks.

MILLWRIGHT—The person who dresses or sharpens the stones and sees to the maintenance of these venerable machines. It takes many years to learn this trade to do it right. This skill is passed on to others by hands-on demonstration and guidance. We have several well-trained millwrights on our staff, including Bob himself.

FRENCH BUHR STONES— The world's finest flint-hard quartz millstones, quarried in the region of La Fert-sous-Jouarre, France, since the early 1400s.

DRESSING THE STONES—The process, also called "sharpening," whereby mill picks or pneumatic chisels are used to periodically redefine the furrows and roughen the surface of a set of millstones.

WHOLE GRAINS, FIBER, AND GOOD HEALTH

Studies show, and the USDA recommends, that while we need about 48 grams of fiber a day for optimal health, most Americans only consume a small percentage of this recommendation on a daily basis. The answer to this problem is to fill your diet with the whole grains, fruits, and vegetables that will increase your intake of both insoluble and soluble fiber. Insoluble fiber (found in wheat bran, and many fruits and vegetables) greatly benefits the digestive tract by helping to push along waste. Soluble fiber (fiber that dissolves in water) helps prevent cholesterol from being absorbed into the blood stream. Soluble fiber is found in oats and oat bran, dried beans and peas, barley, flaxseed, and nuts.

A study published in February 2003 by the American Journal of Clinical Nutrition* shows that men who eat just one serving of whole-grain cereal a day are as much as 20 percent less likely to die from heart disease, diabetes, or cancer than those who do not. The research, which began in 1982, involved information collected for twenty years from more than 85,000 doctors. The results were clear:

- The more whole grain cereal the men ate, the lower their risk of heart disease.
- The men who ate whole grain had a 28 percent lower risk of death due to heart disease, and a 23 percent lower risk of heart attack.
- The health benefits remained even taking into account other health factors, such as high alcohol intake, smoking, etc.

The Mayo Clinic recognizes the value of including whole grains into our diets. They note that consumers should look for whole grain products, and make sure the whole grain appears as the first ingredient listed. Here are some of the Clinic's recommendations for getting whole grains into every meal:

- Eat high-fiber cereals for breakfast.
- Replace bagels and toast with whole grain versions, and substitute whole grain low-fat muffins for pastries.
- Substitute whole grain breads for white bread.
- Add wild rice, barley, and other grains to soups, stews, salads, and casseroles.
- Use whole wheat tortillas.
- Serve a side of kasha, brown rice, wild rice, quinoa, or bulgur instead of potatoes, or add these cooked whole grains to a salad.
- Add whole wheat breadcrumbs, rolled oats, or brown rice to ground meat.

As we learn more about the health benefits of a diet rich in whole grains, more Americans are incorporating them into their diets. Many Americans eat some sort of whole grain food everyday, and the numbers grow daily. Just a note about our grain industry—the recent increase in demand for whole grains is reflected in the appearance of whole grain products made by the snack industry and sugary breakfast cereals now made with whole grains. But like everything else, not all whole grain products are created equal, so it's important to read the nutritional labels before you make your purchase. A breakfast cereal or snack item that touts whole grains in one inch block letters across the front of the box may be better for your body than one made with processed grains devoid of fiber and germ, but the high percentage of sugar, corn syrup, dextrose, and artificial fruit syrups is still sugar added to your body. High sugar intake leads to diabetes, obesity, and hyperactivity in children. A large intake of sugar raises your blood sugar level rapidly and just as quickly lets it down again, leading to hunger in a very short time, making us ever hungry and ever eating.

* SOURCE: American Journal of Clinical Nutrition, February 2003.
http://www.webmd.com/content/article/61/67445.htm?lastselectedguid=%7B5FE84E90-BC77-4056-A91C 9531713CA348%7D.

BOB'S RED MILL GRAINS FROM A TO Z

Amaranth

The name *amaranth* comes from the Greek word for immortal, but while eating amaranth won't necessarily make you live forever, the seed itself is practically indestructible. Amaranth is not a cereal grass or a grain, but a broad-leafed annual related to leafy greens, including chard and spinach. The tall plant has a brilliant maroon color (the leaves are used for food coloring) and its heads each contain thousands of seeds.

The Aztecs built their empire on amaranth, which they prized for providing their warriors with energy and strength; the seeds evolved to rival corn as the New World's most important crop. On ritual holidays, the Aztecs combined Amaranth flour with honey and shaped it into deities, birds, and animals. They also made celebratory cakes with it. However, to ensure Spain's conquest of the New World, the Spanish conquistador Hernán Cortes ordered the crops and seed burned and destroyed, marking the end of the Aztec empire.

Today, Amaranth has made a comeback. Seeds discovered in Aztec ruins a thousand years old have been cultivated and sprouted in North America. Amaranth flour has a taste described as earthy, woodsy and even grassy. Its tiny seeds can only be processed into flour by stone grinding, which is why Bob's is one of the few providers of amaranth flour in the world.

Amaranth's popularity is growing in part because it is an excellent source of high quality, balanced protein, thanks to its enormous amount of lysine, the amino acid that controls protein absorption. It has almost twice the fiber of wheat, and is high in vitamin E, iron, and calcium. It is also very low in sodium and contains no saturated fat.

Although Amaranth has no gluten, Amaranth flour is often used in quick breads, cookies, and baked goods, but is not quite as useful for yeast breads. It must be mixed with wheat flour to make leavened breads. Amaranth flour increases moisture retention and shelf life in your baked goods. Bob's Red Mill packages whole grain Amaranth grain and stone ground Amaranth flour.

Barley

Barley has fed us through the millennia with flour and cereals, and helped us imbibe by providing us with the makings for beers and malt spirits. Barley has been a staple for many ancient cultures in need of dense, chewy flatbreads. It is believed to be among the first cereals cultivated in the Middle East. The Egyptians, Vikings, and Romans all had considerable amounts of barley in their diets. Four thousand years ago, barley grew wild in northern Asia, but food gatherers had to watch the ripening kernels very closely. They often shattered and their value was lost to the winds.

Barley is popular with farmers because it is one of the hardiest perennials, able to withstand flood, frost, and drought. It also has a short growing season and can be grown almost anywhere—from icy

Finland to the warm Mediterranean shores.

Barley flour is low in gluten and thus provides a more textured and heavier loaf when baked. The flour has a slightly sweet, malty taste and adds moisture to whatever you combine it with, creating a loaf that will last a little longer than breads baked with flour. However, too much barley can make for too chewy a loaf, so mix it up with other flours. Adding about 1/2 cup of barley flour to white flour in your favorite loaf is enough to give it more flavor and nutrition.

Barley contains up to three times the protein of an equal serving of rice, is high in fiber, selenium, and triptophan, and may help lower cholesterol. It has been shown to help prevent gallstones and many people believe it significantly reduces the risk of colon cancer.

Barley's nutty flavor is somewhat similar to brown rice, and it is a better breakfast choice than oats for persons with Type 2 diabetes because studies have shown that it effectively reduces glucose and insulin responses.

Barley has a tough, tenacious hull that must be removed by friction, a process called *pearling*. Heavy pearling removes the nutritious bran and germ. At Bob's Red Mill, we use simple, de-hulled barley to mill our flour and make rolled grain, leaving all the nutritious bran and germ intact.

Bob's Red Mill produces Barley Flour from 100% stone ground, whole grain barley. We also make Malted Barley Flour, made from sprouted whole grain barley, package Barley Grits/Meal (tiny chunks of the barley grain), and Rolled Barley Flakes, which can be used in recipes in place of rolled oats and also makes a great hot breakfast cereal. Bob's Red Mill carries Pearl Barley and a Whole, Hull-less Barley, a type of barley which allows the whole grain to be used, retaining the bran layers.

Bulgur

Bulgur is simply wheat that has been steamed whole, dried and then cracked. Since it is essentially pre-cooked it is easy to use; it needs no cooking, just soaking time. Bulgur is made from hard red wheat, and from soft white wheat for a slightly lighter taste and texture. Bob's features both, and both have the traditional nutty flavor. The process for making bulgur goes back to at least 4,000 years ago, when it was created in areas around the Middle East. After steaming, the grain was spread in the sun to dry, making it a food that traveled very well and was easy to prepare anywhere water was found. High in fiber and protein, bulgur is used in soups, baked goods, and as stuffing. It is best known by most Americans as the staple in tabbouleh, the Middle Eastern salad.

Fava

Until the discovery of the broad diversilty of beans from the New World, Fava beans were the most prominent and widely used beans in Europe. Related to the pea, they are one of the oldest known cultivated plants—fava seeds have been found in the Middle East dating to 2400 B.C. Called, among other things, horse beans, pigeon beans, and daffa beans, fava beans are high in fiber and iron, and low in sodium and fat. If you can find them fresh, parboil them, remove the tough outer skin, simmer them for 30 minutes, and then puree them with extra-virgin olive oil, garlic, and lemon, for a wonderfully healthy and delicious spread. At Bob's Red Mill, we stone grind dried fava beans into flour and combine this with garbanzo bean flour to produce a much-favored, all-purpose gluten-free baking mix. We finely stone grind Fava Flour and Garbanzo & Fava Bean Flour, both of which are gluten free, and package Fava Beans (blanched) which have had the seed coat removed.

Garbanzo

This Middle Eastern bean has a recorded history going back almost 7,000 years, and a record of cultivation going back 5,000 years. It isn't surprising that most garbanzos today are grown and eaten in India, Pakistan, Turkey, and Ethiopia given the famous garbanzo-based dishes emanating from those countries, like hummus, falafel, and curry. But garbanzos are also grown in the Americas, where they are called chickpeas.

Garbanzos are high in soluble fiber and protein, which makes them good for lowering cholesterol. They also contain molybdenum, which detoxifies sulfites in the body. If you've reacted to sulfites—preservatives found in salad bars, deli foods, wine, and many other common foods—it may be because your body doesn't have enough molybdenum. Garbanzo beans are also a good choice for those with hypoglycemia and diabetes. Garbanzo beans, dried and finely stone ground, are used primarily in gluten-free recipes. Many of our gluten-free mixes at Bob's Red Mill also use 100% stone ground garbanzo flour as the primary ingredient.

Soy

Soybeans had an inauspicious beginning in America, arriving early in the nineteenth century as ballast for a ship. It wasn't until the end of that century that farmers began growing the bean, mostly as a crop to feed livestock. Needless to say, the soybean has been much more revered in other parts of the world, where it has been cultivated as far back as seventeenth century B.C. In 2853 B.C., Emperor Shen-Nung of China named the soybean one of five sacred plants, along with millet, rice, wheat and barley. Sea and land trade routes brought the soy bean to Japan, Southeast Asia and India by the fifteenth century B.C. Highly regarded in the Far East where much of the world's crop is consumed, it has nonetheless become very popular in the United States, which is now responsible for about half of the world's soy bean production.

Soy flour, from milled soybeans, is highly nutritious, cholesterol-free, full of vitamins, minerals, and especially protein. It significantly reduces blood pressure and cholesterol. For everyday baking, soy flour should not be substituted entirely for wheat. However, you can replace up to 25 percent for more protein and a longer shelf life. A growing percentage of today's soybean crop is used in the manufacture of tofu (soy cheese). Bob's Red Mill stone grinds dried soy beans into Soy Flour, retaining all the nutritious fiber and oils. We also package Low Fat Soy Flour, Soy Beans, and Defatted Soy Grits, all of which add nutrition and texture to casseroles, soups, and cooked cereals.

Buckwheat

Buckwheat is the seed of an herb, nutritionally similar to wheat, but gluten-free. Bob's Red Mill buckwheat flour is ground from buckwheat groats, and is perfect for pancakes, to which it adds a malt flavor. It thrives in adverse conditions, managing to survive drought, frost, and floods. Unlike its cousin, rhubarb, buckwheat is not prized for its stalk. Instead, the shell of the grain is dried and crushed, thereby creating buckwheat groats.

Buckwheat comes from Central Asia, on the border between Siberia and Manchuria, where it has fed the locals since the tenth century A.D. It didn't reach Europe until the Middle Ages, when it was probably brought by the Moors. The French, Italian, and Spanish still call buckwheat *sarrasin*, derived from the name for Arab nomads, *saracen*. The Dutch, who brought buckwheat to the New World (legend holds that it was part of a dowry) where it thrived in the Hudson Valley, gave us the modern day name. They thought so much of buckwheat they felt it must have come from God, so they called it *boek weit* (book wheat, after the Scriptures).

Buckwheat is one of the best-known sources of complex carbohydrates. It fuels the body and saves protein for other things, like tissue repair and cell building. All eight amino acids—lysine, leucine, methionine, isoleucine, tryptophan, threonine, phenylalanine, and valine—are in buckwheat. There are few more complete proteins. Buckwheat is also high in thiamine, riboflavin, and other B complex vitamins, and rich in calcium and phosphorus.

Buckwheat is believed to lower risks associated with high blood pressure and high cholesterol in part because it is high in magnesium, which relaxes blood vessels and therefore improves blood flow. Buckwheat is simply great for your cardiovascular system. It even helps prevent diabetes—in a six-year Iowa study,* women who ate foods high in magnesium, like buckwheat, had a 24 percent lower risk of diabetes. Part of buckwheat's benefits stem from its supply of flavonoids. These phyto-chemicals extend the action of vitamin C and act as antioxidants.

Buckwheat has a strong, nutty flavor and should be combined with other ingredients. Buckwheat is digested more slowly and thus may leave you feeling full even though you're eating less. That makes it great for dieting. Buckwheat is a gluten-free grain. At Bob's Red Mill, we stone grind Organic Buckwheat Flour from our Buckwheat Groats, the whole grain, hulled seeds of the buckwheat plant. We also offer stone ground Buckwheat Pancake and Waffle Mix and Organic Kasha, which are the roasted, hulled buckwheat kernels.

Corn

Indigenous to the Americas, corn has been a staple in native civilizations for thousands of years. Even Christopher Columbus' crew members were amazed by this incredible crop: their notes indicate attempts to describe the odd green stalks full of yellow or white kernels the natives called *maize*. They reported that

* Meyer KA, Kishi LH, Jacobs DR Jr., Slavin J, Sellers TA, Folsom AR. Carbohydrates, dietary fiber, and incident type 2 diabetes in older women. Am J Clin Nutr 1999;71:921-30.

it tasted good raw, cooked, or even dried, ground into a flour and baked. Columbus carried as much as he could back to Europe along with his other New World treasures including tomatoes and squash. The relatively small amount he brought back produced five thousand ears of corn three years later. Today, the United States continues to lead the world in corn production.

Cornmeal is made from dried corn kernels that are ground into flour. Many commercial cornmeals have had the germ removed during the milling process, which also removes the character, the flavor, and some of the nutrition. Bob's Red Mill's stone ground cornmeal contains the bran and germ, and is far more nutritious. Blue cornmeal is slightly sweeter, and absorbs a bit more liquid than yellow cornmeal, so be sure to compensate if you're substituting. Cornmeal is great for baking because it becomes a whole food with essential amino acids when combined with other grains and animal proteins—including butter, milk, and cheese.

Whole corn and stone ground cornmeal are high in fiber, and have significant amounts of folate, which prevents damage to blood vessels. It also contains beta-cryptoxanthin, which studies show prevents lung cancer.

Cornstarch is the ground starch from the corn kernel and used primarily as a thickener. It needs to be cooked before being added to a recipe, or the resulting dish will have a chalky taste. It reaches its full expansion at boiling, and may be boiled a minute longer to thicken. After that, the granules begin to collapse and the cornstarch will thin out. It should not be stirred vigorously, or the same effect will occur—a collapse and lack of thickening. Adding cornstarch to recipes can create fragile and delicate cookies and cakes. Rice and potato starch flour may be used in place of recipes calling for cornstarch, as can arrowroot.

From the Native American tales of "Mother Corn" leading the people to safety, to terms like "off the cob" (a little crazy), corn has given us nourishment for our language and our bodies. In baseball a "can of corn" is an easily caught ball, the old "Jimmy Crack Corn" was a minstrel song, "corn-fed" means well fed, and a cornball is, well, a cornball.

Corn was originally the English word for grain. The new Americans apparently didn't like the native word, *maize*, so they called it "Indian corn" and then shortened it to corn. Corn was such an important part of the nineteenth century diet that the term was used to describe many things of value—you could jingle the corn in your pockets, chew with your corn grinders, admit you were wrong by acknowledging the corn, and get attention by being all for corn. Oh, and those prone to boasting were "as full of wind as a corn eating horse." In the Southwest, they went even further, with terms such as "corn weather" (hot), and "corn twisters" (dry spells), "corn on the tongue" (looking for a wife), and "corn shaker" (someone who is so good looking, the corn stalks shake when he or she is nearby). And they don't find a darn thing about all of that to be corny.

Corn was so popular, recipes using corn were even captured in rhyme. This recipe for cornbread appears in the 1917 book, *American Indian Corn,* by Charles J. Murphy:

Two cups Indian, one cup wheat,

One cup sour milk, one cup sweet,

One good egg that well you beat.

Half cup molasses, too;

Half cup sugar add thereto,

With one spoon of butter new.

Salt and soda each a teaspoon;

Mix up quick and bake it soon.

Then you'll have corn bread complete,

Best of all corn bread you meet.

It will make your boy's eyes shine,

If he's like that boy of mine.

If you have a dozen boys

To increase your household joys,

Double then this rule I should,

And you'll have two corn cakes good.

Corn is gluten-free and gradually working its way into gluten-free diets. Bob's Red Mill turns out a variety of corn products, including Corn Grits (Polenta), and three different granulations of 100% stone ground cornmeal—coarse, medium, and fine. We also stone grind Blue and White Cornmeal, Corn Flour, and we produce a delicious, stone ground Cornmeal Pancake and Waffle Mix. Corn is one of the whole grains in our 10-Grain Pancake and Waffle Mix and in several of our hot cereals, including 8-Grain Wheatless Cereal, 10-Grain Cereal, Mighty Tasty Hot Cereal (gluten-free), and 6-Grain Organic Right Stuff Cereal.

Kamut® Grain

Kamut® grain is an ancient relative of durum wheat, and is very high in protein (30% higher than wheat), zinc, B vitamins, vitamin E, and magnesium. It's great for boosting your immune system and has anti-inflammatory properties. Kamut grain has a high gluten content and can replace whole wheat flour in recipes. It is best to use a mix of Kamut flour and a wheat flour.

Beyond being delicious, Kamut grain has an interesting history. Six thousand years ago, Kamut grain was king of the Nile (at least food-wise). The most important grain in the region, it was lost when the Greeks came to Egypt and replaced the Kamut fields with wheat. In 1949, a Montana airman stationed in Portugal was given, or bought, 36 wheat kernels said to be taken from an ancient tomb in Egypt. The air-man, Earl Deadman, mailed them to his father who planted them. Six years later, the farmer had 1,500 bushes of this Egyptian wheat. They dubbed it "King Tut's Wheat," took it to county fairs where it was a curiosity, but the consumers weren't buying and it ended up as animal feed.

Twenty years later, a young organic wheat farmer named Bob Quinn remembered seeing the grain at a fair and tracked down a single pint of the wheat, enough to save the grain from extinction once again. He named the grain *Kamut*, believed to be the ancient Egyptian word for grain. At Bob's Red Mill, we stone grind this organic Kamut® grain into flour and cereal, and package Organic Kamut® Berries which can be used in pilafs, cold salads, soups, or as a substitute for beans in chili.

Millet

Millet has been around so long that some speculate the dinosaurs may have eaten the grain. This grain is a good source of iron, potassium, and protein. Once almost exclusively used for birdseed in America and Europe, people in our part of the world are only beginning to discover its value. Millet is the seed of a cereal grass and is used around the world as a replacement for rice and barley, and often added to soups and stews. A relative of sorghum, millet is easy to digest.

No one is quite sure where it was first cultivated, many believe it to have been in Asia, since that is where, five thousand years ago, it was considered one of China's sacred crops. Referred to in the Bible as "the gruel of endurance," it may have also come from Africa because it survives drought exceptionally well (it actually hibernates, and reawakens when rains return) and is found all over the continent. The Gauls, Romans, Greeks, Assyrians, and Visigoths considered millet to help clear the mind and build the body.

Eating millet can protect your heart and your head. With high amounts of magnesium, it is heart-healthy, and is also thought to help reduce the severity of asthma and the frequency of migraines. Millet is often called the least allergenic flour, and is gluten-free. It is particularly good in muffins and quick breads, and can be used in gluten-free cooking, but will not make a bread on its own. Bob's Red Mill packages Millet Flour; Millet Grits/Meal, which makes a great hot cereal; and Hulled Millet, which adds a nice crunch to muffins and quick breads.

Flaxseed

Delicious flaxseed has long been recognized around the world as a whole grain food offering amazing health benefits. Flax is a blue-flowered plant crop grown mainly along the western Canadian prairies. Flax is rich in heart-healthy omega-3 fatty acids, alpha-linolenic acid, and fiber. It also contains *lignans*, which provide invaluable help in preventing cancers, especially of the colon and breast. There are three ways to get flax in your diet—flax seeds, flax meal (which is simply flax seeds coarsely ground), and flax oil.

Flax also adds a wonderfully nutty taste when added to foods we eat every day. Simply sprinkle a handful of seeds into bread or pastry dough, or add them to the finished product. You can even toss some of the seeds into your favorite casseroles. Whole flax seeds are a good source of fiber, but grinding the seeds into meal allows our bodies to assimilate all the wonderful nutrients flaxseeds offer. Sprinkle flaxseed meal on salads, over hot cereal, on sandwich fillings, or even stir it into your morning orange juice. If you can't add it directly to your food, take a teaspoon or so of flax oil a day straight from the bottle or try adding it to salad dressings. You can substitute flaxseed meal for eggs in a recipe by combining 1 tablespoon flaxseed meal with 3 tablespoons of water and letting it sit for a couple of minutes until it gels.

Bob's Red Mill packages Whole Flaxseed (both Brown and Organic Golden) and stone grinds these two varieties of flax seeds into Flaxseed Meal.

Oats

Oats were cultivated to feed animals as far back as the Bronze Age. When humans began to feast on the grain is unknown, however, as early as the fifth century A.D. it was reported that Attila's troops were fed a porridge of oats. He believed it made them fierce. It is said that Alexander the Great fed his storied horse Esepheus only oats because the grain flourished in the southern wind, and he thought his horse's speed would increase as a result. Long considered to be a food for the poor, oats were disdained by the middle and upper classes until the Crusaders, who sustained themselves on oats they carried in saddlebags, discovered it gave them more energy and made them feel stronger. This prompted them to plant the crop upon returning to their native lands.

Oats contain seven B vitamins, Vitamin E, calcium, and iron. They are very easy to digest, and are high in protein. Oats are so high in fiber, they can easily help fill the recommended 48 grams of fiber per day.

Bob's Red Mill's oats are uniquely "kiln toasted" whole grain oats with the bran still intact. This intensifies their hearty flavor. Whole grain Steel Cut Oats, also called Irish oats, are tempered and cut between two steel rolls. They make for the chewiest oats. Scottish Oatmeal is the original porridge of ancient Scotland. This true whole grain oatmeal is stone ground, not rolled, on our century-old mills. Rolled oats are made from grain that has been infused with steam and rolled flat between two smooth rolls. The moisture from the steam keeps the grain from fracturing while it is being rolled. The rollers can be adjusted to create a thin, quick-cooking rolled oat, a regular rolled oat, or a thick rolled oat.

Not surprisingly, oats are the whole grain consumed most by North Americans, usually as a bowl of oatmeal in the morning. Oatmeal remains one of the best ways to start the day, especially for anyone concerned about heart disease or diabetes (isn't that all of us?). This wonderful food helps reduce cholesterol and regulate blood sugar.

Oat Bran is the outer layer of the oat groat that has been removed by machine. When cooked as a cereal, it has a wonderful creaminess. Oat bran can be added to most baking recipes in small quantities to increase the fiber.

Because whole grain oat flour is naturally gluten free, it cannot replace all of the flour in a recipe. But it is good in quick and leavened breads, along with many other recipes, when mixed with wheat flour. It does not rise as wheat does so your loaf may be a little smaller.

Bob's Red Mill packages a wide assortment of oat products, including Instant, Quick-Cooking, Old Fashioned, and Thick Rolled Oats; Oat Bran Cereal; Steel Cut Oats; Scottish Oatmeal; and Oat Flour.

These products provide the foundation for many great-tasting dishes that are in no way limited to breakfast alone.

Quinoa

Like amaranth, quinoa (pronounced KEEN-wah) —a nutty and delicious grain that can be used in everything from salad to soups and stews—is packed with lysine, one of the essential amino acids not found in wheat. It also has many B vitamins, vitamin E, iron, and enough calcium in a serving to equal a quart of milk. This little gem of a grain is arguably the most nutritious of all, with as much as 22 percent protein, making it a spectacular addition to any diet. Quinoa also supplies a complete protein—it includes all nine essential amino acids.

To the Incans, quinoa was the "mother grain." It was sacred to them because they believed it gave them long life. Folklore suggests the explorer Pizzaro inadvertently named the grain after tasting it and declaring it to be *quimera* or fantastic. (This was later mistranslated into the name we use today.) Quinoa's revival has been recent. While still growing wild in parts of Ecuador, Peru, and Bolivia, few people outside the region cultivated the grain until the 1980s. Quinoa is one of the few grains that can flourish at very high altitudes. This purplish red plant has leaves similar to spinach, with large seed heads.

Bob's Red Mill stone grinds Organic Quinoa Flour, perfect for those on a gluten-free diet. We also package whole grain Organic Quinoa Grain which is an excellent addition to cold salads, soups, and casseroles.

Rice

It is estimated that six out of ten people in the world eat rice daily, so it is not an overstatement to say that rice feeds the world. Still grown primarily in southeast Asia, where it is believed to have been first cultivated about 4,000 years ago and where heavy rains provide the water necessary to grow the grain, rice is grown on every continent. It came to Europe around the fifth century B.C.

There are two species of rice: Asian (*oryza sativa*) and African red rice (*oryza globerrina*). The short, medium, and long grain varieties Americans eat, mostly grown in Texas and California, come from the Asian species.

Bob's Red Mill stone grinds both whole grain brown rice flour and white rice flour. They can both be used in gluten free recipes and adds tenderness to shortbread and cakes. Whole grain brown rice flour is rich in fiber and low in sodium. It has almost all complex carbohydrates with a little protein, phosphorus, and potassium, and is a great source of manganese, selenium, and B vitamins. White rice begins as brown rice, but its germ and bran layers are mechanically removed. However, the germ and bran makes brown rice more nutritious than white rice. One of the key benefits of brown rice is a healthier nervous system, thanks primarily to the manganese.

Bob's Red Mill stone grinds whole grain Brown Rice Flour, White Rice Flour, and Sweet White Rice Flour, all of which work wonderfully in gluten-free baked goods. We package Rice Bran, the nutritious outer husk and germ of the rice kernel, and "Creamy Rice" Brown Rice Farina Cereal, which is freshly milled from whole grain brown rice. Bob's Red Mill packages a wide assortment of rice, including Arborio, Basmati, Long and Short Grain Rice, Wild Rice and Sweet Rice.

Rye

Rye is a hardy field grass that grew on the edges of the wheat fields in southern Europe and parts of Asia. This tough little plant needed less attention and care than its non-wild counterparts, and was therefore able to grow further north and at higher altitudes, winning the attention of farmers from Russia throughout Western Europe. In fact, rye can be grown in a wide range of conditions. The English and Dutch brought rye to America, planting crops in New England.

The earthy flavor of rye remains a favorite in Europe, making for rich breads, especially in Germany. It is used in a variety of recipes in this book, adding texture and flavor. Whole grain dark rye flour is more nutritious with twice the protein of light rye, since it contains the whole kernel. Light rye flour has had the germ and bran removed for a lighter flavor. Use either in this book, with dark flour making a denser loaf.

Rye is similar to wheat nutritionally, with dark rye having the highest percentage of lysine of any grain, lots of B vitamins, Vitamin E, protein, and iron. Rye flour is good for those watching their intake of food, because it expands in the stomach, giving a feeling of fullness so you eat less (think of having a few rye crackers before dinner). It is also good for energy and endurance.

Rye's distinctive flavor comes during the rise. It ferments and sours as it rises. For a less sour taste, you can use tepid rather than warm water and let it rise in a slightly cooler place in the house. Bob's Red Mill's Organic Dark Rye Flour is 100% stone ground here at our mill. Organic Pumpernickel Dark Rye Meal adds flavor and texture to your favorite rye breads and can be cooked for a nutritious hot cereal while our Light Rye Flour (unbleached) has the germ and bran removed to make a lighter rye bread, both in texture and color. Bob's Red Mill offers Rolled Rye Flakes, whole grain rye that has been gently steamed and rolled into flat flakes; and Organic Cracked Rye, which makes a very satisfying hot whole grain cereal.

Sorghum

Sorghum is the world's fifth largest cereal grass crop and is primarily consumed in Africa, where it has been eaten for as many as 9,000 years. Plant fossils from ceramic vessels dating to 4000 B.C. show that the grass was prized even then for cooking and baking. Sorghum is particularly drought resistant and able to thrive in high temperatures. It grows wild in Ethiopia, Egypt, and Libya. Scholars believe it is native to Ethiopia and was first cultivated along the Nile between 1000 and 3000 B.C.

This close relative to sugar cane became popular in other parts of the African continent around 200 A.D. It remains an important food across Africa, cooked daily in soups or porridges and used for making flatbread. It also goes by many names including *kafir corn, milo, durra,* and *sorgos.*

Sorghum has a taste similar to wheat, but it is gluten-free, and contains many minerals, including calcium, phosphorus, potassium, and niacin. This is a reliable combination for reducing high blood pressure, lowering cholesterol, and fighting depression. Because it contains no gluten, you can't substitute sorghum flour for wheat flour when baking, but you can replace up to 20 percent with sorghum flour for a sweeter and denser final product. Since sorghum has the most wheat-like flavor profile of all the nonglutenous grains, prominent recipe developers for the gluten-free community turn to Bob's Red Mill stone ground Sorghum Flour as they formulate new recipes. Additionally, many of our signature gluten-free mixes, such as Gluten Free Pancake Mix, Gluten Free Chocolate Cake Mix, and our Homemade Wonderful Bread Mix, contain sorghum flour.

Spelt

Spelt, a distant cousin to wheat, is one of the oldest cultivated grains and one of the most nutritious. Five thousand years ago, farmers in the Middle East and southern Europe were growing this wonderful, nutty tasting grain called *farro* in Italy, and dinkle in Germany. Spelt was mentioned in the Bible, and was also an important food for the ancient Greeks. It remains popular in much of northern Europe where it is used for breads and muffins.

Spelt grows with a tough, tenacious husk that must be mechanically removed, making spelt more expensive to process than wheat. This contributed to spelt's decline in popularity. However, the tremendous health benefits in spelt were too much to keep a great grain down for long, and this delicious food is now enjoying quite a comeback. Many folks who are allergic to wheat have found they can tolerate spelt, plus stone ground spelt flour makes a wonderful loaf of bread because of its high gluten content. Now found baked into breads in many supermarkets and health-conscious restaurants, spelt is extremely rich in Vitamin B2 and manganese, and packed with B vitamins (just two ounces gives you 24 percent of the daily requirement for niacin), copper, and tryptophan. Some research suggests that spelt helps fight migraines since Vitamin B2 improves energy metabolism in brain and muscle cells. The high amounts of niacin in spelt will help reduce cholesterol and the risk of heart disease.

Spelt flour can be easily substituted for wheat flour in many recipes. Spelt is highly water-soluble, making its nutrients easily absorbed into the body.

Bob's Red Mill stone grinds 100% whole grain Spelt Flour as well as stone ground Light Spelt Flour, which has a portion of the bran layer removed, making a good, all-purpose flour. We also package whole grain Spelt Berries and Rolled Spelt Flakes, which make a delightful hot breakfast cereal.

Teff

Teff, or *tef*, originated in Ethiopia at the source of the Blue Nile some 6,000 years ago. This very tiny grain—about 150 grains weigh as much as one kernel of wheat—is an important part of Ethiopian culture and tradition. The region's everyday basic bread, *injera*, is made from teff. The flatbread is used in place of tableware: the diner simply scoops the food up using the injera.

Teff is related to millet and because of the grain's size, the word is thought to originate from the Amharic word *teffa*, which means lost—because of its size, and because its thin stalks cannot hold up the seeds and the plants lay down in fields, lost to the eye. As for the rest of the world, teff was also lost until the twentieth century. Very few people enjoyed this powerful little food until the late 1970s, in part because of Ethiopia's self-imposed isolation, and in part because harvesting teff is very labor intensive.

Teff has very high lysine levels, is high in fiber, iron, and potassium, and is gluten-free. It helps lower cholesterol and fight heart disease. You can substitute teff for up to a quarter of the wheat flour in a recipe, boosting nutrition and adding flavor. Bob's Red Mill has contracted to have our teff grown in Idaho by an astute farmer, thereby ensuring the high quality of our teff. We stone grind 100% whole grain teff into flour and also package whole grain teff.

Triticale

Triticale (trit-a-KAY-lee) is a hardy hybrid grain that was created when varieties of wheat and rye were crossbred in Scotland in 1875. The name is a hybrid of wheat (*triticum*) and rye (*secale*). It was developed in the hopes of creating a grain that was hardy like rye, but produced high yields like wheat. The results were not as hoped. Originally, the grain bore no fruit and was very unpredictable in size. However, in the 1930s a French scientist picked up the experiment and, after a number of failures, treated it with colchrine, a crocus derivative. It worked.

Triticale has higher protein than either rye or wheat and a better balance of amino acids than either parent. It also has twice the lysine of wheat.

Triticale tastes of both wheat and rye, and it requires a little less kneading because it has a softer gluten. However, its softer gluten also requires that it shouldn't replace more than half of wheat flour, if substituting in a recipe. Triticale is a good source of protein, thiamin, calcium, and magnesium. The combination is great for energy and a healthy nervous system.

Because of its better balance of amino acids, and therefore better protein, Bob's Red Mill adds triticale to many of our cereals, such as our 5-Grain, 7-Grain, and 10-Grain hot cereals. We also package stone ground Triticale Cereal, Rolled Triticale Flakes, stone ground Triticale Flour, and whole grain Triticale Berries.

Wheat

Wheat is a grass of the genus *Triticum*. It was probably one of the first cereal grains grown by man. For the past 6,000 plus years, it has provided a nutritious food containing the important elements needed for an adequate diet for man and domestic animals. The embryo or germ at the base of the grain is a miniature plant with rudimentary roots and leaves ready to develop into a plant when proper moisture, light, and temperature conditions prevail.

There is archeological evidence that wheat was an important cereal food to the earliest civilizations of

Mesopotamia, Egypt, and China. It became the grain of choice during the Roman Empire, and its stalks were woven into thatch for roofs and lacings for sandals. It was roasted as cereal, fried with meat, cooked in stews, and stone ground for making bread.

Wheat has never been out of favor with Western world cultures. Because of its ease of storage, its simple milling characteristics, and its unique gluten content (making it possible to bake a leavened bread better than any other cereal grain), it has been cultivated and used since ancient times. Europeans introduced wheat to the New World and within 150 years, it was a significant crop. Plymouth settlers brought wheat, as well as oats, rye, and barley to America and planted it with Indian corn. By the mid 1600s, wheat was a major food for the New England colonies, and New York, Pennsylvania, and Maryland were the centers of wheat farming in America by 1760.

Grain milling is, without doubt, the oldest continuously conducted industry in the world. From the earliest efforts of reducing grain to meal between two stones by hand, to the beginning efforts of milling using the weight and action of water falling over a wheel, this peaceful pursuit utilized human ingenuity in a most unique way, providing food for the family and the animals that plowed and supplied transportation. Nutritious grain has given life and kept more people from starvation than any other food on earth. Because wheat plants, grows, harvests, stores, and ships so well, it truly is a miracle food.

Some 100 varieties of wheat are grown in America alone. Ninety-five percent of them belong to *Triticum* aestivem, better known as spring or winter wheat. Wheat is classified according to the season in which it is sown. Winter wheat is planted in September, lies dormant over the winter, and is harvested in June and July. Spring wheat is planted in May, grows for four months, and is harvested in September. Even though the growing season is shorter, Spring wheat contains more protein than winter wheat.

Whole wheat is a highly nutritious food, with a good supply of protein, B vitamins, and minerals such as iron, magnesium, and manganese. Wheat bran is high is fiber which adds bulk to our diets, and aids in our body's regularity. Sixty percent or more of the vitamins and minerals are lost in flours that have had the germ and bran removed. At Bob's Red Mill, we stone grind 100% high protein, U.S. No. 1 dark northern hard red spring wheat on our century-old stone mills. Stone grinding is a cool, slow rubbing of the grain between thick quartz stones, which allows the germ, the bran, and the endosperm to completely fuse together, making the flour less perishable. This whole grain flour containing the germ and bran is a powerhouse of nutrition. At Bob's Red Mill, the whole grain goes into the mill and the whole grain comes out as flour or cereal. We then package a wide assortment of wonderful whole grain wheat products, both conventionally and organically grown. We offer Whole Wheat Flour and Whole Wheat Pastry Flour (stone ground from U.S. No. 1 soft white wheat), Unbleached White Flour, and Unbleached White Pastry Flour. We also offer Wheat Bran, Wheat Germ, Rolled Wheat Flakes, and Whole Wheat Farina Cereal, as well as Hard Red and Hard White Wheat Berries. Our stone ground whole wheat is also an ingredient in many of our cereal and pancake and waffle mixes.

OTHER FLOURS USED

Among the other flours used in this book is *graham flour*, named for nineteenth century dietary reformer Sylvester Graham. Originally, graham flour was created by grinding the endosperm finely for white flour, and then grinding the bran and germ coarsely and mixing it all back together. Bob's Red Mill Graham Flour is our most coarsely ground flour, made from the highest protein, U.S. No.1 dark northern hard red spring wheat.

Potato starch flour is flour made only from the starch of the potato and should never be confused with potato flour. Potato starch flour works as a replacement for arrowroot or cornstarch as a thickener. *Potato flour* is made from dehydrated potato and is much heavier.

Almond flour is simply ground almonds, and is also called almond meal. You can make the flour in a coffee grinder or spice mill from whole almonds, but you won't get as consistent a grind as you will with Bob's Red Mill Almond Meal/Flour.

Finally, *white bean flour*, high in fiber, is often used to make a simple soup but can also be used in gluten-free cooking.

USING THE SUPPORT INGREDIENTS IN THIS BOOK

Liquids

We use a variety of liquids in this book—milk, yogurt, buttermilk, juice, syrup, cream, sour cream, applesauce. Liquids supply the moisture that activates baking powder and baking soda, while in yeast breads, liquid enables the protein to form the gluten necessary for a bread's tenderness and elasticity. In general, lower fat products should not replace full fat ones (see the explanation on the next page) unless indicated, but a slightly higher fat product may replace a lower fat one. (The result will be a little heavier, and certainly higher in calories.) If you choose to use a lower fat product, the result may be a smaller or less airy result.

MILK—The milk used in these recipes is whole milk. You may substitute low fat milk in most recipes, or use rice or soy milk. Nonfat milk is not recommended.

CREAM—Heavy cream and whipping cream are interchangeable in these recipes, even though heavy cream has a slightly higher butterfat content. If you can find cream that has not been ultra pasteurized (lengthens shelf life but hurts taste), buy it.

BUTTERMILK—Buttermilk provides a wonderful tang, and today's buttermilk is low in fat. Because buttermilk tends to separate in its container, be sure to shake it well before using.

SOUR CREAM—Recipes that call for sour cream were made using full-fat sour cream. Low fat sour cream may be substituted (you may lose a little flavor and tenderness) but do not use nonfat sour cream.

YOGURT—Unflavored, plain yogurt also works for a less rich, slightly tangier product. Make sure to use only low fat plain yogurt and read the label to avoid yogurts with artificial gum.

NONFAT DRY MILK—Instant nonfat dry milk is milk that has had the water and most of the fat removed.

WATER—Even the water you use adds flavor to baked goods. Tap water is just fine for most cooking, but if you live in a place where the water is chlorinated, and you can taste it, consider using bottled or filtered water.

WHEY—Whey is a protein-rich byproduct of the cheese-making process. Sweet dairy whey gives yeast dough a satiny and delicate texture. Whey protein concentrate is excellent for protein drinks but may also be used to add more protein to baked goods.

Fats

Fat coats the flour particles in your baking mixture, allowing the gluten strands to become slick, which in turns allows gas bubbles to move about freely. This results in a finer grain and more moisture in your baked goods. When people talk about a baked good being "moist," they are referring to the fat content. Using non-fat ingredients generally means you will have very dry baked goods. Use good quality products for best results since old fats can dramatically affect the taste of your baked goods.

BUTTER—Unsalted butter is recommended in most of our recipes because it gives the best flavor and texture and has less trans fats than margarine. We recommend using unsalted butter because the amount of salt used by producers in salted butters varies from product to product. Using unsalted butter and then adding your own salt lets you control the amount of salt.

SHORTENING—Shortening is liquid vegetable oil that has been hydrogenated, turning it into a solid: hydrogen atoms are attached to the atoms in the oil to turn them into saturated fat. This extends the shelf life and helps make flaky crusts.

OILS—Canola, corn, sunflower, and safflower oil are the oils most commonly used in cooking and any of these will work fine in the recipes in this book. Canola has the lightest consistency and contains no trans fats, making it the most healthy.

Eggs and Cheeses

EGGS—Eggs should be Grade A Large. Keep in mind that stale eggs do not increase in volume as much as fresh eggs, which will keep your doughs from rising to their fullest.

CREAM CHEESE—Supermarket-brand cream cheeses work better for baking than natural cream cheeses, which may curdle. As with sour cream, do not use nonfat cream cheese.

Wheat and Other Flours

Flours are the finely ground and sifted meal of any of the grains discussed in previous pages; they are starches that provide the connection between liquids and fats, evenly distributing the ingredients in the recipe. Most flours contain gluten (some more than others), which forms the network that helps contain the gases that make mixtures rise as they bake. Flour can also be used as a thickener in pies, tarts, and sauces. Flour begins to expand when moistened, forming a web of starch molecules that can absorb liquids and fats. At a certain point, depending on the other ingredients, the starches stop absorbing and they gel. If the recipe calls for flour as a thickener but you want to substitute corn starch or tapioca, then use half of the recommended amount.

Flours are also used for surface dusting to provide a stick-free atmosphere on which to work. When using flour for dusting a rolling surface, it's best to use unbleached white since it provides the best protection against sticking (even if it is not used in the recipe). Some recipes call for cornmeal to add texture or flavor; it too can be used for dusting a rolling surface and can be most often found keeping pizza dough from sticking to its baking stone.

High gluten flours, such as wheat and kamut, produce a high amount of gluten when lubricated and agitated. The more gluten, the more air the dough will hold. Low gluten breads are denser and heavier in consistency and texture.

Wheat germ is the germ of the wheat grain and may be added to cakes, breads, and other recipes to increase their nutritional value. It has a nutty taste good for muffins in particular. Keep your wheat germ in the refrigerator for freshness.

Wheat bran is the outer layer of the wheat kernel, separated during the milling of white flour. It is high in calcium, and coarser and darker than the germ. It's also good added to muffins and quick breads.

Store your flour in the refrigerator, if possible. Whole grain flours contain more oil than white flours, and thus can spoil a little faster than less healthy flours. Bring the flour to room temperature before using.

Leaveners and Thickeners

BAKING SODA—Also called *bicarbonate of soda,* baking soda acts as a leavening agent. In the presence of moisture, heat, acidity, or other triggers, it reacts, producing carbon dioxide that gets trapped as bubbles in the dough. When the dough is baked, the holes are set, giving the bread its sponge-like texture. Too much baking soda can negatively affect the flavor of baked goods, so use it sparingly.

BAKING POWDER— Baking powder is a leavener, which causes non-yeast breads and cakes to rise. Baking powders commonly sold in supermarkets contain sodium aluminum sulfate, calcium sulfate, and monocalcium phosphate. Because long-term exposure to aluminum may cause health problems, Bob's Red Mill Baking Powder contains only sodium phosphate, bicarbonate of soda, cornstarch, and calcium phosphate—no aluminum. When liquid is added to baking powder, a chemical reaction causes it to produce carbon dioxide. When added to a dough, this carbon dioxide is trapped in tiny air pockets in the dough or batter. The heat from the oven causes additional carbon monoxide to release and expands the trapped carbon dioxide gas and air, creating steam. The steam expands the trapped air pockets, thereby expanding the bread. Baking powder gradually loses its potency, so it is good to replace it every 4 months or so. To test it, stir a $\frac{1}{2}$ teaspoon of baking powder into $\frac{1}{4}$ cup of hot water and see if it bubbles. If it doesn't, it's probably not any good.

YEAST—The yeast recommended in this book is active dry yeast. Keep it refrigerated to maintain its freshness.

ARROWROOT—Arrowroot, also called arrowroot starch, is commonly used in place of cornstarch as a thickener. Arrowroot received its unusual name because the root of this South American plant was used in the treatment of poisoned arrow wounds. Its chief benefit is a lack of taste—unlike flour or cornstarch. Therefore, it can be undercooked and not affect the taste of the final product. It is easily digested, important if you are feeding the final product to children. Cornstarch and arrowroot are interchangeable in these recipes. However, arrowroot does not hold your food together as well after having been cooled and reheated.

TAPIOCA—Tapioca is made from the starch from the root of the tropical cassava, or manioc. Quick cooking tapioca has been precooked, then dehydrated. Both tapioca flour and pearled tapioca may be used as a thickener.

Sugars and Sweeteners

SUGAR—The recipes in this book call for granulated sugar (which is the most refined) unless otherwise noted. There are two types commonly sold—cane sugar and beet sugar. They are interchangeable except when melting sugar (say for caramel), when you should use cane sugar.

CONFECTIONERS' SUGAR—Confectioners' sugar, or powdered sugar, is granulated sugar that has been pulverized and mixed with a little cornstarch. If you live in a humid climate, be sure to store it in an airtight container.

BROWN SUGAR—Unless a recipe in this book calls for dark brown sugar, light brown sugar should be used. However, dark brown sugar can be substituted for a stronger flavor. Brown sugar is simply granulated sugar with some of the molasses added back to it (molasses is removed from sugar during the refining process). Dark brown sugar has a higher molasses content, giving it a stronger flavor. To keep brown sugar moist, store it with a cut piece of apple in the bag or container.

TURBINADO SUGAR—Turbinado sugar comes from the minimally processed juice of sugar cane. The juice is spun out of the sugar cane, thus the name *turbinado*. This is a crunchy, light brown sugar that is great for toppings, especially on Bob's Red Mill's hot breakfast cereal.

MOLASSES—A byproduct of cane sugar refinement, molasses is a little more nutritious than sugar, but also comes with a strong flavor, which explains why most recipes only use a tablespoon or two. To extract the sugar from sugar cane, the cane juice is boiled. The initial two boils produce what is packaged as molasses. A third boil produces the more nutritious blackstrap molasses. If you buy a package just marked "molasses," make sure it is unsulphured, which means that sulfur fumes were not used to treat the cane during the extraction process. Sulfured molasses is the lowest grade of molasses.

CORN SYRUP—Corn syrup is not as sweet as sugar but it adds a moistness to baked goods that sugar does not. Corn syrup is fabricated from dextrose and fructose. A dark corn syrup provides the flavor of butterscotch.

MAPLE SYRUP—Maple syrup is available in three grades—Fancy, A, and B. They range in color from light to dark amber. The lighter the syrup, the milder the flavor. Grade B is best for baking. Make sure you bake only with pure maple syrup, not imitation maple syrup or flavored maple syrup.

Other Ingredients

VANILLA—When we call for vanilla in a recipe, we mean real vanilla extract, not imitation vanilla. You can substitute vanilla sugar for the vanilla extract—just replace some of the sugar in the recipe with vanilla sugar. To substitute vanilla powder use half as much as the recipe calls for. To make vanilla sugar at home, slice one vanilla bean lengthwise and scrape the seeds into an airtight container. Add 2 cups sugar, then bury the bean in the sugar. Let the sugar sit for a week or two, then use as you would sugar.

CHOCOLATE— Chocolate comes from cocoa beans, which develop their distinctive chocolate flavor only after being fermented, dried, and roasted. Unsweetened chocolate, also called baking chocolate, is pure chocolate with nothing added and is not used in this book. In the recipes that call for chocolate chips, you can use your choice of milk or semi-sweet chocolate chips.

COCOA POWDER— For recipes using cocoa powder, choose Dutch-process cocoa, which is also packaged as alkalized. Nonalkalized cocoa powder can be acidic and very assertive in flavor where alkalized is darker, milder in taste and more balanced. Don't confuse cocoa powder with instant cocoa which has been pre-cooked with an emulsifier added, and includes up to 75 percent sugar. Cocoa powder and toasted carob powder may be used in these recipes when a chocolate flavor is called for. Toasted carob powder is a wonderful substitute. You can substitute 3 tablespoons of carob powder and one tablespoon water for each square-ounce of chocolate, as well.

CAROB— Carob, also called locust bean, is the pod of an evergreen tree native to the eastern Mediterranean. Carob chips or powder may be used in place of chocolate. Carob pods are roasted and ground into a powder and work as a substitute for cocoa powder. Carob has far less fat, coming in at less than 1 percent versus chocolate, which may be as high as 50 percent.

XANTHAN GUM—This natural carbohydrate, made from a tiny microorganism called *Xanthomonas* campestris, adds volume and viscosity to bread and other gluten-free baked goods.

SALT— For these recipes, use the salt of your choice, kosher, sea, or iodized. Consider the suggested salt content an average; if you are using kosher, you might use a little more than recommended by the recipe (since the grain is bigger) and if you're using sea, use a little less.

A Few Thoughts on Baking Equipment

Always use proper equipment for measuring, cooking, and baking. For example, use measuring spoons, never tableware—measurements are a vital part of baking.

Clear Pyrex measuring cups with a spout are great for measuring liquids. If you are measuring honey or another sticky liquid, brush the inside of the cup with a little vegetable oil or spray it with nonstick cooking spray first.

If possible, use measuring cups with the exact size—¼ cup, ½ cup—for dry ingredients.

A kitchen scale and an oven thermometer come in very handy when baking. We recommend both for the best accuracy. Use the thermometer to check your oven periodically, placing it in the oven and then increasing the temperature by 50°F. as you check the accuracy.

An instant read thermometer is very important for making bread dough. The cost and frustration of tossing out dough that didn't rise is far more than the price of this vital tool for the home baker.

We highly recommend an electric mixer for creaming butter and sugar. It can be done by hand, although not as efficiently. When mixing, use stainless or glass bowls. Plastic bowls tend to retain oils no matter how well they are washed.

We recommend making pastry in a food processor, but it can be done with a pastry blender, an inexpensive tool made of six curved blades attached to a wood or plastic handle. Chop up and down to cut the fat into the flour.

Pans

Heavy aluminum pans, with or without a nonstick surface, provide the best and most even distribution of heat, although lightweight pans work tolerably well. Darker pans conduct heat better and brown cakes very well. Sturdy pans with straight sides are best.

Before buying baking sheets, be sure to measure your oven to make sure they fit. Rimmed sheets are often used for cinnamon rolls while rimless sheets are used for pastries. You can use either for cookies. We prefer heavy aluminum baking sheets over insulated cookie sheets, in which a layer of air is trapped between two layers of aluminum. These sheets prevent burning but the cookies take longer to bake and sometimes remain soft.

Tube and bundt pans (bundt pans generally have fluted or scalloped sides) are almost always made with nonstick finishes.

The traditional aluminum is best for tart pans as darker pans cook faster. If you only have access to darker tart pans, reduce the temperature by approximately 25 degrees (as ovens vary). Our recipes call for a 9- or 10-inch tart pan. Pick one with a removable bottom to make serving easier.

The recipes in this book call for standard muffin tins, not the mini or "Texas" size. Springform pans, great for cakes that bake higher than 2 inches or cakes that are hard to unmold, come in aluminum,

Our Whole Grain Store—a real "destination" in the Pacific Northwest.

stainless steel, or nonstick. We prefer the aluminum ones.

For many recipes, we highly recommend parchment paper, available in rolls so you can cut to the size you need. Parchment makes an excellent nonstick surface and makes clean up easy. The new reusable silicone liners are also great and will last for years.

The temperatures and times given for each recipe are for conventional ovens. If you are using a convection oven, reduce the temperature by 25 degrees and check a few minutes earlier. The times given are the minimum—they are the time you should check for doneness, but the product may not be quite ready. Remember, oven temperatures vary, and even the size of an egg can affect the cooking time. If your loaf crusts tend to burn on the bottom or sides, try a shiny aluminum loaf pan or place the loaf in its pan on a cookie sheet.

To test if your baked good is done, poke a wooden skewer or toothpick into the center of the cake or cookie. If what you're baking isn't done, bits of dough stick to the wood better than they would a metal skewer or a knife; if the toothpick emerges clean, your baked good is ready. Be sure to check out our pan chart on page 427.

Back to quaint! Our new Bob's Red Mill Store has a Whole Grain Bakery and Café, and a real water wheel! We are so happy with our lovely building.

Whole Grain Yeast Breads, Rolls, & Sourdough

Preparing yeast dough can often be intimidating for the beginning baker, with terms such as *proofing* and *rising* to understand and keep in mind. But never fear: we think you'll find that these yeast recipes are not complicated, and with practice, you'll be much more comfortable making homemade yeast breads.

Whole grain yeast breads rise more slowly and, in general, do not achieve the lightness of white flour yeast breads. Whole grain breads also tend to brown more quickly, so if you are adapting a favorite recipe to incorporate whole grains, keep an eye on the cooking time. If the bread begins to brown before it is fully cooked, place a piece of foil over the top.

Whole grain dough also feels stickier than white bread dough. If you are used to the feel of white bread dough, resist the temptation to add more flour. It is better to err on the side of a too moist loaf, than one too dry. Whole grain dough needs to remain moist for lightness.

The best room temperature for dough to rise in is 80°F. or warmer, which isn't likely to be the temperature in most of our homes. Good ideas for warmer places are the top of the refrigerator, a top shelf in the kitchen, a sunny window where you can invert a glass bowl over the dough and create a little greenhouse effect, or on a towel under which you've placed a heating pad set to low. If you want to use a microwave oven to warm the dough, place it in an oiled glass bowl, cover with a kitchen towel, then place the covered bowl in a glass pie pan filled with warm water. Microwave the dough on lowest setting 4 or 5 minutes at a time, checking the dough between each time to make sure it is not getting too hot. The dough should feel just a little warmer than body temperature. To use the oven to warm the dough, turn it to 275°F. for $2\frac{1}{2}$ minutes, then turn it off. Wrap the bowl of dough in a damp dish towel and place it in the oven. Close the door and let it rise until it doubles in size.

For those living at high altitudes, higher baking temperatures and a little more liquid that normal are generally necessary, especially since flours tend to dry out more in these higher altitudes. On the other hand, a little less baking powder, baking soda, and sugar should be used in the recipes. How high is high obviously varies, and experimentation or reference to recipes used in the past will be the ultimate key.

There are several things that can affect baking bread, and oven temperatures are one of the most common.

Ovens vary depending on their age and quality. If your oven is too hot, the outside of your bread will be done before the interior is baked. If this happens, reduce the oven temperature and cover your loaf with foil (shiny side up) to help prevent over-browning while you finish baking. Oven temperature will also vary if you get impatient and open the oven too frequently to check the baking process—oven heat escapes quickly. So be patient.

Other factors that can negatively affect your bread from properly rising include using a pan that is too small (thereby cutting short the rising time), pouring water that is too hot into your yeast (killing it), a lack of precise measurements, or dough that did not achieve the required warmth to rise.

But don't let this scare you. Once you get the hang of it, you'll see that creating your own baked bread can bring unending amounts of joy and, as you've already read, health benefits.

Kneading

Most bread doughs do not require lengthy kneading, just a few minutes is usually all you need. Because most doughs are somewhat sticky when ready, many bakers will be tempted to add flour; we provide the options to add more flour both for stickiness and to achieve the right elasticity in a dough that is too moist. However, most doughs should be somewhat sticky. Adding too much additional flour may result in a dry texture. If you are having trouble kneading, you might want to oil your hands instead of adding more flour.

Bob's Whole Wheat Honey Bread

Low in fat and a snap to make, this bread makes terrific sandwiches. The honey gives it a nice bit of sweetness that is especially prominent when the bread is toasted. Whole wheat and honey goodness, toasted and spread with Oregon blueberry jam—yum.

Makes two 9-inch loaves

- 2¼ teaspoons active dry yeast
- 2 cups warm water (105°F. to 115°F.)
- 1 cup nonfat dry milk
- ⅓ cup honey
- 1½ teaspoons salt
- 2½ tablespoons vegetable oil
- 2 cups hard white whole wheat flour
- 3⅓ cups whole wheat flour

In a large bowl, sprinkle the yeast over the warm water, then add the dry milk and honey. Stir until the yeast is dissolved, then let stand until the yeast begins to foam, about 5 minutes. Add the salt, oil, and hard white whole wheat flour and beat until well blended and smooth.

Add the whole wheat flour one cup at a time, stirring well between each addition. Add until the dough is stiff (you may not need all of the flour) then let it rest for 15 minutes.

Turn the dough out onto a lightly floured surface and knead until smooth and elastic, about ten minutes. Lightly oil a large bowl, place the dough inside, turning it over in the oil, and cover with a clean dish towel. Let the dough rise in a warm place until it doubles in size, about 1 hour.

Lightly oil a baking sheet or line it with parchment paper.

Punch the dough down and divide it in two. Shape each loaf into an oval about 9 inches long. Place the loaves on the prepared baking sheet, cover with the dish towel, and let them rise another 45 minutes, or until they've doubled in size. At this point, the dough, when pressed with a finger, should dent rather than fill back in.

Preheat the oven to 375°F. Using a sharp knife, cut a slash through the top of each loaf lengthwise, about ½ inch deep. Bake for 30 to 35 minutes. Cool on a wire rack.

Buckwheat Bread

Buckwheat has an earthy, nutty flavor and from the time you open the package, through the kneading, baking, and eating, buckwheat's aroma and taste grab center stage. Buckwheat bread makes hearty sandwiches or toast and is fantastic with bananas or whichever fruit you choose.

Makes two 8 x 4-inch loaves

- 4½ teaspoons active dry yeast
- 2½ cups warm water (105°F. to 115°F.)
- 3 tablespoons sorghum or molasses
- 2 cups buckwheat flour
- 4 cups stone ground whole wheat flour, divided
- 2 teaspoons salt
- ⅓ cup vegetable oil
- ½ cup unbleached white flour

In a large bowl, sprinkle the yeast over the warm water, then add the sorghum or molasses. Stir until the yeast is dissolved, then let stand until the yeast begins to foam, about 5 minutes.

Stir in the buckwheat flour and 1 cup of the whole wheat flour, beating vigorously for one minute. Cover with a clean dish towel and place in a warm spot for about 30 minutes to create a sponge.

Fold in the salt and oil, then work in the remaining 3 cups of whole wheat flour. Add the ½ cup of unbleached white flour as needed to prevent it from sticking.

Turn the dough out onto a lightly floured surface and knead until smooth and elastic, about 5 to 10 minutes. Lightly oil a large bowl, place the dough inside, turning it over in the oil, and cover with the dish towel. Let the dough rise in a warm place until it doubles in size, about 1 to 1½ hours.

Lightly oil two 8 x 4-inch loaf pans.

Punch the dough down and divide it in two. Shape the loaves and place them in the prepared pans. Cover the loaves with the dish towel and let them rise again until they double in size, about 45 minutes to 1 hour. At this point, the dough, when pressed with a finger, should dent rather than fill back in.

Preheat the oven to 375°F. Bake the loaves for 35 to 40 minutes, or until a tester comes out clean. Cool the loaves in the pans for 5 minutes, then remove to a wire rack to cool.

Spelt Bread

WHEAT-FREE, CAN BE DAIRY-FREE

Spelt has been at the forefront of America's renewed interest in whole grains and alternatives to the previously limited choices in the market. Its nutty flavor especially comes through in this loaf. Be sure to knead your dough for no more than 5 minutes, because over-kneaded spelt dough can be tough.

Makes two 8 x 4-inch loaves

- 2¼ teaspoons active dry yeast
- 2 cups warm water (105°F. to 115°F.)
- 2 tablespoons honey
- 1 teaspoon xanthan gum
- ½ cup rolled oats
- 5 cups spelt flour
- 3 tablespoons unsalted butter, melted
- 1 teaspoon salt

In a large bowl, sprinkle the yeast over the warm water, then add the honey. Stir until the yeast is dissolved, then let stand until the yeast begins to foam, about 5 minutes.

Combine the xanthan gum, oats, and flour in another bowl.

Stir into the yeast mixture the butter, salt, and half of the flour/oat mixture. Stir vigorously with a wooden spoon. Add the remaining flour/oat mixture until the dough becomes too stiff to stir, then turn out on a lightly floured surface and knead for about 5 minutes, adding additional flour as necessary to keep the dough from sticking. The dough should become smooth and elastic, but be careful not to over-knead.

Place the dough in a lightly oiled bowl, cover with a clean dish towel, and let the dough rise in a warm place until it doubles in size, about two hours.

Lightly oil 2 8 x 4-inch loaf pans. Punch the dough down and divide it in half. Shape the halves into smooth loaves and place them in the pans. Cover the loaves with the dish towel and let them rise for another hour, until the dough has risen nearly to the top of the pans.

Preheat the oven to 350°F. Bake for 45 minutes or until the loaves are brown. Let them rest in the pans for 5 minutes, then remove them to cool on a wire rack.

Multigrain Seeded Bread

This wonderfully flavorful and nutritious bread is naturally chewy as a result of the added cereal, and it's crunchy because of the added flaxseeds. You can substitute other seeds—such as sesame and sunflower. You'll note that we add a pan of water to the oven along with the bread. This water will steam during baking, and it's this steam that allows the yeast to work longer than usual in the dough, creating a larger loaf.

Makes one 12-inch loaf

- ½ cup unsweetened multi-grain cereal (such as 7-Grain)
- 2 cups boiling water
- 2¼ teaspoons active dry yeast
- 2½ cups unbleached white flour, divided
- 1 tablespoon extra-virgin olive oil
- 1 tablespoon dark brown sugar
- 1½ teaspoons salt
- 1½ cups whole wheat flour
- 2 teaspoons each poppy and flax seeds, mixed
- 2 cups water

Place the cereal in a large bowl, and pour the boiling water on top. Stir, and let it stand until the cereal cools to between 105°F. and 115°F., about 15 or 20 minutes.

Sprinkle the yeast over the cereal and stir until the yeast is dissolved. Let stand until the yeast begins to foam, about 5 minutes.

Add 1 cup of the unbleached white flour to the cereal, along with the oil, sugar, and salt, and stir until smooth. Mix in the remaining flour, ½ cup at a time, alternating between unbleached white and whole wheat, to form the dough. Add up to ¼ cup more unbleached white flour if needed. Cover the dough with a clean dish towel and let it rest for 15 minutes.

Turn the dough out onto a lightly floured surface and knead until smooth and elastic, about ten minutes, adding more flour if necessary. Lightly oil a large bowl, place the dough inside, turning it over in the oil, and cover with the dish towel. Let the dough rise until it doubles in size, about 1 hour.

Punch down the dough and turn it out onto a lightly floured surface. Knead for 3 to 4 minutes, then shape into a 12 x 4-inch loaf. Sprinkle a baking sheet with 2 teaspoons of the seed mixture and place the loaf on top of the seeds. Cover the dough with the dish towel and let it rise until almost doubled, about 30 to 45 minutes. At this point, the dough, when pressed with a finger, should dent rather than fill back in.

Set one of the oven racks in the center of the oven and one just below the center. Place a baking pan on the lower rack and preheat the oven to 425°F. Brush the dough with a little water and sprinkle with the remaining seed mixture. Using a sharp knife, cut 3 slashes across the top of the loaf. Pour 2 cups of water into the hot pan on the lower rack in the oven (water will steam) and immediately place the baking sheet with the loaf in the oven.

Bake the loaf until a tester inserted into center comes out clean, about 30 to 35 minutes. Transfer to rack and cool.

Coffee Spelt Rye Bread

The tanginess of rye, the nuttiness of spelt, and the rich flavor of coffee come together in this rich, dense, delicious bread. It's pretty intense, so slice this bread thin.

Makes two 10-inch round loaves

- 4 cups spelt flour
- 2 cups oatmeal
- 2 cups dark rye flour
- 1 tablespoon salt
- 4½ teaspoons active dry yeast
- 1 cup lukewarm brewed coffee
- 1 egg white mixed with 1 tablespoon water
- 2 tablespoons sesame seeds

In a large bowl, combine 3½ cups of the spelt flour with the oatmeal, rye flour, salt, and yeast. Add the coffee and mix well, adding more spelt flour if needed to make a slightly sticky, but firm, dough.

Turn the dough out onto a floured surface and knead until smooth and elastic, about 8 to 10 minutes. Lightly oil a large bowl, place the dough inside, turning it over in the oil, and cover with a clean dish towel. Let the dough rise for 1 hour or until it doubles in size.

Line a baking sheet with parchment paper.

Return the dough to a lightly floured surface, cut the dough in half and form each half into a round ball. Place the balls of dough on the prepared baking sheet, cover with the dish towel, and let them rise for 45 minutes to 1 hour or until they double in size. At this point, the dough, when pressed with a finger, should dent rather than fill back in.

Preheat the oven to 375°F. Brush egg wash onto the dough balls. Sprinkle them with sesame seeds.

Bake for 30 minutes or until each loaf sounds hollow when tapped on the bottom. Remove to a rack to cool.

Barley Bread

This wonderfully wheat- and dairy-free bread, which makes the most out of barley's goodness, has been adapted from a recipe by Phyllis Potts, author of The Complete Guide to Wheat Free Cooking.

Makes two 8 x 4-inch loaves

- 2¼ teaspoons active dry yeast
- 1 cup warm water (105°F. to 115°F.)
- 2 teaspoons brown sugar, divided
- 1 teaspoon salt
- 1 tablespoon vegetable oil
- ⅓ cup soy flour
- 2½ cups barley flour, divided

In a large bowl, stir the yeast in the warm water until the yeast is dissolved, then let stand until the yeast begins to foam, about 5 minutes. Add the sugar, salt, oil, soy flour, and half the barley flour and beat vigorously until blended. Add enough of the remaining barley flour to make a dough that can be kneaded.

Turn the dough out onto a lightly floured surface and knead until smooth and elastic, about ten minutes. Lightly oil a large bowl, place the dough inside, turning it over in the oil. Using a sharp knife, cut a slash across the top of the loaf, then cover the dough with a clean dish towel and let the dough rise until it doubles in size, about 1 hour.

Dust your hands and your work surface with flour and lightly knead the dough again, adding more flour if needed, until the dough is spongy and keeps its shape. Return the dough to the bowl, turn the dough to coat in oil, cover, and let the dough rise again for another hour. At this point, the dough, when pressed with a finger, should dent rather than fill back in. Cut the dough in half and shape into two round loaves.

Preheat the oven to 350°F. Lightly oil a baking sheet.

Place the loaves on the prepared sheet and bake, uncovered, for about 50 to 60 minutes, or until the loaves are golden brown. Cool on a wire rack.

Multigrain Bread

This loaf is a dense, dark bread with an appealing combination of flours, plus cornmeal for crunch and oatmeal for chewiness. This bread is really delicious with apple butter.

Makes two 10-inch round loaves

- 3¼ cups unbleached white flour
- 3 cups graham flour
- 4½ teaspoons active dry yeast
- 4 teaspoons salt
- 3 cups warm water (105°F. to 115°F.)
- ½ cup molasses
- ¼ cup vegetable oil
- ½ cup buckwheat flour
- ½ cup rye flour
- ½ cup soy flour
- ½ cup cornmeal
- ½ cup quick rolled oats
- Melted unsalted butter, for brushing

In a large mixing bowl, combine 1½ cups of the unbleached white flour with 2 cups of the graham flour, the yeast, and salt. Mix well.

Combine the water, molasses, and oil, then add to the flour mixture and beat on low speed until moistened. Increase to medium speed and beat for 3 minutes.

Using a wooden spoon, gradually stir in the buckwheat, rye, and soy flours, cornmeal, oats, remaining graham flour, and just enough remaining unbleached white flour to make a firm dough. You may not end up using all of the flour.

Turn the dough out onto a lightly floured surface and knead until smooth and elastic, about 5 to 8 minutes. Lightly oil a large bowl, place the dough inside, turning it over in the oil, and cover with a clean dish towel. Allow the dough to rise until it doubles in size. Lightly oil a baking sheet.

Punch the dough down and divide it in two. Shape each half into a round loaf and place the loaves on a lightly oiled baking sheet. Cover with the dish towel and let the loaves rise another 30 minutes. At this point, the dough, when pressed with a finger, should dent rather than fill back in.

Preheat the oven to 375°F. Using a sharp knife, cut a slash across the top of each loaf. Place in the oven and bake for 35 to 40 minutes, or until the loaves sound hollow when tapped. If the tops darken too quickly, cover the loaves loosely with foil for the last 5 to 10 minutes of baking.

Remove the loaves from the baking sheet to a wire rack and brush with melted butter.

Rosemary Whole Wheat Baguettes

Rosemary is a fragrant and delicious addition to these long, slender, whole wheat loaves. For a plain whole wheat baguette, just leave out the rosemary.

Makes two 12-inch baguettes

- 1 tablespoon brown sugar
- 1¼ cups warm water (105°F. to 115°F.)
- 2¼ teaspoons active dry yeast
- 2 teaspoons salt
- 1½ cups hard white whole wheat flour
- 2 cups whole wheat flour
- 2 tablespoons minced fresh rosemary leaves
- Cornmeal, for dusting, optional

In a large bowl, dissolve the sugar in the water, then sprinkle the yeast on top and stir. Allow to stand until foamy, about five minutes.

Add the salt and the hard white flour and stir well, then stir in 1½ cups of the whole wheat flour to form a stiff dough, adding more if needed.

Turn the dough out onto a lightly floured surface and knead until smooth and elastic, about 10 minutes. Toward the end of the kneading time, sprinkle the dough with rosemary leaves and knead to incorporate. Lightly oil a large bowl, place the dough inside, turning it over in the oil, and cover with a clean dish towel. Allow the dough to rise until it doubles in size, about 1 hour.

Line a 17 x 14-inch baking sheet with parchment paper, or lightly oil and sprinkle the pan with cornmeal.

Punch the dough down, divide it in half and return it to the floured surface. Shape each half into a long loaf, rolling into 5 x 12-inch rectangle, then pinching each end to make a skinny loaf. Place the loaves seam side down on the prepared sheet, cover, and allow to double again, about another 45 minutes. At this point, the dough, when pressed with a finger, should dent rather than fill back in.

Preheat the oven to 400°F. Using a sharp knife, cut a slash across the top of each loaf, brush with water, and bake for about 15 to 20 minutes, until brown and crisp. Cool on a wire rack.

Wheat Berry Bread

Whole wheat kernels, also known as wheat berries, are added to this wonderful wheat bread. When soaked, the berries soften and intensify the wheat flavor. Be sure to start this recipe at least 8 hours in advance to allow the wheat berries to adequately soak.

Makes two 8-inch round loaves

- ¼ cup hard red or hard white whole wheat berries
- 2¼ teaspoons active dry yeast
- 2½ cups warm water (105°F. to 115°F.)
- ¼ cup honey
- 2 tablespoons unsalted butter, melted and cooled
- ¼ cup wheat germ
- 4 cups whole wheat flour
- 2 teaspoons salt
- 1½ cups hard white whole wheat flour
- ¼ cup milk or 4 tablespoons unsalted butter, melted and cooled

Place the wheat berries in a small bowl, and cover with warm tap water. Allow to stand at least 8 hours, or overnight. Drain.

In a large bowl, sprinkle the yeast over the warm water and stir to dissolve. Stir in the honey, butter, wheat germ, wheat berries, and 1¾ cups of the whole wheat flour. Allow to stand for 15 minutes, or until the yeast foams. Gradually add the remaining whole wheat flour, the salt, and ¾ cup of the hard white flour, until a stiff dough forms. Cover with a clean dish towel and let stand for 30 minutes, then stir in enough of the remaining flour so that the dough is not too sticky to handle.

Turn the dough out onto a lightly floured surface and knead until smooth and elastic, about 8 to 10 minutes. Lightly oil a large bowl, place the dough inside, turning it over in the oil, and cover with the dish towel. Allow the dough to rise until it doubles in size, about 1 to 1½ hours.

Line a baking sheet with parchment paper.

Punch the dough down, return it to the floured surface, and shape into a 9- or 10-inch circle. Divide the dough in half, shape into round balls, and place them on the prepared baking sheet. Let the dough balls rise another hour until they double in size. At this point, the dough, when pressed with a finger, should dent rather than fill back in.

Preheat the oven to 375°F. Using a sharp knife, cut two or three slashes across the top of the loaves, then brush them with a little milk or melted butter. Bake for 30 to 40 minutes or until the loaves sound hollow when tapped. Cool on a wire rack.

Cottage Cheese Loaf

This healthy loaf makes a very dense and strongly flavored dinner bread. If you don't have hard white whole wheat flour on hand (also known as bread flour) you can substitute whole wheat flour.

Makes one 8-inch round loaf

- 2 tablespoons vegetable oil
- ½ small onion, minced (about ⅓ cup)
- 2¼ teaspoons active dry yeast
- ½ cup warm water (105°F. to 115°F.)
- 1 cup cottage cheese
- ⅓ cup fresh parsley, finely chopped
- 2 tablespoons honey
- 1 egg, room temperature, lightly beaten
- ½ cup hard white whole wheat flour
- 2 cups whole wheat flour
- 1 teaspoon salt
- ¼ teaspoon melted unsalted butter or oil

In a medium saucepan set over medium heat, heat the oil and sauté the onion until translucent, about 5 minutes. Allow to cool until just warm.

In a small bowl, sprinkle the yeast over the water and stir to dissolve. Let stand for 5 minutes, until foamy.

Add the cottage cheese to the onions and warm the mixture slightly. Remove from the heat and combine with the parsley, honey, and egg.

In a large bowl, whisk together the flours and the salt, then stir in the yeast and the cottage cheese mixture to form a dough.

Turn the dough out onto a lightly floured surface and knead until smooth and elastic, about 5 to 10 minutes. Cover with a clean dish towel and allow the dough to rise for about 45 to 50 minutes, or until the dough, when pressed with a finger, dents rather than fills back in. (Keep an eye on your dough because it will rise quickly.) Punch the dough down, shape it into another round, cover, and set aside to rise again for about 25 minutes.

Lightly oil an 8- or 9-inch pie dish.

Punch down the dough and press it into the prepared dish. Allow to rise another 15 or 20 minutes. The dough should dent when you press it with your finger.

Preheat the oven to 350°F. Brush the top of the loaf with a little butter or oil and bake for 45 minutes. Cool on a wire rack and serve warm or at room temperature.

Buttermilk Bulgur Bread

This is a pleasantly heavy bread, especially great right out of the oven. You'll love the texture and the sweet aftertaste.

Makes two 9-inch loaves

- 2¼ teaspoons active dry yeast
- ¼ cup warm water (105°F. to 115°F.)
- 3 tablespoons honey
- 2 teaspoons tomato paste
- ½ cup bulgur wheat
- 1½ cups buttermilk, warmed
- 5 tablespoons unsalted butter, melted and cooled
- ½ teaspoon salt
- 2 cups whole wheat flour
- 2 cups unbleached white flour
- Cornmeal, for dusting, optional

In a large bowl, sprinkle the yeast over the warm water. Stir to dissolve, then let stand about 5 minutes until foamy. Stir in the honey and tomato paste, and whisk until smooth. Stir in the bulgur and buttermilk and allow to stand for 20 minutes.

Stir the butter and salt into the bulgur mixture, then add the whole wheat flour and about 1½ cups unbleached white flour to make a stiff dough, adding a little more if the dough is too sticky.

Turn the dough out onto a lightly floured surface and knead until smooth and elastic, about 15 minutes, adding more flour if necessary to keep dough from sticking. Lightly oil a large bowl, place the dough inside, turning it over in the oil, and cover with a clean dish towel. Allow to rise in a warm place until the dough doubles in size, about 90 minutes.

Return the dough to the lightly floured surface, punch it down, and divide it in half. Roll each half like a long cigar, until it resembles a loaf of French or Italian bread.

Sprinkle a baking sheet with cornmeal or line it with parchment paper and place the loaves on the sheet. Lightly brush the top of each loaf with water, cover them loosely with the dish towel, and let them rise again until they double in size, about 45 minutes to 1 hour. At this point, the dough, when pressed with a finger, should dent rather than fill back in.

Preheat the oven to 400°F. Using a sharp knife, cut four or five slashes across the top of the loaves and brush again with water. Bake for 25 minutes or until crisp and hollow sounding when tapped. Cool on a wire rack.

Cinnamon Raisin Bread

This recipe makes a wonderfully moist loaf, thanks in part to the extra moisture in the quinoa flour. If you can keep yourself from eating up this great-smelling bread and save enough for later, it's also great in bread pudding.

Makes two 9 x 5-inch loaves

- ¼ cup sugar
- ¾ cup warm water (105°F. to 115°F.)
- 2¼ teaspoons active dry yeast
- 2½ cups hard white whole wheat flour
- 1 cup quinoa flour
- 2 teaspoons salt
- 1½ teaspoons ground cinnamon
- 1 egg, beaten
- ½ cup whole or low fat milk, room temperature
- 2 tablespoons unsalted butter, melted and cooled, or vegetable oil
- 1½ cups raisins

In a large bowl, stir ⅛ teaspoon of the sugar into the water and sprinkle the yeast on top. Stir to dissolve, then let stand about 5 minutes until foamy.

Sift together the remaining sugar, flours, salt, and cinnamon and add to the yeast mixture along with the egg, milk, and butter. Stir to form a dough, adding a little more hard white flour if the dough is too sticky, or adding a little water if the dough is too dry.

Turn the dough out onto a lightly floured surface and knead until smooth and elastic, about 10 minutes, kneading in the raisins for the last couple of minutes. Lightly oil a large bowl, place the dough inside, turning it over in the oil, and cover with a clean dish towel. Allow the dough to rise until it doubles in size, about 2 hours.

Lightly oil two 9 x 5-inch loaf pans. Punch the dough down and divide in it half, shape into loaves, and place in the pans. Cover with the dish towel and allow to rise again until it doubles in size, about 60 to 75 minutes. At this point, the dough, when pressed with a finger, should dent rather than fill back in.

Preheat the oven to 350°F. Bake for 40 minutes, or until golden brown and the loaves make a hollow sound when tapped. Remove from the pans and cool completely on a wire rack.

Applesauce Pecan Bread

This moist loaf has a long shelf life—which might not matter since it's so good it will probably be gobbled right up. It's especially delicious with cream cheese. Be sure to have all of your ingredients at room temperature except, of course, the water for proofing the yeast. Don't even think about using cold applesauce—it will keep your bread from rising properly or at all.

Makes two 8 x 4-inch loaves

- 2¼ teaspoons active dry yeast
- 1 cup warm water (105°F. to 115°F.)
- 2½ cups whole wheat flour
- 2 cups hard white whole wheat flour
- 2 teaspoons salt
- 1 cup applesauce
- 3 tablespoons oil
- 1 cup buttermilk
- ¾ cup pecans, chopped

In a small bowl, sprinkle the yeast over the warm water, and stir until the yeast is dissolved, then let stand until the yeast begins to foam, about 5 minutes.

In a large bowl, whisk together the whole wheat flour and 1½ cups of the hard white flour with the salt, and form a well in the middle. Combine the applesauce and oil in a small saucepan and warm over low heat, then stir in the buttermilk. Pour this mixture and the yeast into the well in the flour and stir to incorporate. Add remaining flour as needed.

Turn the dough out onto a lightly floured surface and knead until smooth and elastic, about 10 to 15 minutes. Knead in the pecans.

Lightly oil a large bowl, place the dough inside, turning it over in the oil, and cover with a clean dish towel. Let the dough rise in a warm place for 90 minutes. Punch the dough down and shape it into a round. Allow to rise for again 50 minutes. At this point, the dough, when pressed with a finger, should dent rather than fill back in.

Lightly oil two 8 x 4-inch loaf pans.

Divide the dough in two and press into the prepared loaf pans. Allow to rise again, another 30 minutes.

Preheat the oven to 350°F. Bake for 55 minutes, or until lightly browned, remove from the pans, and cool on a wire rack.

Bob's High-Fiber Bread

Bran gives this bread a healthy dose of fiber and a great flavor. Use this bread for savory sandwiches, or spread it with goat cheese for a special treat.

Makes two 12-inch loaves

- ¼ teaspoon sugar
- 1¼ cups warm water (105°F. to 115°F.)
- 2¼ teaspoons active dry yeast
- 2½ cups hard whole wheat flour
- ⅓ cup bran
- ¼ cup barley flour
- ½ cup rolled oats
- ¼ cup wheat germ
- 2 teaspoons salt
- Cornmeal, for dusting pan, optional

In a small bowl, stir the sugar into the water. Sprinkle the yeast on top, stirring to dissolve. Allow to rest until it gets foamy, about 5 minutes.

In a large bowl, whisk together 2 cups of the hard whole wheat flour with the bran, barley flour, oats, wheat germ, and salt. Make a well in the middle and pour in the yeast mixture. Stir, gradually incorporating the wet and dry, to form a dough, adding a little more of the hard flour if needed.

Turn the dough out onto a lightly floured surface and knead until smooth and elastic, about 10 to 15 minutes. Lightly oil a large bowl, place the dough inside, turning it over in the oil, and cover with a clean dish towel. Let stand for about 45 minutes, until the dough has doubled in volume.

Line a baking sheet with parchment paper or sprinkle with cornmeal.

Punch the dough down and return it to the floured surface. Divide the dough into two pieces, then roll each piece into a loaf about 12 inches long, with tapered ends. Place the loaves on the prepared baking sheet and cover with the dish towel. Allow to rise again, for 45 minutes to 1 hour, until they almost double in size. At this point, the dough, when pressed with a finger, should dent rather than fill back in.

Preheat the oven to 425°F. Bake for 30 minutes, or until the loaf produces a hollow sound when tapped. Cool on a wire rack.

Bob's Overnight 100 Whole Wheat Bread

Refrigerating this dough overnight gives the yeast a chance to produce its own flavors and convert the starch to sugar. Since yeast acts differently in a cool environment, the resulting acids and enzymes combine beautifully with the strong wheat flavors for a delightfully complex loaf.

Makes two 9 x 5-inch loaves

- 8 cups whole wheat flour
- 3 teaspoons salt
- ¼ cup vegetable oil
- ¼ cup honey
- 3½ cups hot milk or water
- 4½ teaspoons active dry yeast
- 3 tablespoons warm water (105°F. to 115°F.)

Combine the flour, salt, vegetable oil, honey, and the milk and mix well. Cover with plastic wrap and allow to sit overnight at room temperature.

Combine the yeast with the warm water, stir to blend, and allow to rest 5 minutes until foamy. Add the yeast mixture to the dough and blend in thoroughly. Let it rest 10 minutes.

Turn the dough out onto a lightly floured surface and knead until smooth and elastic, about 10 minutes. Lightly oil a large bowl, place the dough inside, turning it over in the oil, and cover with a clean dish towel. Let the dough rise for 1 to 1½ hours, until it doubles in size.

Lightly oil two 9 x 5-inch loaf pans.

Punch the dough down, return it to the floured surface, divide it in half, and shape into loaves to fit the prepared pans. Place the loaves in the pans, cover with the dish towel, and allow to rise again until they double in size, about 45 minutes to 1 hour. At this point, the dough, when pressed with a finger, should dent rather than fill back in.

Preheat the oven to 325°F. Bake the bread for 1 hour, or until hollow sounding when tapped. Remove from pans and cool on wire racks.

Pumpernickel Walnut Bread

True pumpernickel takes about 16 hours to bake, but this recipe cuts that time while still maintaining the rich coffee and chocolate flavors naturally found in a true German pumpernickel—we just add coffee with cocoa and rye. This is a spectacularly hearty loaf of bread, made even more so with the additions of wheat bran and caraway seeds.

Makes two 9-inch loaves

- 4½ teaspoons active dry yeast
- 2¼ cups warm water (105°F. to 115°F.)
- ¼ pound (1 stick) unsalted butter, melted and cooled
- 2 tablespoons honey
- 2 tablespoons instant coffee or espresso powder
- 1 tablespoon caraway seeds
- 1 tablespoon orange zest
- 3 tablespoons unsweetened cocoa powder or carob powder
- 3 cups unbleached white flour
- 2½ cups light rye flour
- ½ cup wheat bran
- 1 tablespoon salt
- ¾ cup walnuts, coarsely chopped
- Cornmeal, for dusting, optional

In a large bowl, sprinkle the yeast over the warm water and stir. Allow it to stand until it gets foamy, about 5 minutes. Stir in the butter, honey, coffee powder, caraway seeds, orange zest, and cocoa.

In a separate bowl, combine the flours, bran, and salt, then add to the yeast mixture to form a dough. Turn the dough out onto a lightly floured surface and knead until smooth and elastic, about 5 to 10 minutes. Lightly oil a large bowl, place the dough inside, turning it over in the oil, and cover with a clean dish towel. Let the dough rise in a warm place until it doubles in size, about 1½ to 2 hours.

Line a baking sheet with parchment paper or dust with cornmeal.

Punch down the dough and turn out onto a lightly floured work surface. Knead in the walnuts, then divide the dough in two and shape each half into a round loaf. Place the rounds on the prepared baking sheet, leaving space between them. Cover with the dish towel and allow the dough to rise until it doubles in size again, about 50 to 60 minutes. At this point, the dough, when pressed with a finger, should dent rather than fill back in.

Preheat the oven to 375°F. Bake the loaves about 35 to 40 minutes, or until they sound hollow when tapped. Transfer to a wire rack and cool completely.

Holiday Bread

This sweet bread is great for holiday celebrations or brunch, especially slathered with sweet cream butter. It's also easy to make, so kids can help make it and are sure to help eat it.

Makes two 9 x 5-inch loaves

- ¼ pound (1 stick) unsalted butter
- ½ cup milk
- 2¼ teaspoons active dry yeast
- ⅓ cup sugar
- ¾ cup warm water (105°F. to 115°F.)
- 1½ cups hard white whole wheat flour
- Zest from 1 large orange
- 2 teaspoons salt
- 3 eggs, lightly beaten
- 2 teaspoons vanilla extract
- 3 cups unbleached white flour
- 1 cup whole wheat flour
- ½ cup slivered almonds
- 1 cup chopped candied fruit of your choice

Combine the butter and milk in a small saucepan and gently heat to melt the butter, then let cool to 105°F. to 115°F.

In a medium bowl, sprinkle the yeast and ⅛ teaspoon of the sugar over the warm water and stir to dissolve, then let stand until foamy, about 5 minutes.

In a large bowl, combine the remaining sugar, the hard white flour, zest, and salt. Add the yeast mixture, the milk mixture, the eggs, and the vanilla extract, and beat using a wire whisk for two minutes or until creamy, scraping down the sides of the bowl occasionally.

In a separate bowl, combine the unbleached white with the whole wheat flour. In ½ cup increments, add the flour mixture to the large bowl, beating for a minute or two after each addition, to make a soft dough (use a wooden spoon if the whisk becomes too clogged). You may not need all of the flour.

Turn the dough out onto a lightly floured surface and knead until smooth and elastic, about 3 to 5 minutes. Lightly oil a large bowl, place the dough inside, turning it over in the oil, and cover with a clean dish towel. Let the dough rise in a warm place until it doubles in size, about 2 hours.

Lightly oil two 9 x 5-inch loaf pans.

Turn the dough out onto a lightly floured surface and flatten into a large rectangle. Sprinkle with almonds and candied fruit and knead to distribute. Divide the dough into two equal portions and roll each to a size that will fit the prepared pans. Place the loaves in the pans, cover with plastic wrap, and allow to rise again, for about 40 to 50 minutes.

Preheat the oven to 350°F. Bake for 45 minutes or until golden brown. Cool on a wire rack.

Brioche Triangles

This eggy bread is a French favorite, great in the morning with a cup of good coffee and even better toasted with butter. Leftover brioche also makes terrific French toast.

Makes about 1 dozen brioche

- ⅓ cup milk
- 2¼ teaspoons active dry yeast
- ¾ cup sugar
- ½ cup whole wheat flour
- 3 cups hard white whole wheat flour, plus more as needed
- 2 teaspoons salt
- 12 tablespoons (1½ stick) unsalted butter
- 4 eggs, beaten
- 1 egg white, beaten with 1 tablespoon water
- Confectioners' sugar for sprinkling

Heat the milk in a medium saucepan until just before boiling, then let it cool to lukewarm, 105°F. to 115°F. Sprinkle the yeast along with ⅛ teaspoon of the sugar over the warm milk, stir to dissolve, then let stand until foamy, about 5 minutes.

In a large bowl, combine the remaining sugar, the flours, and salt. Make a well in the center, add the yeast mixture, butter, and eggs, and stir vigorously to make a stiff dough, adding a little more hard white whole wheat flour if needed.

Turn the dough out onto a lightly floured surface and knead until smooth and elastic, about 5 to 7 minutes. Lightly oil a large bowl, place the dough inside, turning it over in the oil, and cover with a clean dish towel. Allow to rise for at least 6 hours or overnight in the refrigerator.

Preheat the oven to 350°F. Line a baking sheet with parchment paper.

Return the dough to a lightly floured surface and flatten, then roll out to about ⅛ inch-thick, making a rectangle about 8 x 15-inches. From the rectangle, cut out triangles that are 7½- to 8-inches on the sides, with a 2½-inch base. Roll each triangle from the bottom to the point and place about 2½ inches apart on the prepared sheet. Allow to rise for 2 hours. At this point, the dough, when pressed with a finger, should dent rather than fill back in.

Brush the brioche with the egg wash and bake for about 15 minutes, until golden. Remove to a wire rack and allow to cool for a few minutes. Sprinkle with confectioners' sugar. Serve warm.

Tomato Basil Bread

Nothing says summer like the combination of tomatoes and basil, and here you can savor the two baked into a healthy bread. Serve this with an Italian dinner or use for quick sandwiches—the bread has a lot of flavor here so what you put inside doesn't have to be fancy.

Makes two 9 x 5-inch loaves

- 2 tablespoons sugar
- ¾ cup warm water (105°F. to 115°F.)
- 2¼ teaspoons active dry yeast
- 30 basil leaves, stems removed
- 3½ cups hard white whole wheat flour
- 2 teaspoons salt
- ¾ cup canned crushed tomatoes
- 2 tablespoons extra-virgin olive oil
- Cornmeal, for dusting, optional

In a large bowl, dissolve ⅛ teaspoon of sugar in the water and sprinkle the yeast on top. Stir and then let rest until foamy, about 5 minutes.

Using kitchen scissors to prevent bruising, snip the basil leaves into small ribbons and set aside.

Add to the yeast mixture 3 cups of flour along with the remaining sugar, salt, tomatoes, and olive oil, and stir vigorously to form a dough, adding the remaining flour, as needed.

Turn the dough out onto a lightly floured surface and knead until smooth and elastic, about 5 to 10 minutes. Sprinkle the dough with the basil and incorporate as you knead. Lightly oil a large bowl, place the dough inside, turning it over in the oil, and cover with a clean dish towel. Allow the dough to rise for 1 hour.

Return the dough to the floured surface and punch it down. Flatten and divide the dough into two pieces. Shape each piece into a 9 x 5-inch loaf, cover with the dish towel, and allow the loaves to rise for an additional hour.

Line a large baking sheet with parchment paper, or dust it with cornmeal and place it in the oven. Preheat the oven to 425°F. Place the bread on the hot baking sheet and bake for 30 minutes, or until hollow sounding when tapped. Cool on a wire rack.

7-Grain Molasses Bread

The rich flavor of molasses combines wonderfully with seven healthy grains in this unbelievable loaf. For a denser loaf, substitute rolled oats for the 7-Grain cereal.

Makes one 9 x 5-inch loaf

- ½ cup Bob's Red Mill 7-Grain Cereal
- 1 cup plus 3 tablespoons water
- 4 tablespoons unsalted butter
- 3 tablespoons molasses
- 2¼ teaspoons active dry yeast
- 3 cups unbleached white flour
- 3 cups hard white whole wheat flour
- 2 teaspoons salt

Place the cereal or oats in a large bowl.

In a small saucepan, bring the water and butter to a boil, then pour over the cereal. Stir in the molasses and let stand until it cools to 105°F. to 115°F. Stir in the yeast and let stand for 5 or 6 minutes until foamy.

Combine the flours and salt, then stir 3½ cups of the flour mixture into the yeast mixture. Continue adding the flour mixture ½ cup at a time to form a dough. You may not need all of the flour.

Turn the dough out onto a lightly floured surface and knead until smooth and elastic, about 5 to 10 minutes. Lightly oil a large bowl, place the dough inside, turning it over in the oil, and cover with a clean dish towel. Let the dough rise in a warm place until it doubles in size, about 1 hour.

Lightly grease a 9 x 5-inch loaf pan.

Punch the dough down and form it into an oval. Place the dough in the prepared pan, cover, and allow to rise again for 45 minutes to 1 hour, until it doubles in size. At this point, the dough, when pressed with a finger, should dent rather than fill back in.

Preheat the oven to 375°F. Bake the bread for 40 minutes, or until golden and hollow sounding when tapped. Remove the bread from the pan and let it cool on a wire rack.

Honey Granola Bread

Made with sugar-free or low sugar granola, this delightful bread is great for breakfast. It keeps well—up to 3 or 4 days—sealed in a plastic bag.

Makes two 9 x 5-inch loaves

- 4½ teaspoons active dry yeast
- 1¼ cups warm water (105°F. to 115°F.)
- ⅓ cup honey
- 1 cup warm milk (105°F. to 115°F.)
- 2 teaspoons salt
- 2 tablespoons vegetable oil
- 2 cups whole wheat flour
- 4½ cups unbleached white flour
- 1 cup granola

In a large bowl, sprinkle the yeast over ½ cup of the warm water. Add 1 teaspoon of the honey and stir to dissolve. Allow to stand until foamy, about 5 minutes. Stir in remaining ¾ cup of warm water, the honey, milk, salt, and oil.

Add the whole wheat flour, along with 2½ cups of the unbleached white flour, and mix with a wooden spoon until well blended. Stir in the granola, then gradually add 1 cup or more of the remaining flour to make a soft dough.

Turn the dough out onto a lightly floured surface and knead until smooth and elastic, about 10 to 15 minutes, adding remaining flour if the dough is too sticky.

Lightly oil a large bowl, place the dough inside, turning it over in the oil, and cover with a clean dish towel. Allow to rise in a warm place until it doubles in size, about 1 hour.

Lightly oil two 9 x 5-inch loaf pans.

Punch the dough down and divide it into two equal portions. Shape the dough into loaves, place the loaves into the prepared pans, and cover them with the dish towel. Allow the loaves to rise until they double in size, about 45 minutes. At this point, the dough, when pressed with a finger, should dent rather than fill back in.

Preheat the oven to 350°F. Bake for 40 minutes, or until the bread is well-browned and sounds hollow when tapped. Remove from pans and cool on wire racks.

Apple Cinnamon Bread

Apple and cinnamon must be the most basic of sweet bread combinations, one we can't imagine turning our noses up at—unless, of course, it's to smell the wonderful aroma of this bread as it bakes.

Makes two 10-inch loaves

- 2¼ teaspoons active dry yeast
- ⅓ cup warm water (105°F. to 115°F.)
- ½ cup sugar
- 3 medium apples, preferably Granny Smith
- 2½ teaspoons ground cinnamon
- 2 teaspoons salt
- 3 cups hard white whole wheat flour
- 1 cup unbleached white flour
- ⅓ cup milk
- 3 eggs, beaten
- ¼ pound (1 stick) unsalted butter, softened

In a large bowl, sprinkle the yeast over the warm water, add ⅛ teaspoon of sugar, and stir to dissolve. Allow to rest until foamy, about 5 minutes.

Peel, core, and coarsely grate the apples. Set aside.

Whisk together the remaining sugar, cinnamon, salt, and the flours, and add half of this dry mixture to the yeast. Stir the grated apples, milk, and eggs into the yeast mixture, then gradually add the remaining flour, along with the butter, to form a dough. You may not need all of the flour.

Turn the dough out onto a lightly floured surface and knead until smooth and elastic, about 5 to 10 minutes. Lightly oil a large bowl, place the dough inside, turning it over in the oil, and cover with a clean dish towel. Let the dough rise in a warm place until it doubles in size, about 1 hour.

Return the dough to the floured surface. Punch the dough down, then divide it into equal portions. Knead each half for 2 minutes, then form into a round loaf and allow to rest for 10 minutes.

Line 2 baking sheets with parchment paper.

Roll the dough into an oval of about 10 inches by 3½ inches with tapered ends. Place on the prepared sheets and allow to rise for 1 hour. At this point, the dough, when pressed with a finger, should dent rather than fill back in.

Preheat the oven to 350°F. Using a sharp knife, cut 3 or 4 slashes across the top of each loaf. Bake for 30 minutes, or until golden. Cool on a wire rack.

Light Rye with Caraway Seeds

This light, slightly sweet rye bread is great for slathering with mustard and topping with cold cuts. The combination of the whole grain nuttiness and the caraway seeds makes this homemade bread worth the effort.

Makes two 12-inch loaves

- 5 teaspoons active dry yeast
- 1¾ cups warm water (105°F. to 115°F.)
- 2 tablespoons vegetable oil
- 1 teaspoon caraway seeds
- 2½ teaspoons salt
- 2 cups light rye flour
- 3 cups unbleached white flour
- Cornmeal, for dusting, optional

In a large bowl, sprinkle the yeast over the warm water and let stand until foamy, about 5 minutes. Stir in the oil, caraway, salt, rye flour, and 2½ cups of the unbleached white flour to form a dough.

Turn out onto a lightly floured surface and knead, adding more white flour if needed (but not too much; the dough should be a little sticky), until smooth and elastic, about 5 to 10 minutes. Lightly oil a large bowl, place the dough inside, turning it over in the oil, and cover with a clean dish towel. Let the dough rise in a warm place until it doubles in size, about 90 minutes.

Line a baking sheet with parchment paper or lightly dust with cornmeal.

Punch the dough down and place it on a lightly floured surface. Shape and roll the dough to form two oval loaves.

Place the loaves on the prepared baking sheet. Cover with the dish towel and let the loaves rise until they double in size, about 1½ to 2 hours. At this point, the dough, when pressed with a finger, should dent rather than fill back in.

Preheat the oven to 425°F. Using a sharp knife, make 3 or 4 slashes across the top of each loaf. Place the loaves in the oven and reduce the heat to 400°F. Bake for 30 to 35 minutes, until nicely browned, or until the loaves sound hollow when tapped. Cool completely on a wire rack.

Old-Fashioned Triticale Bread

Triticale not only adds a lot of vitamins to this flavorful loaf, but it also adds minerals and fiber. As expected, this hybrid grain gives a bit of a rye flavor mixed with the taste of wheat.

Makes two 9 x 5-inch loaves

- 2 cups water
- 1 cup rolled triticale, plus more for dusting
- 4½ teaspoons active dry yeast
- ½ cup warm water (105°F. to 115°F.)
- ¼ cup vegetable oil
- ½ cup honey
- 2 tablespoons salt
- 1 cup triticale flour
- 5 cups unbleached white flour
- 1 egg white mixed with 1 tablespoon water

Boil the water in a medium saucepan, then add the triticale to the water. Stir, cover, and simmer for 30 minutes. Remove from the heat and allow to cool to 105°F. to 115°F.

In a large bowl, sprinkle the yeast over the warm water and stir to dissolve. Allow to rest 5 minutes or until foamy. Add the oil, honey, salt, triticale flour, and 2 cups of the unbleached white flour. Beat vigorously for 2 minutes, then gradually add additional flour, ½ cup at a time, until the dough begins to pull away from the sides of the bowl. You may not need all of the flour.

Turn the dough out onto a floured work surface and knead, adding flour as needed, until the dough is smooth and elastic, about 10 minutes. Lightly oil a large bowl, place the dough inside, turning it over in the oil, and cover with a clean dish towel. Let the dough rise in a warm place until it doubles in size, about 1 hour.

Lightly oil two 9 x 5-inch loaf pans and press triticale against the insides of the pans. Set aside.

Return the dough to a lightly floured work surface and divide in it half. Shape each half into a loaf and place into the prepared bread pans. Cover with plastic wrap and let the dough rise until almost doubled, about 45 minutes. At this point, the dough, when pressed with a finger, should dent rather than fill back in.

Preheat the oven to 375°F. Just before baking, brush each loaf lightly with the egg wash and sprinkle with additional rolled triticale.

Bake for 30 minutes, or until brown and hollow sounding when tapped. Immediately remove bread from the pans and cool on a wire rack.

Sourdough

A sourdough starter is a mixture—usually of flour, water, and yeast—that is allowed to sit in a warm place to ferment and develop a sour flavor. Once fermented, the starter is used to provide a characteristic sour flavor for breads, pancakes, and other doughs. Without a fully activated sourdough starter (or sourdough culture), your success in making these delicious, tangy baked goods will be sharply limited. The following sourdough recipes call for the starter to be done during the first proof: that is, the starter is warm and active.

Whether you use our Bob's Red Mill packaged sourdough culture or our starter recipe, you will want an aggressively active culture in order to make the best finished product.

To use packaged starter, simply follow the instructions on the Bob's Red Mill Sourdough Starter label. If you want to try your hand at making homemade starter, here are a couple of basic recipes. Sourdough starter isn't necessarily hard to make, but it can fail if attention is not paid to the process. The first recipe below is more traditional, but takes a little more care by the maker. Save leftover starter in the refrigerator for future use. A starter will last virtually forever with proper care and continual feeding. At cooler temperatures, they become less active, but are still in a stage of fermentation and acidity production. However, left alone for too long, starters get too sour and acidic, become bacterial, are not pleasant to taste, and will eventually die. To keep your starter fresh, remove about 1 cup of starter each week and discard it. Add to your started ¼ cup water and ½ cup flour to replenish the culture.

Starter #1

- 3 cups hard white whole wheat flour or unbleached white flour
- 1½ cups warm water (105°F. to 115°F.)

Combine 2 cups hard white whole wheat flour with the water in a 2-quart jar or bowl. Whisk vigorously to stir in air, then loosely cover with cheesecloth, but not plastic wrap (which prevents live organisms from forming in the starter), and allow to sit in a warm place.

Stir the mixture a couple of times a day and in two or three days, bubbles will begin to appear, and it should smell slightly sweet (if it smells bad you may need to start over; in some places where air pollution is a problem, starters can pick up the wrong organisms). Add another cup of flour and another ½ to ⅔ cup warm water or enough to bring it back to the consistency of pancake batter, and stir again. In a day or two it should form a layer of foam. The starter is now ready for use in these recipes.

Starter #2

- 1 cup warm water (105°F. to 115°F.)
- 1¼ cups hard white whole wheat or unbleached white flour
- 1 teaspoon salt
- 1 teaspoon sugar
- 1 medium Russet potato, peeled and grated

Combine the warm water with the flour, salt, and sugar. Add enough potato to the flour mixture to make two cups. Whisk vigorously to stir in air, then cover with cheesecloth and allow to sit in a warm place for 24 hours.

Stir the mixture and cover with plastic wrap; continue to stir once or twice a day. The mixture should become foamy in 2 or 3 days.

Place in the refrigerator and in 3 or 4 days, a liquid on top will indicate that the starter is ready to be activated. Remove the starter from the refrigerator, add up to one cup of flour and ½ to ⅔ cup of lukewarm water (75°F. to 85°F.), and mix briefly.

Leave the starter out in a warm place for 6 to 12 hours to get the yeast very active; you'll know it's ready because it will be covered by foam. Without that foamy cover, the starter is most likely not ready to be used. Store the unused starter in a jar in the refrigerator.

Bob's Red Mill Sourdough Bread

This modest, yet classic, recipe makes a spectacular sourdough.

Makes one 12-inch loaf

- 1½ cups sourdough starter (pages 68-69)
- 1 cup lukewarm water (about 100°F.)
- 2 teaspoons salt
- 1 teaspoon active dry yeast
- 4 cups unbleached white flour, divided
- Cornmeal, for dusting, optional

Stir the starter with the water, salt, yeast, and one cup of the flour. Combine to make a thick dough. Add in additional flour ½ cup at a time until the dough begins to come together. You may not need all of the flour.

Turn the dough out onto a floured surface and knead until smooth and elastic, about 5 to 10 minutes. Lightly oil a large bowl, place the dough inside, turning it over in the oil, and cover with a clean dish towel. Allow the dough to rise until it doubles in size, about 1 to 2 hours.

Return the dough to the floured surface and knead for 30 seconds. Cover and let rest for 5 minutes.

Sprinkle a baking sheet with cornmeal or line it with parchment paper. Shape the dough into a round or long loaf, place on the baking sheet, cover with the dish towel, and allow to rise again until it doubles in size, about 1 hour.

Preheat the oven to 425°F. Using a sharp knife, cut 2 or 3 slashes across the top of the loaf and brush with water. About 5 minutes before baking, place a baking pan with water on the bottom shelf of the oven. This will give the loaf a thick, crispy crust.

Bake the bread about 20 minutes, or until golden brown and hollow sounding when tapped. Cool on a wire rack.

Sourdough Rye Bread

This tangy sourdough is made even better with the added flavors of the rye flour. It can't be beat when served with good sharp Cheddar cheese or, if you really like caraway, Havarti—which is also flavored by caraway.

Makes one 9 x 5-inch loaf

- 2 cups sourdough starter (pages 68-69)
- 1 teaspoon salt
- 1 tablespoon unsalted butter, melted and cooled
- ½ cup water at room temperature
- 2 tablespoons molasses
- ¼ cup honey
- 1 tablespoon caraway seeds
- 1 cup light rye flour
- 2 cups hard white whole wheat flour

In a large bowl, combine the starter with the salt, butter, water, molasses, honey, and caraway, and blend well. Add the rye flour and mix, then add the white whole wheat flour, ½ cup at a time, stirring to form a stiff dough. When it becomes too stiff to stir, turn the dough out onto a lightly floured surface and knead in remaining flour until smooth and elastic, about 5 to 10 minutes.

Lightly oil a 9 x 5-inch loaf pan.

Shape the dough into a loaf, and place it into the prepared pan. Cover and allow the dough to rise in a warm place for 2 to 3 hours. The dough should rise an inch or so above the edge of the pan.

Preheat the oven to 375°F. Bake the loaf for 55 minutes, or until golden and hollow sounding when tapped. Remove from pan and cool on a wire rack.

Sourdough Rye Beer Bread

The beer in this recipe gives the rye a nice tanginess and adds the necessary yeast. Use a good beer for this recipe; the better the beer, the better your bread.

Makes two 9 x 5-inch loaves

- 1 cup porter, stout, or other good ale, room temperature
- 1½ teaspoons salt
- 2 tablespoons sugar
- 2 tablespoons unsalted butter, melted and cooled
- 4 cups sourdough starter (pages 68-69)
- 2 cups rye flour
- 4 cups hard white whole wheat flour

Pour the beer, salt, sugar, and butter into a mixing bowl and stir to dissolve.

Place the starter in a large mixing bowl, add the beer mixture, and mix well. Stir in the rye flour and 1 cup of the hard white flour and mix. Continue adding the white flour, 1 cup at a time, stirring to form a stiff dough. When the dough becomes too stiff to stir, turn it out to a floured surface and knead in remaining flour until the dough is smooth and elastic, about 5 to 10 minutes.

Lightly oil two 9 x 5-inch loaf pans. Divide the dough in half, shape into loaves, and place into the prepared pans. Cover and allow to rise in a warm place for 2 to 3 hours. The dough should rise an inch or so above the edge of the pan.

Preheat the oven to 375°F. Bake the loaves for 50 minutes, or until golden and hollow sounding when tapped. Remove from the pans and cool on a wire rack.

Sourdough Spelt Bread

The earthy flavor of spelt makes for a truly robust sourdough bread. We like it sweetened with a touch of brown sugar and honey. Slice it thin to make sandwiches or for use in French toast.

Makes two 9 x 5-inch loaves

- 2½ tablespoons brown sugar
- 2 teaspoons salt
- ¾ cup warm water (105°F. to 115F.)
- 2 tablespoons honey
- 2 tablespoons unsalted butter, melted and cooled
- 1 tablespoon fennel seeds
- 4 cups sourdough starter (pages 68-69)
- 2 cups whole wheat flour
- 4 cups spelt flour

In a large bowl, combine the sugar and salt with the water and stir to dissolve. Stir in the honey, butter, and fennel seeds. Blend together, then add the starter and combine well.

Add the whole wheat flour and stir to combine. Add the spelt flour, 1 cup at a time, stirring to form a stiff dough. When the dough becomes too stiff to stir, turn it out to a floured surface and knead in the remaining flour to form a smooth and elastic dough, about 5 to 10 minutes.

Lightly oil two 9 x 5-inch loaf pans. Divide the dough in half, shape into loaves, and place into the prepared pans. Cover with a clean dish towel and allow to rise in a warm place for 2 to 3 hours. The dough should rise an inch or so above the edge of the pan.

Preheat the oven to 375°F. Bake the loaves for 50 minutes, or until golden and hollow sounding when tapped. Remove from pans and cool on a wire rack.

Sourdough Kamut® Herb Bread

Kamut® grain flour gives a sweet, nutty flavor to any bread, and paired here with a mix of herbs, it is truly remarkable. For an especially alluring treat, serve this sourdough with figs or fig preserves. The delicate sweetness of the figs pairs wonderfully with the rich, rustic sourdough.

Makes two 9 x 5-inch loaves

- 1 cup warm water (105°F. to 115°F.)
- 2 tablespoons sugar
- ¼ cup vegetable oil
- 4 cups sourdough starter (pages 68-69)
- 2 teaspoons salt
- 3 tablespoons fresh minced, or 3 teaspoons dried mixed herbs such as thyme, oregano, basil, and marjoram
- 1½ cups Kamut® flour
- 4½ cups hard white whole wheat flour

Combine the water with the sugar and oil, then mix with the starter in a large bowl.

In a separate bowl, whisk together the salt, herbs, and flours.

Add two cups of the flour mixture to the starter mixture and stir to combine. Add the flour mixture, 1 cup at a time, stirring to form a stiff dough. When the dough becomes too stiff to stir, turn it out to a floured surface and knead in remaining flour to form a smooth and elastic dough, about 5 to 10 minutes.

Lightly oil two 9 x 5-inch loaf pans. Divide the dough in half, shape into loaves, and place into the prepared pans. Cover with a clean dish towel and allow to rise in a warm place for 2 to 3 hours. The dough should rise an inch or so above the edge of the pan.

Preheat the oven to 350°F. and bake the loaves for 50 minutes, or until golden and hollow sounding when tapped. Remove from pans and cool on a wire rack.

ROLLS

Whole Wheat Rolls

Good on its own, this recipe can be used as a base for a variety of differently flavored rolls. The dough easily incorporates added seeds, raisins, nuts, and even olives or onions, giving you endless options for practically any meal. The variations follow the recipe.

Makes 2 dozen rolls

- ½ teaspoon sugar
- 2 cups warm water (105°F. to 115°F.)
- 2¼ teaspoons active dry yeast
- 2 cups hard white whole wheat flour
- 1 tablespoon salt
- 3 tablespoons honey
- 4 tablespoons unsalted butter, melted and cooled
- 3¼ cups whole wheat flour
- 1 egg beaten with 1 tablespoon water

In a large bowl, combine the sugar and water, and sprinkle on the yeast. Stir to dissolve and allow to rest until foamy, about 5 minutes.

Mix in the hard white flour and stir for one minute. Then add the salt, honey, and butter. Add the whole wheat flour ½ cup at a time to form a stiff dough.

Turn the dough out onto a lightly floured surface and add additional flour to form a tacky (but not sticky) dough. You may not need all of the flour. Knead for 10 minutes, or until smooth and elastic. Lightly oil a large bowl, place the dough inside, turning it over in the oil, and cover with a clean dish towel. Let the dough rise in a warm place until it doubles in size, about 1 hour.

Lightly oil 2 baking sheets or line them with parchment paper.

Punch the dough down and return it to a floured surface. Press the dough down, shape it into a 12- to 14-inch square, then cut into two pieces, and divide those two pieces to form four pieces. Roll each piece into a rope, about 2-inches in diameter. Cut each rope into six pieces. Form each piece into a round, smooth ball, flatten slightly and place on the prepared sheets. Allow to rise in a warm place until they double in size, about 45 minutes.

Preheat the oven to 375°F. and brush egg wash on the tops of the rolls. Bake for 20 minutes, or until nicely browned. Cool on a wire rack.

VARIATIONS

Whole Wheat Orange Poppy Seed Rolls

These are especially good with a bit of whipped cream cheese.

Replace half of the water with orange juice. When you turn the dough out to knead, knead in 1 tablespoon of orange zest and 2½ tablespoons of poppy seeds.

Whole Wheat Cardamom Rolls

Try these rolls with sliced vegetables or eggs scrambled with cream cheese and chives.

Add ½ teaspoon ground cardamom into the melted butter.

Whole Wheat Raisin Rolls

Gently press ½ cup raisins into the dough before the last minute or two of kneading.

Whole Wheat Onion Rolls

Sauté 1 cup minced onion in 1 tablespoon of oil until soft, about 5 minutes (or simply use fresh). Allow to cool, stir into the butter.

Walnut Olive Rolls

Replace the butter with extra-virgin olive oil and add ⅔ cup chopped, pitted Kalamata olives and ⅔ cup chopped walnuts to the batter.

Whole Wheat Rye Rolls

For a twist, try these rolls with roast beef.

Replace 1½ cups of the whole wheat flour with light rye flour and ¾ cup of the water with brewed coffee at 105°F. to 115°F. Add 1 tablespoon caraway or fennel seeds, or a combination.

Seeded Rolls

With any roll recipe above you may sprinkle with a mixture of sesame, poppy, or other seeds to taste after brushing with the egg wash.

Basic Dinner Rolls

These mouthwatering rolls are perfect for dinner, in a basket with jams, or to eat at afternoon tea. Let your guests pile cold cuts and cheeses on them and make scrumptious mini sandwiches.

Makes about 18 rolls

- 1 tablespoon active dry yeast
- ¼ cup warm water (105°F. to 115°F.)
- ¾ cup sugar
- 2 cups hard white whole wheat flour
- 1½ cups whole wheat flour
- 2 teaspoons salt
- ¾ cup milk
- 1 egg, beaten
- 4 tablespoons unsalted butter, softened
- 1½ cups golden raisins
- Cornmeal, for dusting, optional

In a large bowl, sprinkle the yeast over the warm water, add ⅛ teaspoon of sugar, and stir to dissolve. Let stand until foamy, about 5 minutes.

Combine the flours and salt in a large bowl, and make a well in the center. Add the yeast, remaining sugar, milk, egg, and butter and whisk vigorously to form a dough, adding more whole wheat flour if needed.

Turn out onto a lightly floured surface and knead, adding the raisins toward the end of the kneading, for 5 to 7 minutes or until smooth and elastic. Lightly oil a large bowl, place the dough inside, turning it over in the oil, and cover with a clean dish towel. Allow the dough to rise until it doubles in size, about 1 hour.

Line 2 baking sheets with parchment paper or dust with cornmeal.

Punch the dough down, then return to the floured surface and divide the dough into six equal pieces. Divide each of the six pieces into three small balls.

Place the balls, evenly spaced, on the prepared sheets and cover with the dish towel. Allow the dough to rise for 1 hour, until almost tripled in size.

Preheat the oven to 350°F. and bake for 15 minutes, or until golden brown. Cool on a wire rack. Serve warm or at room temperature.

Kamut® Rolls

Kamut grain flour provides a bit of a sweet, nutty flavor and a subdued sunshiny yellow color. Some people even think Kamut has a buttery flavor, but you can decide for yourself with a bite or two . . . or three. . . . Be sure to plan ahead when preparing this bread; the dough must rest for at least 8 hours prior to baking.

Makes about 3 dozen rolls

- ⅛ teaspoon of sugar
- 2¼ teaspoons active dry yeast
- 2½ cups warm water (105°F. to 115°F.)
- 2 cups hard whole wheat flour
- 1 teaspoon salt
- 5 cups Kamut grain flour
- Cornmeal, for dusting, optional

In a large bowl, combine the sugar and yeast with the water and stir to dissolve. Allow to rest until foamy, about five minutes.

Add the hard whole wheat flour and salt to the yeast and stir vigorously, then add 3 cups of the Kamut flour, 1 cup at a time, stirring after each addition. Continue to add the Kamut flour ½ cup at a time, until a firm dough forms. Cover with plastic wrap and refrigerate for at least 8 hours and up to 24 hours.

Punch the dough down and remove it from the bowl to a floured surface. Shape the dough into a large rectangle, about 10 x 14-inches. Cover with a dish towel and allow to rise for 40 minutes.

Place a baking pan with a little water on the bottom of the oven, and preheat the oven to 425°F. (This water will turn to steam, allowing the yeast in your dough to work a little longer than usual, creating a larger loaf.)

Line 2 baking sheets with parchment paper or dust with cornmeal.

Cut the dough in half and each piece in half again. Divide each quarter into 9 or 10 pieces and shape each piece into a ball, then flatten slightly.

Place the rolls on the prepared baking sheets and bake for 20 to 25 minutes, or until golden. Cool on a wire rack.

Pinwheel Bread

This recipe, created by Iris Chambers of Albany, Oregon, was among the winners in the 2005 Bob's Red Mill bread contest at the Oregon State Fair.

Makes three 9 x 5-inch loaves

- 4½ teaspoons active dry yeast
- 2 cups warm water (105°F. to 115°F.)
- 2 cups milk
- ½ cup sugar
- ½ cup shortening
- 2 tablespoons salt
- 7½ cups unbleached white flour
- 1 cup spelt flour
- ¼ cup molasses
- ½ cup 10-Grain Cereal
- 4 cups whole wheat flour

In a large bowl, sprinkle the yeast over the warm water and stir to dissolve. Allow to stand until foamy, about five minutes.

In a saucepan, heat together the milk, sugar, shortening, and salt just until warm (110°F. to 115°F.), stirring constantly until the shortening partially melts. Add to the yeast mixture, then stir in 3 cups of the white flour and 1 cup of the spelt flour until smooth.

Cover the bowl with a clean dish towel and let the dough rise in a warm place for about 1 hour.

Punch the batter down, then transfer about half of the batter (4 cups) to another mixing bowl. To this half, stir in enough of the remaining white flour to make a moderately stiff dough. Turn the dough out onto a lightly floured surface and knead until smooth and elastic, about 6 to 8 minutes, then form into a ball. Lightly oil a large bowl, place the dough inside, turning it over in the oil, and cover with the dish towel.

Into the remaining half of the batter, stir the molasses until well blended. Add the 10-Grain cereal and enough of the whole wheat flour to make a moderately stiff dough. Turn the dough out onto a lightly floured surface and knead until smooth and elastic, about 6 to 8 minutes, then form into a ball. Lightly oil a large bowl, place the dough inside, turning it over in the oil, and cover with the dish towel. Allow dough to rise in a warm place until it doubles in size, about 45 to 60 minutes. Punch the dough down, then let it rise another 10 minutes.

Lightly oil three 9 x 5-inch pans.

Divide each dough ball into thirds. On a lightly floured surface, roll out each portion of dough to a 12 x 8-inch rectangle. Place one dark portion of dough on top of one light portion and roll up tightly into a loaf, beginning at the short side.

Place the loaf in a prepared pan. Repeat with the remaining portions to make three loaves. Cover and let the dough rise again until almost doubled, about 45 to 60 minutes.

Preheat the oven to 375°F. Bake for 30 to 35 minutes, covering with foil after 20 minutes. Brush the tops of the loaves with melted butter. Remove from the pans and cool thoroughly on a wire rack.

Multigrain Buns

These buns not only incorporate loads of health benefits from the four different types of flour, cornmeal, and wheat germ, but they taste great, as well. As complexly flavored as are the many grains used, these rolls are great for sandwiches. They also freeze well; after baking them, let them cool and freeze them in a heavy-duty freezer bag.

Makes 32 buns

- 4½ teaspoons active dry yeast
- 3 cups warm water (105°F. to 115°F.)
- ½ cup honey
- 2 teaspoons salt
- 3 tablespoons vegetable oil
- 1 cup rolled oats
- ½ cup cornmeal
- ½ cup wheat germ
- 2 cups whole wheat flour
- ½ cup rye flour
- ½ cup millet flour
- 3½ cups unbleached white flour
- Cornmeal, for dusting, optional

In a large bowl, sprinkle the yeast on the warm water. Stir until the yeast is dissolved, then let stand until foamy, about 5 minutes.

Stir in the honey, salt, oil, oats, cornmeal, wheat germ, whole wheat flour, rye flour, and millet flour. Beat vigorously until blended, then gradually add the unbleached white flour to form a dough. You may not need all of the flour.

Turn the dough out onto a floured surface and knead until smooth and elastic, about 10 minutes, adding a bit more unbleached white flour if needed. Lightly oil a large bowl, place the dough inside, turning it over in the oil, and cover with a clean dish towel. Let the dough rise in a warm place until it doubles in size, about 1 hour.

Lightly oil 2 baking sheets, line them with parchment paper, or sprinkle with cornmeal.

Return the dough to a lightly floured surface and divide into two pieces. Divide in it half again and again, repeating until you have 32 pieces. Cover half of the pieces, then roll the remaining pieces into balls and flatten. Arrange the flattened balls on the prepared baking sheets, cover and allow to rise for another 45 minutes. Repeat with the remaining 16 pieces, placing them on a floured surface.

Preheat the oven to 375°F. Bake the first batch of buns for 20 minutes, or until golden brown. Transfer to a wire rack to cool. Place remaining dough on the baking sheets and repeat.

Whole Grain Sourdough Muffins

These muffins are a tangy way to begin your day. Start the recipe the night before you plan to serve them, and let the batter rest. In the variations that follow, you'll see you can turn them into fruit, herb, or cheese sourdough muffins.

Makes 12 muffins

- 1¾ cups whole wheat flour
- 1 cup unbleached white flour
- 1 teaspoon baking soda
- 1 teaspoon salt
- ¼ cup sugar
- ½ cup sourdough starter (page 68-69)
- 1½ cups warm milk (105°F. to 115°F.)
- 2 eggs, beaten
- ¼ cup vegetable oil

In a large bowl, blend together the flours, baking soda, salt, and sugar.

In a medium bowl, mix together the starter, milk, eggs, and oil. Pour the wet ingredients into the dry, and stir just to moisten. Cover the lumpy batter with a clean dish towel and let sit at room temperature for 12 hours.

Preheat the oven to 400°F. Grease a 12-cup muffin tin or line with paper muffin tin liners.

Stir the batter just to combine, then spoon into the prepared muffin tins and bake for 20 minutes, or until a tester comes out clean. Serve warm.

VARIATIONS

Add 1½ tablespoons fresh or 1½ teaspoons dried *Herbes de Provence* or a mix of oregano, basil, and thyme to the dry ingredients.

Add 1¾ cups grated Emmenthal, Gruyere, Swiss, or Cheddar cheese to the dry ingredients, and use 1 tablespoon less sugar, and ½ teaspoon less salt

Add 1¼ cups chopped dried apricot to the dry ingredients.

Whole Wheat Bagels

This recipe makes a pleasantly chewy bagel, great topped with sour cream, fresh sliced tomatoes and cucumber, and a grinding of pepper. If you're a seeded bagel fan, simply sprinkle sesame or poppy seeds on a plate and dip the bagels in the seeds, or sprinkle the seeds over the dough just before placing it on the baking sheet.

Makes 18 bagels

- 2¼ teaspoons active dry yeast
- 1 cup warm water (105°F. to 115°F.)
- 1 egg, beaten
- ¼ cup plus 2 tablespoons honey
- 2 tablespoons vegetable oil
- 2 teaspoons barley malt extract
- 1 teaspoon salt
- 2 cups unbleached white flour
- 2½ cups whole wheat flour
- Cornmeal, for dusting, optional

In a large bowl, sprinkle the yeast over the warm water. Stir until the yeast is dissolved, then let stand until foamy, about 5 minutes.

Add the egg, ¼ cup of honey, oil, barley malt, salt, white flour, and 1 cup of the whole wheat flour, beating vigorously for one minute. Add the remaining whole wheat flour, ¼ cup at a time, until a dough forms. You may not need all of the flour.

Turn the dough out onto a floured surface and knead until smooth and elastic, about 10 minutes, adding a bit more flour if needed. Lightly oil a large bowl, place the dough inside, turning it over in the oil, and cover with a clean dish towel. Let the dough rise in a warm place until it doubles in size, about 1 hour.

Punch the dough down and return it to a lightly floured surface. Divide the dough in two, then divide it in two again and repeat until you have 18 pieces. Roll each piece into a 10-inch rope, bring the ends together, and overlap by about ³⁄₄-inch. Press the ends together to form a circle. Cover and repeat with the remaining pieces. Allow to rest 25 minutes.

Meanwhile, fill a stockpot with 6 quarts of water and bring to a boil over high heat. Stir in the remaining 2 tablespoons of honey.

Preheat the oven to 375°F. Lightly oil 2 baking sheets, line them with parchment paper, or dust with cornmeal.

Carefully lower 2 or 3 bagels into the water and boil for about a minute, turn over and boil for another 2 minutes. Remove with a slotted spoon and drain on a cloth towel. Place on a prepared baking sheet. Repeat with remaining dough.

Bake for 20 minutes or until lightly browned. Transfer to a wire rack to cool.

Whole Wheat Potato Bread

Aside from being hearty and delicious, this bread is a great way to use leftover mashed potatoes.

Makes one 10-inch round loaf

- 2¼ teaspoons active dry yeast
- ¼ cup warm water (105°F. to 115°F.)
- ½ cup mashed potatoes, at room temperature
- 1 cup warm milk (105°F. to 115°F.)
- 2 tablespoons brown sugar
- ½ teaspoon salt
- 2 tablespoons vegetable oil
- 1½ cups whole wheat flour
- 2 cups unbleached white flour
- 1 egg beaten with 1 tablespoon water

In a large bowl, sprinkle the yeast on the warm water. Stir until dissolved, and let stand until foamy, about 5 minutes.

Stir in the potatoes, milk, brown sugar, salt, oil, whole wheat flour, and ½ cup of unbleached white flour, beating vigorously for one minute, until smooth. Add the remaining unbleached white flour, ¼ cup at a time, to make a dough. You may not need all the flour.

Turn the dough out onto a floured surface and knead until smooth and elastic, about 10 minutes, adding a bit more flour if needed. Lightly oil a large bowl, place the dough inside, turning it over in the oil, and cover with a clean dish towel. Let the dough rise in a warm place until it doubles in size, about 1 hour.

Line a large baking sheet with parchment paper. Shape the dough into a 10-inch round loaf and place on the baking sheet. Cover and allow to rise for another 45 minutes.

Preheat the oven to 375°F. Brush the top of the loaf with egg wash. Using a sharp knife, cut 3 slashes in the surface of the loaf. Bake until a tester inserted into the center comes out clean, about 25 to 30 minutes. Transfer to a wire rack to cool.

Gluten-Free Rice Bread

This rice bread, like most, is a bit gritty and porous, something that may surprise those unused to baking with rice flour. But once you try it, you're sure to make it again and again. It makes great toast. Although you need to start this bread a day ahead of time, it is a relatively easy recipe. Stored in a plastic bag at room temperature, it will last up to 5 days.

Makes two 8 x 4-inch loaves

- 5½ cups rice flour
- ½ cup garbanzo and fava flour
- 2 teaspoons salt
- 2¾ cups water, at room temperature
- 2¼ teaspoons active dry yeast
- 2 tablespoons sugar
- ½ cup warm water (105°F. to 115°F.)
- 3 tablespoons xanthan gum
- ¼ cup vegetable oil

In a large bowl, combine the flours and salt. Make a well in the center, add the water and beat with an electric mixer for 8 minutes, until well aerated. Cover loosely with a clean dish towel and allow to rest at room temperature for at least 12 hours or overnight.

Preheat the oven to 350°F. Lightly oil or butter two 8 x 4-inch loaf pans.

In a small bowl, sprinkle the yeast, along with ⅛ teaspoon of sugar, over the warm water and stir to dissolve, then let stand until foamy, about 5 minutes. Stir the yeast mixture into the batter, then add the rest of the sugar, the xanthan gum, and the oil, mixing to combine well.

Spoon the batter into the prepared pans and let it rise until it reaches the top of the pans and pinholes appear on top. Depending on the room temperature and how well aerated the batter is, this will take anywhere from 20 to 40 minutes.

Bake for 50 minutes, or until a tester comes out clean.

Cool in the pans on a wire rack for 10 minutes, then remove from the pans and continue cooling on the wire rack until completely cooled.

Whole Wheat Pretzels

It is said that the first pretzels were made by a monk as a reward for children who learned their lessons; the three holes were said to represent the Trinity. These pretzels are made from whole wheat flour but still have the characteristic pretzel crunch.

Makes 32 pretzels

- 2¼ teaspoons active dry yeast
- ¼ cup warm water (105°F. to 115°F.)
- 1 cup warm milk (105°F. to 115°F.)
- ¼ cup sugar
- ¼ cup vegetable shortening, softened
- 4½ cups whole wheat flour
- 1 teaspoon salt
- Kosher salt for sprinkling

In a large bowl, sprinkle the yeast over the warm water, then add the milk and sugar. Stir until the yeast is dissolved, then let stand until foamy, about 5 minutes. Add the shortening and 2 cups of the flour and beat vigorously until smooth. Cover with plastic wrap and allow to rise for 30 minutes.

Add another 1½ cups of flour along with the salt, and beat vigorously for 3 minutes. Gradually add the remaining flour to form a dough. You may not need all of the flour. Turn the dough out onto a lightly floured surface and knead until smooth and elastic, about 10 minutes. Lightly oil a large bowl, place the dough inside, turning it over in the oil, and cover with a clean dish towel. Let the dough rise in a warm place until it doubles in size, about 1 hour.

Return the dough to a lightly floured surface and divide in two, then divide in two again and repeat until you have 32 pieces. Roll each piece into a rope, about 24-inches in length. Form one rope into a u-shape, place the open ends at the top, then cross the open ends twice. Looking at the dough as though it were the face of a clock, bring the ends down to the 5 and 7 o'clock positions. Repeat with the remaining dough, covering each pretzel with a towel as you finish it. Allow to rest 15 minutes.

Preheat the oven to 400°F. Lightly oil 2 baking sheets or line them with parchment paper. Bring 2½ quarts of water to a boil in a large pot. Drop a few pretzels at a time into the water for 10 seconds, then remove with a slotted spoon and place on the prepared baking sheet. Sprinkle with salt. Repeat with remaining pretzels.

Bake for about 15 minutes, or until golden brown. Transfer to a wire rack to cool.

10-Grain French Bread

This recipe, using Bob's Red Mill 10-Grain Cereal, was created by Marie Patten, of Keizer, Oregon. We thought it was so good, we gave her an award at the 2005 Oregon State Fair's Bob's Red Mill sponsored bread contest. Now you, too, can make this award-winning, healthful bread.

Makes two 12-inch loaves

- 4½ teaspoons active dry yeast
- 2 cups warm water (105°F. to 115°F.)
- 2 tablespoons sugar
- 1 tablespoon sea salt
- 2 tablespoons vegetable oil
- 4 cups unbleached white flour
- 1 cup whole wheat flour
- 2⅓ cup Bob's Red Mill 10-Grain cereal
- 1 egg white mixed with 1 tablespoon water
- ½ cup sunflower seeds, shelled
- Cornmeal, for dusting, optional

In a large bowl, sprinkle the yeast over the warm water and stir to dissolve. Allow to stand until foamy, about five minutes.

Stir in the sugar, salt, oil, and three cups of the unbleached white flour. Beat vigorously 2 to 3 minutes, scraping the sides of the bowl occasionally. Gradually add the remaining flours and ⅓ cup of the 10-Grain cereal to make a stiff dough. You may not need all of the flour.

Allow the dough to rest for 10 minutes, then stir down. Repeat four times, allowing the dough to rest for 10 minutes each time between stirring it down.

Lightly oil 2 large baking sheets, line them with parchment paper, or dust with cornmeal.

Turn the dough out onto a lightly floured surface and knead just enough to coat with flour (two or three times) so it can be handled. Divide the dough in half, roll out each half into a 12 x 9-inch rectangle, then roll up from the long side like a jellyroll and pinch the seams to seal.

Combine the remaining 2 cups of 10-Grain cereal with the sunflower seeds. Brush each loaf with the egg wash and coat with the cereal mixture. Place the loaves on the prepared baking sheets. Using a sharp knife, make 3 diagonal slashes along the top of each loaf. Cover with a clean dish towel and let the dough rise at room temperature until it nearly doubles in size, about 30 to 45 minutes.

Preheat the oven to 375°F. Bake for 25 to 30 minutes or until golden brown. Transfer to a wire rack to cool.

Tangy Cheese & Nut Wheat Bread

Another of our 2005 Oregon State Fair bread contest winners, this slightly spicy loaf, created by Frances Benthin, of Scio, Oregon, incorporates sharp Cheddar cheese and full-bodied beer for a sharp and tangy taste.

Makes two 9 x 5-inch loaves

- 1 (12-ounce) bottle of full-bodied beer
- 2¼ teaspoons active dry yeast
- 1 teaspoon sugar
- 1 cup graham flour
- 1 cup wheat germ
- 5 cups unbleached white flour
- 1 cup water
- ¼ cup brown sugar
- 2 teaspoons salt
- 2 teaspoons freshly ground black pepper
- ½ teaspoon cayenne pepper
- 2 cups walnuts, chopped
- 1½ cups sharp cheddar cheese, grated

In a large bowl, mix together the beer, yeast, sugar, and graham flour. Cover lightly with a clean dish towel and allow to sit at room temperature overnight.

The next day, in the same bowl, mix in the wheat germ, white flour, water, brown sugar, salt, pepper, cayenne, walnuts, and cheese, stirring well to combine.

Turn the dough out onto a lightly floured surface and knead until smooth and elastic, about 10 minutes. Lightly oil a large bowl, place the dough inside, turning it over in the oil, and cover with a clean dish towel. Let the dough rise in a warm place until it doubles in size, about 1 hour.

Lightly oil two 9 x 5-inch loaf pans.

Punch the dough down, turn it onto a lightly floured surface, and divide it in half. Shape each half into a loaf and place the loaves in the prepared pans. Cover lightly and let the dough rise again in a warm place until it doubles in size, about 40 minutes

Preheat the oven to 375°F.

Bake the loaves for 35 to 45 minutes, or until firm and golden brown. Transfer to a wire rack to cool. Brush tops of loaves with butter before serving.

Freckles & Warts Bread

Brian Thorp, of Newberg, Oregon, was creative with both the name and the delicious outcome of this recipe that was another 2005 Oregon State Fair award winner. It's a great take on the basic cinnamon and raisin bread that your kids are sure to love eating.

Makes one 9 x 5-inch loaf

- 1¼ cups hot water
- 1 cup Bob's Red Mill 5-Grain rolled cereal
- 1 package rapid rise yeast
- ½ cup orange juice
- 2 tablespoons brown sugar
- 2 tablespoons unsalted butter
- 1¼ teaspoons salt
- 1½ teaspoons ground cinnamon
- 2 cups unbleached white flour
- ¾ cup whole wheat flour
- 3 tablespoons whey protein concentrate
- ¾ cup raisins

In a large bowl, pour the hot water over the 5-Grain cereal, then add the yeast, orange juice, brown sugar, butter, salt, cinnamon, flours, and whey, stirring until well combined.

Turn the dough out onto a lightly floured surface and knead for 8 minutes. Add the raisins and knead for 2 more minutes. Lightly oil a large bowl, place the dough inside, turning it over in the oil, and cover with a clean dish towel. Let the dough rise in a warm place until it doubles in size, about 1 hour.

Preheat the oven to 375°F. Lightly oil a 9 x 5-inch pan.

Punch the dough down, turn it onto a lightly floured surface, shape it into a loaf, and place it in the prepared pan, turning once to coat with oil.

Bake for 35 to 40 minutes, covering with aluminum foil during the last part of baking if it gets too brown. Transfer to a wire rack to cool.

Whole Wheat Oatmeal Bread

This hearty, healthy, and very delicious oatmeal bread comes from Kimella Modrall, of Fairview, Oregon. Her recipe was another of the winners at the 2005 Oregon State Fair.

Makes one 8 x 4-inch loaf

- 2 cups unbleached white flour
- 1 cup whole wheat flour
- ½ cup unsweetened oat bran cereal
- 2 tablespoons brown sugar
- 2¼ teaspoons active dry yeast
- 1 teaspoon salt
- 1 teaspoon ground cinnamon
- 1¼ cups water
- 2 tablespoons unsalted butter

In a large bowl, whisk together the flours, oat bran, brown sugar, yeast, salt and cinnamon.

In a small saucepan, heat the water and butter until warm (105°F. to 115°F.), then gradually stir the water mixture into the flour mixture.

Turn the dough out onto a lightly floured surface and knead until smooth and elastic, about 6 to 8 minutes. Cover the dough with a clean dish towel and let it rest for 10 minutes.

Lightly oil an 8 x 4-inch pan.

On the lightly floured surface, roll the dough out to a 12 x 7-inch rectangle. Beginning at the short end, roll up tightly as for a jellyroll. Pinch the seam and ends to seal. Place, seam side down, in the prepared pan. Cover the pan with the dish towel and let the dough rise in a warm place until it doubles in size, about 1 hour.

Preheat the oven to 375°F.

Bake for 30 to 35 minutes, or until a tester comes out clean. Remove from the pan and cool completely on a wire rack.

High-Protein Dairy Bread

Cottage cheese too heavy, you say? Well, we paired the cottage cheese in this recipe with rice flour to make this pleasantly light loaf. With a touch of sweetness from the honey, and a high level of protein from the dairy ingredients, this bread will be a truly tasty energy booster.

Makes two 8 x 4-inch loaves

- 1/8 teaspoon sugar
- 1/2 cup warm water (105°F. to 115°F.)
- 2¼ teaspoons active dry yeast
- 1½ cups cottage cheese
- 2 eggs, beaten
- 2 tablespoons honey
- 1 tablespoon sugar
- 2/3 cup water
- 1 cup rice flour
- 4 cups whole wheat flour
- 1/2 cup milk powder
- 1 teaspoon salt
- 2½ tablespoons unsalted butter, chilled and diced

In a small bowl, stir the sugar into the water to dissolve, then sprinkle with the yeast and stir. Allow to stand until foamy, about five minutes.

In a saucepan, warm the cottage cheese, taking care not to overheat it. Remove from the heat and stir in the eggs, honey, sugar, and water.

In a large bowl, whisk together the flours, milk, and salt. Stir in the yeast and cottage cheese mixtures to form a sticky dough. The dough should be sticky but if it is unworkable, add whole wheat flour a little at a time.

Turn the dough out onto a lightly floured surface and knead until smooth and elastic, about 5 minutes. Sprinkle the butter over the dough and continue to knead for another 5 minutes or so until incorporated.

Lightly oil a large bowl, place the dough inside, turning it over in the oil, and cover with a clean dish towel. Let the dough rise in a warm place for about 1 hour 15 minutes. At this point, the dough, when pressed with a finger, should dent rather than fill back in.

Punch the dough down, shape it into a ball, cover with the dish towel and let the dough rise again, for another hour.

Lightly oil two 8 x 4-inch loaf pans.

Divide the dough in half. Shape each half into a loaf, place the loaves in the prepared pans, cover, and allow to rest for 30 minutes.

Preheat the oven to 325°F. Bake for 50 minutes, or until a tester comes out clean. Allow to cool completely on a wire rack before slicing.

Luscious Lemon Rolls

These rolls are a zingo zango lemony burst of flavor. For a twist, we make them in muffin tins, but you can also bake them as two loaves at 325°F. for 40 minutes. These rolls also freeze quite well; just bake them, let them cool, and freeze them in a freezer bag. Allow them to defrost at room temperature to prevent mushiness and to keep that zingy flavor.

Makes 24 rolls or two 8 x 4-inch loaves

- 2¼ teaspoons active dry yeast
- ½ cup warm water (105°F. to 115°F.)
- 4 cups whole wheat flour
- 1½ cups oat flour
- 2 teaspoons salt
- Zest of one lemon, about 1 tablespoon
- 1⅓ cups cottage cheese, drained if necessary
- ¾ cup hot water (105°F. to 115°F.)
- 1 tablespoon honey
- 2 tablespoons vegetable oil
- 1 tablespoon sugar

In a medium bowl, sprinkle the yeast over the warm water and stir to dissolve. Allow to rest until foamy, about five minutes.

In a large bowl, whisk together the flours, salt, and zest.

Mix in the cottage cheese, hot water, honey, oil, and sugar into the yeast mixture, then add the new mixture to the flour to form a dough. Add a little more water or flour as needed.

Turn the dough out onto a lightly floured surface and knead until smooth and elastic, about 15 minutes. Lightly oil a large bowl, place the dough inside, turning it over in the oil, and cover with a clean dish towel. Let the dough rise in a warm place until it doubles in size, about 90 minutes.

Punch the dough down, knead for about 2 to 3 minutes, then shape it into a ball again, cover, and let the dough rise another 45 minutes.

Lightly oil two 12-cup muffin tins or line with paper liners. Divide the dough into two pieces, then in two again and repeat until you have 24 pieces. Place the dough pieces in the prepared tins, cover, and let the dough rise in a warm place for 25 minutes.

Preheat the oven to 400°F.

Bake for 15 to 20 minutes, or until a tester comes out clean. Transfer to a wire rack to cool.

Quick Breads, Muffins, Biscuits, & Scones

This chapter includes some of our favorite whole grain breakfast foods and easy-to-make breads. Aside from being delicious, one of the great things about quick breads is that you can assemble the dry ingredients the night before and then simply combine them with the wet ingredients and bake the next morning.

We've included unbleached white flour in many of our recipes because—in general, quick breads, muffins, biscuits, or scones containing only whole grains are too crumbly and dry. But definitely experiment with your favorite family recipes to add whole grain flour to them. Start by substituting up to half of the unbleached white flour with whole wheat or whole wheat pastry flour, slightly increase the wet ingredients, add a bit more baking powder, and cut back on the sugar just a touch. It may take a few tries to get the adjusted recipe just right, but don't give up. The health benefits are worth the extra effort.

Baking Tips for this Chapter

When making quick breads, it's best to level the playing field when it comes to the temperature of your ingredients—everything should start out at room temperature. If you keep your flours in the refrigerator, take the flour out of the refrigerator before using and bring it to room temperature. If you forget or are in a hurry, you can compensate by using slightly warmer liquids.

Cool butter after melting it. Pouring hot butter over cold eggs can result in scrambled eggs. Because cold eggs and milk can also slightly retard the rising, they also work best when brought to room temperature.

For a slightly lighter batter, you can separate the eggs and add just the yolks when the recipe calls for eggs. Beat the whites until they are light and fold them in at the end. Some breads should be denser and chewier, especially savory ones, so keep that in mind when considering whether to add the egg whites later using this method.

If possible, use an electric mixer for creaming the sugar and butter and for combining the egg mixture.

Mix the dry and wet ingredients thoroughly *before* combining them so the ingredients are evenly distributed. For most quick breads, you want to avoid overmixing when you combine wet and dry ingredients just mixing long enough to moisten the dry ingredients. Don't worry if the batter is lumpy. Stir, whisk, or fold, rather than beat, wet ingredients into the dry, unless the recipe specifies otherwise. Beating the batter can cause the gluten to stiffen, resulting in tough bread. Mix until just moistened—whole grain quick breads can be mixed a little more thoroughly than those made with just unbleached white flours because they have less gluten.

Once you've mixed the wet ingredients, don't let them sit at room temperature for more than 20 minutes. If you want to do some advance preparation, combine the dry ingredients and have all of the wet ingredients out. After you have combined the wet with the dry, bake immediately.

Because oven temperature is important, always be sure to properly preheat your oven. Quick breads need a hot oven to rise properly. These temperatures and times are for conventional ovens, so if you are using a convection oven, reduce the temperature by twenty-five degrees and check on your baked good a few minutes before the recipe says it should be done. The times given in this book are minimum times—they are the time you should check for doneness, but the bread may not be quite ready. Remember, oven temperatures vary, and even the size of a large egg can affect your baking time.

Spritz breads with a water-filled spray bottle as you bake for a crunchier crust. You can also place a small baking pan filled halfway with water on the lowest rack in your oven. This will create steam, crisping the sides as the bread rises. Fill unused muffin cups with water to help the muffins bake evenly and to add a little steam.

Let breads and muffins cool in their pan for a few minutes before unmolding. This helps them keep their structure as any steam is released.

You can substitute brown sugar for granulated sugar, and vice-versa in bread, muffin, and scone recipes, but add the brown sugar to the wet ingredients and the granulated sugar to the dry.

If you'd like to substitute oil for butter, use about 10 percent less oil.

If you don't have the pan called for in the recipe, simply adjust the baking time. Bake until a toothpick inserted in the center comes out clean no matter what the time calls for. If you use a smaller pan than called for in the recipe, the cooking time will be a few minutes longer. If you use a larger pan, the time will be shorter. (Don't miss our Pan Chart on page 427!)

Most quick breads freeze very well, except those with fresh berries which tend to release water into the bread as they thaw, making them sticky. To freeze, seal cooled quick breads in a freezer bag and store for up to 4 weeks. Defrost to room temperature: if you try to heat the bread, it will turn gummy.

QUICK BREADS

Cranberry Bread

Tart cranberries, one of the few fruits native to North America, are grown in the northeast, upper Midwest, and here in our great Pacific Northwest, not far from our mills in Portland. This bread is a perfect match of slightly sour cranberries and sweet bread. It tastes even better the day after you bake it.

Makes one 9 x 5-inch loaf

- 2½ cups sifted whole wheat flour
- 1½ cups sifted whole wheat pastry flour
- 1 cup sugar
- 4 teaspoons baking powder
- 1 teaspoon salt
- 1 egg, lightly beaten
- 4 tablespoons unsalted butter, melted and cooled
- 1½ cups milk
- 1 cup fresh cranberries, coarsely chopped
- ½ cup toasted almonds or pecans, coarsely chopped

Preheat the oven to 350°F. Grease a 9 x 5-inch loaf pan, or line it with parchment paper.

In a large bowl, whisk together the flours, sugar, baking powder, and salt.

In another bowl, beat together the egg, butter, and milk, then combine with the dry ingredients. Stir in the cranberries and almonds, then pour the batter into the prepared pan and bake for about 60 minutes, or until a tester inserted into the center comes out clean. Let the bread rest for a few minutes, then remove from the pan and cool on a wire rack.

Persimmon Bread

Persimmons, which are pretty much inedible in their raw state, cook beautifully with a flavor reminiscent of apricots and honey. This luscious bread was created by Jan Mancuso of Portland, who makes this bread each fall, when persimmons flood the produce departments of local stores. If you can find some in your own local markets, don't forget to try this bread.

Makes two 9 x 5-inch loaves

- 1 cup unbleached white flour
- 1½ cups whole wheat pastry flour
- 1½ teaspoon salt
- 2½ teaspoons baking soda
- 2 cups sugar
- 4 teaspoons ground cinnamon
- 1 teaspoon ground nutmeg
- 4 eggs, lightly beaten
- ⅔ cup bourbon, brandy, or orange juice
- 2 cups (about 8 persimmons) Hachiya persimmon pulp, pureed
- 2 cups walnuts, coarsely chopped
- 2 cups golden raisins
- ½ pound (2 sticks) unsalted butter, melted and cooled

Preheat the oven to 350°F. Grease two 9 x 5-inch loaf pans or line them with parchment paper.

Sift together the flours, salt, baking soda, sugar, and spices into a medium bowl.

In a large bowl, beat the eggs with the bourbon, then stir in the persimmon pulp, walnuts, and golden raisins.

Add the persimmon mixture to the flour mixture and whisk, gradually adding the butter.

Spoon the batter into the prepared pans and bake for 55 to 60 minutes, or until a tester comes out clean. Let the bread rest for a few minutes, then remove from the pan and cool on a wire rack.

Apple Nut Bread

Apples are never far from us in Portland, Oregon, where the numerous apple and pear orchards near Mt. Hood have inspired a particular route to be dubbed the "Fruit Loop." We think the sweetness from plenty of honey mixes perfectly with the apple and spice in this bread. Hazelnuts, toasted and chopped, may stand in for the walnuts.

Makes one 9 x 5-inch loaf

- 2½ cups hard white whole wheat flour
- ½ cup unbleached white flour
- 1½ tablespoons ground cinnamon
- 1 teaspoon ground allspice
- ½ teaspoon ground ginger
- 2½ teaspoons baking powder
- ¼ cup sugar
- 2 eggs
- ¾ cup honey
- 1 cup milk
- 5 tablespoons unsalted butter, melted and cooled
- ¾ cup walnuts or pecans, chopped
- 2½ cups Granny Smith apple, peeled, cored and coarsely grated

Preheat the oven to 350°F. Grease a 9 x 5-inch loaf pan or line it with parchment paper.

Whisk together the flours, spices, baking powder, and sugar in a large bowl.

In a separate bowl, beat the eggs then beat in the honey, milk, and butter.

Combine the wet ingredients with the dry, then stir in the walnuts and apple.

Spoon the batter into the prepared pan and bake for 55 minutes, or until a tester comes out clean. Let the bread rest for a few minutes, then remove it from the pan and cool it on a wire rack.

Healthy Honey Tea Bread

Katie Schulze of Portland, Oregon, provided us with this recipe for a healthy honey and tea-flavored bread that she enjoys with orange marmalade along with her morning cup of tea. She uses English or Irish breakfast tea to make this loaf, but feel free to experiment with your own favorite brews.

Makes one 9 x 5-inch loaf

- 1 cup unbleached white flour
- 2/3 cup hard white whole wheat flour
- 1/3 cup wheat germ
- 1/2 teaspoon salt
- 1/2 teaspoon ground cinnamon
- 1/2 teaspoon ground ginger
- 1 1/2 teaspoons baking powder
- 3/4 cup milk
- 1/2 cup honey
- 1/3 cup brewed tea
- 1/3 cup vegetable oil
- 1 egg

Preheat the oven to 350°F. Grease a 9 x 5-inch loaf pan, or line it with parchment paper.

Combine the flours, wheat germ, salt, cinnamon, ginger, and baking powder in a small bowl. Beat the remaining ingredients in a large bowl until well blended, then whisk in the flour mixture 1/2 cup at a time, incorporating well before each new addition.

Spoon into the prepared pan and bake for 45 minutes, or until a tester comes out clean. Let the bread rest for a few minutes, then remove it from the pan and cool on a wire rack.

Tangerine Tea Cake

This citrusy and moist cake is much like a pound cake and is great for dessert with a little ice cream, or as a breakfast treat. While tangerines provide a strong citrus flavor, oranges make a fine substitute.

Makes one 8¹/₂ x 4¹/₂-inch loaf

- 1¹/₂ cups sifted unbleached white flour
- 1¹/₂ cups sifted whole wheat flour
- 1 teaspoon baking soda
- ¹/₂ teaspoon salt
- Zest of 3 tangerines
- ¹/₄ cup tangerine juice (from about 2 tangerines)
- 1 tablespoon lemon juice
- ¹/₄ pound (1 stick) unsalted butter, softened
- ¹/₂ cup vegetable shortening
- 1³/₄ cups sugar
- 3 eggs
- 1 cup buttermilk

Preheat the oven to 350°F. Grease the bottom of an 8¹/₂ x 4¹/₂-inch baking pan, or line it with parchment paper.

Sift together the flours, baking soda, and salt. In a separate bowl stir the zest and juices together.

Cream the butter and shortening together with the sugar until the mixture is lemon-yellow in color, about 4 minutes. Add the eggs one at a time, incorporating each fully and scraping down the sides of the bowl after each addition. Add ¹/₃ of the flour to the butter mixture, followed by half of the buttermilk. Repeat, then finish by folding in the rest of the flour. Add the juice mixture and stir.

Pour the batter into the prepared pan and bake for 55 minutes, or until a tester comes out clean. Cool in the pan on a wire rack.

Walnut Bread

Mary Monson, of Columbus Junction, Iowa, created this walnut bread that bakes to a lovely mahogany color and has a rich flavor and chewy texture.

Makes one 9 x 5-inch loaf

- 1¾ cups walnuts
- 2 tablespoons unsalted butter, softened
- 1 tablespoon walnut oil, or extra-virgin olive oil
- ¾ cup sugar
- 1 egg, lightly beaten
- ¾ cup unbleached white flour
- 1¼ cups whole wheat flour
- 1½ teaspoons baking powder
- ¼ teaspoon salt
- 1¼ cups milk

Preheat the oven to 350°F.

Put the walnuts on an ungreased and rimmed baking sheet or jellyroll pan and bake for 5 to 10 minutes, keeping an eye on them, until they look golden brown. Be careful—nuts burn very quickly because of their high oil content, so it's important to watch them carefully. Remove the nuts from the pan and cool them before roughly chopping them and setting them aside.

Leave the oven set at 350°F. Grease a 9 x 5-inch loaf pan, or line it with parchment paper.

Cream the butter, oil, and sugar for 4 minutes, then add the egg and beat for another minute, scraping down the sides of the bowl.

Sift together the flours, baking powder, and salt, then add to the butter mixture along with the milk. Stir to combine, gently folding in the chopped nuts.

Pour the batter into the prepared pan and bake for 40 minutes, or until a tester comes out clean. Let the bread rest for a few minutes still in the pan, then remove it from the pan and cool it on a wire rack.

Pumpkin Cranberry Bread

Hold a slice of this moist and aromatic bread in your hand, and close your eyes—it's just like holding a slice of pumpkin pie and a side of cranberry sauce in your hand, but without the mess.

Makes two 9 x 5-inch loaves

- 1³/4 cups unbleached white flour
- 1¹/4 cups whole wheat pastry flour
- ¹/8 teaspoon ground cloves
- ¹/4 teaspoon ground ginger
- ¹/2 teaspoon ground cinnamon
- 2¹/2 teaspoons baking soda
- 1¹/2 teaspoons salt
- 2³/4 cups sugar
- 1 (15-ounce) can pumpkin
- 4 eggs
- 1 cup vegetable oil
- ¹/2 cup milk
- 1 cup fresh or dried cranberries

Preheat the oven to 350°F. Grease two 9 x 5-inch loaf pans, or line them with parchment paper.

Combine the flours, spices, baking soda, and salt in a large bowl. In a separate bowl, beat together the sugar, pumpkin, eggs, oil, and milk until just blended.

Combine the wet ingredients with the dry until just moistened, then fold in the cranberries.

Pour the batter into the prepared pan and bake for about 60 minutes, or until a tester comes out clean. Let the bread rest for a few minutes, then remove it from the pan and cool on a wire rack.

Strawberry Nut Bread

Forget pre-packaged fruit bars. This nutty, fruity bread is a healthy breakfast treat, made even better spread with cream cheese (think strawberries and cream). Or enjoy it on a warm summer day, when strawberries are in full bloom, with an ice cold glass of lemonade.

Makes one 9 x 5-inch loaf

- 2 pints strawberries, hulled
- 1 cup sugar
- 5 tablespoons unsalted butter, softened
- 2 eggs
- 1 cup unbleached white flour
- ¾ cup whole wheat pastry flour
- 1½ teaspoon baking powder
- 1 teaspoon baking soda
- ½ teaspoon salt
- ½ teaspoon ground cinnamon
- ⅓ cup milk
- ½ cup walnuts, chopped

Preheat the oven to 350°F. Grease a 9 x 5-inch loaf pan, or line it with parchment paper.

Place half of the strawberries in a blender and puree. Add enough strawberries to make 1 cup of puree. Set aside the rest of the strawberries. Pour the puree into a saucepan, bring to a boil, and cook stirring constantly for 1 minute. Remove the puree from the heat and cool. Slice the remaining strawberries.

In a large bowl, cream the sugar, butter, and eggs. In a separate bowl, whisk together the flours, baking powder, baking soda, salt, and cinnamon.

Add one-third of the flour mixture to the butter and egg mixture, and incorporate, then add half the milk and incorporate. Repeat until all of the flour and milk is added, then stir in the strawberry puree and walnuts.

Pour the batter into the prepared pan and bake for about 1 hour, or until a tester comes out clean. Let the bread rest for a few minutes, then remove it from the pan and cool it on a wire rack.

Zucchini Bread

Our moist, whole grain version of this American classic always makes the kitchen smell good when it's in the oven. This recipe is a great way to use the overabundance of zucchinis grown during the summer months.

Makes two 9 x 5-inch loaves

- 2 cups unbleached white flour
- 1¼ cups whole wheat pastry flour
- ½ teaspoon salt
- 2½ teaspoons baking powder
- 1 teaspoon baking soda
- 2 teaspoons ground cinnamon
- 2 tablespoons lemon zest
- 3 eggs
- 1 cup vegetable oil
- 1¾ cups sugar
- 1½ teaspoons vanilla
- 3 cups grated zucchini
- 1 cup walnuts, coarsely chopped

Preheat the oven to 350°F. Grease two 9 x 5-inch loaf pans, or line them with parchment paper.

In a small bowl, combine the flours, salt, baking powder, baking soda, cinnamon, and zest. In a large bowl, beat the eggs with the oil, sugar, and vanilla.

Whisk the dry ingredients into the wet, then fold in the zucchini and walnuts.

Pour the batter into the prepared pans and bake for 50 minutes, or until a tester comes out clean. Let the bread rest for a few minutes, then remove it from the pan and cool it on a wire rack.

Banana Flax Bread

The flaxseed meal in this bread creates a fantastic nutty flavor that nicely compliments the bananas. It also creates a pleasantly coarse texture. The bananas help sweeten the bread which means you use less sugar.

Makes two 9 x 5-inch loaves

- 1½ cups unbleached white flour
- ¼ cup hard white whole wheat flour
- ¾ cup golden flaxseed meal
- 1 teaspoon ground cinnamon
- ¾ cup sugar
- 1½ teaspoons baking powder
- ½ teaspoon baking soda
- ¼ teaspoon salt
- ⅓ cup walnuts, chopped
- 2 eggs
- ⅓ cup vegetable oil
- 3 medium bananas, very ripe, peeled and mashed to pulp

Preheat the oven to 350°F. Grease two 9 x 5-inch loaf pans, or line them with parchment paper.

Combine the flours, flaxseed meal, cinnamon, sugar, baking powder, baking soda, and salt in a medium bowl. Stir in the nuts.

In a large bowl, beat together the eggs and the oil. Add half of the dry ingredients to the egg and oil mixture, then add the mashed bananas, combining well. Add the remaining dry ingredients to moisten.

Pour the batter into the prepared pans and bake, checking the loaf after 45 minutes. If it is browning quickly but not yet fully baked, cover the loaves loosely with foil and continue to bake for another 10 minutes, or until a tester comes out clean. Let the breads rest for a few minutes, then remove them from the pan and cool on a wire rack.

10-Grain Yogurt Quick Bread

Bob's Red Mill 10-Grain Flour contains freshly milled wheat, rye, triticale, oats, corn, barley, soy beans, brown rice, millet, and flax seeds. This flour makes a moist and flavorful loaf that is also nutritious and full of fiber. Use it in your favorite recipes for breads, pancakes, cookies, biscuits, and other baked goods and try substituting a little of this flour for unbleached white or other flour. For example, in bread recipes, use 1/4 to 1/2 cup of Bob's 10-Grain Flour in place of regular flour per loaf of bread.

Makes two 9 x 5-inch loaves

- 3 cups Bob's Red Mill 10-Grain Flour
- 1 teaspoon salt
- 2 teaspoons baking soda
- 1/2 cup brown sugar
- 1/4 cup vegetable oil
- 3 eggs, lightly beaten
- 2 cups plain yogurt

Preheat the oven to 350°F. Grease two 9 x 5-inch loaf pans, or line them with parchment paper.

In a large bowl, combine the flour, salt, baking soda, and brown sugar.

In another bowl, beat the oil into the eggs, then fold in the yogurt thoroughly. Pour the wet ingredients into the dry and stir until moistened.

Pour the batter into the prepared pans and bake for 55 minutes, or until a tester comes out clean. Let the breads cool in the pan for a few minutes, then remove them from the pan and cool on a wire rack.

Cheese Spoon Bread

GLUTEN-FREE

This is a very soft, filling bread with the consistency of a firm pudding. It's called a spoon bread because you have to eat it with, what else? A spoon. Traditional in the American South, spoon breads are great for breakfast or as a side dish with dinner.

Makes one 8 x 8-inch loaf

- 1 cup cornmeal
- 1 tablespoon soy flour
- 1 teaspoon salt
- 1¼ cups boiling water
- 4 tablespoons unsalted butter, melted and cooled
- 2 eggs
- 1¼ cups milk
- ¼ cup grated cheddar cheese
- 2 teaspoons baking powder

Preheat the oven to 350°F. Grease an 8 x 8-inch 2-quart baking dish.

Combine the cornmeal, soy flour, and salt in a bowl and, stirring constantly, gradually pour in the boiling water. Stir in the butter.

In a separate bowl, whisk the eggs until thick, then add the milk. Stir in the cheddar cheese and baking powder and add to the cornmeal mixture. Whisk well to combine. Pour the batter into the prepared dish and bake for 30 minutes, or until firm. Let the bread cool in the pan for at least 10 minutes before serving, directly out of the pan.

Candied Fruit Bread

Because this recipe uses only citrus, it's not as dense as the fruit bread eaten around the holidays. Candied fruit peel is widely available in markets, or you can make your own—the recipe follows the bread recipe.

Makes two 9 x 5-inch loaves

- ²/₃ cup sugar
- 2 cups unbleached white flour
- ½ cup whole wheat flour
- ½ cup millet flour, or substitute with same amount whole wheat flour
- 1¾ teaspoons baking powder
- ½ teaspoon salt
- 1 cup candied lemon or orange peel (recipe follows)
- 6 tablespoons unsalted butter, melted and cooled
- 1 egg
- 1 cup milk

Preheat the oven to 375°F. Grease two 9 x 5-inch loaf pans, or line them with parchment paper.

In a large bowl, whisk together the sugar, flours, baking powder, and salt. Transfer ¼ cup of this mixture to a small bowl and stir in the candied peel.

In a small bowl, whisk together the butter, egg, and milk, then add this to the flour mixture, stirring until just combined. Whisk in the candied fruit.

Pour the batter into the prepared pans and bake for 50 minutes, or until a tester comes out clean. Let the breads rest for a few minutes, then remove them from the pan and cool on a wire rack.

Candied Fruit Peel

- 4 lemons (or 2 oranges)
- ²/₃ cup sugar
- ¼ cup water

Cut the lemons into sixths (or the oranges into eighths), and peel, reserving the flesh of the fruit for another use. Using a sharp knife, remove the white pith, leaving just the outer colored skin.

Place the peel in a sauce pan with cold water to cover, bring to a boil, lower the heat, and simmer, uncovered, for 20 minutes. Drain in a colander, then add the sugar and water to the saucepan and cook over medium heat, stirring occasionally, until the sugar is dissolved. Lower the heat to a bare simmer and cook about 15 minutes more, until the syrup is thick. Remove the peel from the pan and transfer to a rack to cool and dry completely, at least 2 hours. Mince the peel and use in the recipe above. The peel may be made two days ahead and stored in an airtight container at room temperature.

Whole Wheat Irish Soda Bread

Made with mostly whole wheat flour, this soda bread is rich and dark, and is as equally marvelous with stew as it is for breakfast with butter and jam.

Makes one 8-inch round

- 4½ cups whole wheat flour
- 1½ cups unbleached white flour
- 1 teaspoon salt
- 3 teaspoons sugar
- 1½ teaspoons baking soda
- 2⅓ cups buttermilk
- ⅔ cup raisins

Preheat the oven to 400°F. Lightly oil a baking sheet, or line it with parchment paper.

Whisk together the flours, salt, sugar, and baking soda in a large bowl. Pour in the buttermilk and raisins and mix until stiff. Shape the dough into a ball, then place on the baking sheet and flatten into a round about 2 inches thick. Using a sharp knife, cut 2 or 3 slashes across the top of the loaf.

Bake for 35 minutes or until a tester comes out clean. Cool completely on a wire rack before slicing.

Chocolate Hazelnut Bread

This chocolate treat marries hazelnuts and chocolate—a match made in heaven. Drizzle a slice of this bread with a little raspberry syrup or serve it with vanilla ice cream, and you'll feel like you're at their wedding.

Makes one 9 x 5-inch loaf

- 1½ cups unbleached white flour
- 1 cup whole wheat pastry flour
- ⅔ cup unsweetened Dutch process cocoa powder
- 1¼ teaspoons baking powder
- 1 teaspoon baking soda
- ½ teaspoon ground cinnamon
- ½ teaspoon salt
- 5 tablespoons unsalted butter, softened
- ½ cup (4 ounces) cream cheese, room temperature
- 1¼ cups sugar
- 2 eggs
- 1⅓ cups buttermilk
- 1 teaspoon vanilla extract
- ¾ cup hazelnuts, skinned, toasted, and chopped
- Raw sugar for sprinkling, optional

Preheat the oven to 350°F. Grease a 9 x 5-inch loaf pan, or line it with parchment paper.

In a medium bowl, sift together the flours, cocoa, baking powder, baking soda, cinnamon, and salt.

In a large bowl, cream the butter with the cream cheese, then beat in the sugar for 3 minutes. Add the eggs one at a time, beating well and scraping the sides of the bowl after each addition.

In a separate bowl, combine the buttermilk and vanilla.

Add half of the dry ingredients to the butter mixture and incorporate, then add half of the buttermilk mixture. Incorporate well, then repeat with the remaining flour mixture, followed by the remaining buttermilk mixture. Fold in the hazelnuts.

Pour the batter into the prepared pan and smooth the top. Sprinkle with raw sugar. Bake for 1 hour; if the bread begins to brown before it is fully cooked, cover the loaf with foil. Continue to bake another 15 minutes, or until a tester comes out clean. Let the bread rest for a few minutes, then remove it from the pan and cool on a wire rack.

Stollen

Stollen is a very sweet German bread pastry that is traditionally served at Christmas; its shape represents the Christ child wrapped in swaddling clothes. This recipe is a healthier version of this most popular holiday bread.

Makes one 10 x 7½-inch loaf

- 1½ cups unbleached white flour
- 1 cup whole wheat pastry flour
- ¾ cup sugar
- 2 teaspoons baking powder
- ½ teaspoon baking soda
- ¼ teaspoon ground mace
- ½ teaspoon ground nutmeg
- ½ teaspoon salt
- ¼ pound (1 stick) unsalted butter, softened
- 1 (8 ounce) package cream cheese, room temperature
- 1 egg
- 1 teaspoon almond extract
- 1 teaspoon vanilla extract
- ⅓ cup golden raisins
- ½ cup dried apricots
- ½ cup dried cherries

Preheat the oven to 350°F. Grease a baking sheet, or line it with parchment paper.

Combine the flours, sugar, baking powder, baking soda, spices, and salt in a large bowl.

Cream the butter and cream cheese until light lemon-yellow in color, then add the egg, almond and vanilla extracts, and beat until smooth. Beat in the dry ingredients ⅓ cup at a time, scraping the sides of the bowl occasionally. Stir in the raisins, apricots, and cherries.

Turn the batter onto a floured surface and knead 5 or 6 times to make a stiff dough. Transfer to the baking sheet and form into a 10 x 7½-inch loaf, with tapered ends.

Bake for 40 minutes or until lightly brown and a tester comes out clean. Let the bread rest for a few minutes, then remove it from the pan and cool it on a wire rack.

Yogurt Whole Grain Coffee Cake

This is a delicious coffee cake that's got the perfect balance of sweetness and healthiness. It even makes your life easy by allowing you to mix the streusel and the dry ingredients the night before and just put it all together the next morning. The whole wheat pastry flour is very finely ground, giving a lighter texture to your cakes and cookies.

Makes one 13 x 9-inch cake

Topping

- ³/₄ cup brown sugar, packed
- ½ cup unbleached white flour
- ¼ cup whole wheat flour
- ¼ pound (1 stick) unsalted butter, softened
- 2 teaspoons ground cinnamon
- 1 cup pecans or walnuts, coarsely chopped

Cake

- 1 cup unbleached white flour
- ²/₃ cup whole wheat pastry flour
- 1½ teaspoons baking powder
- 1 teaspoon baking soda
- ½ teaspoon salt
- 1¼ cups plain yogurt or sour cream
- ½ teaspoon vanilla extract
- 5 tablespoons unsalted butter, softened
- ³/₄ cup sugar
- ¼ cup honey
- 2 eggs

Preheat the oven to 350°F. Oil or butter a 13 x 9-inch baking dish or cake pan.

TO MAKE THE STREUSEL TOPPING: Combine the sugar, flours, butter, and cinnamon in a bowl and mix with a fork until the mixture resembles coarse crumbs. Stir in the pecans and set aside.

TO MAKE THE CAKE: In a large bowl, whisk or sift together the flours, baking powder, baking soda, and salt. Combine the yogurt and vanilla in a small bowl.

In a large bowl, beat the butter and sugar together until light lemon-yellow in color, about 3 or 4 minutes. Beat in the honey and then the eggs, one at a time, until incorporated. Add half the flour mixture, beating on low, then half the yogurt mixture. Scrape the sides of the bowl and repeat, scraping as necessary to remove any lumps in the batter. Scrape the batter into the prepared pan and top with the streusel.

Bake for 25 minutes or until lightly brown and a tester comes out clean. Let the cake rest for 15 minutes before cutting.

Boston Brown Bread

Many Americans remember this famous bread baked in a can. Our version uses rye flour—not unheard of, but still somewhat uncommon in this loaf. We think it adds a wonderful tangy flavor.

Makes one 13 x 9-inch loaf

- 1½ cups whole wheat flour
- ½ cup rye flour
- 1 cup unbleached white flour
- 2 teaspoons baking soda
- 1 teaspoon salt
- ½ cup brown sugar, packed
- ¼ cup unsulfured molasses
- ¼ cup honey
- 2 cups buttermilk
- ¾ cup raisins
- ¾ cup walnuts, coarsely chopped

Preheat the oven to 350°F. Grease or butter a 13 x 9-inch baking dish.

Whisk together the flours, baking soda, salt, and brown sugar in a large bowl.

In a separate bowl, combine the molasses, honey, and buttermilk. Pour over the dry ingredients, add the raisins and walnuts, and stir just enough to combine. Scrape the batter into the prepared baking dish.

Bake for 1 hour or until lightly brown and a tester comes out clean. Let the bread rest for at least 20 minutes before cutting.

Blueberry Applesauce Coffee Cake

This moist and flavorful coffee cake, created by Jan Brazeau of West Linn, Oregon, has a sweet surprise—a layer of blueberries in the middle.

Makes one 13 x 9-inch cake

Topping

- ⅓ cup whole wheat flour
- ⅓ cup unbleached white flour
- ⅔ cup walnuts, finely chopped
- ⅓ cup sugar
- ¼ cup brown sugar, packed
- 7 tablespoons unsalted butter, melted and cooled

Blueberry Filling

- 1¼ cups fresh or frozen blueberries
- ¼ cup water
- 2 tablespoons sugar
- 2 tablespoons arrowroot or cornstarch
- ¼ teaspoon ground nutmeg

Cake

- ¾ cup whole wheat pastry flour
- ¾ cup unbleached white flour
- ⅓ cup brown sugar, packed
- 2½ teaspoons baking powder
- ½ teaspoon baking soda
- ½ teaspoon salt
- 1 egg
- ½ cup applesauce
- ⅓ cup buttermilk
- 2½ tablespoons vegetable oil

Preheat the oven to 350°F. Oil or butter a 13 x 9-inch baking dish or cake pan.

TO MAKE THE TOPPING: Place all of the topping ingredients in a bowl and combine with a fork, or place in a food processor and pulse to combine until it resembles coarse crumbs.

TO MAKE THE FILLING: Combine the berries and water in a small saucepan. In a small bowl, stir together the sugar, arrowroot, and nutmeg. Bring the berry mixture to a boil, reduce the heat to medium, and stir in the sugar mixture. Cook and stir until the mixture boils and thickens, then cook and stir another minute or so. Remove from the heat.

TO MAKE THE CAKE: sift together the flours, sugar, baking powder, baking soda, and salt into a large bowl. In a medium bowl, beat the egg and then beat in the applesauce, buttermilk, and oil. Add the wet ingredients to the dry and stir until just moistened.

Pour half the batter into the prepared pan. Use a spatula to spread the blueberry mixture on top, then spread the remaining batter over the blueberry sauce.

Sprinkle topping over the batter and bake until lightly brown and a tester comes out clean. Let the cake rest for 15 minutes before cutting.

Blue Cornbread

GLUTEN-FREE

Blue cornbread is a Native American staple, and this simple recipe lets the corn flavor shine—it's especially delicious with soups and stews.

Makes one 8 x 8-inch loaf

- 1½ cups blue cornmeal
- 2 teaspoons baking powder
- 1 tablespoon sugar
- 1 egg
- ¾ cup milk
- 3 tablespoons vegetable oil

Preheat the oven to 350°F. Oil or butter an 8 x 8-inch baking dish.

In a large bowl, whisk or sift together the cornmeal, baking powder, and sugar until well blended.

Beat the egg together with the milk and vegetable oil, then stir into the dry ingredients and mix well.

Pour into the prepared dish and bake for 30 minutes, or until a tester comes out clean. Let the bread rest for 15 minutes before turning out to cool on a wire rack.

Bob's Cornbread

Native Americans were making cornbread long before the Pilgrims landed at Plymouth Rock. This bread's popularity was boosted by the Civil War since it was inexpensive and easy to make. Blue cornmeal is slightly higher in protein than yellow cornmeal, and it has a coarser texture and nuttier flavor. Choose either for this bread, or a combination of the two.

Makes one 8 x 8-inch loaf

- 1 cup cornmeal
- 1 cup unbleached white flour
- ½ cup sugar
- 1 tablespoon baking powder
- 1 teaspoon salt
- ⅓ cup vegetable oil
- 1 egg
- 1 cup milk

Preheat the oven to 400°F. Oil or butter an 8 x 8-inch baking dish.

In a large bowl, whisk or sift together the cornmeal, flour, sugar, baking powder, and salt. Beat the oil, egg, and milk together in a separate bowl, then stir into the dry ingredients.

Pour the batter into the prepared pan and bake for 25 minutes or until lightly brown and a tester comes out clean. Let the bread rest in the pan for 5 minutes before serving.

Amaranth Raisin Nut Bread

We've added amaranth to raisin nut bread to boost the protein content. We also think the slight graham-cracker-like taste the grain gives the loaf makes for a bread that's even better than the original.

Makes one 9 x 5-inch loaf

- ½ cup whole grain amaranth, uncooked
- ½ cup raisins
- 1 cup boiling water
- 1¼ cups hard white whole wheat flour
- ¾ cup whole wheat pastry flour
- 2 teaspoons baking powder
- ½ cup walnuts or pecans, chopped
- 3 tablespoons unsalted butter, melted and cooled
- 2 eggs
- 1 teaspoon vanilla extract
- ½ cup honey

Preheat the oven to 350°F. Oil or butter a 9 x 5-inch loaf pan, or line it with parchment paper.

Soak the amaranth and the raisins in the water in a medium bowl for 20 minutes.

In a large bowl, whisk together the flours, baking powder, and walnuts. Drain the amaranth and raisin mixture, then stir in the butter.

In a small bowl, beat together the eggs, vanilla, and honey. Add to the flour mixture along with the amaranth and raisins. Beat until blended, then pour into the prepared pan.

Bake for 40 minutes, or until lightly brown and a tester comes out clean. Let the bread rest for a few minutes, then remove it from the pan and cool on a wire rack before serving.

MUFFINS

All-Barley Muffins

WHEAT-FREE

These are very, very dense little muffins with a mild yet nutty flavor. Barley lovers will find these muffins gratifying.

Makes 12 muffins

- 2 cups barley flour
- 1 tablespoon baking powder
- ½ teaspoon salt
- 2 tablespoons sugar
- 2 eggs
- 2 tablespoons vegetable oil
- ½ cup water
- ½ cup apple juice or additional water
- ½ cup raisins

Preheat the oven to 425°F. Oil or butter a 12-cup muffin tin or line with paper muffin tin liners.

Whisk or sift together the flour, baking powder, salt, and sugar in a large bowl.

In a small bowl, beat together the eggs, oil, water, and juice until well blended. Pour the wet ingredients into the dry and stir to moisten. Fold in the raisins and then spoon into the prepared muffin tin.

Bake for 15 minutes or until browned and a tester inserted comes out clean. Let the muffins rest for 5 minutes, then turn them out onto a wire rack to cool.

Amaranth Applesauce Muffins

GLUTEN-FREE

These gluten-free muffins are pleasantly light, thanks to the combination of amaranth and white rice flours. Grating rather than chopping the apple allows it to become more thoroughly incorporated into the batter, infusing apple flavor into every bite.

Makes 12 muffins

- 1 cup amaranth flour
- 1 cup white rice flour
- 2 teaspoons baking soda
- 1 teaspoon cream of tartar
- 2 teaspoons cornstarch or arrowroot
- ½ teaspoon ground cinnamon
- ¼ teaspoon ground allspice
- ¼ teaspoon salt
- ⅓ cup vegetable oil
- ½ cup applesauce, room temperature
- ½ cup apple cider or water
- 1 egg
- 1 small apple, peeled, cored, and grated

Preheat the oven to 375°F. Oil or butter a 12-cup muffin tin or line with paper muffin tin liners.

In a large bowl, sift together the flours, baking soda, cream of tartar, cornstarch or arrowroot, spices, and salt.

In a medium bowl, beat together the oil, applesauce, apple cider, and egg. Stir in the apple, then fold the wet ingredients into the dry.

Spoon the batter into the prepared muffin tin and bake for 17 minutes, or until a tester comes out clean. Let the muffins rest for 5 minutes, then turn them out onto a wire rack to cool.

Blue Corn & Chile Muffins

These muffins are spectacular when served hot and spread with honey, and they go very well with eggs, or as a side dish to your favorite southwestern or Mexican-style meal.

Makes 12 muffins

- 1⅓ cups unbleached white flour
- 1 cup blue (or yellow) cornmeal
- 2 tablespoons baking powder
- ½ teaspoon salt
- 1½ cups coarsely grated Cheddar cheese, loosely packed
- ¼ pound (1 stick) unsalted butter, room temperature
- ⅓ cup sugar
- 2 tablespoons brown sugar
- 5 eggs
- ½ cup milk
- ½ cup canned diced green chilies, seeds and ribs removed

Preheat the oven to 375°F. Oil or butter a 12-cup muffin tin or line with muffin tin liners.

Whisk or sift together the flour, cornmeal, baking powder, and salt in a medium bowl, blending well. Stir in the cheese.

Beat together the butter and sugars until light-lemon-yellow in color. Add the eggs one at a time, scraping down the sides of the bowl after each addition. Beat in the milk, then stir in the chilies and the cornmeal flour mixture.

Spoon the batter into the prepared muffin tin and bake 20 minutes or until a tester comes out clean. Let the muffins rest for 5 minutes, then turn them out onto a wire rack to cool.

Lemon Poppy Seed Muffins

The classic British teacake combination of lemon and poppy is reborn here as a muffin. There is no better way to enjoy these than fresh out of the oven with plenty of butter and a very traditional spoonful of lemon curd.

Makes 12 muffins

- 1 cup unbleached white flour
- 3/4 cup whole wheat pastry flour
- 1/4 cup wheat germ
- 3 tablespoons poppy seeds
- 1/2 teaspoon salt
- 1/2 teaspoon baking soda
- 1 teaspoon baking powder
- 1 cup sugar
- Zest from one lemon
- 2 eggs
- 1/3 cup vegetable oil
- 1/2 cup milk
- 1/4 cup lemon juice

Preheat the oven to 375°F. Oil or butter a 12-cup muffin tin or line with muffin tin liners.

Whisk together the flours, wheat germ, poppy seeds, salt, baking soda, baking powder, sugar, and zest in a large bowl. In a separate bowl, beat the eggs together with the oil, milk, and lemon juice, then combine with the dry ingredients until moistened.

Spoon the batter into the prepared muffin tin and bake for 20 minutes, or until a tester comes out clean. Let the muffins rest for 5 minutes before serving warm, right out of the pan.

Brown Rice Muffins

Cooked rice adds far more rice flavor than just rice flour to these rich muffins. The blend of cardamom, ginger and fenugreek used in Indian and Pakistani cooking give these muffins a warm spiciness that goes well with a cup of chai tea.

Makes 12 muffins

- 1 cup whole wheat pastry flour
- 1 cup unbleached white flour
- 2 teaspoons baking powder
- ¼ teaspoon baking soda
- 1 teaspoon ground cinnamon
- 1 teaspoon ground ginger
- ½ teaspoon ground cardamom
- ¼ teaspoon ground fenugreek
- 2 teaspoons lemon zest
- ¾ cup sugar
- 1½ cups cooked brown rice, cooled
- 2 eggs
- 1½ cups buttermilk
- 2 tablespoons lemon juice
- 5 tablespoons unsalted butter, melted and cooled

Preheat the oven to 400°F. Oil or butter a 12-cup muffin tin or line with muffin tin liners.

Whisk together the flours, baking powder, baking soda, spices, zest, and sugar in a large bowl. Work the rice in with a fork, stirring until well blended.

Beat the eggs together with the buttermilk and lemon juice and pour into the dry ingredients. Add the butter and mix until just blended.

Spoon the batter into the prepared muffin tin and bake for 20 minutes, or until a tester comes out clean. Let the muffins rest for 5 minutes, then turn them out onto a wire rack to cool.

Pumpkin Quinoa Muffins

Cooked quinoa is packed with protein and gives these muffins a moist, crumbly texture. If the quinoa is too moist and sticky, wrap the grains in several layers of paper towels and press out any excess liquid.

Makes 12 muffins

- 1¼ cups whole wheat pastry flour
- ¾ cup light brown sugar, packed
- 1 teaspoon pumpkin pie spice
- 1 teaspoon baking powder
- ½ teaspoon baking soda
- ½ teaspoon salt
- ¾ cups quinoa, cooked and drained (see below)
- 2 eggs
- ¾ cup unsweetened canned pumpkin
- ½ cup buttermilk
- 4 tablespoons unsalted butter, melted and cooled
- 2 teaspoons vanilla extract
- ¼ cup shelled sunflower seeds or pepitas

Preheat the oven to 400°F. Oil or butter a 12-cup muffin tin or line with muffin tin liners.

In a large bowl, combine the flour, sugar, pie spice, baking powder, baking soda, and salt. Add the quinoa, separating the grains with a fork to distribute evenly.

In another bowl, beat the eggs, then add the pumpkin, buttermilk, butter, and vanilla extract. Whisk until the mixture is smooth. Gradually stir into the dry ingredients until just incorporated.

Spoon the batter into muffin tins and sprinkle sunflower seeds on top of each muffin. Bake for about 30 minutes, or until the muffins are browned around edges and a tester comes out clean. Let the muffins rest for 5 minutes, then turn them out onto a wire rack to cool.

COOKING QUINOA

To make about 4 cups of quinoa, place 1 cup of quinoa in a bowl of cold water and gently rub it with your palms for about ten seconds. Rinse in a strainer. Bring a scant 2 cups vegetable stock or water and ¼ teaspoons salt to a boil. Add quinoa, lower to simmer and cover. Cook for 12 minutes or until all of the water has been absorbed. The quinoa should be translucent. Let it rest, covered, for about 5 minutes, then fluff with a fork.

Ginger Pear Barley Muffins

Tiny pieces of crystallized ginger and pear pair to make a delightfully sweet and spicy muffin, and with the added barley flour, these muffins taste great and are very moist (and a bit more nutritious).

Makes 12 muffins

- 1 cup unbleached white flour
- 1 cup whole wheat pastry flour
- ⅓ cup barley flour
- 2 teaspoons baking powder
- ½ teaspoon salt
- ½ cup sugar
- 7 tablespoons minced, unsweetened crystallized ginger
- 1 egg
- 1⅓ cup buttermilk
- 6 tablespoons unsalted butter, melted and cooled
- 2 to 3 pears, peeled, cored, and finely chopped, to yield 1⅓ cup
- 4 teaspoons freshly squeezed lemon juice

Preheat the oven to 375°F. Oil or butter a 12-cup muffin tin or line with muffin tin liners.

Whisk together the flours, baking powder, salt, sugar, and ginger. In a separate bowl, beat the egg together with the buttermilk, then stir in the butter. Add the wet mixture to the dry ingredients.

Toss the pear and lemon juice together and fold in to the batter, until just blended.

Spoon the batter into the prepared muffin tin and bake for 20 minutes, or until a tester comes out clean. Let the muffins rest for 5 minutes, then turn them out onto a wire rack to cool.

Raspberry Ricotta Muffins

Ricotta cheese helps transform ordinary muffins to luscious cheesecake-like treats. Substitute some blueberries for raspberries and you have a festive muffin for the Fourth of July, the height of berry season.

Makes 12 muffins

- 1¼ cups unbleached white flour
- 1 cup whole wheat pastry flour
- ½ teaspoon salt
- 2 teaspoons baking powder
- ½ teaspoon baking soda
- ¾ cup sugar
- 2 eggs
- 1⅓ cups buttermilk
- 1¼ cups ricotta cheese, drained if necessary
- 1½ tablespoons lemon juice
- 6 tablespoons unsalted butter, melted and cooled
- 1½ cups fresh or frozen raspberries (if you're using frozen, let them defrost and then drain them)

Preheat the oven to 350°F. Oil or butter a 12-cup muffin tin or line with muffin tin liners.

In a large bowl, sift or whisk together the flours, salt, baking powder, baking soda, and sugar.

In a mixing bowl, beat one egg with the buttermilk and ricotta, scraping down the sides of the bowl once, then beat in the second egg, scraping the bowl once again. Beat in the lemon juice. Whisk in the butter, then add this mixture to the dry ingredients along with the raspberries.

Spoon the batter into the prepared muffin tin and bake 20 minutes, or until a tester comes out clean. Let the muffins rest for 5 minutes, then turn them out onto a wire rack to cool.

Oat Bran Muffins

These healthy muffins are rich and full of nourishment. Strawberry jam always tastes good on bran muffins. Store any leftovers in a plastic bag so they stay moist.

Makes 12 muffins

- ¾ cup unbleached white flour
- ¼ cup whole wheat flour
- ¼ cup rolled oats
- ¾ cup unsweetened bran flakes
- 1 teaspoon baking soda
- ½ teaspoon baking powder
- ½ teaspoon salt
- ¼ cup raisins
- ¼ cup dried apricots, chopped
- ¼ cup flax seeds
- 1 egg
- 2½ tablespoons honey
- ¾ cup buttermilk
- ¼ cup vegetable oil

Preheat the oven to 375°F. Oil or butter a 12-cup muffin tin or line with muffin tin liners.

Combine the flours, oats, bran, baking soda, baking powder, salt, raisins, apricots, and flax seeds in a small bowl. In a separate bowl, beat the egg with the honey, buttermilk, and oil until well blended, then whisk in the dry ingredients.

Spoon the batter into the prepared muffin tin and bake for 17 minutes, or until a tester comes out clean. Let the muffins rest for 5 minutes, then turn them out onto a wire rack to cool.

Blueberry Triticale Muffins

This delicious and healthy alternative to traditional blueberry muffins tastes great with a little honey.

Makes 12 muffins

- ¼ cup whole wheat flour
- ¾ cup unbleached white flour
- 1 cup triticale flour
- 3 teaspoons baking powder
- ½ teaspoon baking soda
- ½ teaspoon salt
- ½ teaspoon ground cinnamon
- 2 eggs, lightly beaten
- 5½ tablespoons vegetable oil or unsalted butter, softened
- Scant ½ cup honey
- 1 cup milk
- 1 cup blueberries, fresh or frozen

Preheat the oven to 400°F. Oil or butter a 12-cup muffin tin or line with paper muffin tin liners.

Combine the flours, baking powder, baking soda, salt, and cinnamon in a large bowl. In a separate bowl, beat together the remaining ingredients, then stir into the flour mixture until well blended. Stir in the blueberries.

Spoon the batter into the prepared muffin tin and bake for 12 minutes, or until a tester comes out clean. Let the muffins rest for 5 minutes, then turn them out onto a wire rack to cool.

Blueberry Muffins

These fluffy muffins have a delicate texture and are delightfully crumbly.

Makes 14 to 16 muffins

- 2 cups rice flour
- 1¼ cups oat flour
- ¾ cup millet flour
- ¼ teaspoon salt
- 2 teaspoons baking powder
- 2 eggs, lightly beaten
- 1½ cups milk
- ¼ cup honey
- ¼ cup pure maple syrup
- 3 tablespoons vegetable oil
- 5 tablespoons unsalted butter, melted
- 1 cup blueberries, fresh or frozen

Preheat the oven to 375°F. Oil or butter one 12-cup and one 6-cup muffin tin or line with muffin tin liners.

In a large bowl, sift or whisk together the flours with the salt and baking powder.

In a separate bowl, beat the eggs with the milk, honey, maple syrup, and oil until blended. Add to the dry ingredients, along with the butter, and stir until combined. Stir in the blueberries.

Spoon the batter into the prepared muffin tin and bake for 20 minutes, or until a tester comes out clean. Let the muffins rest for 5 minutes, then turn them out onto a wire rack to cool.

Ham and Cheese Yogurt Muffins

Ah, breakfast in a muffin. These go great with a bowl of Bob's Steel Cut oats. You can always leave out the ham for a meatless version.

Makes 12 muffins

- ³/₄ cup unbleached white flour
- ½ cup whole wheat flour
- 1½ teaspoons baking powder
- ½ teaspoon baking soda
- ½ teaspoon salt
- 1 egg, lightly beaten
- 1 cup plain yogurt
- 1 tablespoon vegetable oil
- 2 tablespoons sugar
- ½ teaspoon Dijon mustard
- ³/₄ cup diced cooked ham
- ½ cup grated Gruyere or Swiss cheese

Preheat the oven to 375°F. Oil or butter a 12-cup muffin tin or line with muffin tin liners

In a medium bowl, whisk or sift together the flours, baking powder, baking soda, and salt. In a separate bowl, beat together the egg, yogurt, oil, sugar, and mustard until well blended. Whisk in the dry ingredients, then stir in the ham and cheese.

Spoon the batter into the prepared muffin tin and bake for 20 to 25 minutes, or until a tester comes out clean. Serve immediately.

Amaranth Whole Wheat Muffins

Don't let the honey in this recipe fool you—these are not cupcakes disguised as muffins. They are definitely savory little guys. Because amaranth flour is slightly higher in fat than normal flour, this is a nicely moist muffin.

Makes 12 muffins

- 1 cup amaranth flour
- ½ cup whole wheat pastry flour
- 2 teaspoons baking powder
- 1 egg
- ½ cup milk
- ¼ cup vegetable oil or 4 tablespoons unsalted butter, softened
- 1 teaspoon vanilla extract
- ¼ cup honey
- ⅓ cup raisins
- ⅓ cup walnuts or pecans, optional

Preheat the oven to 375°F. Oil or butter a 12-cup muffin tin or line with muffin tin liners.

In a large bowl, sift or whisk together the flours and baking powder.

In a medium bowl, beat together the egg, milk, oil, vanilla, and honey. Combine the wet ingredients with the dry until just moistened. Fold in the raisins and nuts.

Bake for 15 minutes or until a tester comes out clean. Let the muffins rest for 5 minutes, then turn them out onto a wire rack to cool.

Maple Pecan Muffins

Pairing pecans with maple syrup has been done in everything from pancakes to popcorn. This recipe adds whole grains, making these muffins scrumptious and good for you.

Makes 12 muffins

- 1½ cups whole wheat pastry flour
- ½ cup unbleached white flour
- ½ cup wheat germ
- 3 teaspoons baking powder
- ¼ cup plus 1 tablespoon brown sugar
- ¼ teaspoon salt
- 1 cup pecans, coarsely chopped
- ½ cup milk
- ⅓ cup maple syrup
- ½ cup vegetable oil
- 1 egg, lightly beaten

Preheat the oven to 400°F. Oil or butter a 12-cup muffin tin, or line with muffin tin liners.

In a large bowl, whisk together the flours, wheat germ, baking powder, ¼ cup brown sugar, and salt. Stir in ¾ cup of pecans. In another bowl, whisk together the milk, syrup, oil, and egg.

Pour the wet ingredients into the dry and mix to combine. Spoon the batter into the prepared tin and sprinkle with remaining nuts and brown sugar.

Bake for 15 to 20 minutes or until a tester comes out clean. Let the muffins rest for 5 minutes, then turn them out onto a wire rack to cool.

Fig Muffins

If you've ever tried to bake with fresh figs, you know they have a lot of water. However, we find that fig jam, combined with a bit of apricot jam, makes a great combination and allows us to add these fantastic flavors to our healthful muffins.

Makes 12 muffins

- ¾ cup light brown sugar
- ¾ cup vegetable oil
- 1 egg
- 1 cup buttermilk
- 1½ cups unbleached white flour
- ½ cup rye flour
- 1 teaspoon ground cinnamon
- 1 teaspoon salt
- 1½ teaspoons baking soda
- 1 teaspoon lemon zest
- ¾ cup fig Jam
- ¼ cup apricot jam
- ½ cup golden raisins

Preheat the oven to 350°F. Oil or butter a 12-cup muffin tin or line with muffin tin liners.

In a large bowl, beat the sugar, oil, egg, and buttermilk until well combined. In a separate bowl, sift together the flours, cinnamon, salt and baking soda. Stir in the lemon zest then whisk the dry ingredients into the sugar mixture. Fold in the fig and apricot jams and raisins. Spoon the batter into the prepared muffin tin.

Bake about 30 minutes, or until golden and a tester comes out clean. Let the muffins rest for 5 minutes, then turn them out onto a wire rack to cool.

Pine Nut Muffins

Pine nuts are the edible seeds of the pine tree. Most Americans are familiar with them in Italian pasta dishes, like pesto. Here, their toasty flavor is a perfect combination with the flavors of the whole wheat and millet flours.

Makes 12 muffins

- ½ cup pine nuts
- 1 cup unbleached white flour
- ¾ cup whole wheat pastry flour
- ¼ cup millet flour
- ⅓ cup sugar
- ½ teaspoon ground cinnamon
- 1½ teaspoons baking soda
- ¼ teaspoon salt
- 1 cup plain yogurt
- ⅔ cup milk
- 5 tablespoons unsalted butter, melted and cooled
- 1 egg, lightly beaten
- ½ teaspoon vanilla extract
- 1 cup dried fruit, chopped, optional
- Ground cinnamon, for dusting
- Sugar, for dusting

Preheat the oven to 350°F. Scatter the pine nuts on a baking sheet and place them in the oven for about 10 minutes. Shake the tray once or twice during baking, keeping a close eye on the nuts so they don't burn. You could also toast them in a skillet, stirring over medium low heat. Remove them from the heat when they're fragrant and golden.

Increase the oven temperature to 400°F. Oil or butter a 12-cup muffin tin or line with muffin tin liners.

In a large bowl, sift together the flours, sugar, cinnamon, baking soda, and salt.

In a medium bowl, whisk together the yogurt, milk, butter, egg, and vanilla. Combine the wet with the dry ingredients, and fold together to moisten. Stir in the pine nuts and fruit.

Spoon the batter into muffin tins and sprinkle with a little cinnamon and sugar. Bake for 15 minutes, or until a tester comes out clean. Let the muffins rest for 5 minutes, then turn them out onto a wire rack to cool.

Soybean Muffins

Soybeans are easy to cook and are a wonderful addition to soups and stews. Mashing and adding them to these muffins makes for a rich texture, and a lot of protein.

Makes 12 muffins

- ²/₃ cup soybeans
- ¹/₃ cup honey
- 2 eggs, lightly beaten
- 1½ cups buttermilk
- 1 cup whole wheat pastry flour
- ½ cup unbleached white flour
- 2 teaspoons baking powder
- ½ teaspoon baking soda
- 1 teaspoon salt
- 1 teaspoon ground cinnamon
- ²/₃ cup pecans or walnuts, chopped

To cook the soybeans, soak the beans in 3 cups of water for 8 hours or overnight. Drain the beans, replace the water with 3 cups of fresh water and simmer for about 3 hours, or until soft.

Preheat the oven to 350°F. Oil or butter a 12-cup muffin tin or line with paper muffin tin liners.

Puree or mash the beans and then blend with honey, eggs, and buttermilk and mix well. In a separate bowl, mix together the remaining ingredients, except the pecans. Combine the dry with the wet ingredients until just moistened, then stir in the pecans.

Spoon the batter into the prepared muffin tin and bake for 45 minutes or until a tester comes out clean. Let the muffins rest for 5 minutes, then turn them out onto a wire rack to cool.

Banana-Bran Nut Muffins

These banana-bran muffins use less sugar than most because the yogurt and bananas give them plenty of natural sweetness. Speaking of yogurt, they make a nice breakfast with a little yogurt and fresh fruit.

Makes 12 muffins

- 1¼ cups wheat bran
- 1 cup whole wheat flour
- ¼ cup whole wheat pastry flour
- 1 teaspoon baking powder
- 1½ teaspoons baking soda
- ½ teaspoon salt
- ¼ cup brown sugar, packed
- ¾ cup walnuts, chopped
- 2 tablespoons vegetable oil
- 1¼ cups plain yogurt
- 1 overripe banana, peeled and mashed

Preheat the oven to 400°F. Butter or oil a 12-cup muffin tin or line with muffin tin liners.

In a large bowl, combine the bran, flours, baking powder, baking soda, salt, brown sugar, and walnuts and stir until well mixed.

Process the oil, yogurt, and banana in a food processor or blend in a blender at medium speed, until well mixed. Pour into the dry ingredients and stir until just moistened.

Spoon the batter into the prepared tin and bake for 15 to 20 minutes, or until a tester comes out clean. Let the muffins rest for 5 minutes, then turn them out onto a wire rack to cool.

Parmesan Muffins

These savory muffins are great with soup or salad. Try adding ¼ teaspoon dried or ½ teaspoon fresh minced herbs, such as marjoram, oregano, rosemary or basil. Simply whisk the herbs in with the rest of the dry ingredients.

Makes 12 muffins

- 2 eggs
- ¾ cup milk
- ½ cup extra-virgin olive oil
- 1 cup (about 2 ounces) freshly grated Parmesan cheese
- 1 cup unbleached white flour
- ½ cup whole wheat pastry flour
- 1½ tablespoons sugar
- ½ teaspoon salt
- ¼ teaspoon pepper
- 2 teaspoons baking powder
- ⅓ teaspoon baking soda
- 1 teaspoon minced garlic

Preheat the oven to 350°F. Oil a 12-cup muffin tin or line with muffin tin liners.

In a small bowl, beat together the eggs, milk, and oil. In a large bowl, whisk together the cheese, flours, sugar, salt, pepper, baking powder, and baking soda. Add the egg mixture and the minced garlic to the dry mixture and stir to combine.

Pour into the prepared muffin tin and bake for about 20 minutes, or until a tester comes out clean. Let the muffins rest for 5 minutes, then turn them out onto a wire rack to cool.

Date-Nut Muffins

These muffins include a French spice blend called Quatre Epices *(which means four spices), which includes white pepper, cloves, ginger, and nutmeg (of course, you can make up your own spice blend and call it "Sharon's Spice Blend," or use your own name if your name doesn't happen to be Sharon). The spice goes nicely with the dates and nuts in this muffin. We have reliable reports that these muffins, split in half and spread with softened cream cheese, are especially delicious.*

Makes 12 muffins

- 1 ¼ cups whole wheat pastry flour
- ½ teaspoon salt
- ¾ teaspoon Quatre Epices, or ½ teaspoon ground cinnamon and ¼ teaspoon ground allspice
- 2 teaspoons baking powder
- ½ teaspoon baking soda
- ½ cup dried dates, chopped
- ½ cup walnuts, chopped
- ½ cup wheat germ
- 2 tablespoons light molasses
- 1 tablespoon brown sugar
- 2 tablespoons vegetable oil
- 1 cup apple juice or ½ cup juice and ½ cup milk or water
- 1 tablespoon lemon zest

Preheat the oven to 375°F. Oil or butter a 12-cup muffin tin or line with muffin tin liners.

Sift the flour, salt, spices, baking powder, and baking soda into a large bowl, then stir in the dates, walnuts, and wheat germ.

In a separate bowl, beat the molasses, brown sugar, oil, juice, and zest until smooth, then combine with the dry ingredients, stirring just enough to moisten.

Spoon the batter into the prepared muffin tin and bake for about 15 to 20 minutes, until a tester comes out clean. Let the muffins rest for 5 minutes, then turn them out onto a wire rack to cool.

Rye Muffins

If you like rye bread, you'll gobble up these naturally sweetened rye muffins. Use unsweetened apple juice if you can, or just cut the honey to 1 tablespoon. For a savory treat, grate a little cheddar cheese and sprinkle it on a still warm muffin.

Makes 12 muffins

- ³/₄ cup unbleached white flour
- ¹/₂ cup rye flour
- ¹/₂ cup rice flour
- ¹/₂ teaspoon salt
- 3 teaspoons baking powder
- 2 tablespoons honey
- 1 cup apple juice
- 3¹/₂ tablespoons canola oil

Preheat the oven to 375°F. Oil or butter a 12-cup muffin tin or line with muffin tin liners.

In a large bowl, sift together the flours, salt, and baking powder. In a small bowl, combine the honey, juice, and oil, and stir until well blended. Mix into the dry ingredients.

Spoon the batter into the prepared muffin tin and bake for 20 to 25 minutes or until a tester comes out clean. Let the muffins rest for 5 minutes, then turn them out onto a wire rack to cool.

Kamut® Walnut Muffins

This high protein muffin has a natural buttery flavor which comes from the Kamut® grain flour. We've made it with buttermilk for that extra bit of moistness. If you don't have buttermilk on hand, mix one tablespoon of lemon juice or white vinegar to a cup of milk, and let it stand for about 10 minutes.

Makes 12 muffins

- 1½ cups Kamut® grain flour
- 2 tablespoons baking powder
- 1 teaspoon salt
- 1 teaspoon ground cinnamon
- ¼ pound (1 stick) unsalted butter, softened
- ½ cup sugar
- 2 eggs, lightly beaten
- ⅔ cup buttermilk
- ¼ cup walnuts, chopped
- Sugar and ground cinnamon for dusting, optional

Preheat the oven to 375°F. Oil or butter a 12-cup muffin tin or line with muffin tin liners.

Sift or whisk together the flour, baking powder, salt, and cinnamon in a large bowl. In a medium bowl, cream the butter and sugar for two minutes, then add the eggs one at a time, scraping the sides of the bowl after each addition. Pour the buttermilk into the butter mixture and combine. Add the wet mixture to the dry mixture and mix until moistened. Stir in the walnuts.

Spoon the batter into the prepared muffin tin, sprinkle with sugar, and cinnamon, and bake for 15 minutes or until a tester comes out clean. Let the muffins rest for 5 minutes, then turn them out onto a wire rack to cool.

Whole Wheat Pumpkin-Rye Muffins

Imagine your favorite pumpkin pie in a rye crust, and you can imagine what these muffins taste like. The sweet pumpkin flavor and the warm spices contrast nicely with the slightly sour taste of the rye.

Makes 12 muffins

- 1 cup light rye flour
- ³/₄ cup whole wheat pastry flour
- 2 teaspoons baking powder
- 1¹/₂ teaspoons ground cinnamon
- ¹/₄ teaspoon ground cloves
- ¹/₄ cup sugar
- ¹/₄ teaspoon salt
- ¹/₂ cup raisins or currants
- ¹/₃ cup apple juice, or other fruit juice
- 2 tablespoons vegetable oil
- 1 egg
- 1 cup unsweetened pumpkin puree

Preheat the oven to 400°F. Oil or butter a 12-cup muffin tin or line with muffin tin liners.

In a medium bowl, whisk or sift together the flours, baking powder, spices, sugar, and salt. Stir in the raisins.

In a small bowl or blender, combine the juice and oil, then whisk in the egg and pumpkin puree. Mix well, then add the liquid mixture to the flour mixture and stir just to moisten.

Spoon the batter into the prepared muffin tin and bake for 20 minutes or until a tester comes out clean. Let the muffins rest for 5 minutes, then turn them out onto a wire rack to cool.

Applesauce Muffins

There are 2,500 types of apples grown commercially in the United States, so unless you're Johnny Appleseed, you've probably missed out on about 99 percent. In this recipe, we don't use any unusual types of apples, just unsweetened applesauce. Of course, you can always find some unusual types of apples, make your own applesauce, and see how they change the flavors of these muffins. If all you have on hand is sweetened applesauce, just cut the brown sugar to 2 tablespoons.

Makes 12 muffins

- ¾ cup whole wheat pastry flour
- 1½ cups unbleached white flour
- 1 tablespoon sugar
- 2½ teaspoons baking soda
- ½ teaspoon ground cinnamon
- ½ teaspoon ground allspice
- 1½ cups unsweetened applesauce
- ¼ cup brown sugar
- 2 eggs
- 3 tablespoons vegetable oil

Preheat the oven to 400°F. Grease a 12-cup muffin tin or line with paper muffin tin liners.

Whisk or sift together the flours, sugar, baking soda, and spices. In a large bowl, beat together the applesauce, brown sugar, eggs, and oil. Sift the flour mixture into the wet ingredients and stir until moistened.

Spoon the batter into the prepared tins and bake for 20 minutes or until a tester comes out clean. Let the muffins rest for 5 minutes, then turn them out onto a wire rack to cool.

Apple Streusel Muffins

These muffins are a little like mini-coffee cakes, and are crumbly and flavorful. A combination of sour cream and yogurt offers a magnificent piquancy, but you can use either one exclusively if that's more convenient.

Makes 12 muffins

Streusel Topping

- ⅓ cup light brown sugar, packed
- 3½ tablespoons unbleached white flour
- 4 tablespoons unsalted butter, chilled and diced

Muffins

- ¼ cup whole grain flour
- ½ cup whole wheat pastry flour
- 1¼ cups unbleached white flour
- ¾ cup sugar
- 1 tablespoon baking powder
- 1 teaspoon baking soda
- ½ teaspoon salt
- 2 teaspoons of Quatre Epices blend (see headnote on page 136) or 1 teaspoon ground cinnamon, ½ teaspoon ground allspice, and ½ teaspoon ground nutmeg
- 2 eggs
- 4 tablespoons unsalted butter, melted, or vegetable oil
- ¾ cup plain yogurt
- ¾ cup sour cream
- 1 apple, seeded, peeled and coarsely grated

Preheat the oven to 400°F. Oil or butter a 12-cup muffin tin or line with muffin tin liners.

TO MAKE THE STREUSEL: Combine all streusel ingredients in a food processor or bowl, cutting in the butter by pulsing until it resembles coarse crumbs. Refrigerate until you're ready to use.

TO MAKE THE MUFFINS: Sift or whisk together the flours, sugar, baking powder, baking soda, salt, and spices.

In another bowl, beat the eggs with the butter, yogurt, and sour cream until well blended. Stir in the apple and then add this mixture to the dry mixture, stirring until just moistened.

Spoon the batter into the muffin cups and sprinkle with streusel topping. Bake for 20 minutes or until a tester comes out clean. Let the muffins rest for 5 minutes, then turn them out onto a wire rack to cool.

Cornmeal Raspberry Muffins

Oregon and Washington lead the nation in production of raspberries, and we love to make use of our wonderful summer bounty. They are a sweet match to freshly baked cornmeal in these muffins. We recommend you use yellow cornmeal here, but you can substitute blue for a stronger flavor (and an unusual color).

Makes 12 muffins

- ½ cup whole wheat pastry flour
- 1 cup unbleached white flour
- 1 cup fine cornmeal
- ½ cup sugar
- 2½ teaspoons baking powder
- ½ teaspoon baking soda
- ¼ teaspoon salt
- 1¼ cups milk
- 2 eggs
- ⅓ cup vegetable oil
- 1½ cups fresh or frozen raspberries (if you're using frozen, defrost and drain them)

Preheat the oven to 400°F. Oil or butter a 12-cup muffin tin or line with muffin tin liners.

In a large bowl, sift or whisk together the flours, cornmeal, sugar, baking powder, baking soda, and salt.

In a medium bowl, combine the milk, eggs, and vegetable oil and beat together. Pour the wet ingredients into the dry and stir until combined.

Fold the raspberries into the batter and then spoon into the prepared tin. Bake for 20 minutes or until a tester comes out clean. Let the muffins rest for 5 minutes, then turn them out onto a wire rack to cool.

Quinoa Muffins

GLUTEN-FREE

Start these nutty, protein-packed muffins the night before and you can look forward to enjoying them for breakfast. These are not especially sweet muffins, since they have a minimal amount of honey and no sugar, but you can always add a little more honey or top them with jam to suit that sweet tooth of yours.

Makes 12 muffins

- 1 cup quinoa grains, uncooked
- 1 cup yellow cornmeal
- 1¼ cups boiling water
- ¼ cup honey
- 1 cup milk
- 1 egg, beaten
- Zest from 1 lemon
- ½ teaspoon salt
- 1¼ cups whole wheat pastry flour
- 2 teaspoon baking powder

Thoroughly rinse the quinoa through a sieve and combine with the cornmeal. Pour the water over the grains, cover, and let stand for at least 1 hour or overnight.

Preheat the oven to 375°F. Oil or butter a 12-cup muffin tin or line with muffin tin liners.

Combine the honey, milk, egg, and lemon zest and stir into the grains. Combine the salt, flour, and baking powder in a small bowl, then stir into the wet ingredients.

Spoon the batter into the prepared muffin tins and bake for 25 minutes or until lightly browned and a tester comes out clean. Let the muffins rest for 5 minutes, then turn them out onto a wire rack to cool.

Teff Peanut Butter Muffins

These muffins taste much like peanut butter cookies, but are much healthier with the addition of teff grains and whole wheat flours. They taste great with a slice of banana layered on a cooled muffin. For even more banana, stir ¼ cup of dried bananas into the liquid ingredients. Chocolate or carob chips are other great additions—just toss them in with the dry ingredients.

Makes 12 muffins

- ⅓ cup to ½ cup teff grains (uncooked)
- 1½ cups whole wheat flour
- ½ cup whole wheat pastry flour
- 1 tablespoon baking powder
- ½ teaspoon salt
- ¼ cup peanut butter, crunchy or creamy
- 2 tablespoons vegetable oil
- 1½ cups water
- 4 tablespoons molasses, honey, or pure maple syrup

Preheat the oven to 350°F. Grease a 12-cup muffin tin or line with paper muffin tin liners.

Place the teff, flours, baking powder, and salt in a food processor and pulse until well blended. Add the peanut butter and oil, pulsing until the mixture is like crumbs. Pour the mixture out into a bowl and add the water and molasses, stirring just until well mixed.

Spoon the batter into muffin cups and bake for 14 minutes or until a tester comes out clean. Let the muffins rest for 5 minutes, then turn them out onto a wire rack to cool.

Cranberry Nut Muffins

Cranberries freeze very well, so to make up for their short season, buy an extra bag or two when they are in season and toss them in the freezer. When you're ready to use them, you don't even have to defrost them, just toss them in. If you'd like a bit of citrus flavor in these muffins, stir two teaspoons of orange zest into the dry ingredients and then serve with orange marmalade.

Makes 12 muffins

- 2 eggs
- ¼ pound (1 stick) unsalted butter, melted, or ½ cup vegetable oil
- ½ cup honey
- 1½ teaspoons vanilla extract
- 1¼ cups whole wheat pastry flour
- ¼ cup amaranth, oat or barley flour
- ⅓ cup sugar
- 1½ teaspoons baking powder
- 1 cup dried cranberries or other dried fruit, chopped
- ⅓ cup walnuts, toasted and chopped

Preheat the oven to 375°F. Grease a 12-cup muffin tin or line with muffin tin liners.

In a medium bowl, beat the eggs, butter, honey, and vanilla.

In a large bowl, whisk together the flours, sugar, and baking powder. Stir in the liquid ingredients until just mixed. Add the cranberries and walnuts and stir until incorporated.

Pour the batter into the prepared muffin tin and bake for 20 minutes or until a tester comes out clean. Let the muffins rest for 5 minutes, then turn them out onto a wire rack to cool.

Oatmeal Muffins

This recipe gives you the option of using amaranth or barley flour. The amaranth flour gives these muffins a slightly lighter texture and taste than barley flour. Of course, barley adds a nice nutty flavor. Try both to find which style you like best. Oat flour is a natural antioxidant, which is not only good for you, but it also means these muffins will last a little longer than others when stored in an airtight bag.

Makes 12 muffins

- 1 cup rolled oats
- 1 cup oat flour
- ½ cup amaranth or barley flour
- 1 teaspoon baking powder
- ½ teaspoon salt
- 2 eggs
- ¾ cup brown sugar, packed
- Scant 1 cup milk
- 4 tablespoons unsalted butter, melted and cooled
- 1 teaspoon vanilla extract

Preheat the oven to 400°F. Oil or butter a 12-cup muffin tin or line with muffin tin liners.

In a large mixing bowl, whisk together the oats, flours, baking powder, and salt.

In another bowl, beat the eggs and brown sugar until light, 2 to 3 minutes. Whisk in the milk, butter, and vanilla. Pour the wet mixture into the flour mixture and fold in just until moistened.

Spoon the batter into the prepared muffin tin and bake for 15 minutes, or until a tester comes out clean. Let the muffins rest for 5 minutes, then turn them out onto a wire rack to cool.

Southwestern Cheddar Muffins

These slightly spicy muffins are perfect with a bowl of chili on a cold day.

Makes 12 muffins

- ¼ cup unbleached white flour
- ¼ cup amaranth, millet or soy flour
- 1 cup stone ground yellow cornmeal
- 2 tablespoons sugar
- 1 teaspoon baking powder
- ½ teaspoon baking soda
- 1 teaspoon salt
- ½ teaspoon chili powder
- 1 cup buttermilk
- ¼ cup vegetable oil
- 2 eggs
- 1 cup shredded cheddar cheese
- ¼ cup canned green chilies, chopped, optional

Preheat the oven to 425°F. Oil or butter a 12-cup muffin tin or line with muffin tin liners.

In a medium bowl, sift or whisk together the flours, cornmeal, sugar, baking powder, baking soda, salt, and chili powder. In another bowl, whisk the buttermilk, oil, and eggs. Add the wet mixture to dry mixture, stirring until just mixed. Gently fold in cheese and chilies.

Spoon the batter into the prepared muffin tin and bake for 20 minutes or until a tester comes out clean. Let the muffins rest 5 minutes, then turn out onto a wire rack to cool.

Bulgur Muffins

You may be familiar with bulgur from the delicious Middle Eastern parsley and wheat salad called tabouli. This nutritious grain is used in baking as well, for breads and in these tasty muffins.

Makes 12 muffins

- 1 cup unbleached white flour, sifted
- ½ cup whole wheat pastry flour, sifted
- ¼ cup sugar
- 3½ teaspoons baking powder
- 1½ teaspoons salt
- ⅓ cup raisins or other dried fruit, chopped
- 1 egg
- 1 cup milk
- 3 tablespoons vegetable oil
- ¾ cup hard red or soft white dark bulgur, cooked

Preheat the oven to 425°F. Grease a 12-cup muffin tin or line with muffin tin liners.

In a large bowl, sift or whisk together the flours, sugar, baking powder, and salt. Stir in the raisins.

In a medium bowl, beat the egg, milk, and oil. Pour into the flour mixture and combine until just moistened. Stir in the cooked bulgur.

Spoon the batter into the prepared muffin tin and bake for 15 minutes or until a tester comes out clean. Let the muffins rest for 5 minutes, then turn them out onto a wire rack to cool.

Orange Spelt Muffins

DAIRY-FREE

This low gluten muffin mixes apples and oranges—well, applesauce and oranges—to come up with a delightful and dairy-free treat.

Makes 12 muffins

- 2 cups spelt flour
- 1¾ teaspoons baking powder
- 1½ teaspoons orange zest
- ¼ teaspoon ground allspice
- ½ teaspoon salt
- ½ cup orange juice
- ¼ cup applesauce
- ⅓ cup vegetable oil
- ½ cup brown sugar
- 1½ teaspoons vanilla extract
- 2 eggs

Preheat the oven to 375°F. Oil or butter a 12-cup muffin tin or line with muffin tin liners.

Sift or whisk together the flour, baking powder, zest, allspice, and salt in a large bowl.

In a medium bowl, beat together the orange juice, applesauce, oil, sugar, vanilla, and eggs until well combined. Stir into the flour mixture until just combined. The batter will be somewhat lumpy.

Spoon the batter into the prepared muffin tin and bake for 15 minutes or until a tester comes out clean. Let the muffins rest for 5 minutes, then turn them out onto a wire rack to cool.

Barley Buttermilk Muffins

Buttermilk makes particularly tender muffins. When paired with baking soda, the baking soda reacts with the acidity in the buttermilk, which creates carbon dioxide bubbles, which creates steam—which gives us moist, tender muffins. Add barley to the mix and you've got a great muffin. Delicious.

Makes 12 muffins

- 1 cup whole wheat pastry flour
- ½ cup barley flour
- 1 teaspoon baking soda
- 1 teaspoon baking powder
- ½ teaspoon salt
- ⅓ cup sugar
- 1⅓ cups buttermilk
- ¼ cup vegetable oil
- 1 egg, slightly beaten

Preheat the oven to 400°F. Oil or butter a 12-cup muffin tin or line with muffin tin liners.

In a large bowl, sift or whisk together the flours, baking soda, baking powder, salt, and sugar.

In another bowl, beat together the buttermilk, oil, and egg, then pour this mixture into the dry ingredients and stir until just mixed.

Spoon the batter into the prepared muffin tin and bake for 18 minutes or until a tester comes out clean. Let the muffins rest for 5 minutes, then turn them out onto a wire rack to cool.

Carrot Muffins

Carrot cake calls for a lot of oil to keep the cake moist. While these muffins have no shortage of oil, they contain less oil than carrot cake, yet they still deliver a moist, rich muffin that's just as good as the heavier cake.

Makes 12 muffins

- 4 eggs
- ½ cup vegetable oil
- 1 teaspoon vanilla extract
- 1¼ cups unbleached white flour
- ½ cup whole wheat pastry flour
- ¼ cup barley flour, or substitute with same amount whole wheat pastry flour
- 1⅔ cups sugar
- 1½ teaspoons ground cinnamon
- 2 tablespoons flax seeds
- 1½ teaspoons baking powder
- 1 teaspoon baking soda
- ½ teaspoon salt
- 2½ cups peeled and grated carrots (about 3 carrots)

Preheat the oven to 350°F. Oil or butter a 12-cup muffin tin or line with muffin tin liners.

In a large bowl, beat together the eggs, oil, and vanilla.

In another large bowl, whisk together the flours, sugar, cinnamon, flax seeds, baking powder, baking soda, and salt until well combined. Add the dry ingredients to the egg mixture, whisking to combine. Stir in the carrots.

Spoon the batter into the prepared muffin tin and bake for 15 minutes, or until a tester comes out clean. Let the muffins rest for 5 minutes, then turn them out onto a wire rack to cool.

Spelt Muffins

These muffins are rich and dense, both healthy and hearty with wheat germ mixed in for even more nutrition. It's simple to turn these into blueberry spelt muffins—just reduce the milk by ¼ cup, and stir in a cup of fresh or frozen blueberries just before baking.

Makes 12 muffins

- 2 cups spelt flour
- ¼ cup wheat germ
- 1 tablespoon baking powder
- ½ teaspoon salt
- 1¼ cups milk
- 3 eggs, beaten
- ¼ cup brown sugar, packed
- 1 tablespoon vegetable oil

Preheat the oven to 425°F. Oil or butter a 12-cup muffin tin or line with muffin tin liners.

In a large bowl, whisk together the flour, wheat germ, baking powder, and salt.

In another bowl, beat together the milk, eggs, brown sugar, and oil. Stir into the wet ingredients to blend.

Spoon the batter into the prepared muffin tin and bake for 17 minutes or until a tester comes out clean. Let the muffins rest for 5 minutes, then turn them out onto a wire rack to cool.

BISCUITS

Buttermilk Biscuits

This whole grain version of the classic recipe is just as good, and better for you. How can you resist? Take care not to overbeat the batter, or your biscuits will be tougher in consistency.

Makes 18 biscuits

- 2 cups unbleached white flour
- 1 cup whole wheat flour
- 3 tablespoons sugar
- 3 teaspoons baking powder
- 1 teaspoon baking soda
- 1 teaspoon salt
- 12 tablespoons (1½ stick) unsalted butter, chilled and diced
- 1 cup buttermilk

Preheat the oven to 425°F. Lightly oil a baking sheet or line it with parchment paper.

Whisk or sift together the flours, sugar, baking powder, baking soda, and salt in large bowl to blend. Using your fingers, rub the butter into the flour mixture until it resembles coarse crumbs.

Add the buttermilk and stir until moistened, then knead just until the dough comes together. Drop about ¼ cup dough for each biscuit onto the baking sheet and flatten slightly. Alternatively, roll the dough to ½-inch thickness, cut into 2-inch rounds, and place on the baking sheet.

Bake for about 12 minutes, or until the biscuits are brown on top and a tester comes out clean. Cool on a wire rack.

Gluten-Free Buttermilk Biscuits

GLUTEN-FREE

These moist, yet gluten-free biscuits are a spectacular alternative to the classic buttermilk biscuit. You can turn them into luscious almond biscuits—delicious alongside fruit—by adding 2½ tablespoons of slivered almonds to the dry ingredients, and a scant ⅛ tablespoon almond extract to the wet ingredients.

Makes about 12 biscuits

- 1 cup rice flour
- ¼ cup tapioca flour
- ⅓ cup potato starch
- ¼ teaspoon xanthan gum
- 4 teaspoons baking powder
- 1 teaspoon baking soda
- 1 teaspoon sugar
- 2 eggs, lightly beaten
- ⅓ cup vegetable oil
- ⅓ cup buttermilk

Preheat the oven to 400°F. Lightly oil a baking sheet or line it with parchment paper.

In a large bowl, whisk or sift together the flours, potato starch, xanthan gum, baking powder, baking soda, and sugar. In a medium bowl, beat together the eggs, oil, and buttermilk.

Add the wet ingredients to the flour mixture, and stir until combined. Add a small amount of water if the batter is too thick.

Using a large mixing spoon, drop about ¼ cup dough for each biscuit onto the baking sheet and flatten slightly. Bake for about 12 minutes, or until the biscuits are brown on top and a tester comes out clean.

Sour Cream Orange Biscuits

These biscuits are moist from the sour cream and wonderfully citrusy as a result of the added orange juice and zest. While there are many ways to zest an orange, microplane zesters, which are very sharp graters, make the job as easy as can be. Whether you have a microplane zester or not, these light biscuits are wonderful in a bread basket for brunch or served alongside scrambled eggs and other savory morning dishes.

Makes about 12 biscuits

- ½ cup sour cream
- 1½ tablespoons orange juice
- 1 tablespoon orange zest
- ½ teaspoon baking soda
- ¼ pound (1 stick) unsalted butter, softened
- 1¼ cups sugar
- 1 egg
- 1¾ cups unbleached white flour
- ¾ cup whole wheat flour
- 1 tablespoon baking powder
- ½ teaspoon salt

Preheat the oven to 350°F. Lightly oil a baking sheet or line it with parchment paper.

Combine the sour cream, orange juice, zest, and baking soda. Cream the butter with the sugar about 2 or 3 minutes, until it is light and fluffy. Beat in the egg.

In a separate bowl, combine the flours, baking powder, and salt. Sift half of the flour mixture into the butter mixture and fold in, then beat in half the sour cream mixture. Repeat with remaining flour and sour cream.

Using a large spoon, drop tablespoon-size pieces of dough onto the baking sheet. Bake for about 12 to 15 minutes, or until the biscuits are brown on top and a tester comes out clean. Cool on a wire rack.

Sage Biscuits

Redolent of earthy herbs, these savory biscuits are a wonderful accompaniment to roasted meats. Make them as a side dish for Thanksgiving or any other fall dinner, and suggest that guests put a little chutney on them.

Makes about 12 biscuits

- 1 ⅓ cup unbleached white flour
- ⅔ cup whole wheat flour
- 1 tablespoon baking powder
- ½ teaspoon salt
- 1 tablespoons fresh sage, finely chopped
- ½ cup cold milk
- 1 egg
- ¼ pound (1 stick) unsalted butter, chilled and diced
- ¼ cup shortening, chilled and diced

Preheat the oven to 400°F. Lightly oil a baking sheet or line it with parchment paper.

Place the flours, baking powder, salt, and sage in a food processor and pulse to blend, or whisk together in a large bowl. In a small bowl, combine the milk and egg.

Scatter the butter and shortening on top of the flour mixture and pulse a few times, or cut in with two knives, until it resembles coarse crumbs. If you are using a food processor, remove the flour mixture to a large bowl and add the milk and egg mixture. Mix until just combined, then transfer the dough to a floured surface and knead until it comes together, about 5 or 6 times. Roll the dough to ½-inch thickness and cut into 2-inch rounds.

Place the biscuits on the prepared baking sheet and bake for about 12 minutes, or until biscuits are brown on top and a tester comes out clean. Cool on a wire rack before serving.

Cornmeal Biscuits

Light in texture and pleasantly crunchy, these biscuits have a bit of rye flour for added flavor. To make them a great accompaniment to a barbecue, add ½ teaspoon or more of red pepper flakes to the dry ingredients—that'll be sure to spice things up.

Makes about 12 biscuits

- ¼ cup rye flour
- ¾ cup unbleached white flour
- 1 cup cornmeal
- ½ teaspoon salt
- ¾ teaspoon baking soda
- ¼ cup shortening, chilled and diced
- 2 eggs, lightly beaten
- ¾ cup milk

Preheat the oven to 425°F. Lightly oil a baking sheet or line it with parchment paper.

Place the flours, cornmeal, salt, and baking soda in a food processor and pulse, or whisk together in a large bowl. Sprinkle with the shortening and pulse, or use two knives to cut the shortening in, until the mixture resembles coarse crumbs. Whisk together the eggs and milk. In a large bowl, pour the milk mixture into the flour mixture, stirring until the dough comes together. If the dough is too sticky, add a bit more cornmeal.

Turn the dough out onto a floured surface and knead the dough 3 or 4 times, then roll out to about ½-inch thickness and cut into 1½-inch rounds. Place on the prepared baking sheet and bake for about 15 minutes, or until the biscuits are brown on top and a tester comes out clean. Cool on a wire rack before serving.

Feta Dill Biscuits

Feta and dill are often used together in Greek cuisine. Here, they are combined into a quick, easy, and delicious biscuit.

Makes about 12 biscuits

- 1 1/3 cups unbleached white flour
- 2/3 cup whole wheat flour
- 1/2 teaspoon salt
- 3 1/2 teaspoons baking powder
- 1 tablespoon sugar
- 6 tablespoons unsalted butter, chilled and diced
- 3/4 cup plus one tablespoon milk
- 2/3 cup feta cheese, crumbled
- 1 1/2 teaspoons fresh chopped or 1/2 teaspoon dried dill

Preheat the oven to 400°F. Lightly oil a baking sheet or line it with parchment paper.

Place the flours, salt, baking powder, and sugar in a food processor and pulse to blend, or sift together in a large bowl. Add the butter and pulse, or use two knives to cut the shortening in, until the mixture resembles coarse crumbs.

In a separate bowl, combine the milk, cheese, and dill. In a large bowl, pour the milk mixture into the flour mixture, stirring until the dough comes together.

Turn the dough out onto a floured surface and knead the dough 7 or 8 times. Roll out to about 1/2-inch thickness and cut into 2-inch rounds.

Place the biscuits on the prepared baking sheet and bake for about 12 minutes, or until the biscuits are brown on top and a tester comes out clean. Cool on a wire rack before serving.

Bran Biscuits

These slightly coarse, savory biscuits don't rise as much as many other biscuits do, but they are a good accompaniment to meat dishes. For more flavor, add ⅓ cup of minced, dried fruit, such as apricots or cherries.

Makes about 12 biscuits

- ½ cup wheat bran
- 1 cup plus 1 tablespoon milk
- 1 cup unbleached white flour
- 1 cup whole wheat flour
- 1 teaspoon salt
- 1 tablespoon baking powder
- 1 teaspoon sugar
- 6 tablespoons unsalted butter, chilled and diced

Preheat the oven to 400°F. Lightly oil a baking sheet or line it with parchment paper.

Combine the bran with the milk in a small bowl and let stand for 5 minutes.

Place the flours, salt, baking powder, and sugar in a food processor and pulse to blend, or whisk together in a large bowl. Pulse or cut the butter in until the mixture resembles coarse crumbs. In a large bowl, pour the milk mixture into the flour mixture and combine to form a dough.

Turn the dough out onto a floured surface and knead the dough 4 or 5 times. Roll out to about ½-inch thickness and cut into 2-inch rounds.

Place the biscuits on the prepared baking sheet and bake for about 15 minutes, or until the biscuits are brown on top and a tester comes out clean. Cool on a wire rack before serving.

Triticale Biscuits

Triticale's mix of wheat and rye flavor is front and center in this gem of a biscuit. Enjoy the health benefits of the hybrid grain, but treat the biscuit just like you would any other—slather it with butter and/or jam.

Makes about 12 biscuits

- 1 cup triticale flour
- 1 cup whole wheat flour
- ½ teaspoon salt
- 3¼ teaspoons baking powder
- 5 tablespoons unsalted butter or shortening, chilled and diced
- ⅔ cup milk

Preheat the oven to 400°F. Lightly oil a baking sheet or line it with parchment paper.

Place the flours, salt, and baking powder in a food processor and pulse to blend, or whisk together in a large bowl. Pulse or cut in the butter or shortening until the mixture resembles coarse crumbs. If you're using a food processor, remove the mixture to a large bowl and stir in the milk to form a dough.

Turn the dough out onto a floured surface and knead 5 or 6 times. Roll out to about ½-inch thickness and cut into 2-inch rounds. Place the biscuits on the prepared baking sheet and bake for about 10 minutes, or until the biscuits are brown on top and a tester comes out clean. Cool on a wire rack before serving.

Whole Wheat Biscuits

This classic biscuit is easy to make and so darn satisfying. This recipe works very well for those wanting a dairy-free biscuit—just substitute soy or rice milk for the cow's milk.

Makes about 12 biscuits

- 1 cup whole wheat flour
- 1 cup unbleached white flour
- ½ teaspoon salt
- 1 tablespoon baking powder
- 4 tablespoons vegetable shortening or unsalted butter, chilled and diced
- ¾ cup milk

Preheat the oven to 425°F. Lightly oil a baking sheet or line it with parchment paper.

Combine the flours, salt, and baking powder in the bowl of a food processor or a large bowl. Pulse or cut the shortening into the flour, until it resembles coarse crumbs. If you're using a food processor, remove the mixture to a large bowl and stir in the milk to form a dough.

Turn the dough out onto a floured surface and knead 5 or 6 times. Roll out to a ½-inch thickness and cut into 2-inch rounds.

Place the biscuits on the prepared baking sheet and bake for about 12 minutes, or until the biscuits are brown on top and a tester comes out clean. Cool on a wire rack before serving.

Cornmeal Buttermilk Biscuits

These biscuits are particularly great served alongside a bowl of chili. Or, turn these into dumplings—just spoon the dough onto a simmering pot of chili. Just be sure the dumplings rest on something solid in the soup and don't just fall to the bottom (remove some liquid if necessary). Cover and simmer for about 15 minutes, or until done.

Makes about 12 biscuits

- ³/₄ cup unbleached white flour
- ¹/₄ cup whole wheat flour
- ¹/₂ cup yellow cornmeal
- 1 teaspoon baking powder
- ¹/₄ teaspoon baking soda
- ¹/₂ teaspoon salt
- 6 tablespoons unsalted butter, chilled and diced
- ³/₄ cup buttermilk, chilled

Preheat the oven to 425°F. Lightly oil a baking sheet or line it with parchment paper.

Combine the flours, cornmeal, sugar, baking powder, baking soda, and salt in a food processor or large bowl. Pulse or cut in the butter, until it resembles coarse crumbs. Remove to a bowl, add the buttermilk, and stir.

Turn the dough out onto a floured surface and knead 5 or 6 times. Roll out to about ¹/₂-inch thickness and cut into 2-inch rounds.

Place the biscuits on the prepared baking sheet and bake for about 15 minutes, or until the biscuits are brown on top and a tester comes out clean. Cool on a wire rack before serving.

Cheese Biscuits

These biscuits go great alongside a pot of homemade soup, and are great shared with a few friends over a late, lazy weekend lunch. Perfect.

Makes about 16 biscuits

- 2½ cups unbleached white flour
- 1 cup whole wheat flour
- 2 tablespoons baking powder
- 1 teaspoon baking soda
- 1 tablespoon sugar
- ½ teaspoon salt
- 1¼ cups grated cheddar cheese
- ⅔ cup grated Romano cheese
- ¾ cup vegetable shortening or 12 tablespoons (1 ½ stick) unsalted butter, chilled and diced
- 1¼ cups buttermilk, chilled

Preheat the oven to 450°F. Lightly oil a baking sheet or line it with parchment paper.

Sift the flours, baking powder, baking soda, sugar, and salt into a medium bowl, then stir in the cheeses. Cut in the shortening until the mixture resembles coarse crumbs. Add the buttermilk and stir to form a dough.

Turn the dough out onto lightly floured surface and knead until smooth, about 5 or 6 times. Roll out to a ¾-inch thick circle and cut into 3-inch rounds.

Place the biscuits on the prepared baking sheet and bake for about 15 minutes, or until the biscuits are brown on top and a tester comes out clean. Cool on a wire rack before serving.

SCONES

Sourdough Scones

It's hard to improve on the simplicity of the sourdough scone. Adding something sweet on top, such as fruit preserves or honey, brings it darn near perfection.

Makes about 12 scones

- 1 cup hard white whole wheat flour
- 1 cup unbleached white flour
- 3 tablespoons sugar
- ½ teaspoon salt
- ⅓ cup unsalted butter, chilled and diced
- ½ cup sourdough starter (pages 68-69)
- 1 egg, beaten
- 2 tablespoons milk, room temperature

In the bowl of a food processor, combine the flours, sugar, and salt, then cut in the butter by pulsing a few times until the mixture resembles coarse crumbs.

Place the flour mixture in a mixing bowl and add the starter, egg, and milk, and mix well.

Turn the dough out onto a lightly floured surface and knead until smooth, about 2 minutes. Roll the dough out into a circle no more than ¾-inch thick, then cut into 12 wedges. Cover with a clean dish towel and allow to rest for 30 minutes.

Preheat the oven to 425°F.

Line a baking sheet with parchment paper and place the scones, spaced an inch apart, on the sheet. Bake for 15 minutes, or until golden, and a tester comes out clean. Cool on a wire rack before serving.

Buckwheat Scones

Buckwheat is delicious, but it sure isn't thought of as a grain that makes things "fluffy," so handle the dough as little as possible to keep these scones light. They will be dense no matter what, of course, but they will also be loaded with nutty, sweet flavor.

Makes 6 to 8 scones

- 1 cup unbleached white flour
- ½ cup whole wheat flour
- ⅔ cup buckwheat flour
- ½ teaspoon salt
- 1 tablespoon baking powder
- 6 tablespoons unsalted butter, chilled and diced
- 1 egg
- ⅓ cup brown sugar, packed
- ½ cup milk
- ¾ cup unsweetened granola
- Milk or melted butter for glazing
- Ground cinnamon and sugar for dusting, optional

Preheat the oven to 400°F. Lightly oil a baking sheet or line it with parchment paper.

In a food processor or large bowl, pulse or whisk together the flours, salt, and baking powder. Cut in the butter until the mixture resembles coarse crumbs.

In a medium bowl, beat the egg with the brown sugar and milk. Pour the egg mixture into flour mixture and combine until moistened.

Turn the dough out onto a lightly floured surface, sprinkle with granola and knead 8 or 9 times to incorporate. Pat the dough into a ½-inch thick round, brush with milk or melted butter, and cut into 6 or 8 wedges. Sprinkle with cinnamon and sugar.

Place the scones on the prepared pan and bake for 20 minutes or until a tester comes out clean. Cool on a wire rack before serving.

Pumpkin Scones

Not only are they fantastically delicious, pumpkins are rich in Vitamin A and potassium. We've used them here to make a great scone.

Makes 6 to 8 scones

- ¾ cup unbleached white flour
- ¾ cup whole wheat pastry flour
- ¼ cup rye flour
- 1 tablespoon baking powder
- ½ teaspoon salt
- ¼ cup brown sugar, packed
- 6 tablespoons unsalted butter, chilled and diced
- 2 teaspoons ground cinnamon
- ½ teaspoon ground ginger
- 1 cup unsweetened pumpkin puree
- ⅓ cup plus 2 tablespoons milk
- Milk or melted butter for glazing
- Ground cinnamon and sugar for dusting, optional

Preheat the oven to 400°F. Lightly oil a baking sheet or line it with parchment paper.

In a food processor or large bowl, pulse or stir together the flours, baking powder, salt, and brown sugar. Add the butter and pulse or cut in until the mixture resembles coarse crumbs.

Combine the spices with the pumpkin and mix well. Pour the pumpkin mixture into the flour mixture along with ⅓ cup of the milk and stir well. If the dough is too dry, add the additional milk as needed.

Turn the dough out onto a lightly floured surface and knead 5 or 6 times. Pat the dough into a ½-inch thick round, brush with milk or melted butter, and cut into 6 or 8 wedges. Sprinkle with cinnamon and sugar.

Place the scones on the prepared pan and bake for 20 minutes, or until a tester comes out clean. Cool on a wire rack before serving.

Gluten-Free Lemon Scones

GLUTEN-FREE

This recipe was inspired by the gluten-free scones created by Carol Fenster, author of Gluten-Free 101. *The lemon flavor intensifies as the days pass, which is great for lemon lovers. Store them in an airtight container.*

Makes 6 to 8 scones

- 1 ¼ cups sweet white sorghum flour
- ½ cup tapioca flour
- 1 ½ teaspoons cream of tartar
- 1 ½ teaspoons baking soda
- 1 ½ teaspoons xanthan gum
- ¼ teaspoon salt
- 1 tablespoon lemon zest
- 3 tablespoons sugar
- 1 egg
- ⅔ cup plain yogurt
- ¼ cup lemon juice
- Milk or melted butter for glazing
- Sugar and ground cinnamon for dusting, optional

Preheat the oven to 400°F. Lightly oil a baking sheet or line it with parchment paper.

In a large bowl, combine the flours, cream of tartar, baking soda, xanthan gum, salt, lemon zest, and sugar.

Beat the egg well with the yogurt, then stir in the lemon juice. Pour into the flour mixture and mix until moistened.

Turn the dough out onto a lightly floured surface and knead 5 or 6 times. Pat the dough into a ½-inch thick round, brush with milk or melted butter, and cut into 6 or 8 wedges. Sprinkle each scone with cinnamon and sugar.

Place the scones on the prepared pan and bake for 15 minutes or until a tester comes out clean. Cool on a wire rack before serving.

Millet Scones

These millet scones are a good, healthy, and delicious start to the day, especially when they are topped with lots of apricot preserves. Yum.

Makes 6 to 8 scones

- 1½ cups unbleached white flour
- ¾ cup millet flour
- 1 tablespoon baking powder
- ½ teaspoon baking soda
- ¼ cup sugar
- ½ teaspoon salt
- ½ cup golden raisins
- 2 eggs
- ⅓ cup plain yogurt
- ½ cup vegetable oil
- Milk or melted butter for glazing
- Sugar and ground cinnamon for dusting, optional

Preheat the oven to 400°F. Lightly oil a baking sheet or line it with parchment paper.

In a large bowl, combine the flours, baking powder, baking soda, sugar, and salt. Stir in the raisins. Beat the eggs, yogurt, and oil until well mixed, then add to the flour mixture and stir until moistened.

Turn the dough out onto a lightly floured surface and knead 5 or 6 times. Pat the dough into a ½-inch thick round, brush with milk or melted butter, and cut into 6 or 8 wedges. Sprinkle with cinnamon and sugar.

Place the scones on the prepared pan and bake for 22 minutes or until a tester comes out clean. Cool on a wire rack and serve warm or at room temperature.

White Chocolate Cherry Scones

This delightful dessert scone is quicker to make than cookies, so you don't have to wait that long to get your sweet fix. Serve this luscious treat warm, topped with vanilla ice cream.

Makes 6 to 8 scones

- 1⅓ cups unbleached white flour
- ⅔ cup whole wheat pastry flour
- 1 tablespoon baking soda
- 1 teaspoon cream of tartar
- ½ teaspoon salt
- 3 tablespoons sugar
- 6 tablespoons unsalted butter, chilled and diced
- 1 egg
- ½ cup buttermilk
- 5 ounces white chocolate, chilled and diced
- ½ cup dried cherries, coarsely chopped
- Milk or melted butter for glazing
- Sugar and ground cinnamon for dusting, optional

Preheat the oven to 425°F. Lightly oil a baking sheet or line it with parchment paper.

In a food processor or large bowl, pulse or whisk together the flours, baking soda, cream of tarter, salt, and sugar. Cut in the butter until the mixture resembles coarse crumbs.

Beat the egg with the buttermilk, then stir in the chocolate and cherries. Stir the buttermilk mixture into the flour until moistened.

Turn the dough out onto a lightly floured surface and knead 5 or 6 times. Pat the dough into a ½-inch thick round, brush with milk or butter, and cut into 6 or 8 wedges. Sprinkle with cinnamon and sugar if desired.

Place the scones on the prepared pan and bake for 15 minutes or until a tester comes out clean. Cool on a wire rack and serve warm or at room temperature.

Whole Wheat Herb Scones

The list of herbs in this recipe is merely a suggestion, of course; you can mix and match to your heart's desire. Another option is a sprinkling of Herbs d'Provence, that French combination of herbs that varies some with whomever is putting it together.

Makes 6 to 8 scones

- ½ cup barley flour
- ½ cup whole wheat pastry flour
- 1 cup unbleached white flour
- 1 tablespoon baking powder
- ¼ teaspoon salt
- 2 teaspoons fresh minced or ¾ teaspoon dried basil
- 1½ teaspoons fresh minced or ½ teaspoon dried thyme
- 1 teaspoon fresh minced or ¼ teaspoon dried marjoram
- 6 tablespoons unsalted butter, chilled and diced
- 2 eggs
- ½ cup milk
- Milk or melted butter for glazing

Preheat the oven to 425°F. Lightly oil a baking sheet or line it with parchment paper.

In a food processor or large bowl, pulse or whisk together the flours, baking powder, salt, and herbs. Cut in the butter until the mixture resembles coarse crumbs.

Beat the eggs with the milk, then add to the dry ingredients and combine to moisten.

Turn the dough out onto a lightly floured surface and knead 5 or 6 times. Pat the dough into a ½-inch thick round, brush with milk or butter, and cut into 6 or 8 wedges.

Place the scones on the prepared pan and bake for 18 minutes or until a tester comes out clean. Cool on a wire rack and serve warm or at room temperature.

Sour Cream Scones

Sour cream isn't the only star in these scones—the buckwheat flour adds a nice nutty flavor.

Makes 6 to 8 scones

- 1 cup unbleached white flour
- ¾ cup whole wheat pastry flour
- ½ cup buckwheat flour
- ¼ cup brown sugar
- 1 tablespoon baking powder
- ½ teaspoon baking soda
- 1 teaspoon ground nutmeg
- ½ teaspoon salt
- 6 tablespoons unsalted butter, chilled and diced
- 1 cup sour cream
- 2 tablespoons milk
- Milk or melted butter for glazing
- Sugar and ground cinnamon for dusting, optional

Preheat the oven to 425°F. Lightly oil a baking sheet or line it with parchment paper.

In a food processor or large bowl, pulse or whisk together the flours, brown sugar, baking powder, baking soda, nutmeg, and salt. Cut in the butter until mixture resembles coarse crumbs.

In a separate bowl, combine the sour cream and milk. Pour the sour cream mixture into the flour mixture and, using a fork, combine until moist.

Turn the dough out onto a lightly floured surface and knead 5 or 6 times. Pat the dough into a ½-inch thick round, brush with milk or melted butter, and cut into 6 or 8 wedges. Sprinkle with cinnamon and sugar.

Place the scones on the prepared pan and bake for 20 minutes or until a tester comes out clean. Cool on a wire rack and serve warm or at room temperature.

Cardamom Rye Scones

Cardamom is one of the classic flavors found in Indian food. Warm without being spicy, it lends a distinctive flavor to these scones, which are delicious topped with a bit of honey.

Makes 6 to 8 scones

- 2 cups unbleached white flour
- 1 cup rye flour
- ½ cup brown sugar
- 4 teaspoons baking powder
- 1 teaspoon baking soda
- 2 teaspoons ground cardamom
- ½ teaspoon salt
- 12 tablespoons (1 ½ stick) unsalted butter, chilled and diced
- 3 eggs
- ⅓ cup buttermilk, chilled, plus more as necessary
- Milk or melted butter for glazing
- Sugar and ground cinnamon for dusting, optional

Preheat the oven to 425°F. Lightly oil a baking sheet or line it with parchment paper.

In a food processor or large bowl, pulse or whisk together the flours, sugar, baking powder, baking soda, cardamom, and salt. Cut in the butter until mixture resembles coarse crumbs.

Beat the eggs with the buttermilk. Stir the egg mixture into the flour mixture until moistened. Add more buttermilk if the dough is too dry.

Turn the dough out onto a lightly floured surface and knead 5 or 6 times. Pat the dough into a ½-inch thick round, brush with milk or melted butter, and cut into 6 or 8 wedges. Sprinkle with cinnamon and sugar.

Place the scones on the prepared pan and bake for 15 minutes or until a tester comes out clean. Cool on a wire rack and serve warm or at room temperature.

Quinoa Hazelnut Scones

Quinoa flour makes for a chewier scone, and hazelnuts add great flavor. Although you can substitute pecans or walnuts here, our first choice remains Oregon hazelnuts (also known as filberts).

Makes 6 to 8 scones

- 1¼ cups whole wheat pastry flour
- ¾ cup quinoa flour
- ¼ cup sugar
- 2 teaspoons baking powder
- ½ teaspoon salt
- ½ teaspoon ground cinnamon
- 6 tablespoons unsalted butter, chilled and diced
- ¾ cup hazelnuts, toasted and coarsely chopped
- ⅔ cup whole milk
- 1 egg
- Milk or melted butter for glazing
- Sugar and ground cinnamon for dusting, optional

Preheat the oven to 400°F. Lightly oil a baking sheet or line it with parchment paper.

In a food processor or large bowl, pulse or whisk together the flours, sugar, baking powder, salt, and cinnamon. Cut in the butter until the mixture resembles coarse crumbs, then stir in the hazelnuts.

Beat the milk and egg together, then stir into the dry ingredients until it forms a dough.

Turn the dough out onto a lightly floured surface and knead 7 or 8 times. Pat the dough into a ½-inch thick round, brush with milk or melted butter, and cut into 6 or 8 wedges. Sprinkle with cinnamon and sugar.

Place the scones on the prepared pan and bake for 20 minutes or until a tester comes out clean. Cool on a wire rack and serve warm or at room temperature.

Whole Wheat Cream Scones

Cream-based scones are traditionally found in England (where they know their scones). Rich, tender, and flavorful, these delicate treats are everything you look for in that perfect morning or tea time scone.

Makes 12 scones

- 1¼ cups unbleached white flour
- 1 cup whole wheat pastry flour
- ½ teaspoon salt
- 1 tablespoon baking powder
- ½ teaspoon baking soda
- 6 tablespoons unsalted butter, chilled and diced
- 1 egg
- ½ cup heavy cream
- 1 teaspoon vanilla extract
- 3 tablespoons sugar
- Milk or melted butter for glazing
- Sugar and ground cinnamon for dusting, optional

Preheat the oven to 400°F. Lightly oil 2 baking sheets or line them with parchment paper.

In a food processor or large bowl, pulse or whisk together the flours, salt, baking powder, and baking soda. Cut in the butter until the mixture resembles coarse crumbs.

In a medium bowl, beat the egg with the cream, vanilla, and sugar until the mixture is well blended. Add to the flour mixture and stir to make a dough. Divide into two pieces.

Turn one piece of the dough out onto a lightly floured surface and knead 5 or 6 times. Pat the dough into a ½-inch thick round, brush with milk or melted butter, and cut into 6 or 8 wedges. Sprinkle with cinnamon and sugar. Repeat with the second piece. Place the scones on the prepared baking sheets.

Place the baking sheets in the oven and bake for 15 minutes or until a tester comes out clean. Cool on a wire rack and serve warm or at room temperature.

VARIATION:

Scones Filled with Blueberry Jam

Make the dough above, but roll to ½- to ⅓-inch thickness. Make a slight indent in one of the rounds and place a little blueberry or other jam inside. Top with the second round of dough to seal and cut into 6 or 8 pieces. Finish as directed, baking 18 minutes or until a tester comes out clean.

Ginger Scones

Both crystallized and fresh ginger are used here to create a tremendously gingery scone.

Makes 6 to 8 scones

- 1 1/4 cups unbleached white flour
- 3/4 cup whole wheat pastry flour
- 1/3 cup sugar
- 1 tablespoon baking powder
- 1/4 teaspoon baking soda
- 1/4 teaspoon salt
- 1/4 pound (1 stick) unsalted butter, chilled and diced
- 1/3 cup crystallized ginger, diced
- 2 tablespoons grated fresh ginger
- Zest from 2 lemons, minced
- 1 egg
- 2/3 cup buttermilk
- Milk or melted butter for glazing
- Sugar and ground cinnamon for dusting, optional

Preheat the oven to 400°F. Lightly oil a baking sheet or line it with parchment paper.

In a food processor or large bowl, pulse or whisk together the flours, sugar, baking powder, baking soda, and salt. Cut in the butter until the mixture resembles coarse crumbs. Stir in the ginger and lemon zest.

In a separate bowl, beat the egg with the buttermilk. Add to the flour mixture and combine until moistened.

Turn the dough out onto a lightly floured surface and knead 5 or 6 times. Pat the dough into a 1/2-inch thick round, brush with milk or melted butter, and cut into 6 or 8 wedges. Sprinkle with cinnamon and sugar.

Place the scones on the prepared pan and bake for 18 minutes or until a tester comes out clean. Cool on a wire rack and serve warm or at room temperature.

Apricot Cream Scones

Oat flour gives these scones a slightly chewier texture, and its flavor is a perfect match for the apricots. If you're a true apricot lover, add a slice of fresh apricot on top.

Makes 6 to 8 scones

- 1 cup unbleached white flour
- ³/₄ cup whole wheat pastry flour
- ¹/₄ cup oat flour
- ¹/₄ cup sugar
- 1 tablespoon baking powder
- Pinch of ground nutmeg
- ¹/₂ teaspoon salt
- ²/₃ cup dried unsweetened apricots, chopped
- 1¹/₄ cups heavy cream
- Milk or melted butter for glazing
- Sugar and ground cinnamon for dusting, optional

Preheat the oven to 400°F. Lightly oil a baking sheet or line it with parchment paper.

In a food processor or large bowl, pulse or whisk together the flours, sugar, baking powder, nutmeg, and salt. Remove to a large bowl and stir in the apricots. Add the cream and stir just until moistened.

Turn the dough out onto a lightly floured surface and knead 5 or 6 times. Pat the dough into a ¹/₂-inch thick round, brush with milk or melted butter, and cut into 6 or 8 wedges. Sprinkle with cinnamon and sugar.

Place the scones on the prepared pan and bake for 15 minutes or until a tester comes out clean. Cool on a wire rack and serve warm or at room temperature.

Dried Cherry Spelt Scones

These scones pair dried cherries with spelt flour, and a delicious match is made. Who said healthy had to be boring?

Makes 6 to 8 scones

- 2¼ cups spelt flour
- 1¼ tablespoons baking powder
- 1 teaspoon baking soda
- ½ teaspoon salt
- 6 tablespoons unsalted butter, chilled and diced
- ½ cup dried cherries
- 1 egg
- ½ cup buttermilk
- 1 teaspoon vanilla extract
- 3 tablespoons light brown sugar
- Milk or melted butter for glazing
- Sugar and ground cinnamon for dusting, optional

Preheat the oven to 400°F. Lightly oil a baking sheet or line it with parchment paper.

In a food processor or large bowl, pulse or whisk together the flour, baking powder, baking soda, and salt. Cut or pulse in the butter until the mixture resembles coarse crumbs. Remove to a large bowl and stir in the dried cherries.

In another bowl beat together the egg, buttermilk, vanilla, and brown sugar, then stir into the flour mixture until a dough forms.

Turn the dough out onto a lightly floured surface and knead 8 or 9 times. Pat the dough into a ½-inch thick round, brush with milk or melted butter, and cut into 6 or 8 wedges. Sprinkle with cinnamon and sugar.

Place the scones on the prepared pan and bake for 15 minutes or until a tester comes out clean. Cool on a wire rack and serve warm or at room temperature.

Rosemary Parmesan Scones

In Italy, the combination of rosemary and parmesan cheese is a tried-and-true delight, found everywhere from hearty pastas to chicken dishes. This savory scone combines both flavors for an out-of-this-world treat.

Makes 6 to 8 scones

- 1 cup unbleached white flour
- ½ cup whole wheat pastry flour
- 2 tablespoons sugar
- 1 tablespoon baking powder
- ½ teaspoon baking soda
- ½ teaspoon salt
- 2 tablespoons fresh rosemary leaves, chopped
- 4 tablespoons unsalted butter, chilled and diced
- 1 egg, lightly beaten
- ⅔ cup buttermilk
- ½ cup grated Parmesan cheese

Preheat the oven to 400°F. Lightly oil a baking sheet or line it with parchment paper.

In a food processor or large bowl, pulse or whisk together the flours, sugar, baking powder, baking soda, and salt. Stir in the rosemary leaves. Cut in the butter until the mixture resembles coarse crumbs.

In a separate bowl, beat together the egg and buttermilk. Add to the flour mixture and stir with a fork.

Turn the dough out onto a lightly floured surface and knead 5 or 6 times. Pat the dough into a ½-inch thick round and cut into 6 or 8 wedges. Sprinkle with the Parmesan cheese.

Place the scones on the prepared pan and bake for 15 minutes or until a tester comes out clean. Cool on a wire rack and serve warm or at room temperature.

Oatmeal Scones

These delicious and chewy little scones taste just like an oatmeal cookie.

Makes 12 scones

- 1 cup unbleached white flour
- 3/4 cup whole wheat pastry flour
- 1/4 cup brown sugar
- 1/2 teaspoon ground cinnamon
- 1 1/4 tablespoons baking powder
- 3/4 teaspoon baking soda
- 1/2 teaspoon salt
- 1 1/3 cups old-fashioned rolled oats
- 1/4 pound (1 stick) unsalted butter, chilled and diced
- 1/3 cup applesauce, room temperature
- 3/4 cup buttermilk
- Milk or melted butter for glazing
- Sugar and ground cinnamon for dusting, optional

Preheat the oven to 400°F. Lightly oil a baking sheet or line it with parchment paper.

In a food processor, combine the flours, brown sugar, cinnamon, baking powder, baking soda, and salt. Add the oats and pulse 15 to 20 times, one second each. Cut in the butter by pulsing a few times more, until the mixture resembles coarse crumbs.

Transfer the mixture to a large bowl. Stir in the applesauce and buttermilk until a dough forms.

Turn the dough out onto a lightly floured surface and knead 5 or 6 times. Pat the dough into a 1/2-inch thick round, brush with milk or melted butter, and cut into 6 or 8 wedges. Sprinkle with cinnamon and sugar.

Place the scones on the prepared pan and bake for 15 minutes or until a tester comes out clean. Cool on a wire rack and serve warm or at room temperature.

PANCAKES, CREPES & WAFFLES

Sourdough Pancakes

These are great after the starter mix has been sitting overnight. Of course, you can make them the same day you make the starter, and we'll even approve of your dropping blueberries into the pancakes before you flip them over.

Makes about 12 to 14 pancakes

- 1 cup sourdough starter (pages 68-69)
- 1½ cups milk, room temperature
- 1 cup whole wheat flour
- 1 cup hard white whole wheat unbleached white flour
- 1 egg, lightly beaten
- 1½ teaspoons baking powder
- 1 tablespoon sugar
- ½ teaspoon salt

In a large bowl, combine the starter, 1 cup of the milk, and the whole wheat flour. Allow to sit for at least 1 hour, or cover and place in the refrigerator overnight.

Preheat and oil a griddle. Beat into the batter the remaining milk and flour, and the egg, baking powder, sugar, and salt. Depending on how large or small you want your pancakes, pour ¼ or ⅓ cup onto the griddle and cook on both sides, until brown, about 2 to 3 minutes.

Wheat Berry Pancakes

Start this recipe by soaking the wheat berries after dinner, and you'll have an easy breakfast from a blender the next morning. These are wonderful served with our quick berry syrup.

Makes 10 pancakes

Quick Berry Syrup

- 1 cup water
- ¼ to ⅓ cup sugar
- 1½ cups mixed berries

Pancakes

- ½ cup wheat berries
- ½ cup water
- 1 cup plus 2 tablespoons milk
- 3 eggs
- 1 tablespoon honey
- 2 tablespoons unsalted butter, melted, or vegetable oil
- ¼ teaspoon salt
- ⅓ teaspoon baking powder
- ¼ teaspoon baking soda
- ¼ cup unbleached white flour

To make the syrup, place the water and sugar in a small saucepan over medium heat. Heat until the sugar dissolves, then add the berries and continue to cook down for 5 to 10 minutes, to desired consistency. Serve as is, strain, or puree.

Soak the wheat berries in the water for 12 hours or overnight, covered in the refrigerator. Drain and rinse the berries, place in a blender with the milk, and blend for 3 or 4 minutes.

Oil and preheat a griddle.

Add to the blender the eggs, honey, butter, salt, baking powder, baking soda, and flour and blend for another minute.

Ladle about ¼ to ⅓ cup of batter for each pancake onto the hot griddle and cook over medium heat until bubbles appear, turn, and cook until done, about 2 to 3 minutes.

Johnnycakes

GLUTEN-FREE

There is some debate about the origin of the name "johnnycakes," with one camp believing it came from Shawnee Cake, made by that particular tribe. Others think it was originally "journey cake," since it travels well and was eaten by those coming to settle in the new continent. We'll never really know, since in 1796, when Amelia Simmons published what is considered to be America's first recipe for johnnycakes, she called them "Johny Cake or Hoe Cake." What we do know is that they taste great.

Makes 10 johnnycakes

- 1½ cups cornmeal
- 1 teaspoon salt
- 1 teaspoon sugar
- 2 cups boiling water
- ⅓ cup milk, room temperature

Oil and preheat a griddle.

Combine the cornmeal, salt, and sugar in a large bowl, then pour the water over the mixture and stir. Let stand for ten minutes, then stir in the milk.

Ladle about ¼ to ⅓ cup batter for each pancake onto the griddle and cook over low heat for 5 to 10 minutes, until brown. When bubbles begin to appear on the surface, flip and repeat on the other side.

Banana Pecan Buttermilk Pancakes

These pancakes include a classic trio: bananas, pecans, and maple syrup. You could eat breakfast all day. Whole wheat pastry flour helps make this pancake lighter than the usual pancakes, but you can use whole wheat flour, too. Serve these with syrup, jam, or our quick berry syrup (page 181).

Makes about 24 pancakes

- ½ cup unbleached white flour
- ½ cup whole wheat pastry flour
- ½ cup whole wheat flour
- 3 tablespoons sugar
- 2 teaspoons baking powder
- ½ teaspoon baking soda
- ¼ teaspoon salt
- 1 ripe banana
- 1½ cups buttermilk
- 3 tablespoons unsalted butter, melted, or vegetable oil
- 2 eggs
- ½ teaspoon vanilla extract
- ½ cup pecans, chopped

In a large bowl, sift or whisk together the flours, sugar, baking powder, baking soda, and salt. Slice the banana into ½-inch rounds, then slice each round into four pieces and set aside.

Oil and preheat a griddle.

In a separate bowl, beat together the buttermilk, butter, eggs, and vanilla. Fold into the flour mixture until just combined, then stir in the banana and pecans.

Ladle about ¼ to ⅓ cup batter onto the griddle and cook over medium heat until bubbles appear. Turn and cook until golden brown, about 2 to 3 minutes.

Buckwheat Pancakes

GLUTEN-FREE

We think of pancakes as a relatively new food—after all, how could they have been made without baking powder, which wasn't even invented until around 1843? Believe it or not, pancakes are actually an ancient food—the word "pancake" appears in print as early as 1430. When they made those fifteenth-century pancakes, it might very well have been with delicious buckwheat, which is thought to have been one of the earliest grains used for pancakes. For variety, we've added quinoa as an option here. Using buckwheat alone, you should know, makes for a very strong-flavored pancake. You'll get a lighter pancake and, of course, a different flavor using either grain, but both make great breakfasts.

Makes about 24 pancakes

- 2 cups buckwheat or quinoa flour
- 3 tablespoons sugar
- 1 tablespoon baking powder
- ½ teaspoon salt
- 1 cup water
- 1 cup milk
- 2 tablespoons unsalted butter, melted, or vegetable oil

Oil and preheat a griddle.

Sift or whisk together the flour, sugar, baking powder, and salt. In a small bowl, whisk together the water and milk, then slowly whisk in the butter. Combine the wet with the dry ingredients, adding a little more water, if necessary. The batter may thicken as it sits; add a little more water if necessary.

Ladle about ¼ to ⅓ cup batter onto the griddle and cook over medium heat until bubbles appear, about 2 to 3 minutes. Turn and cook until golden brown on the underside.

Buckwheat Blini

GLUTEN-FREE

Buckwheat blini, a version of the traditional Russian pancake cooked in celebration of the end of winter, is pretty tasty served with sour cream or, of course, caviar if you just happen to have it on hand (doesn't everyone?). Try these with savory or sweet toppings and fillings, from smoked salmon to maple syrup.

Makes about 12 blini

- 1¼ cups rice flour
- ½ cup buckwheat flour
- ¼ cup flaxseed meal
- 2 teaspoons baking powder
- 2 eggs, well beaten
- 1 tablespoon sugar
- 1⅓ cups milk
- ¼ cup vegetable oil

Oil and heat a griddle over medium heat.

In a large bowl, whisk together the flours, flaxseed meal, and baking powder.

In a small bowl, combine the eggs and sugar. Stir the egg mixture into the flour mixture, then gradually add the milk, beating until batter is smooth. Stir in the oil.

Ladle about ¼ to ⅓ cup batter onto the griddle and cook over medium heat until bubbles appear, about 2 to 3 minutes. Turn and cook until done.

Teff Pancakes

GLUTEN-FREE

Ethiopians make a delicious flatbread with teff, called injera *(page 222), but here, we thought we'd put its incredible flavor to use in pancakes.*

Makes 14 to18 pancakes

- 2 cups teff flour
- 4 teaspoons baking powder
- 2 tablespoons sugar
- ½ teaspoon salt
- 2 cups water or half milk and half water
- 2 tablespoons unsalted butter, melted, or vegetable oil

Oil and preheat a griddle.

In a medium bowl, sift or whisk together the flour, baking powder, sugar, and salt. In a separate bowl, whisk the butter into the water, then stir into the dry ingredients and combine well. The batter may thicken as it sits; add a little more water if necessary.

Ladle about ¼ to ⅓ cup batter onto the griddle and cook over medium heat until bubbles appear, about 2 to 3 minutes. Turn and cook until done.

Delicately Delicious Sour Cream Pancakes

The good news about these pancakes is that teenagers absolutely love them. The bad news is, well, teenagers love them. That means you may find yourself making batch after batch as "those young people with hollow legs" consume vast quantities of them. These pancakes are very delicate and cook quickly, so have a thin, flexible spatula on hand—and hopefully, no more than two or three teenagers.

Makes about 24 pancakes

- 4 eggs
- 2 cups sour cream or plain yogurt
- ¼ cup unbleached white flour
- ¼ cup whole wheat pastry flour
- 1½ teaspoons baking soda
- 2 tablespoons sugar
- ¼ teaspoon salt

Lightly oil and heat a griddle over medium heat.

Place all ingredients in a blender and puree, stopping every few pulses to wipe down the sides with a rubber spatula.

Ladle about ¼ to ⅓ cup batter onto the griddle and cook over medium heat until bubbles appear, about 2 to 3 minutes. Turn and cook until golden brown on underside.

Spiced Pancakes

We've used ginger, nutmeg, and cinnamon in this whole wheat breakfast treat, but allspice and a pinch of ground cloves work just as well. Try serving these with fresh applesauce for a very wholesome start to your day.

Makes 14 to 18 pancakes

- 1½ cups unbleached white flour
- 1 cup whole wheat flour
- 1¼ teaspoons baking powder
- 1½ teaspoons baking soda
- ½ teaspoon salt
- ½ teaspoon freshly grated nutmeg
- 1 teaspoon ground ginger
- 1½ teaspoons ground cinnamon
- 3 eggs
- ⅓ cup sugar
- 1¼ cups buttermilk
- 1 cup water
- 5 tablespoons unsalted butter, melted and cooled

Oil and heat a griddle over medium heat.

Sift or whisk together the flours, baking powder, baking soda, salt, and spices in a large bowl.

In a separate bowl, cream the eggs and sugar until light lemon-yellow color, about 4 minutes. Beat in the buttermilk, water, and butter. Add this mixture to the dry ingredients and fold together just to moisten. The batter may thicken as it sits; add a little more water if necessary.

Ladle about ¼ cup batter onto the griddle and cook until bubbles appear, about 2 to 3 minutes. Turn, and cook until light golden on underside.

Oat Pancakes

Made with wheat pastry flour, these pancakes are nice and light; made with barley or millet flour, their consistency will be denser and chewier. Each option is spectacular.

Makes about 48 thin pancakes

- 1 cup oat flour
- ½ cup barley, millet, or whole wheat pastry flour
- ½ teaspoon baking powder
- ⅓ cup cornstarch or arrowroot
- ½ teaspoon salt
- 2 teaspoons sugar
- 1 egg, lightly beaten
- 1⅓ cups milk
- 2 tablespoons unsalted butter, melted and cooled

Oil and heat a griddle over medium heat.

Sift or whisk together the flours, baking powder, cornstarch, salt, and sugar in a large bowl. In a separate bowl, beat the egg with the milk, then whisk in the butter and fold into the dry ingredients. Stir together just to blend.

Ladle about ¼ cup batter onto the griddle and cook for about 3 minutes, until brown. Turn and cook until golden brown.

Oatmeal Pancakes

These very traditional pancakes are similar to ancient Scottish oatcakes and are made with Scottish oatmeal instead of rolled oats. At Bob's Red Mill, we produce a coarse meal made the way it was in Scotland centuries ago.

Makes 18 to 20 pancakes

- 1¼ cups whole wheat pastry flour
- ¾ cup Bob's Red Mill Scottish oatmeal
- 2 tablespoons sugar
- 2 tablespoons baking powder
- ½ teaspoon baking soda
- 1 teaspoon salt
- 1¾ cups buttermilk
- 1 egg, beaten
- 4 tablespoons unsalted butter, melted or ¼ cup vegetable oil

Oil and heat a griddle over medium heat.

In a large bowl, whisk together the flour, oatmeal, sugar, baking powder, baking soda, and salt. In a small bowl, combine the buttermilk, egg, and butter, then stir into the dry ingredients until smooth.

Ladle about ¼ cup batter onto the griddle and cook until bubbles appear, about 2 to 3 minutes. Turn and cook until golden on underside.

Blue Corn Crepes

This recipe is for a savory crepe you can stuff with cheese, meat, or beans—well, lots of things—and use as an entrée. For a sweeter crepe to serve with fresh fruit or maple syrup, add 2 teaspoons sugar to the dry ingredients and ½ teaspoon of vanilla extract to the wet ingredients.

Makes about 12 crepes

- 2 eggs
- 5 tablespoons water, plus more as needed
- 1 cup milk
- ⅓ cup hard unbleached white flour
- ⅓ cup whole wheat pastry flour
- ⅔ cup blue cornmeal
- Pinch of salt
- 2 tablespoons unsalted butter, melted and cooled
- 2 tablespoons superfine sugar, optional for sweet crepes

Combine the eggs, water, milk, flours, cornmeal, salt, and butter in a blender and pulse for about 7 seconds, scraping down the sides half way through. Add a little more water if you need to thin the batter. (Add the sugar if you want to make sweet crepes.) Pour the batter into a large measuring cup or batter bowl, cover with plastic wrap, and refrigerate for at least 1 hour, up to 12 hours.

Preheat the oven to 200°F. Drape a large ovenproof plate with a clean kitchen towel.

Heat a crepe pan or a small skillet over medium-high heat and coat with butter. Stir the batter, then pour about ¼ cup of batter into the pan. Tilt the pan to spread the batter and cook the crepe until it just begins to turn brown at the edges, about one minute. Loosen the edges and flip the crepe, cooking the other side for a few seconds.

Remove the crepe from the pan, place on the prepared plate, cover loosely with foil, and place in the oven. Repeat with remaining batter. Roll each crepe like a burrito around the filling of your choice.

VARIATION:

For garbanzo crepes, substitute ½ cup garbanzo flour and ¾ cup unbleached white flour for the flours and cornmeal in this recipe, and increase the milk by 1 tablespoon.

Buttermilk Whole Wheat Waffles

Here's our whole grain version of the classic buttermilk waffle. For a little lighter waffle, separate the egg, adding just the yolk where the egg is indicated, and then beat the egg white to fold in just before baking.

Makes 4 waffles

- ½ cup whole wheat flour
- ½ cup hard unbleached white flour
- 1 tablespoon cornmeal
- ½ teaspoon salt
- ½ teaspoon baking soda
- 1 egg
- 1 cup buttermilk
- 2½ tablespoons unsalted butter, melted and cooled

Preheat a waffle iron.

In a medium bowl, sift or whisk together the flours, cornmeal, salt, and baking soda. In a separate bowl, beat together the egg, buttermilk, and butter, then gradually add to the dry ingredients to form a batter.

Spoon the batter into the waffle iron and cook until golden brown.

Kamut® Waffles

We haven't found any ancient hieroglyphics to make us believe the Egyptians were baking waffles with their beloved Kamut grain. However, had they managed to invent electricity, we're sure they would have invented this waffle immediately thereafter. Puree a few of your favorite berries with just a little sugar, and drizzle on top.

Makes 6 to 8 waffles

- 1⅓ cups Kamut grain flour
- ⅔ cup whole wheat flour
- 2 teaspoons baking powder
- 2 tablespoons sugar
- ¼ teaspoon salt
- 2 eggs, beaten until foamy
- 2 cups milk
- 5 tablespoons unsalted butter, melted, or vegetable oil

Preheat a waffle iron.

In a large bowl, sift or whisk together the flours, baking powder, sugar, and salt. In another bowl, beat the eggs until foamy, then beat in the milk and butter or oil. Gradually stir the wet ingredients into the dry ingredients to make the batter.

Spoon the batter into the waffle iron and cook until golden brown.

Whole Grain Millet Pancakes

Here's a delicious pancake. Make it with the great flavor of barley or the flavor and chewiness of oats. Decisions, decisions.

Makes 12 to 14 pancakes

- 1 cup millet flour
- ½ cup barley or oat flour
- 1 teaspoon baking powder
- 2 tablespoons cornstarch or arrowroot
- ½ teaspoon salt
- 2 teaspoons sugar
- 2 eggs
- 1⅓ cups milk
- 3 tablespoons unsalted butter, melted and cooled

Oil and heat a griddle over medium heat.

In a large bowl, sift or whisk together the flours, baking powder, cornstarch or arrowroot, salt, and sugar. In a separate bowl, beat the eggs with the milk then whisk in the butter and add to the dry ingredients. Fold together just to blend.

Ladle about ¼ cup batter onto the griddle and cook until bubbles appear. Turn and cook until golden brown on underside.

Corn and Flaxseed Waffles

You would never guess when you take a bite that these lovely waffles are packed with heart-healthy Omega-3 oils. Just enjoy the crunchy delicious flavors without the guilt.

Makes about 4 waffles

- ½ cup corn flour
- ¼ cup whole wheat flour
- ¼ cup flaxseed meal
- 1 teaspoon baking powder
- ½ teaspoon baking soda
- ½ teaspoon salt
- 1 egg, lightly beaten
- ½ cup buttermilk
- 1 cup plain yogurt
- 2 tablespoons canola oil
- ¼ teaspoon vanilla extract

Preheat a waffle iron.

In a large bowl, sift or whisk together the flours, flaxseed meal, baking powder, baking soda, and salt. In a separate bowl, beat the egg with the buttermilk, yogurt, oil, and vanilla, then combine with the dry ingredients.

Spoon the batter into the waffle iron and cook until golden.

Popovers

Popovers can be a bit on the tricky side, and these—while by no means difficult—are no exception. There are about as many tips for popovers as there are people who bake them. The most important thing to remember is to make sure all ingredients are at room temperature before starting.

Makes 6 large or 9 small popovers

- 2 eggs
- ¾ cup milk
- ¼ cup water
- 1 tablespoon unsalted butter, melted
- ½ cup unbleached white flour
- 6 tablespoons whole wheat pastry flour
- ½ teaspoon salt

Preheat the oven to 375°F. Oil or butter 6 popover tins or 9 muffin tins.

Whisk together the eggs, milk, and water. Slowly whisk in the butter, followed by the flours and salt, until well combined. The batter should be slightly lumpy.

Spoon the batter into the prepared tins and bake for 40 minutes, or until nicely browned.

Banana Rice Bread

GLUTEN-FREE

This makes a very light loaf, so let it cool completely before cutting or you will flatten it with the knife.

Makes one 8 x 4-inch loaf

- 1½ cups rice flour
- 1 tablespoon potato starch flour
- 1 tablespoon garbanzo and fava bean flour
- 2 teaspoons baking powder
- ½ teaspoon xanthan gum
- ½ teaspoon baking soda
- ½ teaspoon salt
- 2 tablespoons quick cooking tapioca
- 2 tablespoons vegetable oil
- 3 tablespoons honey
- ¼ cup buttermilk
- 2 eggs, lightly beaten
- 2 bananas, mashed

Preheat the oven to 350°F. Lightly oil an 8 x 4-inch loaf pan.

In a medium bowl, sift together the flours, baking powder, xanthan gum, baking soda, and salt, then stir in the tapioca.

In a large bowl, beat together the oil, honey, buttermilk, and eggs, then beat in the bananas. Stir in the dry ingredients and mix well.

Pour the batter into the prepared pan and bake for 50 minutes, or until a tester comes out clean. Allow to cool in the pan for 10 minutes, then remove to a wire rack to cool completely.

Irish Soda Bread

GLUTEN-FREE

This recipe was adapted from one by Carol Fenster, author of several books on gluten-free cooking. This gluten-free version is more porous than a traditional Irish Soda Bread, but is still great with an Irish stew.

Makes one 9 x 5-inch loaf

- ¾ cup garbanzo and fava flour
- ⅓ cup rice flour
- ¼ cup potato starch
- ⅓ cup tapioca flour
- 1 tablespoon sugar
- 2 teaspoons xanthan gum
- 1 teaspoon salt
- 1 teaspoon baking powder
- ½ teaspoon baking soda
- ½ teaspoon unflavored gelatin
- 1 egg, lightly beaten
- ⅔ cup buttermilk
- 4 tablespoons unsalted butter, melted and cooled, or vegetable oil
- ½ cup currants or raisins

Preheat the oven to 350°F. Lightly oil a 9 x 5-inch pan.

In a large bowl, sift or whisk together the flours, potato starch, sugar, xanthan gum, salt, baking powder, baking soda, and gelatin. In a separate bowl, beat the egg, buttermilk and butter, then add to the dry ingredients, along with the currants. Mix well.

Spoon the batter into the prepared pan and bake for 50 to 55 minutes, or until the top is deeply browned and the loaf sounds hollow when tapped. Allow to cool in the pan for 15 minutes, then remove to a wire rack to cool completely.

Lemon Blackberry Bread

Linda Langley won first place with this recipe in the Quick Bread category at our 2005 Summer Loaf Bread Baking Contest in Portland, Oregon. It's perfect with fresh summer berries.

Makes one 9 x 5-inch loaf

Topping

- ½ cup sugar
- ⅓ cup unbleached white flour or unbleached white pastry flour
- 4 tablespoons unsalted butter, softened
- 1 teaspoon grated lemon zest
- ½ teaspoon ground cinnamon

Bread

- ¾ cup sugar
- ½ cup milk
- 4 tablespoons unsalted butter, softened
- 1 egg
- 2 cups unbleached white flour or unbleached white pastry flour
- 2 teaspoons baking powder
- ¼ teaspoon salt
- 2 cups fresh blackberries
- 1 tablespoon grated lemon zest

Preheat the oven to 375°F. Lightly grease or oil a 9 x 5-inch loaf pan.

FOR THE TOPPING: in a small bowl, stir together the sugar, flour, butter, zest, and cinnamon. Set aside

FOR THE BREAD: in a medium bowl, stir together the sugar, milk, butter, and egg until smooth. In a separate bowl, whisk the flour with the baking powder and salt, then stir the flour mixture into the milk mixture. Fold in the blackberries and the lemon zest.

Scrape the batter into the prepared pan and sprinkle with the topping. Bake until the topping is a deep golden brown and has formed a thick crust, approximately 50 minutes. Cool in the pan for 5 minutes, than transfer to a wire rack to cool completely before serving.

Walnut Coffee Cake

GLUTEN-FREE

We like to use walnuts in this recipe, but other nuts like pecans or hazelnuts work just fine in this gluten-free treat.

Makes one 9-inch round cake

Topping

- ³/₄ cup brown sugar, packed
- 3¹/₂ tablespoons rice flour
- 1¹/₂ tablespoons garbanzo and fava flour
- 4 tablespoons unsalted butter, chilled and diced
- ³/₄ cup walnuts, chopped

Cake

- 1 cup rice flour
- 3 tablespoons potato starch flour
- ¹/₄ cup tapioca flour
- 1 tablespoon garbanzo and fava flour
- 2 teaspoons cornstarch
- ³/₄ teaspoon xanthan gum
- 1¹/₂ teaspoons baking powder
- 1 teaspoon ground nutmeg
- ¹/₄ teaspoon salt
- ¹/₄ pound (1 stick) unsalted butter, softened
- ³/₄ cup brown sugar, packed
- 1 teaspoon vanilla extract
- 4 eggs, room temperature
- ³/₄ cup buttermilk

Preheat the oven to 350 F and grease a 9-inch bundt or tube pan.

TO PREPARE THE TOPPING: In a medium bowl, combine the brown sugar and flours, then cut in the butter until the mixture is like coarse crumbs. Stir in the walnuts and refrigerate.

TO PREPARE THE CAKE: In a medium bowl, stir together the flours, cornstarch, xanthan gum, baking powder, nutmeg and salt.

In a large bowl, cream the butter with the brown sugar for about 3 minutes, then add the vanilla. Add the eggs, one at a time, scraping down the sides of the bowl as needed. Beat half of the flour mixture into the butter mixture, then add half of the buttermilk, stirring until incorporated. Repeat with the remaining flour mixture and buttermilk.

Scrape half of the batter into the prepared pan and sprinkle with half of the topping. Repeat with the remaining batter and topping.

Bake for 50 minutes, or until a tester comes out clean. Allow to cool in the pan for 20 minutes before turning out on a wire rack.

Confetti Cornbread

This recipe, contributed by Jim Bennet, was another winner in the Quick Bread category at the 2005 Summer Loaf Bread Baking Contest in Portland, Oregon. In an inspired cornbread moment, he chose to use our grits-polenta as the base for his fun recipe, and as you'll see, he made a wise choice.

Makes one 9 x 9-inch bread

- 1¼ cups corn grits-polenta
- 1½ cups buttermilk
- 1¾ cups unbleached white flour
- 1½ tablespoons baking powder
- ¼ teaspoon baking soda
- 1 teaspoon salt
- ½ cup brown sugar, packed
- 2 tablespoons honey
- 2 tablespoons unsalted butter, melted and cooled
- 2 eggs
- 1¼ cups combination of diced red pepper, fresh or frozen corn, and jalapeño pepper

Soak the grits-polenta in 1½ cups of the buttermilk, cover, and refrigerate overnight. Remove from the refrigerator 1 hour before proceeding.

Preheat the oven to 350°F. Lightly grease or oil a 9 x 9-inch cake pan.

In a large bowl, sift together the flour, baking powder, baking soda, and salt. Stir in the soaked grits-polenta and the brown sugar.

In a small bowl, combine the honey in the butter. In another small bowl, whisk the eggs with the remaining ¼ cup buttermilk.

Add the honey and egg mixtures to the flour mixture. Stir in the corn and peppers until evenly distributed.

Pour the batter into the prepared pan and bake for 30 to 45 minutes, or until the center is springy and a tester comes out clean. Cool in the pan on a wire rack for 20 minutes before serving.

Yogurt Bread

GLUTEN-FREE

This bread is a little on the sweet side, with a deep cinnamon and brown sugar flavor. The yogurt gives it a nice tang.

Makes one 9 x 5-inch loaf

- 1½ cups white rice flour
- 2 tablespoons potato starch
- ¼ cup rice bran
- ¾ teaspoon baking soda
- ½ teaspoon ground cinnamon
- ¼ teaspoon salt
- ½ cup brown sugar
- 1 egg
- 1 cup plain yogurt
- 2 tablespoons milk

Preheat the oven to 350°F. Lightly oil a 9 x 5-inch pan.

In a large bowl, sift together the flour, potato starch, rice bran, baking soda, cinnamon, and salt.

In a medium bowl, mix together the brown sugar, egg, yogurt, and milk. Pour the egg mixture into the flour mixture and stir until just mixed.

Pour the batter into the prepared pan and bake for 40 minutes, or until a tester comes out clean. Allow to cool in the pan for 15 minutes, then remove to a wire rack to cool completely before slicing.

Orange Cranberry Bread

This is a perfect winter bread, when both cranberries and oranges are at their peak. Over the holidays, it makes a nice indulgence when friends come calling.

Makes one 8 x 4-inch loaf

- ³/₄ cup fresh cranberries, coarsely chopped
- ¹/₂ cup raisins, chopped
- 1 tablespoon lemon zest
- 1¹/₄ cups orange juice
- ¹/₄ cup honey
- ¹/₄ cup vegetable oil
- 1 cup rice flour
- ¹/₃ cup tapioca flour
- ¹/₃ cup potato starch flour
- 2 tablespoons cornstarch
- 1¹/₂ tablespoons garbanzo and fava flour
- ³/₄ teaspoon xanthan gum
- 2 teaspoons baking powder
- ¹/₂ teaspoon baking soda
- ¹/₂ teaspoon salt
- ¹/₂ cup wheat germ
- ¹/₂ cup walnuts, chopped

Preheat the oven to 375°F. Lightly oil an 8 x 4-inch loaf pan.

Combine the cranberries, raisins, zest, orange juice, and honey in a sauce pan and bring to a boil. Remove from the heat and stir in the oil. Allow to cool.

In a large bowl, whisk together the flours, cornstarch, xanthan gum, baking powder, baking soda, salt, wheat germ and all but 2 tablespoons of the walnuts.

Stir the cranberry mixture into the flour mixture, spread the batter into the prepared pan, and sprinkle with the reserved nuts, pressing them into the batter.

Bake for 50 minutes, or until a tester comes out clean. Allow to cool in the pan for 15 minutes, then remove to a wire rack to cool completely.

Quick Orange Bread

GLUTEN-FREE

The lively flavor of orange makes a spectacular bread, and it really comes out in this one. Here, soy lecithin is used as an emulsifier and softener. It does the binding job of the missing gluten.

Makes one 9 x 5-inch loaf

- 4 eggs, separated
- 1 tablespoon frozen orange juice concentrate
- 1 teaspoon lecithin granules (plain soy)
- ½ cup tapioca flour
- ½ cup white rice flour
- 1 tablespoon sugar
- 2 teaspoons baking powder
- 1 teaspoon baking soda

Preheat the oven to 375°F. Lightly oil a 9 x 5-inch pan.

In a large bowl, whip the egg whites until they're stiff. Add the egg yolks, one at a time, and then whip in the orange juice concentrate. Add the soy lecithin and mix just until incorporated.

In a medium bowl, sift together the flours, sugar, baking powder, and baking soda. Add the flour mixture to the egg mixture and mix well. Pour the batter into the prepared pan and bake for 25 minutes (the dough will not rise to the top of the pan). Allow to cool in the pan for 15 minutes, then remove to a wire rack to cool completely.

Zucchini Sweet Potato Bread

GLUTEN-FREE

Zucchini adds a nice texture to this gluten-free loaf, and the sweet potato adds some delightful flavor. This bread is perfect in the fall when both vegetables are plentiful. Quickly cook the sweet potato in a microwave for about 4 to 5 minutes, or until it's soft. Allow it to cook before you use it.

Makes one 9 x 5-inch loaf

- 1 cup garbanzo and fava flour
- ³/₄ cup rice flour
- ¹/₄ cup sorghum flour
- 1 teaspoon xanthan gum
- 2 teaspoons ground cinnamon
- 1 teaspoon baking soda
- ¹/₄ teaspoon baking powder
- ¹/₄ teaspoon salt
- 1³/₄ cups sugar
- ³/₄ cup vegetable oil
- 3 eggs
- 1 teaspoon vanilla extract
- 1¹/₂ cups zucchini, grated
- 1¹/₂ cups sweet potato, cooked, peeled, and grated

Preheat the oven to 350°F. Grease a 9 x 5 x 3-inch loaf pan.

In a medium bowl, sift together the flours, xanthan gum, cinnamon, baking soda, baking powder, and salt.

In a large bowl, beat together the sugar, oil, eggs, and vanilla. Stir in the zucchini and sweet potato, then add the dry ingredients and stir until well blended.

Spoon the batter into the prepared pan and bake for about 1 hour and 10 minutes, or until a tester inserted into the center comes out clean.

Cool in the pan on a wire rack for 10 minutes, then remove from the pan and continue cooling on the wire rack until completely cooled.

Peach Muffins

GLUTEN-FREE

Who says you can't find a great-tasting, gluten-free muffin? The perfect peach for this recipe is one that is ripe but not soft.

Makes 12 muffins

- ¼ cup plus 1 tablespoon garbanzo and fava bean flour
- 2½ tablespoons sorghum flour
- ½ cup tapioca flour
- ½ cup cornstarch
- ½ teaspoon salt
- ½ teaspoon baking powder
- ½ teaspoon baking soda
- 2 eggs
- ½ cup vegetable oil
- 1 cup sugar
- ½ teaspoon vanilla extract
- 2 to 3 medium peaches, peeled, pitted, and chopped, to yield 1¼ cups
- ½ cup almonds, chopped

Preheat the oven to 375°F. Grease a 12-cup muffin tin or line with paper muffin tin liners.

In a small bowl, sift or whisk together the flours, cornstarch, salt, baking powder, and baking soda.

In a large bowl, beat together the eggs, oil, sugar, and vanilla until well blended.

Stir the flour mixture into the egg mixture until just combined, then fold in the peaches and almonds.

Spoon the batter into the prepared muffin tins and bake 10 minutes, or until a tester comes out clean. Cool on a wire rack.

Lemon Muffins

GLUTEN-FREE

These muffins are quick and easy to make, with a real blast of lemon flavor. Eat them warm and pass the strawberry preserves.

Makes 12 muffins

- ¼ cup garbanzo and fava flour
- 2 tablespoons sorghum flour
- 6 tablespoons tapioca flour
- 6 tablespoons cornstarch
- ¾ teaspoon xanthan gum
- 1 teaspoon baking powder
- ½ teaspoon baking soda
- ¼ pound (1 stick) unsalted butter, softened
- ½ cup sugar
- ½ cup vegetable oil
- 2 eggs
- 3 tablespoons fresh lemon juice
- Zest of one lemon
- ⅛ teaspoon of ground cinnamon

Preheat the oven to 350°F. Grease a 12-cup muffin tin or line with paper muffin tin liners.

In a small bowl, sift or whisk together the flours, cornstarch, xanthan gum, baking powder, and baking soda. Remove 2 tablespoons of the mixture and discard.

In a large bowl, cream the butter and sugar until light lemon-yellow in color, about 3 minutes, then gradually add the oil and beat in the eggs, one at a time, scraping down the sides of the bowl after each addition.

Add the flour mixture to the egg mixture until just combined, then stir in the juice, zest and cinnamon.

Spoon the batter into the prepared muffin tins and bake for 20 minutes, or until a tester comes out clean. Cool on a wire rack.

Rice Muffins

GLUTEN-FREE

For a fun way to get your kids to help in the kitchen, have them make this batter in a quart-sized Mason jar—just stir or shake to mix, then pour into muffin tins.

Makes 6 large muffins

- 1 egg, lightly beaten
- ½ cup fruit juice, milk, or water
- 2 tablespoons sugar
- 2 tablespoons canola oil
- 1 cup white rice flour
- 2 teaspoons baking powder
- ½ teaspoon salt
- 2 tablespoons pecans, finely chopped
- ¼ cup dried blueberries

Preheat the oven to 425°F. Oil or butter a 6-cup muffin tin or line with paper muffin tin liners.

Place all of the ingredients in a large bowl or quart jar and mix very well. Spoon or pour the batter into the prepared muffin tin.

Bake for 17 minutes, or until a tester comes out clean. Allow the muffins to cool in the tin for 5 minutes, then remove and cool on a wire rack.

Rice Pancakes

GLUTEN-FREE

These savory pancakes are a tasty way to use leftover rice. Add a few chopped scallions to the batter for a nice twist.

Makes about 12 to 14 pancakes

- ½ cup rice flour
- ½ teaspoon baking soda
- ½ teaspoon salt
- 1 egg
- ½ cup whole milk plain yogurt
- ½ cup whole milk
- 1 cup cooked long-grain white rice, cooled

In a small bowl, sift or whisk together the flour, baking soda, and salt.

In a large bowl, beat the egg, then stir in the yogurt and the milk. Fold in the rice, then add the flour mixture ¼ cup at a time, adding more milk if needed.

Oil and preheat a griddle.

Ladle about ¼ to ⅓ cup batter onto the griddle and cook over medium heat until bubbles appear and pancakes are brown on one side. Turn and cook until light golden on the underside.

OPTIONAL: add chopped scallions, or lightly sautéed minced garlic, or both, to the batter.

Apple Cinnamon Deep-Dish Pancake

This delicious pancake, created by Gregory Doucette, won the Grand Prize of our "Every Meal of the Day" recipe contest, which was hosted by Cooking Light Magazine.

Makes one 9-inch pancake

- ¾ cup Bob's Red Mill 10-Grain pancake and waffle mix
- ½ cup milk
- 3 eggs
- ⅓ cup sugar
- 1 tablespoon ground cinnamon
- 3 apples, peeled and sliced
- ⅓ cup pecans, chopped

Preheat the oven to 450°F. Grease a 9-inch pie plate.

In a large bowl, stir together the 10-Grain pancake mix, milk, eggs, and 1 teaspoon of sugar, and mix until combined.

In a small bowl, mix the cinnamon and the remaining sugar together.

Arrange the apple slices on the bottom of the prepared pie plate, cover with plastic wrap and microwave for 5 minutes, or until the apples are tender. Distribute the pecans over the apples, then pour the pancake batter over the apples and pecans. Sprinkle the cinnamon and sugar mixture on top of the batter.

Cover with foil and bake for 10 to 12 minutes, until set. Serve warm with butter and syrup.

Whole Grain Waffles

These waffles from Don Payne are another prize winner in our "Every Meal of the Day" recipe contest, which was hosted by Cooking Light Magazine.

Makes 6 waffles

- ³/₄ cup brown rice flour
- ¹/₃ cup sweet white sorghum flour
- ¹/₃ cup oat flour
- 2 teaspoons baking powder
- ¹/₄ teaspoon ground cinnamon
- ¹/₈ teaspoon salt
- 1 tablespoon maple syrup
- 2 tablespoons canola oil
- 1 tablespoon pure vanilla extract
- 1 egg, separated
- 1¹/₃ cups milk

Preheat a waffle iron.

In a large bowl, sift or whisk together the flours, baking powder, cinnamon and salt.

In a medium bowl, beat together the maple syrup, oil, vanilla, egg yolk, and milk.

Beat the egg white until lightly stiff, but not dry. Stir the milk mixture into the flour mixture, then fold in the egg white. Spoon the batter into the waffle iron and cook until done, according to the manufacturer's instructions.

VARIATIONS:

Add grated orange rind or fruit, such as blue-berries, to the batter before baking.

Amaranth Pancakes / Flatbread

GLUTEN-FREE

Pancake? Flatbread? We just can't decide what to call them—except good, that is!

Makes 24 pancakes

- ½ cup almond meal
- 1 cup amaranth flour
- ½ cup arrowroot starch
- ½ teaspoon baking soda
- ¼ teaspoon salt
- 1 teaspoon ground cinnamon
- 2 tablespoons pure maple syrup or honey
- 1½ cups water
- 2 tablespoons fresh lemon juice
- 2 teaspoons cream of tartar
- 2 tablespoons canola oil

In a large bowl, sift or whisk together the almond meal, amaranth flour, arrowroot starch, baking soda, salt, and cinnamon.

Combine the syrup, water, lemon juice, cream of tartar, and oil in a blender and blend for 10 seconds. Stir this wet mixture into the flour mixture. As the batter thickens you may need to add another tablespoon or two of water to keep the pancakes thin (they should be no more than ¼ inch thick).

Preheat an ungreased nonstick griddle or frying pan over medium heat. Ladle about ¼ to ⅓ cup of batter for each pancake onto the griddle or pan and cook until the pancake browns and bubbles appear; turn and cook until light brown on the underside.

VARIATIONS:

For flatbread, prepare the pancakes the same way, but remove them to wire racks to cool. When cold, stack them, then wrap in plastic wrap and refrigerate. Prior to serving, toast the flatbreads or place them on wire racks on cookie sheets in a moderately hot (350°F. to 375°F.) oven for a few minutes.

Flatbreads, Focaccia, Crackers, & Pizza

A thousand years ago, *picea*, a flatbread sprinkled with fresh herbs, was a popular food in southern Italy. It was, as were all flatbreads, an ancestor to the enormously popular pizza we enjoy today. In fact, it took a long time to get to the ubiquitous tomato-based pizza we know today. Introduced in the sixteenth century to Italy from the New World, most of Europe believed the tomato to be poisonous. Another hundred years passed before Italy embraced the fruit. While pizza may be king, flatbreads and focaccia are rapidly gaining popularity in the United States, as are homemade crackers. Here are tips on making and baking all four.

Baking Tips

If you've ever made a pizza from scratch, you probably know that one of the frustrations first timers experience is successfully stretching the dough to the desired size. (It keeps snapping back.) Yeasted dough snaps back because of the gluten strands created during proofing. To stretch it out, roll it out and let it rest for 10 to 20 minutes. It will shrink a bit, but the gluten will be relaxed enough for you to roll it out even further the next time. If necessary, let it rest again for another 10 minutes, and roll it once more.

The amount of liquid recommended in this chapter is just that, a recommendation (unless we say otherwise). Generally speaking, when working with glutinous doughs, you may need a little more or less flour, or a little more or less liquid for a variety of reasons which run the gamut from the altitude you're baking at to the age of your flour (older flour absorbs more water than fresh flour). So the length of time you've had that bag of *Bob's Red Mill* makes a difference in your baking.

When using non-wheat flours, let them rest for 15 minutes with their fluids since they may not absorb liquids as quickly as wheat flours. This will make the dough easier to work with.

When making a sponge, add about half the flour to the yeast and the liquid, and include any sugar or honey called for in the recipe. Never include the oil and salt in the sponge as they inhibit growth. The longer you allow a sponge to rest, the better the bread tastes and the easier the dough will be to knead. In general you can let a sponge rise for up to 8 hours.

Stir in one direction to build strong strands of gluten. Changing direction or mixing in different ways can break those strands and affect the texture of the bread.

If a recipe calls for stovetop baking, a heavy, well-seasoned cast iron skillet works far better than a griddle. The skillet will distribute heat more evenly.

While true for all breads, the quality of the water is especially important for flatbreads, which often just have three or four dough ingredients. If your tap water has a chlorine taste or is sour, the bread may as well. If your local water tastes good, by all means use it, but if it doesn't, consider using bottled water. Never use distilled water, which is far too soft.

The purpose of kneading is to incorporate air into the bread. Flatbread dough especially requires proper kneading so that the bread will puff up and cook evenly for a good texture. See more about kneading in Chapter 1 (page 42).

Pricking flatbreads with a fork makes for a denser bread, since the dough cannot puff up. For some flatbreads, especially when you are filling or topping them, you may want to prick only the middle and leave the edges to puff, like a pizza does. If you slash the bread, it will rise higher and expand more.

For best results, use a baking stone, which distributes oven heat. Baking stones also absorb excess moisture, creating a better crust. The thicker the stone, the better the heat distribution. If you're using a stone, place the stone in the oven and preheat it for 10 extra minutes so that the stone heats up properly. You can also use a standard baking sheet and still enjoy good results with these recipes.

Pizza dough, focaccia, and flatbreads all freeze well. Don't thaw or reheat the bread in a microwave, which will make the bread too wet. Thaw it first, then place it in a slow oven at about 300°F., or on a charcoal or gas grill, which works well for reheating bread that had been frozen.

FOCACCIA

Focaccia is similar to pizza crust in the way it is made—traditionally, foccacia is not kneaded although we think it makes a lighter loaf when it is, especially when made with whole wheat flour. It is especially great with herb and extra-virgin olive oil toppings. We've included one stuffed focaccia recipe here. Feel free to use any kind of filling you'd like for that recipe, but allow your filling to cool (if it is cooked) and drain it well before filling the focaccia.

Basic Whole Wheat Focaccia

Makes one 17 x 11-inch or two 8-inch loaves

- 1 cup plus one tablespoon warm water (105°F. to 115°F.)
- ½ teaspoon sugar
- 1¾ teaspoons active dry yeast
- 1½ cups hard white whole wheat flour
- 1 cup whole wheat flour
- Scant 1 teaspoon salt
- 3 tablespoons plus 2 tablespoons extra-virgin olive oil
- 3 garlic cloves, peeled and minced
- 1½ teaspoons fresh herbs, chopped, or ½ teaspoon dried
- Kosher salt, for sprinkling

Pour the water into a small bowl, add the sugar, and sprinkle the yeast on top. Stir to dissolve, then let stand until the yeast begins to foam, about 5 minutes.

Oil a 17 x 11-inch baking dish or two 8-inch round pans.

In a large mixing bowl, combine 1¼ cups of the hard white flour with the wheat flour and salt. Make a well in the center of the flour mixture. Pour in the yeast mixture and the 3 tablespoons of oil. Using a wooden spoon and beginning at the center and working your way outward, vigorously stir the flour into the well, stirring in one direction, until the flour mixture is incorporated and the dough just begins to come together.

Turn the dough out onto a lightly floured surface. Dust your hands with flour and knead the dough gently, pressing down with the heels of your hands and pushing the dough away from you before partially folding it back over itself. Use a dough scraper to pry up bits of dough that stick to the work surface. Shift the dough a quarter turn and repeat. As you knead, gradually add just enough of the remaining flour until the dough is no longer sticky; you may not need all of it. Continue to knead until the dough is smooth and shiny, with good elasticity, about 10 or 15 minutes more.

Oil a large bowl, shape the dough into a smooth ball and place the ball in the bowl. Turn to coat the dough with the oil, cover the bowl with plastic wrap and set aside to rise in a warm location for 60 to 90 minutes, or until almost doubled in size.

Roll the dough to the desired size(s), cover with a clean towel and allow to rest for 15 minutes.

Move the dough to the prepared dish(es) and flatten to fit. Cover with the towel again and allow to proof for about 1 hour.

If using, place a baking tile or stone in the oven and preheat the oven to 425°F. Use your fingertips to dimple the dough. Combine the remaining oil with the garlic and herbs and brush over the top of the dough. Spread any oil that has pooled on the dough and then sprinkle with salt.

Bake for 20 minutes, or until the bread is crisp and golden. Cool on a wire rack for 15 minutes, or to room temperature, before serving.

VARIATIONS:

Tapenade Focaccia

- Basic Whole Wheat Focaccia dough (page 215)
- Tapenade (page 243)
- 30 small Kalamata olives, pitted and cut in half

Add two tablespoons of tapenade to the yeast mixture just before pouring into the flour.

Just before baking, press the olives into the top of the dough. After the bread has been baked and cooled, spread the additional tapenade on the focaccia.

Stuffed Focaccia

- Basic Whole Wheat Focaccia dough (page 215)
- 2 tablespoons extra-virgin olive oil
- 2 small sweet onions, such as Vidalias, thinly sliced
- 1 packed cup baby spinach leaves, washed and dried
- 1 sweet red bell pepper, roasted and sliced

Follow the focaccia directions on page 215 until it's ready to place in the prepared dish or pans. Instead, divide the dough into two pieces if you're using a 17 x 11-inch dish, or four pieces, if you're making two 8-inch rounds. Flatten half the dough into the prepared dish or pans, and shape the remaining dough to fit on top. Cover with a clean dish towel and allow to rise again in a warm location, for about 1 hour.

Meanwhile, place the oil in a medium-sized skillet over medium high heat and add the onions. Sauté for about 5 minutes, stirring frequently, then reduce the heat to low and continue to cook, stirring occasionally, until golden brown, about 30 to 40 minutes. Remove from the heat to a paper-towel-lined plate, pat to remove excess moisture, and let cool completely.

Preheat the oven to 450°F. Layer the spinach, peppers, and onion on the dough in the dish or pan(s), then top with the remaining dough. Follow the baking instructions in the focaccia recipe.

Rosemary & Potato Focaccia

- ¼ cup extra-virgin olive oil
- 1 sprig rosemary plus 1 tablespoon rosemary leaves, minced
- Basic Whole Wheat Focaccia dough (page 215), without the herbs
- 7 ounces (about 1 large) new potatoes

In a small sauté pan set over low heat, gently warm the olive oil and add the rosemary. Stir and warm for about 15 minutes. Remove from heat and let the oil come to room temperature. Discard the rosemary sprig and reserve the oil.

Meanwhile, prepare the focaccia dough. While the dough is rising, boil the potatoes in a medium saucepan until done, about 10 minutes. Let cool, and thinly slice into rounds approximately ⅛ inch thick. Arrange the potatoes over the dough just before the final proof.

Preheat the oven to 450°F. Before placing the dough in the oven, drizzle with the rosemary oil and chopped rosemary. Bake for 20 to 25 minutes, or until the bread is crisp and golden and the potatoes have lightly browned. Cool on a wire rack for 15 minutes, or to room temperature, before serving.

Cornmeal & Walnut Focaccia

- Basic Whole Wheat Focaccia dough (page 215), without the herbs and replacing ½ cup of the whole wheat flour with cornmeal
- ½ cup walnuts, toasted and coarsely chopped

Before the final proof, sprinkle the walnuts over the dough.

Spelt Focaccia

Spelt makes a dense and chewy focaccia.

Makes one 17 x 11-inch or two 8-inch loaves

- 1 cup plus one tablespoon warm water (105°F. to 115°F.)
- ½ teaspoon sugar
- 1¾ teaspoons active dry yeast
- 2½ cups spelt flour
- 1 teaspoon salt
- 4 tablespoons plus 2 tablespoons extra-virgin olive oil
- 3 garlic cloves, peeled and minced
- 1½ teaspoons fresh herbs, chopped, or ½ teaspoon dried
- Kosher salt, for sprinkling

Pour the warm water into a small bowl, add the sugar and sprinkle the yeast on top. Stir to dissolve, then let stand until the yeast begins to foam, about 5 minutes.

Oil a 17 x 11-inch baking dish or two 8-inch round pans.

In a large mixing bowl, combine 2¼ cups of the spelt flour with the salt. Make a well in the center, pour in the yeast mixture and the 4 tablespoons of oil, and, using a wooden spoon, stir the flour into the well. Begin stirring at the center and work outward, until the flour mixture is incorporated and the dough just begins to come together.

Turn the dough out onto a lightly floured surface. Dust your hands with flour and knead the dough gently, pressing down with the heels of your hands and pushing the dough away from you before partially folding it back over itself. Use a dough scraper to pry up bits of dough that stick to the work surface. Shift the dough a quarter turn and repeat. As you knead, gradually add just enough of the remaining flour until the dough is no longer sticky; you may not need all of it. Continue to knead until the dough is smooth and shiny, with good elasticity, about 10 or 15 minutes more.

Lightly oil a large bowl, place the dough inside, turning it over in the oil, and cover with a clean dish towel. Let the dough rise in a warm location until it's almost doubled in size, about 1 to 1½ hours.

Roll the dough to the desired size, cover with the dish towel, and allow to rest for another 15 minutes.

Move the dough to the prepared dish or pans and flatten it to fit. Cover with the towel again and allow the dough to proof in a warm location for about 1 hour.

Preheat the oven to 450°F. Use your fingertips to dimple the dough.

Combine the remaining olive oil with the garlic and herbs, and brush over the top of the dough. Spread any oil that has pooled on the dough and sprinkle with salt.

Bake for 20 minutes, or until the bread is crisp and golden. Cool on a wire rack for 15 minutes, or to room temperature, before serving.

Yeast-Free Focaccia

GLUTEN-FREE

This recipe is adapted from one by Carol Fenster, author of several gluten-free cookbooks.

Makes one 17 x 11-inch or two 8-inch round loaves

Dough

- 1 cup rice flour
- ⅓ cup tapioca flour
- ⅔ cup potato starch
- 2 teaspoons sugar
- 2 teaspoons xanthan gum
- ¾ teaspoon salt
- ½ teaspoon unflavored gelatin powder
- 1 teaspoon baking powder
- 1¼ teaspoons baking soda
- 1 tablespoon fresh minced or 1 teaspoon dried rosemary leaves
- 2 eggs
- 1 cup milk
- 2 tablespoons extra-virgin olive oil

Topping

- 1½ tablespoons fresh chopped, or 1½ teaspoons dried herbs such as oregano, marjoram, basil
- ½ teaspoon salt
- 1 tablespoon extra-virgin olive oil
- ¼ cup grated Parmesan cheese

Preheat the oven to 375°F. Oil a 17 x 11-inch baking dish or two 8-inch round pans.

In a large mixing bowl, whisk together the flours, potato starch, sugar, xanthan gum, salt, gelatin powder, baking powder, baking soda, and rosemary.

In a separate bowl, beat the eggs, milk, and oil together, then add to the dry ingredients and beat with an electric mixer for 2 minutes on medium speed. The dough will be sticky. Spread in the prepared pan(s).

Combine the herbs for the topping with the salt and olive oil and spread over the dough. Bake for 20 minutes, until the top is brown and a tester comes out clean. Dust with the cheese prior to serving.

FLATBREADS AND CRACKERS

Flatbreads are popular the world over with different versions coming from every corner of every continent. But most are a variation of the same three basic ingredients: yeast, flour, and water. How they are baked can make all the difference in the texture and taste.

Crackers, similar to flatbreads, are surprisingly easy to make and can have a long shelf life in an airtight container. If you have an air-bake cookie sheet, use it for crackers. The average cracker size is about 2 square inches, but at the end of the day, they are your crackers, so feel free to cut them in any shape or size you want.

Injera

GLUTEN-FREE

This bread, which is a staple in Ethiopian homes and restaurants, is a thin but sponge-like flatbread that is simple to make, but does take at least a day to prepare. The delicious result is worth it.

Makes 4 or 5 large injera

- 1 cup teff flour
- 1½ cups warm water
- ½ teaspoon salt

Mix the flour and water in a bowl, cover with a clean dish towel and allow to rest for 24 to 48 hours in a warm place.

Pour off any excess liquid and stir in the salt. Heat a non-stick skillet over medium heat and cook ½ cup of the batter for about 2 or 3 minutes or until air bubbles appear and the bread is done on top. Flip and cook another 2 or 3 minutes until done. Store in a clean towel to keep warm.

Aloo Paratha

There are many versions of this potato-stuffed flat bread from India. You can find a masala at an Indian spice store, or substitute a curry powder of your choice.

Makes 8 medium-sized breads

Dough

- 3½ cups whole wheat flour
- 2 teaspoons salt
- 1 cup water

Filling

- 2 teaspoons plus 1 teaspoon vegetable oil
- ½ cup onion, finely minced
- 1 tablespoon ground coriander
- 1 teaspoon ground cumin
- ½ teaspoon red pepper flakes, or to taste
- 2 tablespoons fresh ginger, grated
- 1 tablespoon chaat masala, garam masala, or curry powder
- 2 small starchy potatoes, boiled, peeled, and mashed

To make the dough, combine the flour and salt in a bowl, then add about ¾ cup of water and stir. Add more water if necessary to form a dough. Cover the bowl with a clean dish towel and allow to rest for 30 minutes.

To make the filling, heat 2 teaspoons of the vegetable oil in a skillet and add the onion. Sauté for 5 minutes or until just beginning to soften, then stir in the coriander, cumin, pepper flakes, ginger, and masala, and stir for 1 minute or so, until fragrant. Remove from the heat and stir the mixture into the mashed potatoes.

Divide the dough into 8 pieces. Pat one piece of dough into a 3- or 4-inch disc. Place 2 teaspoons or so of the filling in the center of the dough, then gather the edges of the dough up to seal on top of the filling. Flip the dough over so the seal is on the bottom, then roll the dough out to about a 5 or 6 inch circle. Repeat with the rest of the dough and filling.

Heat a griddle or a large skillet, and add a little of the remaining oil for the first bread only. Add one of the breads and cook for 30 seconds, while spreading a little oil on the top. Flip, spread the other side with more oil, and cook for another 30 seconds or so. Continue to cook and flip, without adding more oil, until it is brown. Repeat with remaining bread. Cool on a wire rack. Serve warm or at room temperature.

Caribbean Roti

This flatbread recipe, while not a roti in the true sense of the word—a real Indian roti uses no leavening— is adapted from recipes popular in the West Indies.

Makes four 12-inch rounds

- 1½ cups hard white whole wheat flour
- 1 teaspoon baking powder
- 1 teaspoon salt
- 3 tablespoons unsalted butter, softened
- ⅔ cup water
- ½ cup clarified butter, melted and cooled (see below)

Sift or whisk together the flour, baking powder, and salt. Cut in the butter, mixing with your fingers until the mixture resembles coarse crumbs. Add ½ cup of the water and mix to form a dough, adding more water if necessary. The dough should be firm, and not too wet.

Turn the dough out onto a lightly floured surface and knead for about 5 minutes, until smooth. Lightly oil a large bowl, place the dough inside, turning it over in the oil, and cover with a clean dish towel. Let the dough rise in a warm location for 45 minutes.

Return the dough to a floured surface and knead for 1 minute. Divide the dough into 4 pieces and then roll each piece into a 12-inch round. Brush each rolled out piece with clarified butter. Fold each round in half, then in half again. Place the round on a plate, cover with the dish towel, and let it rest for 15 minutes.

Heat a cast iron skillet over medium heat and place a roti in the pan, then brush with more butter. Cook on one side for about 1 minute, until just browned, then flip and cook for another minute. Flip again to just brown the top. Remove from the heat and repeat with remaining roti. Cool slightly and then press to break into pieces before serving.

CLARIFIED BUTTER

Clarified butter is simply the process of melting butter so the butterfat separates from the milk and water. To make clarified butter, place the necessary amount of unsalted butter in a saucepan over low heat. Do not stir and keep the heat low enough to prevent the butter from sizzling. Allow the butter to cook at a very low simmer for about 10 minutes, then remove from the heat and strain, or allow the solids to sink to the bottom of the pan and remove the clarified butter on top. Clarified butter is great to use in sautéing because it has a higher smoking point than normal butter and it doesn't burn, but should not be used as a spread.

Flatbrød

This is the basic recipe for making this easy and delicious Scandinavian bread, but with a bit of oat flour added for flavor. It can also be made with just hard white whole wheat flour.

Makes 4 large flatbreads

- ½ cup oat flour
- ½ cup light rye flour
- 1 cup hard white whole wheat flour
- 2 tablespoons vegetable shortening
- 1½ teaspoons salt
- 1½ cups hot water (above 110°F)

Combine the flours, shortening, and salt in a food processor and pulse to cut in the shortening. Gradually add just enough hot water to form a stiff dough.

Remove the dough to a bowl and let it cool enough to handle, then knead for 5 minutes. Divide the dough into 4 pieces. Roll each out very thin.

Heat a lightly oiled griddle or skillet over medium-high heat and add the dough. Cook until just beginning to brown, flip, and brown the other side.

Wrap the bread in a clean towel while cooking the remaining dough. Serve warm or at room temperature.

Pita Bread

Pita is a most wonderful bread for stuffing (and for stuffing yourself, for that matter). It's the traditional bread used to scoop up hummus, baba ghanouj, and other Middle Eastern delights. You'll know these are done when they blow up like big balloons in the oven.

Makes about 60 pitas

- 2 teaspoons active dry yeast
- 2½ cups warm water (105°F. to 115°F.)
- 5¾ cups hard white whole wheat flour
- 1 tablespoon salt
- 1 tablespoon extra-virgin olive oil

Sprinkle the yeast over the warm water in a small bowl, and let it stand until the yeast begins to foam, about 5 minutes.

Combine 5¼ cups of the flour with the salt in a large bowl. Make a well in the center and add the yeast mixture and olive oil. Stir in one direction, drawing in the flour, until the dough is stiff. Add more flour as necessary.

Turn the dough out to a floured surface and knead for about 10 minutes. Lightly oil a large bowl, place the dough inside, turning it over in the oil, and cover with a clean dish towel. Allow the dough to rise in a warm location for about 90 minutes.

Place an ungreased baking sheet on the bottom rack of the oven and remove all other racks. Preheat the oven to 450°F.

Punch down the dough, divide in it half, and return half to the bowl. Divide one half into 10 pieces. Roll one piece out into a 6- or 7-inch circle and place on the baking sheet, covered with a dish towel. Roll out a second piece, to the same size and place on the baking sheet. Reserve the remaining dough covered with a dish towel.

Bake for just 2 or 3 minutes, watching the bread carefully, until it balloons. Remove from the oven and wrap in a towel to keep warm. Repeat with remaining dough. Serve warm or at room temperature.

Onion Flatbread

Plenty of onion flavor makes this bread a nice accompaniment to soups and stews. This versatile and tasty little flatbread also goes great with cheese or dips.

Makes six 9-inch rounds

- 2 teaspoons active dry yeast
- 2½ cups warm water (105°F. to 115°F.)
- 5 to 6 cups hard white whole wheat flour
- 2 teaspoons salt
- ½ teaspoon extra-virgin olive oil
- 2 tablespoons green onions (scallions), minced
- Kosher salt, for sprinkling

Sprinkle the yeast over the warm water in a small bowl, and let it stand until the yeast begins to foam, about 5 minutes.

Combine 5¼ cups of the flour with the salt in a large bowl. Make a well in the center and add the yeast mixture and olive oil. Stir in one direction, drawing in the flour, until the dough is stiff. Add more flour as necessary.

Turn the dough out onto a floured surface and knead until smooth, about 7 or 8 minutes, adding flour as necessary to prevent sticking.

Lightly oil a large bowl, place the dough inside, turning it over in the oil, and cover with a clean dish towel. Allow the dough to rise until it doubles in size, about 1½ hours.

Preheat the oven to 475°F. Lightly oil 2 baking sheets.

Punch down the dough, then allow it to rest for 5 minutes. Divide the dough into 6 pieces and flatten each piece into a 4-inch round. Take one of the rounds, leaving the others covered with the dish towel. Roll the round into a 9- or 10-inch round (if it springs back, allow it to rest for 1 or 2 minutes to stretch the glutens and then roll again). Place on a prepared baking sheet. Repeat with remaining rounds, then cover all with plastic wrap and allow to rise another 15 minutes.

Press the middle of each round to make a 1-inch lip around the edge of each round. Prick the middle of each round all over with the tines of a fork, then sprinkle with the onions and salt. Bake for about 7 minutes, or until browned. Cool slightly on a wire rack and wrap in a clean towel to keep warm. Best served warm.

Bread Rings

This is another traditional Middle Eastern flat bread, which is rolled into a rope and baked in a ring. There are filled versions in Morocco, holiday versions in Israel, and many others far too numerous to mention. The finished ring can be sprinkled with sesame seeds for an authentic touch.

Makes 6 small round loaves

- 1 teaspoon active dry yeast
- 1½ cups warm water (105°F. to 115°F.)
- 2 cups hard white whole wheat flour
- 1¾ cups whole wheat flour
- 1 tablespoon fresh or 1 teaspoon dried thyme
- 1 teaspoon salt
- 1 egg white combined with 1 tablespoon water
- Sesame seeds, for sprinkling, optional

Sprinkle the yeast over the warm water in a small bowl, stir, and let stand until the yeast begins to foam, about 5 minutes. Combine the hard white and 1 cup of the whole wheat flour with the thyme in a large bowl. Make a well in the center and add the yeast mixture and salt. Stir in one direction, drawing in the flour, until the dough is stiff. Add more flour as necessary.

Turn the dough out onto a floured surface and knead until smooth, about 7 or 8 minutes, adding flour if necessary to prevent sticking.

Lightly oil a large bowl, place the dough inside, turning it over in the oil, and cover with a clean dish towel. Allow the dough to rise in a warm place until it doubles in size, about 1 hour.

Lightly oil 2 baking sheets.

Punch down the dough and divide it into 6 pieces. Roll each piece into a 20-inch rope, form into a circle, and press to connect the ends. Place the dough circles on a baking sheet without crowding. Cover with the dish towel and let the dough rest for 15 minutes.

Preheat the oven to 400°F. Brush the bread well with the egg wash and bake for 15 minutes, or until brown. Remove from the pan and cool on a wire rack.

Barley Flatbread

This recipe has Finnish origins, and is adapted from the fascinating and inspiring recipes in Flatbreads & Flavors, *by Jeffrey Alford and Naomi Duguid.*

Makes one 10-inch round loaf

- 2 cups pearl barley
- 2¼ cups buttermilk
- 1¾ cups water
- 1½ cups barley flour
- ½ cup hard white whole wheat flour
- 1 teaspoon baking soda
- 1 teaspoon salt

Combine the pearl barley and the buttermilk and allow to stand at room temperature for 4 hours, or overnight.

Preheat the oven to 350°F. and lightly oil a 10-inch cast iron skillet.

Add the water to the pearl barley mixture and place in a blender. Purée for 1 minute (it won't break down completely).

In a large bowl, sift or whisk together the flours, baking soda, and salt, then stir in the pearl barley mixture. Pour the dough into the skillet and bake for 45 minutes, or until brown.

Spicy Southwest Flatbread

Around many parts of the country, especially in Santa Fe, the smell of roasting chiles perfumes the air at farmer's markets in the fall. This bread is delicious with freshly roasted chiles but, if they are not available or you don't have time to roast your own, you can leave them out and still have a fabulous flatbread to go with your southwest dinner—or simply with cheese.

Makes 18 to 20 flatbreads

- 1 cup warm water (105°F. to 115°F.)
- 1 tablespoon sugar
- 1 teaspoon active dry yeast
- ¼ pound (1 stick) unsalted butter, chilled and diced
- ¼ cup shortening, chilled and diced
- 1½ cups whole wheat flour
- 1 cup unbleached white flour
- ⅓ cup cornmeal
- 2 teaspoons chili powder
- ¼ teaspoon ground cayenne pepper
- 1 teaspoon salt
- 1 egg
- 2 tablespoons cold water
- 1 teaspoon sugar
- ¾ cup hulled green pumpkin seeds or pepitas, finely chopped

Combine the water, sugar, and yeast in a large bowl, and let stand about 5 minutes until foamy. In a separate bowl, combine the butter, shortening, flours, cornmeal, spices, and salt, then add to the yeast mixture until it just forms a dough.

Turn the dough out onto a lightly floured surface and knead the dough until smooth, about 5 minutes. Form the dough into two balls and place in two lightly oiled bowls, turning to coat. Cover with a clean dish towel and chill for 1 hour.

Preheat the oven to 400°F. Line 2 large baking sheets with parchment paper or lightly sprinkle with cornmeal.

In a small bowl, beat together the egg, water, and sugar.

On a lightly floured surface, roll out half of the dough into a thin rectangle, about ⅛ inch thick, and sprinkle with half of the pumpkin seeds. Use a rolling pin to press the pumpkin seeds into the dough. Brush the dough with some of the egg wash and cut into irregular strips. Carefully transfer the dough to the baking sheets and sprinkle with salt.

Bake until crisp, 10 to 15 minutes. Transfer to racks to cool. Repeat with remaining dough and pumpkin seeds.

ROASTING CHILES

Roasting chiles and peppers enhances their flavors and makes them easier to peel. To roast, place the chiles on a wire rack over a gas flame or barbecue grill, or right under the broiler in your oven. Use tongs to rotate them as their skins blister and blacken, cooking the flesh as little as possible. Transfer the roasted peppers to a paper bag (or to a bowl, covered in plastic wrap) and close the bag, allowing the peppers to steam for 15 minutes or so. Remove from the bag (or bowl) and skin the peppers with the tip of a knife or your fingers. Cut the peppers, and remove and discard the seeds and stem. Be sure to use rubber gloves and do not touch your face, eyes, or other skin after handling chiles until you have thoroughly washed your hands.

Armenian Bread

Also called lavosh, this is our version of the bread popular from this land of southwestern Asia. Try it with wild rice, or with a soft cheese such as brie.

Makes 8 small rounds

- 2¼ teaspoons active dry yeast
- 1⅓ cups warm water (105°F. to 115°F.)
- 1 teaspoon sugar
- 4 cups hard white whole wheat flour
- 1 tablespoon salt
- ⅓ cup extra-virgin olive oil
- ⅓ cup whole milk, at room temperature
- 3 tablespoons sesame seeds

Sprinkle the yeast over the water in a small bowl, add the sugar, stir, and let stand until the yeast begins to foam, about 5 minutes.

Combine 3½ cups of the flour with the salt in a large bowl. Make a well in the center and add the yeast mixture and olive oil. Stir in one direction, drawing in the flour, until the dough is stiff. Add more flour as necessary.

Turn the dough out onto a lightly floured surface and knead for 15 minutes, until smooth. Lightly oil a large bowl, place the dough inside, turning it over in the oil, and cover with a clean dish towel. Let the dough rest in a warm location until it doubles in size, about 90 minutes.

Punch the dough down, return it to the floured surface, and divide into 8 pieces. Cover with the dish towel and let it stand for 15 minutes.

Preheat the oven to 375°F. Take one of the pieces of dough, roll it out to about a 12-inch round, and place it on a baking sheet. Repeat with remaining dough to fit the baking sheet, then brush each round with a little milk, and sprinkle with sesame seeds. Prick the dough with the tines of a fork in several places.

Bake for 8 minutes, or until light brown. Cool on a wire rack, serve warm or at room temperature. Repeat with remaining dough.

Pide

This flatbread comes from Turkey and is much like pizza, although it is often served with meat in that country. Our version is topped with a cheesy blend of feta and ricotta, but you know how it is with pizza— or pide for that matter—so many topping ideas, so little time!

Makes six 6-inch rounds

- 2 tablespoons warm water (105°F. to 115°F.)
- ½ teaspoon sugar
- ½ cup warm milk
- 2¼ teaspoons active dry yeast
- 2½ cups hard whole wheat flour
- 1 teaspoon salt
- 3 eggs
- 2½ tablespoons unsalted butter, softened
- ¼ cup feta cheese, drained if necessary
- ½ cup ricotta cheese, drained if necessary
- ⅓ cup pine nuts
- ⅛ teaspoon hot pepper flakes

Lightly oil 2 baking sheets and set aside.

Combine the water, sugar, and milk in a small bowl. Sprinkle the yeast over the mixture, stir, and let stand until the yeast begins to foam, about 5 minutes.

Combine 2¼ cups of flour with the salt in a large bowl. Beat 2 of the eggs in a small bowl. Make a well in the center of the flour mixture and add the yeast mixture and the 2 eggs to make a stiff dough, adding more flour if needed.

On a lightly floured surface, knead the butter into the dough until smooth, about 10 minutes. Lightly oil a large bowl, place the dough inside, turning it over in the oil, and cover with a clean dish towel. Let the dough rise until it doubles in size, about 90 minutes.

Punch the dough down and divide it into 6 pieces. Shape each piece into a circle, about 6 inches around, then press down the center and crimp up the edges. Place each piece on a prepared baking sheet. Let the bread rest for 20 minutes.

Preheat the oven to 400°F.

Stir together the remaining egg with the cheeses, pine nuts, and pepper flakes. Spread some of the topping on each dough circle, leaving a small margin between the filling and the edge of the dough.

Bake for 20 minutes, cool on a wire rack. Serve the pide warm or at room temperature.

Turkish Flatbread

This bread is very thin and pliable. Use it to roll a meat filling (page 245) for a great lunch, or serve it with salad and rice for dinner.

Makes 8 flatbreads

- 2¼ teaspoons active dry yeast
- 1⅓ cups warm water (105°F. to 115°F.)
- 3 cups hard white whole wheat flour
- ½ teaspoon paprika, hot or mild
- 2 teaspoons salt
- 1 tablespoon extra-virgin olive oil
- Meat or other topping (page 245)

Sprinkle the yeast over the warm water in a small bowl, stir, and let stand until the yeast begins to foam, about 5 minutes.

In a large bowl, sift or whisk together the flour with the paprika and salt. Make a well in the center and add the yeast mixture and olive oil. Stir in one direction, drawing in the flour, until the dough is somewhat stiff.

Turn the dough out onto a lightly floured surface and knead until smooth, about 10 minutes. Lightly oil a large bowl, place the dough inside, turning it over in the oil, and cover with a clean dish towel. Let the dough rise in a warm place until it doubles in size, about 1 hour.

Punch down the dough, then return it to the floured surface, and divide into 4 pieces. Cover the dough with a clean towel and let it rest for 10 minutes.

Preheat the oven to 400°F. and lightly oil a baking sheet.

Roll out a piece of dough onto a baking sheet until very thin, about ⅛ inch thick or less. The dough should be the size of the baking sheet. Brush the dough with a little olive oil, sprinkle or spread with the meat topping, and bake until light brown, about 10 minutes. Remove from the oven and carefully fold the dough over or roll up. Repeat with remaining dough and filling. Cut or tear in half and serve hot.

Naan

From Northwest India comes this flatbread, usually cooked in an 800°F. tandoor oven and served with various dishes. No tandoor is required here; in fact, even the Indian dishes are optional. Enjoy this naan with a Middle Eastern dish or any other food you choose.

Makes 3 large naan

- 4½ tablespoons warm milk (105°F. to 115°F.)
- 1½ teaspoons active dry yeast
- 1 cup unbleached white flour
- 1 cup whole wheat flour
- ½ teaspoon salt
- 1 tablespoon vegetable oil
- 2½ tablespoons plain yogurt
- 1 egg, lightly beaten

In a medium bowl, combine the milk with the yeast and set aside for 5 minutes.

Sift the flours and salt together into a large bowl and then add the yeast mixture, oil, yogurt, and egg and stir to make a soft dough.

Turn the dough out onto a lightly floured surface and knead until smooth, about 10 minutes. Lightly oil a large bowl, place the dough inside, turning it over in the oil, and cover with a clean dish towel. Let the dough rise in a warm location until it doubles in size, about 45 minutes.

Preheat the oven to 500°F. Lightly oil a heavy duty baking sheet and place in the oven.

Return the dough to a lightly floured surface and punch down. Divide the dough into 3 pieces and shape each piece into a ball. Wrap 2 of the balls in plastic and roll out the third into a piece about 5 x 10-inches.

Place the naan on a baking sheet and bake for about 3 minutes, or until nicely puffed. Repeat with remaining dough.

Turn the broiler on, then place the naan under the broiler for a few seconds to brown. Cover with a dish towel to keep warm while repeating with the remaining dough.

Icelandic Flatbread

Although this flatbread is often cooked in sheep tallow or lard, we're guessing you don't have a lot of that on hand—nor would you want to. We're with you there. Vegetable oil works just fine to create this delectable bread, thank you very much.

Makes 24 flatbreads

- 1 teaspoon salt
- 4 teaspoons baking powder
- 3 tablespoons sugar
- 3½ cups whole wheat flour
- ½ cup rye flour
- 1½ cups milk
- 2½ tablespoons unsalted butter, softened
- Vegetable oil, as needed

In a large bowl, sift or whisk together the salt, baking powder, sugar, and flours. Heat the milk until just scalded, then remove from heat and stir in the butter until melted.

Form a well in the center of the dry ingredients and add the milk mixture. Stir vigorously to mix, then turn out onto a lightly floured work surface and knead for 5 minutes.

Divide the dough in half, roll into balls, then cover and allow to rest for 30 minutes.

Shape each ball into a cylinder about 12-inches long, then divide each into 12 pieces. Roll each piece into a 7- or 8-inch circle, place on parchment paper, and repeat, layering on sheets of parchment. Refrigerate the dough for 1 hour.

Place enough oil in a skillet to reach a depth of 3-inches, and preheat to 375°F.

Place one flatbread into the pan. The dough will sink, and then rise to the top. When it rises, turn and fry on the other side. Cook until golden in color, for about a minute.

Remove from the skillet and drain on paper towels. Repeat with remaining dough.

Whole Grain Crackers, Breadsticks, or Flatbread

This recipe can be used to make breadsticks, crackers, or flatbread. Make simple, basic seeded ones for a variety of meals: use garlic to go with hearty soups and poultry dishes, pick smoky cumin if you have a Texas or southwestern dinner planned, or opt for cheese to match with dips. If you want to add more than one option, the garlic and cheese match well, and the seeds will go with any of the other three.

Makes about 100 crackers

- 1 cup unbleached white flour
- 1 cup dark or light rye flour
- 1 cup garbanzo and fava flour
- 1½ teaspoons salt
- ⅓ cup olive or vegetable oil
- 1 to 1½ cups water

Optional Toppings

- ½ cup mixed seeds
- 10 garlic cloves, minced
- 2 teaspoons cumin
- ½ cup grated Asiago cheese

In a large bowl, whisk together the flours and salt (and cumin, if desired), then add the oil and 1 cup of water (add the garlic and/or cheese at this point, if desired).

Turn the dough out onto a lightly floured surface and knead for 5 to 10 minutes, until soft and elastic, adding a little additional water if needed. Cover with a clean dish towel and allow the dough to rest in a warm place for 15 minutes.

Preheat the oven to 450°F. and place a rack on the upper third of the oven. Lightly oil a heavy baking sheet.

Divide the dough into 4 equal portions and leave 3 covered with the dish towel. Flatten 1 piece of dough and coat both sides with 1 tablespoon of seeds. Roll the dough to ¼-inch thick or less on the prepared baking sheet, adding more seeds to coat both sides. (For flatbread, roll the dough into rounds. For breadsticks, cut into long shapes.)

Score the crackers where you plan on cutting them, and bake for 7 minutes, or until the crackers are lightly browned. Cool on a wire rack and break apart. Continue with remaining dough. Store the finished baked goods in an airtight container.

Kamut® Cumin Crackers

These spicy, easy-to-make crackers made of healthy Kamut grain are great with a wide variety of cheeses, and salami and pepperoni slices. Or try them with a spicy sauce or dip.

Makes about 2 dozen crackers

- 1 cup Kamut grain flour
- 1 teaspoon baking powder
- ½ teaspoon salt
- ¼ teaspoon ground cumin
- 2½ tablespoons vegetable oil
- ½ cup plus 2 tablespoons water
- 2 tablespoons lemon juice

Preheat the oven to 425°F. Lightly oil a baking sheet.

In a large bowl, sift or whisk the flour with the baking powder, salt, and cumin. Add the oil, ½ cup of the water, and lemon juice, and stir to make a dough.

Knead the dough for one minute, then divide it into 3 pieces. Reserve two pieces of the dough under a clean dish towel and roll the third piece very thin. Cut the dough into squares or whatever shape you'd like, so that each cracker is about 2 inches in size.

Place the dough on the prepared baking sheet and bake for 15 minutes until just starting to brown. Repeat with remaining dough. Cool on a wire rack.

Almond Flatbread Crackers

The great taste of almond and the wonderful crunch of crackers make a scrumptious combination, especially when you spread them with fruit preserves. If you don't have any almond meal on hand, process about ½ cup of almonds in a clean coffee grinder or food processor and store in a tightly-sealed container in the refrigerator.

Makes about 3 dozen crackers

- ⅓ cup almond meal
- ½ cup whole wheat flour
- ½ cup unbleached white four
- ½ teaspoon salt
- ½ teaspoon baking soda
- 2 tablespoons unsalted butter, softened
- ⅓ cup plain yogurt or sour cream

Preheat the oven to 400°F.

In a large bowl, sift or whisk together the almond meal, flours, salt, and baking soda. In a separate bowl, combine the butter and yogurt, then stir into the dry ingredients.

Knead the dough for about 30 seconds, separate into 2 pieces, and roll each piece very thin. Cut the dough into squares or whatever shape you'd like, so that each cracker is about 2 inches in size.

Bake the crackers on an ungreased baking sheet for 6 minutes, or until just beginning to brown. Cool on a wire rack.

Cornmeal & Cheddar Crackers

Delicious and simple to make, these crackers are great served with crudités. A teaspoon of dried herbs, mixed into the flour at the very start adds flavor and complexity.

Makes about 4 dozen crackers

- 2 cups shredded cheddar cheese
- 6 tablespoons unsalted butter, softened
- ²/₃ cup whole wheat flour
- ½ cup cornmeal
- ¼ teaspoon salt

In a food processor, process the cheese with the butter, pulsing until combined. Add the flour, cornmeal, and salt and process until a dough begins to form.

Roll the dough into a ball, then divide it in half and roll each half into a log, about 1½ inches around. Wrap the logs in plastic and refrigerate for at least 2 hours, or overnight.

Preheat the oven to 350°F. Grease 2 baking sheets or line them with parchment paper.

Slice the logs thinly and place the dough circles on the baking sheets. Bake for 10 minutes, or until just brown around the edges. Cool on a wire rack.

Oat Crackers

These simple yet flavorful oat crackers go well with a plate of cheeses, a warm spring evening, and a group of friends. Delightful.

Makes about 3 dozen crackers

- 1¼ cups Scottish oats or 1½ cups rolled oats
- ¾ cup whole wheat flour
- 1 teaspoon baking soda
- ½ teaspoon salt
- 4 tablespoons unsalted butter, melted and cooled
- ⅔ cup buttermilk

Place the oats in a food processor or blender and finely chop. In a large bowl, whisk together the oats with the flour, baking soda, and salt.

Combine the butter with all but 2 tablespoons of the buttermilk. Pour the wet into the dry ingredients and mix to form a stiff dough, adding more buttermilk if needed.

Turn the dough out onto a lightly floured surface and knead 3 or 4 times. Cover the dough with a clean dish towel and allow it to rest for 15 minutes.

Preheat an oven to 350°F.

Divide the dough into 4 pieces. Roll 1 piece as thin as possible on an ungreased baking sheet. Score the dough into squares or whatever shape you'd like, and bake for 8 minutes or until lightly browned. Remove to a wire rack to cool. Break into desired shapes. Repeat with remaining dough.

Swedish Oatmeal Crackers

Also known as Knackerbrod, *these crackers are sweeter oatmeal crackers than the previous recipe. Cut the sugar if you want a more savory cracker. Like almost all of these crackers, they keep well when stored in an airtight container.*

Makes about 90 crackers

- ¼ pound (1 stick) unsalted butter, softened
- ¼ cup vegetable shortening
- ½ cup sugar
- 2 cups rolled oats
- 1 cup hard white whole wheat flour
- 1 cup whole wheat flour
- 1 cup unbleached white flour
- 2 teaspoons salt
- 1 teaspoon baking soda
- 1½ plus 2 tablespoons buttermilk

In a medium bowl, cream the butter, shortening, and sugar until light lemon-yellow in color, about 4 minutes. In a separate bowl, sift or whisk together the oats, flours, salt, and baking soda.

Add half of the dry ingredients to the butter mixture, then stir in ¾ cup of the buttermilk. Repeat with the remaining flour mixture and the rest of the buttermilk. Blend until stiff, adding additional buttermilk if necessary.

Divide the dough into 6 pieces, flatten each piece into a disc, wrap in plastic, and refrigerate for 1 hour.

Preheat the oven to 375°F. Lightly oil a baking sheet.

Remove 1 disc and place on the baking sheet. Roll to ⅛-inch or as flat as possible. Cut into desired shapes and place on prepared baking sheet. Bake for 10 minutes or until browned and crisp. Allow to cool for 1 or 2 minutes on the sheet, then remove to a wire rack to cool. Repeat with remaining dough.

Onion Crackers

Each crispy, oniony bite of these crackers will bring a smile to your face. They go great with soup, especially minestrone. Be sure to mince the onions as finely as possible—a food processor works best.

Makes about 5 dozen crackers

- 1 cup hard white whole wheat flour
- 1 cup unbleached white flour
- 1½ teaspoons baking powder
- 2 teaspoons sugar
- 1 teaspoon cumin seed
- 2 teaspoons salt
- Pepper to taste
- 1 egg, at room temperature
- ⅓ cup vegetable oil
- 1 cup onions, finely minced and, if necessary, drained

In a large bowl, sift or whisk together the flours, baking powder, sugar, cumin, salt, and pepper.

In a separate bowl, whisk together the egg, oil, and onions.

Slowly pour the egg mixture into the flour mixture, stirring vigorously until the dough is firm.

Turn the dough out onto a lightly floured surface and knead for 4 to 5 minutes, until smooth. Add additional flour if needed to keep the dough from being too sticky. Lightly oil a large bowl, place the dough inside, turning it over in the oil, and cover with a clean dish towel. Allow the dough to rest for 30 minutes.

Preheat the oven to 375°F. Lightly grease a baking sheet.

Divide the dough into 2 pieces, leaving 1 piece covered in the bowl until ready to use. Roll the other piece out onto the baking sheet until very thin. Cut into desired cracker size, and prick with the tines of a fork.

Bake until light brown, about 10 minutes. Cool on a wire rack. Repeat with remaining dough.

TOPPINGS

for Flatbread and Crackers

Tapenade

Spread a bit of softened goat cheese on a cracker before topping it with this luscious, traditionally Mediterranean spread. Tapenade is also delicious tossed with warm pasta and fresh cherry tomatoes.

Makes about 1½ cups

- 2 cups pitted Kalamata olives
- ¼ cup extra-virgin olive oil
- 1 tablespoon fresh oregano, minced
- ¼ cup capers, drained
- 1 garlic clove, peeled and minced

Purée all of the ingredients in a food processor. Stored in a tightly sealed jar in the refrigerator, tapenade will keep for up to 10 days.

White Bean & Roasted Pepper Purée

Healthy and filling, this hummus-like spread is perfect on anything from crackers to flatbreads to focaccia. If you'd like, sprinkle this with feta cheese before serving.

Makes about 1 cup

- 1 cup white beans, cooked and drained
- 1 tablespoon fresh thyme, minced
- 2 tablespoons extra-virgin olive oil
- 1 sweet red pepper, roasted and peeled
- 1 garlic clove, peeled and minced
- Salt and pepper to taste

Purée all of the ingredients in a food processor or blender. Stored in a tightly sealed container, the purée will keep in the refrigerator for up to 7 days.

Apricot Cream Cheese

This delightfully sweet topping goes especially well with the Swedish Oatmeal Crackers (page 241), but try it with any flatbread.

Makes about 1½ cups

- ¼ cup dried apricots, coarsely chopped
- 1 (8-ounce) container cream cheese, at room temperature
- 1 tablespoon honey
- 3 tablespoons goat cheese, softened
- 3 tablespoons sour cream or plain yogurt

Combine all ingredients in a food processor or mix by hand.

Tuna Topper

This hearty, Mediterranean-inspired appetizer calls for a strong cracker, like our Onion Crackers (page 242) or Barley Flatbread (page 229).

Makes about ¾ cup

- 1 (6-ounce) can Italian tuna packed in extra-virgin olive oil
- 1 garlic clove, minced
- 2 teaspoons capers, drained
- 4 teaspoons lemon juice
- 2 tablespoons mayonnaise

Combine all ingredients, including the olive oil from the tuna, in a food processor or blender and purée.

Meat Filling

In Turkey, a meat filling like this is eaten in pide bread, sometimes pizza-style, sometimes calzone style. You can scoop it up or use it with other breads too.

Makes about 3 cups

- 1 tablespoon extra-virgin olive oil
- ³/₄ pound ground lamb or beef
- ½ cup onion, minced
- ½ cup bell pepper, finely chopped
- 2 garlic cloves, minced
- ¼ teaspoon red pepper flakes
- 1½ teaspoons paprika
- 1 teaspoon oregano
- Salt and pepper

Heat the oil in a skillet and add the meat. Sauté until no longer pink, about 5 minutes. Remove from the skillet with a slotted spoon and wipe out all but ½ tablespoon of fat from the pan.

Add the onion and bell pepper to the pan and sauté until the onion is soft, about 3 or 4 minutes. Add the garlic and stir until fragrant, about 30 seconds. Return the meat, without any oil that may have accumulated on the plate, to the pan along with the red pepper flakes, paprika, oregano, and salt and pepper to taste. Stir until well mixed, remove from heat.

Spread on Turkish flatbread or other bread and roll up jelly-roll style, or fold into pockets. Serve warm.

Tzatziki

This Greek basic often accompanies fresh cut vegetables or lamb kabobs. Its garlicky taste goes well with many of our savory crackers and flatbreads.

Makes about 2½ cups

- 1 cucumber, peeled, seeded, and minced
- 2 cups plain yogurt
- 2 small garlic cloves, peeled and minced
- 1½ tablespoons red wine vinegar
- 1 tablespoon fresh mint, chopped
- Salt and pepper

Combine all of the ingredients in a bowl and chill for at least 1 hour. Use as a dip or spread for breads.

PIZZA

Pizza doesn't always have to be high fat junk food, especially when you begin with a whole grain pizza crust. In fact, whole grains add great flavor to pizza dough, and are especially suited to pizzas with stronger flavors—like garlic or pesto, pepperoni or sausage. It is possible to make pizza a healthy treat (just don't tell the kids!). Wrapped well, pizza dough will keep in the freezer for up to 4 months, so you can make it in advance, and then put together a quick, healthy pizza dinner using many of these recipes.

PIZZA BAKING TIPS

Pizza dough benefits from gluten, which is why a crust that is made exclusively with whole wheat or rye can be somewhat dense and tough. Whole wheat flour can be substituted for up to one-third of a pizza crust, but rye and other non-white flours are best kept to a small percentage. The balance of flours is also important to the flavor of pizza dough.

Moisture content varies in flours—as well as in the air we breathe—so you may have to change the amount of flour you use from time to time. Too much moisture can make a heavy dough with a dense or even tough crust. Too little, and the dough is likely to tear during shaping and be sticky. The perfect pizza dough is springy and pliant, but not rubbery.

Baking on a pizza stone helps recreate the intense heat of a professional oven. If you don't have a baking stone or tiles, use a heavy duty baking sheet.

Fast-acting yeast can be a problem if you plan to refrigerate your dough, because although chilling slows the action of the yeast, it doesn't stop it. So be sure to keep an eye on it—it can get away from you in a hurry.

Proof the yeast in your dough for 5 to 10 minutes in warm water (105°F. to 115°F.) that includes a pinch of sugar, until the yeast dissolves and the liquid appears slightly foamy. (For a more puffed up crust, add another ½ to 1 teaspoon of yeast.) The small amount of sugar will feed the yeast and prove that it is active.

Vigorously stir the dough, preferably in the same direction, which will help maintain rather than break the gluten strands.

Pizza Dough

Basic Whole Wheat Pizza Dough

Because an all whole wheat dough can be a little too dense, we suggest using hard white flour (or unbleached white) and half whole wheat. If you want to make it entirely out of whole wheat flour, be aware that the dough will not rise as high, making for a chewy crust. If you're using all whole wheat flour, add an additional tablespoon of water.

Makes one 16-inch, two 12-inch, four 8-inch or eight 4-inch pizzas

- 1/8 teaspoon sugar
- 1 1/4 cups warm water (105°F. to 115°F.)
- 2 1/4 teaspoons active dry yeast
- 1 3/4 cups hard white whole wheat flour
- 1 1/2 cups whole wheat flour
- 1 teaspoon salt
- 4 tablespoons extra-virgin olive oil

In a small bowl, add the sugar to the water and sprinkle the yeast on top. Stir to dissolve and let stand for 5 minutes until foamy.

In a large mixing bowl, combine 1 1/2 cups of the hard white flour with the wheat flour and salt. Make a well in the center of the flour mixture and pour in the yeast mixture and the oil. Vigorously stir the flour into the well, beginning at the center and working slowly outward, until the flour mixture is incorporated and the dough just begins to come together.

Turn the dough out onto a lightly floured surface. Dust your hands with flour and knead the dough gently, pressing down with the heels of your hands and pushing the dough away from you before partially folding it back over itself. Use a dough scraper to pry up bits of dough that stick to the work surface. Shift the dough a quarter turn and repeat. As you knead, gradually add just enough of the remaining flour until the dough is no longer sticky; you may not need all of it. Continue to knead until the dough is smooth and shiny, with good elasticity, about 10 or 15 minutes more. The dough should feel springy and be slightly moist. Too much kneading may result in a tough crust.

Lightly oil a large bowl, shape the dough into a ball, and place the dough in the bowl, turning to coat with the oil. Cover the bowl with a clean dish towel, and set aside to rise in a warm location until it doubles in size, about 90 minutes.

Punch the dough down and use within 2 hours. (If you are not going to use the dough within 2 hours, turn it into an oiled bowl to coat again, tightly cover with plastic wrap, and refrigerate. When the dough has doubled again, in about 5 to 8 hours, punch it down, cover it, and leave it in the refrigerator. You can punch it down a total of 4 times, but after that, it gets tough. Use the dough within 32 hours or wrap tightly in plastic wrap and freeze for up to 4 months.)

Cut the dough into equal-sized pieces for smaller pizzas or keep whole for a large pizza. Use your hands or a rolling pin to shape the dough on a lightly floured surface. Press and stretch it gently to the desired shape and thickness. The thinner the crust, the crispier it will be.

Leave the dough to rest, about 15 minutes, or place in the refrigerator for a thinner crust (since the dough doesn't rise as much in the refrigerator), until you're ready to top the pizza.

To continue, follow the directions in the recipe you choose for Pizza Toppings, starting on page 260.

VARIATIONS

Herb Dough

Add 2 tablespoons fresh minced or 1 tablespoon dried crumbled herbs to the flour and salt and continue with the recipe.

Pepper Dough

Add about 2 tablespoons cracked pepper while kneading the dough.

Sesame Seed Dough

Add ⅓ cup sesame seeds, lightly toasted, to the flour, or while kneading the dough.

Cheese Dough

Add ¼ cup finely grated Parmesan cheese to the flour.

Sweet Pizza Dough

Add 3 tablespoons sugar to the flour mixture, reduce the salt by half, and substitute vegetable oil for the extra-virgin olive oil.

Southwestern Pizza Dough

Add 1 tablespoon chile powder to the flour mixture and substitute vegetable oil for the extra-virgin olive oil.

Whole Wheat Rye Pizza Dough

Rye makes a distinctive and delicious pizza crust, but we don't recommend you use more than ¹/₂ cup of rye flour or that may be all you taste—it's that strong.

Makes one 16-inch, two 12-inch, four 8-inch or eight 4-inch pizzas

- ¹/₈ teaspoon sugar
- 1¹/₄ cups plus one tablespoon warm water (105°F. to 115°F.)
- 2¹/₄ teaspoons active dry yeast
- 1¹/₂ cups unbleached white flour
- 1¹/₄ cups whole wheat flour
- ¹/₂ cup rye flour
- 1 teaspoon salt
- 4 tablespoons extra-virgin olive oil

In a small bowl, add the sugar to the water and sprinkle the yeast on top. Stir to dissolve and let stand for 5 minutes until foamy.

In a large mixing bowl, combine 1¹/₄ cups of the unbleached white flour with the wheat flour, rye flour, and salt. Make a well in the center of the flour mixture. Pour in the yeast mixture and the oil, and vigorously stir the flour into the well. Begin at the center and work slowly outward, until the flour mixture is incorporated and the dough just begins to come together.

Turn the dough out onto a lightly floured surface. Dust your hands with flour and knead the dough gently, pressing down with the heels of your hands and pushing the dough away from you before partially folding it back over itself. Use a dough scraper to pry up bits of dough that stick to the work surface. Shift the dough a quarter turn and repeat. As you knead, gradually add just enough of the remaining flour until the dough is no longer sticky; you may not need all of it. Continue to knead until the dough is smooth and shiny, with good elasticity, about 10 or 15 minutes more. The dough should feel springy and be slightly moist. Too much kneading may result in a tough crust.

Oil a large bowl, shape the dough into a smooth ball, and place the ball in the bowl. Turn to coat the dough with the oil, cover the bowl with plastic wrap, and set aside to rise until it doubles in size, about 90 minutes.

Punch the dough down and use within 2 hours. (If you are not going to use the dough within 2 hours, turn it into an oiled bowl to coat again, tightly cover with plastic wrap, and refrigerate. When the dough has doubled again, in about 5 to 8 hours, punch it down, re-cover it, and leave it in the refrigerator. You can punch it down a total of 4 times, but after that, it gets tough. Use the dough within 32 hours or wrap tightly in plastic wrap and freeze for up to 4 months.)

Break the dough into equal pieces for smaller pizzas or keep whole for a large pizza. Use your hands or a rolling pin to shape the ball of dough on a lightly floured surface. Press and stretch it gently to the desired shape and thickness. The thinner the crust, the crispier it will be.

Leave the dough to rest, about 15 minutes, or place in the refrigerator for thinner crust (since the dough doesn't rise as much in the refrigerator), until you're ready to top the pizza.

To continue, follow the directions in the recipe you choose for Pizza Toppings, starting on page 260.

Kamut® Pizza Dough

Kamut grain makes a dense, chewy pizza dough. This recipe gives a hint of nut butter flavor that goes especially well with olive oil-based pizzas.

Makes one 16-inch, two 12-inch, four 8-inch or eight 4-inch pizzas

- 1¼ cups water (105°F. to 115°F.)
- ⅛ teaspoon sugar
- 2¼ teaspoons active dry yeast
- 3 cups Kamut grain flour
- ½ teaspoon salt
- 2 tablespoons extra-virgin olive oil

In a small bowl, add the sugar to the water and sprinkle the yeast on top. Stir to dissolve and let stand for 5 minutes until foamy.

In a large mixing bowl combine all but ¼ cup of the flour and salt, and make a well in the center. Pour in the yeast mixture and the oil, and using a wooden spoon, vigorously stir the flour into the well. Begin at the center and work slowly outward, until the flour mixture is incorporated and the dough just begins to come together.

Turn the dough out onto a lightly floured surface. Dust your hands with flour and knead the dough gently, pressing down with the heels of your hands and pushing the dough away from you before partially folding it back over itself. Use a dough scraper to pry up bits of dough that stick to the work surface. Shift the dough a quarter turn and repeat. As you knead, gradually add just enough of the remaining flour until the dough is no longer sticky; you may not need all of it. Continue to knead until the dough is smooth and shiny, with good elasticity, about 10 or 15 minutes more. The dough should feel springy and be slightly moist. Too much kneading may result in a tough crust.

Oil a large bowl, shape the dough into a smooth ball, and place the ball in the bowl. Turn to coat the dough with the oil, cover the bowl with plastic wrap, and set aside to rise until it doubles in size, about 90 minutes.

Punch the dough down and use within 2 hours. (If you are not going to use the dough within 2 hours, turn it into an oiled bowl to coat again, tightly cover with plastic wrap, and refrigerate. When the dough has doubled again, in about 5 to 8 hours, punch it down, re-cover it, and leave it in the refrigerator. You can punch it down a total of 4 times, but after that, it gets tough. Use the dough within 32 hours or wrap tightly in plastic wrap and freeze for up to 4 months.)

Break the dough into equal pieces for smaller pizzas or keep whole for a large pizza.

Use your hands or a rolling pin to shape the ball of dough on a lightly floured surface. Press and stretch it gently to the desired shape and thickness. The thinner the crust, the crispier it will be.

Leave the dough to rest, about 15 minutes, or place in the refrigerator for thinner crust (since the dough doesn't rise as much in the refrigerator), until you're ready to top the pizza.

To continue, follow the directions in the recipe you choose for Pizza Toppings, starting on page 260.

Spelt Pizza Dough

We like this dough for the spinach ricotta pizza, and it's good with calzones too. Many people who have mild wheat allergies can tolerate spelt and this delicious crust may be a good option.

Makes one 16-inch, two 12-inch, four 8-inch or eight 4-inch pizzas

- 1 cup plus one tablespoon warm water (105°F. to 115°F.)
- ⅛ teaspoon sugar
- 2¼ teaspoons active dry yeast
- 2½ cups spelt flour
- ¾ cup white bean flour
- 1 teaspoon salt
- 2 tablespoons extra-virgin olive oil

In a small bowl, add the sugar to the water and sprinkle the yeast on top. Stir to dissolve and let stand for 5 minutes until foamy.

In a large mixing bowl combine well 2¼ cups of the spelt flour with the bean flour and salt. Make a well in the center of the flour mixture. Pour in the yeast mixture and the oil, and using a wooden spoon, vigorously stir the flour into the well. Begin at the center and work slowly outward, until the flour mixture is incorporated and the dough just begins to come together.

Turn the dough out onto a lightly floured surface. Dust your hands with flour and knead the dough gently, pressing down with the heels of your hands and pushing the dough away from you before partially folding it back over itself. Use a dough scraper to pry up bits of dough that stick to the work surface. Shift the dough a quarter turn and repeat. As you knead, gradually add just enough of the remaining flour until the dough is no longer sticky; you may not need all of it. Continue to knead until the dough is smooth and shiny, with good elasticity, about 10 or 15 minutes more. The dough should feel springy and be slightly moist. Too much kneading may result in a tough crust.

Oil a large bowl, shape the dough into a smooth ball and place the ball in the bowl. Turn to coat the dough with the oil, cover the bowl with plastic wrap, and set aside to rise until not quite doubled in bulk, about 75 to 90 minutes. Spelt flour will not rise as much as other flours.

Remove the wrap and punch the dough down. (If you are not going to use the dough within 2 hours, turn it into the oiled bowl to coat again, cover with wrap, and refrigerate. Spelt dough does not freeze as well, but may be wrapped tightly and frozen for up to 2 months.) Break the dough into equal pieces for smaller pizzas or keep whole for a large pizza.

Use your hands or a rolling pin to shape the ball of dough on a lightly floured surface. Press and stretch it gently to the desired shape and thickness. The thinner the crust, the crispier it will be.

Leave the dough to rest, about 15 minutes, or place in the refrigerator for thinner crust (since the dough doesn't rise as much in the refrigerator), until you're ready to top the pizza.

To continue, follow the directions in the recipe you choose for Pizza Toppings, starting on page 260.

Yeast-Free Pizza Dough

GLUTEN-FREE

This recipe is adapted from a recipe by cookbook author Carol Fenster. It's a gluten-free alternative that makes for a darn good pizza.

Makes one 8-inch pizza crust

- ½ cup garbanzo and fava flour
- ½ cup tapioca flour
- 1 teaspoon sugar or honey
- 1 teaspoon xanthan gum
- ½ teaspoon sea salt
- ¼ teaspoon unflavored gelatin powder
- ½ teaspoon baking powder
- ½ teaspoon baking soda
- 1 teaspoon dried or 1 tablespoon fresh minced herbs of your choice
- 1 egg
- ½ cup milk, or substitute with rice, soy, or nut milk
- 2 tablespoons extra-virgin olive oil

Preheat the oven to 400°F. Oil a baking sheet or pizza pan.

Combine all ingredients in a medium bowl and beat with an electric mixer for 2 minutes on medium speed. The batter will be sticky.

Spread the batter in the prepared pan. Use a wet spatula to spread and smooth the dough, keeping it away from the edges of the pan. Push the dough to make a ridge around the edge.

Bake for 15 minutes, then remove from the oven, top with toppings, and bake another 10 to 15 minutes or until browned to taste.

Yeast-Free Sweet Milk Dough

Some folks like to make sweet pizzas or include sweet items such as fruit on top. This is the perfect dough for that, but it's also good with tomato sauce. The tomato is, after all, a fruit.

Makes one 16-inch, two 12-inch, four 8-inch, or eight 4-inch pizzas

- 2 cups unbleached white flour
- 1¼ cups whole wheat pastry flour
- ½ teaspoon salt
- 1 tablespoon sugar
- 1 teaspoon baking powder
- 1 cup plus 1 tablespoon milk
- 5 tablespoons unsalted butter, melted and cooled, or vegetable oil

Combine the flours, salt, sugar, and baking powder in a large bowl, and make a well in the center.

In a separate bowl, whisk together the milk and butter, then add this to the well in the flour mixture. Stir in one direction until a dough forms.

Turn the dough out onto a lightly floured work surface and roll it out to the desired size. Place the dough on a baking sheet and push against the edge to form a rim. Leave the dough to rest, about 15 minutes, or until you're ready to top the pizza.

To continue, follow the directions in the recipe you choose for Pizza Toppings, starting on page 260.

Cornmeal Pizza Dough

This dough is very enjoyable, even without the sage, pine nut, or hot pepper flake options. Use a fine grind cornmeal for this dough.

**Makes one 16-inch, two 12-inch,
four 8-inch or eight 4-inch pizzas**

- ⅛ teaspoon sugar
- 1¼ cups warm water (105°F. to 115°F.)
- 2¼ teaspoons active dry yeast
- 1 cup unbleached white flour
- 1½ cups whole wheat flour
- ⅔ cup fine yellow cornmeal
- 1 teaspoon salt
- 1 teaspoon red pepper flakes, or to taste, optional
- 3½ tablespoons extra-virgin olive oil

In a small bowl, add the sugar to the water and sprinkle the yeast on top. Stir to dissolve and let stand for 5 minutes until foamy.

In a large mixing bowl, combine well 1 cup plus 1 tablespoon of the unbleached white flour with the wheat flour, cornmeal, salt, and red pepper flakes. Make a well in the center of the flour mixture. Pour in the yeast mixture and the oil, and using a wooden spoon, vigorously stir the flour into the well. Begin at the center and work slowly outward, until the flour mixture is incorporated and the dough just begins to come together.

Turn the dough out onto a lightly floured surface. Dust your hands with flour and knead the dough gently, pressing down with the heels of your hands and pushing the dough away from you before partially folding it back over itself. Use a dough scraper to pry up bits of dough that stick to the work surface. Shift the dough a quarter turn and repeat. As you knead, gradually add just enough of the remaining flour until the dough is no longer sticky; you may not need all of it. Continue to knead until the dough is smooth and shiny, with good elasticity, about 10 to 15 minutes more. The dough should feel springy and be slightly moist. Too much kneading may result in a tough crust.

Oil a large bowl, shape the dough into a smooth ball, and place the ball in the bowl. Turn to coat the dough with the oil, cover the bowl with plastic wrap, and set aside to rise until it doubles in size, about 90 minutes.

Punch the dough down and use within 2 hours. (If you are not going to use the dough within 2 hours, turn it into an oiled bowl to coat again, tightly cover with plastic wrap, and refrigerate. When the dough has doubled again, in about 5 to 8 hours, punch it down, re-cover it, and leave it in the refrigerator. You can punch it down a total of 4 times, but after that, it gets tough. Use the dough within 32 hours or wrap tightly in plastic wrap and freeze for up to 4 months.)

Break the dough into equal pieces for smaller pizzas or keep whole for a large pizza.

Use your hands or a rolling pin to shape the ball of dough on a lightly floured surface. Press and stretch it gently to the desired shape and thickness. The thinner the crust, the crispier it will be.

Leave the dough to rest, about 15 minutes, or place in the refrigerator for thinner crust (because the dough doesn't rise as much in the refrigerator), until you're ready to top the pizza.

To continue, follow the directions in the recipe you choose for Pizza Toppings, starting on page 260.

VARIATION

Chop 12 fresh sage leaves and combine with ⅓ cup toasted pine nuts. Add to the dry ingredients before mixing.

Pizza Toppings

Of course, you can top your pizzas with anything you like, but here are a few suggestions.

Basic Pizza Sauce

Tomato sauce is not as old as pizza; in fact, the tomato is a New World food that the Italians really didn't start to use until 1750. Nonetheless, tomato sauce has become synonymous with Italian food, and especially with pizza. Here's a simple, easy sauce you can use as a base—use as little or as much as you'd like for any of our pizza dough recipes and save the rest for a pasta dish another night. Spread the sauce, add your toppings, and voila! Homemade pizza!

Makes 2 cups

- 2 tablespoons extra-virgin olive oil
- ½ small onion, minced
- 1 large garlic clove, peeled and minced
- 1 (28-ounce) can of chopped tomatoes, or 4 cups fresh tomatoes, seeded and chopped
- 1 teaspoon fresh minced, or ½ teaspoon dried oregano
- Salt and pepper to taste

In a large saucepan set over medium heat, heat the olive oil and add the onion. Sauté until soft, about 5 minutes. Add the garlic, stir for 30 seconds, then add the tomatoes, oregano, salt, and pepper and stir. Bring to a boil, then simmer for 20 minutes, stirring frequently.

Tomato, Onion, and Rosemary Pizza

Fresh rosemary is believed to have such a calming effect, it is used in some countries as an air freshener. We love the rosemary fragrance ourselves, and especially like it sprinkled on breads and, in this recipe, onto our pizza.

- Pizza dough (pages 247 259)
- Basic Pizza Sauce (page 260)
- 1 medium onion, sliced very thin
- 3 large tomatoes, sliced
- 2 tablespoons fresh rosemary, chopped
- 4 tablespoons extra-virgin olive oil
- Salt and freshly ground pepper

Preheat the oven to 475°F. If you are using a baking stone or tiles, place it/them in the oven now. If you're using a baking sheet, dust it with a little cornmeal or flour.

Roll out the dough to your desired shape and thickness. Place the dough on the baking sheet, if using.

Spread the pizza sauce over the pizza, leaving a ½-inch border free of sauce. Arrange the onions on top, followed by the tomatoes, and sprinkle with the rosemary. Drizzle 3 tablespoons of oil over the toppings. Season to taste with salt and pepper.

If you're using a baking sheet, place the pizza in the oven. If you are using a baking stone or tiles, carefully remove it from the oven and sprinkle with cornmeal. Slide the pizza onto the hot stone. Bake for 15 minutes, or until the crust is brown. Drizzle the remaining 1 tablespoon oil over the top before serving.

Bell Pepper Pizza

This makes for a colorful and lip-smacking pizza. This version is vegetarian, but if you want to add meat, spread ½ pound of pepperoni slices under the peppers, or cook ½ pound of sweet Italian sausage, drain, and place on top of the dough before baking.

- Pizza dough (pages 247-259)
- ½ cup Basic Pizza Sauce (page 260)
- ½ pound mozzarella, sliced very thin or grated
- 1 red bell pepper, roasted, peeled, and julienned
- 1 yellow bell pepper, roasted, peeled, and julienned
- 1 green bell pepper, roasted, peeled, and julienned
- ²/₃ cup coarsely grated Parmesan cheese

Preheat the oven to 475°F. If you are using a baking stone or tiles, place it/them in the oven now. If you're using a baking sheet, dust it with a little cornmeal or flour, then place the dough on top.

Spread the sauce, then the mozzarella over the pizza, covering the surface but leaving a ½-inch border. Distribute the roasted peppers (and pepperoni or sausage, if using) and sprinkle with Parmesan cheese.

If you're using a baking sheet, place the pizza in the oven. If you are using a baking stone or tiles, carefully remove it from the oven and sprinkle with cornmeal. Slide the pizza onto the hot stone. Bake for 15 minutes, or until the crust is brown.

Puttanesca Pizza

This pizza is reminiscent of the popular Italian dish, pasta puttanesca. Anchovy paste makes a decent, albeit less pungent, alternative to mashing or mincing anchovies. Sprinkle this with fresh parsley, if you'd like.

- Pizza dough (pages 247-259)
- 3 tablespoons extra-virgin olive oil
- 2 garlic cloves, peeled and minced
- 1 pound fresh Roma (plum) tomatoes, chopped or 1 (14-ounce) can, drained and chopped
- ⅓ cup Kalamata or Italian black olives, pitted and chopped
- 1 teaspoon fresh oregano, minced, or ½ teaspoon dried
- 3 tablespoons capers, rinsed and drained
- 4 anchovy fillets, minced or 1 tablespoon anchovy paste
- Freshly ground pepper to taste
- 6 ounces mozzarella, sliced very thin or grated

Preheat the oven to 475°F. If you are using a baking stone or tiles, place it/them in the oven now. If you're using a baking sheet, dust it with a little cornmeal or flour, then place the dough on top.

Heat the olive oil in a large skillet over medium heat, then add the garlic, tomatoes, olives, oregano, capers, and anchovies, and cook until thickened, about 7 or 8 minutes. Season with salt and pepper, set aside.

Spread the tomato mixture over the pizza dough, leaving a ½-inch border, then top with mozzarella.

If you're using a baking sheet, place the pizza in the oven. If you are using a baking stone or tiles, carefully remove it from the oven and sprinkle with cornmeal. Slide the pizza onto the hot stone. Bake for 15 minutes, or until the crust is brown.

Grilled or Roasted Vegetable Pizza

Mom may have said to eat more vegetables and less pizza, but surely, she didn't have this pizza in her repertoire. For this dish, it's best to slice the vegetables thickly. If you don't want to grill or roast your vegetables, sauté them in extra-virgin olive oil and garlic, then drain the oil and sprinkle it over the pizza. Or cook the veggies down and tell your friends you created ratatouille pizza.

- 3 medium sweet red, green or yellow peppers, seeded and cut into six pieces
- 1 medium onion, thinly sliced
- 2 zucchinis, thinly sliced
- 3 large tomatoes, thinly sliced
- ¼ cup extra-virgin olive oil
- Pizza dough (pages 247-259)
- Basic Pizza Sauce (page 260) or 3 tablespoons extra-virgin olive oil
- 3 large garlic cloves, peeled and minced
- 4 fresh basil leaves, sliced thin
- 1 teaspoon fresh minced or ½ teaspoon dried oregano
- ½ cup grated Parmesan cheese

Heat a grill or lightly oil a roasting pan. Toss the vegetables with the olive oil to coat. Grill over a medium hot fire for 5 to 10 minutes, turning occasionally until cooked to your taste. Alternately, preheat the oven to 450°F., place the vegetables in the roasting pan, and roast for 15 to 20 minutes, or to taste, turning occasionally.

Preheat the oven to 475°F. If you are using a baking stone or tiles, place it/them in the oven now. If you're using a baking sheet, dust it with a little cornmeal or flour, then place the circle of dough on top.

Spread the pizza sauce or 3 tablespoons of oil over the dough, leaving a ½-inch border. Sprinkle with garlic. Use tongs to place the hot vegetables on top. Sprinkle with the herbs and then Parmesan cheese.

If you're using a baking sheet, place the pizza in the oven. If you are using a baking stone or tiles, carefully remove it from the oven and sprinkle with cornmeal. Slide the pizza onto the hot stone. Bake for 15 minutes, or until crust is brown.

Grilled Eggplant, Leek, and Mozzarella Pizza

Eggplant gives off a lot of water when it cooks, so to make sure it doesn't make your pizza soggy, sprinkle the sliced eggplant with salt and set in a colander to drain for 30 minutes, pressing out excess moisture.

- 1 large or 3 to 4 small Japanese eggplants, sliced ¼ inch thick
- 5 leeks, washed, split lengthwise, woody ends discarded
- ¼ cup plus 3 tablespoons extra-virgin olive oil
- Salt and pepper to taste
- Pizza dough (pages 247-259)
- 3 garlic cloves, peeled and minced
- 1½ cups grated mozzarella cheese

Heat a grill or lightly oil a roasting pan. Toss the vegetables with the ¼ cup of olive oil to coat. Grill over a medium-hot fire for 5 to 10 minutes, turning occasionally until cooked to your taste. Alternately, preheat the oven to 450°F., place the vegetables in the roasting pan, and roast for 15 to 20 minutes, or to taste, turning occasionally.

Preheat the oven to 475°F. If you are using a baking stone or tiles, place it/them in the oven now. If you're using a baking sheet, dust it with a little cornmeal or flour, then place the circle of dough on top.

In a small bowl, mix the garlic with the 3 tablespoons of olive oil and spread over the dough. Add half the mozzarella cheese, then top with the vegetables. Top with the remaining cheese.

If you're using a baking sheet, place the pizza in the oven. If you are using a baking stone or tiles, carefully remove it from the oven and sprinkle with cornmeal. Slide the pizza onto the hot stone. Bake for 15 minutes, or until crust is brown.

Barbecued Chicken & Pepper Pizza with Ginger BBQ Sauce

Tangy ginger barbecue sauce gives this pizza a special southwestern zing.

- Pizza dough (pages 247-259)
- 2 cups cooked chicken, shredded
- ¾ cup Ginger Barbecue Sauce (recipe follows)
- ½ medium sweet onion, thinly sliced
- 1 bell pepper, seeded and cut into thin strips
- 2 cups shredded Monterey Jack cheese

Preheat the oven to 475°F. If you are using a baking stone or tiles, place it/them in the oven now. If you're using a baking sheet, dust it with a little cornmeal or flour, then place the circle of dough on top.

Toss the chicken with about a third of the barbecue sauce. Spread the remaining sauce across the dough, leaving a ½-inch border. Top the pizza with onion, pepper, and the chicken, then top with the cheese.

If you're using a baking sheet, place the pizza in the oven. If you are using a baking stone or tiles, carefully remove it from the oven and sprinkle with cornmeal. Slide the pizza onto the hot stone. Bake for 15 minutes, or until crust is brown.

Ginger Barbecue Sauce

Ginger in barbecue sauce may be to some like barbecue sauce is to pizza—an odd combination. But we think this sauce is great and healthy as a pizza base; just top with grilled chicken or veggies. Save extra for your next barbecue.

Makes about 2 cups

- 1 tablespoon vegetable oil
- 1 medium onion, chopped
- 2 garlic cloves, peeled and minced
- 1 tablespoon grated fresh ginger
- 1 cup tomato sauce
- 1 tablespoon Dijon mustard
- 2 tablespoons vinegar
- ½ cup water
- 2 tablespoons Worcestershire sauce
- 1 tablespoon brown sugar
- 1 tablespoon molasses
- ⅛ teaspoon of salt

Heat the oil in a skillet over medium heat, then add the onion and sauté until soft, 3 to 4 minutes. Add the garlic and ginger and sauté for about 30 seconds, then scrape the mixture into a food processor or blender and puree.

Return the garlic puree to the skillet and add the remaining ingredients. Bring to a boil, reduce the heat, and simmer about 20 minutes, stirring occasionally.

Shrimp and Pesto Pizza

This is a garlicky pizza, which goes surprisingly well with the shrimp.

- Pizza dough (pages 247-259)
- 3 garlic cloves, peeled
- ½ cup pine nuts
- ⅔ cup coarsely grated Parmesan cheese
- 1 teaspoon salt
- ¼ teaspoon pepper
- 3 cups fresh basil, loosely packed
- ⅔ cup plus 2 tablespoons extra-virgin olive oil
- ¾ cup shrimp (about 40 small or 35 medium), peeled, deveined, and butterflied
- 2 teaspoons fresh lemon juice
- 3 bell peppers, roasted and julienned
- 1½ cups shredded mozzarella cheese

Preheat the oven to 475°F. If you are using a baking stone or tiles, place it/them in the oven now. If you're using a baking sheet, dust it with a little cornmeal or flour, then place the circle of dough on top.

Drop the garlic into a food processor and chop finely. Add the pine nuts, Parmesan cheese, salt, pepper, and basil, then process until pureed. With the processor still running, add the ⅔ cup olive oil, blending until incorporated.

Toss the shrimp with the remaining 2 tablespoons of olive oil and the lemon juice.

Spread the pesto mixture over the dough, leaving a ½-inch border, then arrange the roasted peppers on top. Sprinkle with the mozzarella cheese, then place the shrimp over the cheese.

If you're using a baking sheet, place the pizza in the oven. If you are using a baking stone or tiles, carefully remove it from the oven and sprinkle with cornmeal. Slide the pizza onto the hot stone. Bake for 15 minutes, or until crust is brown.

Caramelized Onion and Gorgonzola Pizza

This pizza is simple, terrific, and unrepentantly rich.

- ¼ cup extra-virgin olive oil
- 4 medium onions, thinly sliced
- 1 teaspoon sugar
- Salt and pepper to taste
- Pizza dough (pages 247-259)
- ⅓ pound gorgonzola, crumbled
- ¾ teaspoon fresh oregano, minced, or ¼ teaspoon dried

Heat 3 tablespoons of the olive oil in a large skillet over medium low heat, then add the onions, sugar, salt, and pepper. Sauté, stirring frequently, until the onions are nicely browned and caramelized, about 45 minutes. Remove from the heat and allow to come to room temperature.

Preheat the oven to 475°F. If you are using a baking stone or tiles, place it/them in the oven now. If you're using a baking sheet, dust it with a little cornmeal or flour, then place the circle of dough on top.

Spread the remaining tablespoon of olive oil over the dough. Spread the onion mixture on top, and sprinkle with the gorgonzola and oregano.

If you're using a baking sheet, place the pizza in the oven. If you are using a baking stone or tiles, carefully remove it from the oven and sprinkle with cornmeal. Slide the pizza onto the hot stone. Bake for 15 minutes, or until crust is brown.

Spinach Ricotta Pizza

Here's a cheese pizza that is satisfying to vegetarians and meat eaters alike. Sprinkle some toasted pine nuts on top if the urge strikes (and the pantry is willing).

- Pizza dough (pages 247-259)
- ½ cup Basic Pizza Sauce (page 260)
- ¼ cup grated Parmesan cheese
- 2 cups (about 2 ounces) spinach leaves, lightly packed
- ¾ cup shredded mozzarella cheese
- ¼ cup ricotta cheese

Preheat the oven to 475°F. If you are using a baking stone or tiles, place it/them in the oven now. If you're using a baking sheet, dust it with a little cornmeal or flour, then place the circle of dough on top.

Spread the pizza sauce over the dough, leaving a ½-inch border. Sprinkle the dough with Parmesan cheese, then add the spinach and mozzarella. Dot small pieces of ricotta over the toppings and flatten slightly.

If you're using a baking sheet, place the pizza in the oven. If you are using a baking stone or tiles, carefully remove it from the oven and sprinkle with cornmeal. Slide the pizza onto the hot stone. Bake for 15 minutes, or until crust is brown.

Sausage, Onion, and Mushroom Pizza

This classic combination for a pizza goes really well with a crust with herbs added to the dough.

- Pizza dough (pages 247-259)
- 2 tablespoons extra-virgin olive oil, divided
- 2 pounds sweet Italian sausage, crumbled
- 1 sweet medium onion, thinly sliced
- 8 ounces fresh mushrooms of your choice, sliced
- 1 teaspoon fresh minced rosemary, or ½ teaspoon dried
- 1 teaspoon fresh minced oregano, or ½ teaspoon dried
- Basic Pizza Sauce (page 260)
- 1 cup (about 8 or 9 ounces) coarsely grated mozzarella cheese
- ¾ cup grated Parmesan cheese

Preheat the oven to 475°F. If you are using a baking stone or tiles, place it/them in the oven now. If you're using a baking sheet, dust it with a little cornmeal or flour, then place the circle of dough on top.

Heat 1 tablespoon of olive oil in a skillet over medium-high heat and add the sausage. Break the sausage up with a wooden spoon and cook until brown. Remove the sausage from the pan with a slotted spoon and set aside. Add the onion to the skillet and cook until crisp, about 2 to 3 minutes. Remove from the pan, add the remaining tablespoon of olive oil and add the mushrooms, rosemary, and oregano. Sauté until the mushrooms brown, stirring constantly.

Spread the pizza sauce over the dough, leaving a ½-inch border. Sprinkle with the cheeses, then layer the sausage, onions, and mushrooms on top.

If you're using a baking sheet, place the pizza in the oven. If you are using a baking stone or tiles, carefully remove it from the oven and sprinkle with cornmeal. Slide the pizza onto the hot stone. Bake for 15 minutes, or until crust is brown.

Cajun Pizza

Distinctive and spicy New Orleans andouille sausage gives this pizza a special flavor.

- Pizza dough (pages 247-259)
- Basic Pizza Sauce (page 260)
- ½ teaspoon chili powder
- ½ teaspoon sweet paprika
- 1 tablespoon extra-virgin olive oil
- 12 ounces andouille sausage, sliced into circles
- 1 small onion, finely chopped, to yield ½ cup
- 1 tablespoon minced garlic
- ½ teaspoon red pepper flakes
- 2 cups shredded mozzarella cheese

Preheat the oven to 475°F. If you are using a baking stone or tiles, place it/them in the oven now. If you're using a baking sheet, dust it with a little cornmeal or flour, then place the circle of dough on top.

Heat the pizza sauce over medium heat and stir in the chili powder and paprika. Cook for 2 or 3 minutes and remove from heat.

In a sauté pan or heavy skillet, heat the olive oil and cook the sausage over medium-high heat, stirring frequently, until the meat is lightly browned. Remove the sausage with a slotted spoon and drain on paper towels.

Discard all but 2 tablespoons of the fat in the pan and add the onion. Stir in the garlic and red pepper flakes for 30 seconds and remove from the heat. Return the sausage to the pan and stir to combine.

Spread the pizza sauce over the dough leaving a ½-inch border. Top with mozzarella cheese and then the sausage mixture.

If you're using a baking sheet, place the pizza in the oven. If you are using a baking stone or tiles, carefully remove it from the oven and sprinkle with cornmeal. Slide the pizza onto the hot stone. Bake for 15 minutes, or until crust is brown.

Cheese Calzone

Calzone is really just a pizza folded over, giving you that whole grain crust on the top and the bottom. We think it's just as appropriate to eat calzone on February 9 (National Pizza Day) as it is pizza. Of course, you can stir in ½ cup diced ham or cooked chicken if you are missing the meat in this cheese pie, or a similar amount of vegetable.

Makes 4 calzones

- 2 tablespoons extra-virgin olive oil, divided
- ½ pound mushrooms of your choice, sliced
- 1 bell pepper, red or green, chopped
- Pizza dough (pages 247-259)
- 1 cup ricotta cheese
- ⅔ cup grated mozzarella cheese
- 2 egg yolks
- ¼ teaspoon salt
- Pepper to taste
- 1 egg white mixed with 1 tablespoon water

Preheat the oven to 475°F. If you are using a baking stone or tiles, place it/them in the oven now. If you're using a baking sheet, dust it with a little cornmeal or flour, then place the circle of dough on top.

Heat 1 tablespoon of the oil in a skillet and add the mushrooms. Sauté, tossing frequently, until they begin to release their liquid and darken. Remove from the pan with a slotted spoon, add the remaining tablespoon of oil to the pan, and add the peppers. Sauté until soft, about 5 minutes. Mix the mushrooms and peppers and allow to cool.

Divide the dough into 4 pieces. Roll out each piece of dough into a circle about ¼-inch thick.

Mix the cheeses with the mushroom mixture, egg yolks, salt, and pepper. Divide the filling evenly among the dough circles, spooning it into the bottom half. Brush egg wash around the edge of the circle, fold the top half of the dough over the filling, and press to seal.

If you're using a baking sheet, place the calzone in the oven. If you are using a baking stone or tiles, carefully remove it from the oven and sprinkle with cornmeal. Slide the calzones onto the hot stone. Bake for 20 minutes, or until crust is brown.

Italian Sausage & Fontina Calzone

Sausage and fontina is classic stuffing for calzone. Imported Italian fontina can be pretty expensive, but the flavor is significantly fuller and richer.

Makes 4 calzones

- 1 tablespoon extra-virgin olive oil
- ½ pound bulk Italian sausage
- 1 cup Basic Pizza Sauce (page 260)
- 1 cup grated fontina cheese
- ½ cup mozzarella cheese, grated
- 1 egg yolk
- Pizza dough (pages 247-259)
- 1 egg white mixed with 1 tablespoon water

Heat the oil in a skillet over medium heat and add the sausage. Cook until no longer pink, about 5 to 10 minutes, breaking up with a wooden spoon. Remove it from the pan using a slotted spoon and dry on paper towels. Wipe the pan clean. Return the sausage to the pan, add the sauce, and stir to mix. Add the cheeses and egg yolk and mix well.

Divide the dough into 4 pieces. Roll out each piece of dough until about ¼-inch thick.

Divide the filling evenly among the dough circles, spooning it into the bottom half. Brush egg wash around the edge of the circle, fold the dough over the filling, and press to seal.

If you're using a baking sheet, place the calzones in the oven. If you are using a baking stone or tiles, carefully remove it from the oven and sprinkle with cornmeal. Slide the calzones onto the hot stone. Bake for 20 minutes, or until crust is brown.

Pies, Tarts, Cobblers, & Crisps

A cherry pie cooling on a windowsill. Apple pie at a picnic. Few foods in American culture are more evocative than pie, and in this chapter you'll find some favorite combinations to put inside, and sometimes in between, the whole grain crusts above. We've included classic sweet and savory pies and tarts followed by cobblers and crisps, more great American desserts.

There is a reason we think of pie cooling on that windowsill. Few pies are meant to be eaten right out of the oven. Some pies, such as custard, develop more flavor as they cool. Fruit pies may be runny. Pecan pie is too gooey.

Once your fresh fruit pie or tart is cool enough to eat, however, be sure to eat it as soon as possible. If you'd like to keep it around for 2 or 3 days, store it in the refrigerator. Pies filled with cream and custard will also last 3 days, refrigerated. Pumpkin pies last about 3 days, but nut pies and tarts will go a day longer and dried fruit ones last maybe 5—all refrigerated, of course. However, when it comes to pie topped with whipped cream, you should know that the cream may not fare as well as the pie.

In today's markets, home cooks are blessed with the availability of virtually any fruit year-round, which makes it tempting to bake whatever kind of pie, tart, or fruit-laden dessert that springs to mind. However, just because your grocery has strawberries, it doesn't mean they are full of flavor, especially after possibly traveling your way for several days. The best pies are made with the freshest seasonal ingredients, so if it's fall, perhaps you ought to make an apple pie instead of a rhubarb one.

Pie making is a lot of fun, pie serving even more. We hope you enjoy these pie and tart recipes.

Making the Perfect Piecrust

Creating an exceptional piecrust is all about perfecting the simple combination of flour, water, fat, and salt. Fat and its ratio to flour are the most important considerations for both texture and flavor in a piecrust, particularly when it comes to whole grain baking. A whole grain crust made exclusively of butter might have a great taste, but it won't have much flakiness and will likely be far too hard. One made with shortening alone isn't as flavorful, but it does make for a delicate texture. One made with an animal fat, such as lard (traditional in the South), might have an unusual flavor, but will be wonderfully flaky. At Bob's Red Mill, we use what we find to be the perfect blend of butter and shortening, unbleached white and whole grain flour in our basic pastry crust. This ratio is passed on to you in the recipes in this chapter.

When you are making whole grain pie pastries, the temperature of the fat and the water you use are very important. In most cases, you always want to use very cold (but not frozen) unsalted butter and shortening, and it's good practice to chill the crust completely before baking. It is important that the fat remain cold and not melt until the crust goes into the oven. When a crust bakes, the fat melts and produces steam. The steam creates pockets in the dough that make it flaky. Using ice water helps keep the fat cold when you mix it with the other ingredients. We go one step further and chill the bowl and spatula we use as well, so that everything is cold when we begin mixing. Although this step isn't absolutely necessary, it sure helps keep everything cold. This is also why we suggest that you mix your piecrust ingredients with a spatula instead of your hands—even the heat in your hands can rapidly warm the butter and shortening in your mix causing it to break down and coat the flour, keeping it from absorbing liquid. When the fat coats the flour, your dough will end up crumbly or hard. On the other hand, under-processing will create a tough dough that is less flaky, because the fat hasn't spread evenly through the flour.

When you are working with dough, process it just enough to scatter the butter throughout the dough, not to completely incorporate it into the flour. Your dough should resemble coarse pebbles. This is why we recommend that you use a food processor to mix your pie dough, especially if you're a novice or you make dough only on occasion. A food processor cuts the butter and shortening in quickly and efficiently, taking the guesswork out of the mixing. Of course, the more often you mix dough by hand, the better accustomed you will be to being able to identify when the dough is mixed perfectly. In this chapter, our directions call for a food processor to make mixing easy for everyone, but you should feel free to mix any of these by hand, using two knives, or a pastry blender.

As we mentioned in the first chapter, whole wheat flour does not have as much gluten as unbleached white flour. Therefore, as we did with breads, we suggest that you mix unbleached white flour into most of your whole grain flour doughs. We also recommend you use the smallest amount of water to create the most tender dough. You want to add in just enough water for your dough to come together.

Among our piecrusts are some gluten-free, dairy free, and alternative crusts for your use in the recipes for pies and tarts that follow. However, some of the crust recipes won't work well as a double or top crust, so for those, we've provided single crust directions.

If you would like to adjust an old family favorite piecrust using whole grains, start off by substituting one-third of the unbleached white flour you've been using with whole wheat flour. From there, you can increase the whole wheat flour for up to two-thirds of the white flour. You may need a little more water, but remember to just add enough for the dough to come together.

Unless we say otherwise in the recipes below, be sure to wrap your dough in plastic and refrigerate it for 30 minutes or freeze for 10 to 15 minutes before rolling it out. This relaxes the gluten and firms the fat in your dough, allowing it to be more evenly distributed, thereby ensuring a flaky and tender crust with less shrinkage. If you find that your dough is still too soft after 15 minutes in the refrigerator, don't add more flour to the rolling surface; this will just be quickly absorbed by the dough. Instead, chill your dough a little longer (the only exception to this rule is for a dough that calls for no chilling; many of those are meant to be soft and simply a little harder to roll out). If you need to refrigerate your dough for more than 1 hour, let it warm up for 4 or 5 minutes to before rolling.

When you roll out your dough, there are a few methods you can use to keep your dough from sticking to your mat and rolling pin. Keep in mind that you want to add as little flour as possible to your already perfect dough. The easiest method to do this is to use a silicone rolling mat and rolling pin, found in many kitchen supply stores. We like to cover our dough with plastic wrap before rolling it out. If your dough is cold enough, it won't stick to the wrap. Wax paper is another useful alternative. You can prevent wax paper from sliding on your counter by putting a little water underneath it.

The recipes in this chapter generally call for a 9-inch pie dish or tart pan, but all of them may be rolled a little thinner to stretch into a 10-inch dish. One of the biggest benefits to making whole grain crusts is that not only are they better for you, we think they are better tasting too.

CRUSTS

Basic Single Whole Wheat Piecrust

This is the basic recipe when you need a pre-baked or partially pre-baked crust for a cream or other uncooked pie.

Makes one 9-inch crust

- 3/4 cup whole wheat pastry flour or whole wheat flour
- 1/2 cup unbleached white flour
- 2 teaspoons sugar
- 1/2 teaspoon salt
- 3 tablespoons vegetable shortening, chilled and diced
- 5 tablespoons unsalted butter, chilled and diced
- 5 tablespoons ice water

Place the flours, sugar, and salt in the bowl of a food processor and pulse to combine. Add the shortening and process until combined, about 10 seconds. Sprinkle the butter over the mixture. Process about 7 or 8 one-second pulses, or until the mixture looks like small pebbles.

Pour this mixture into a chilled bowl and sprinkle 6 tablespoons of water over the mixture. Using a cold spatula, press the dough until the dough sticks together. Add more water if the dough will not come together. Flatten the dough into a disk, wrap in plastic, and refrigerate at least 1 hour before rolling.

TO PARTIALLY OR FULLY PRE-BAKE: Roll the dough out to a 12-inch circle on a lightly floured surface, or on a sheet of floured wax or parchment paper. Place the dough over a 9-inch pie plate and gently press the dough into the dish. Trim the edges with scissors or a paring knife, then refrigerate the dish for 30 minutes, or freeze for 15 minutes.

Preheat the oven to 375°F.

Line the pie dough with foil and then fill with pie weights or dried beans. Bake for 15 minutes or until the dough looks dry. Carefully remove hot foil and weights. For a partially baked crust, continue baking another 5 minutes, or until light brown. For a fully baked crust, continue baking for 10 to 12 minutes, or until deep brown. Place on a wire rack to cool.

Basic Double Whole Wheat Piecrust

This is our favorite basic recipe for making a double whole wheat piecrust.

Makes two 9-inch crusts

- 1 cup unbleached white flour
- 1½ cups whole wheat pastry flour or whole wheat flour
- 1 tablespoon sugar
- 1 teaspoon salt
- 7 tablespoons vegetable shortening, chilled and diced
- 12 tablespoons (1 ½ sticks) unsalted butter, chilled and diced
- 9 tablespoons ice water

Place the flours, sugar, and salt in the bowl of a food processor and pulse to combine. Add the shortening and process until the mixture resembles coarse crumbs, about 10 seconds. Sprinkle the butter over the mixture. Process about 7 or 8 one-second pulses, or until the mixture looks like small pebbles.

Pour this mixture into a chilled bowl and sprinkle 6 tablespoons of water over the mixture. Using a cold spatula, press the dough until the dough sticks together. Add more water if the dough will not come together. Divide the dough into two balls, one slightly larger than the other, flatten each piece into a disk, wrap in plastic, and refrigerate at least 1 hour before rolling.

TO PARTIALLY PRE-BAKE: Roll the large disk out to a 12-inch circle on a slightly floured surface. Place the dough over a 9-inch pie plate and gently press the dough into the dish. Trim the edges with scissors or a paring knife, then refrigerate the dish for 30 minutes, or freeze for 15 minutes.

Preheat the oven to 375°F.

Line the pie dough with foil and then fill with pie weights or dried beans. Bake for 15 minutes or until the dough looks dry. Carefully remove hot foil and weights. Continue baking another 5 minutes, or until light brown.

Refrigerate top crust until ready to roll out and use.

Sugar Crust

This is a good crust for sweet tart recipes. The recipe makes two 9-inch crusts, so if you just need one, immediately wrap the unused half in plastic wrap, then in foil, and freeze for up to 2 months. Whole grain pastry flour has less gluten than unbleached white flour, so the egg yolks help hold this dough together.

Makes two 9-inch crusts

- 2⅓ cups whole wheat pastry flour
- ⅓ cup sugar
- 10 tablespoons unsalted butter, chilled and diced
- 6 tablespoons vegetable shortening, chilled and diced
- 2 egg yolks
- ½ teaspoon vanilla extract
- 2 tablespoons heavy cream, divided

Place the flour and sugar in the bowl of a food processor and pulse to blend. Sprinkle the butter over the mixture. Pulse until just incorporated, then add the shortening and pulse until the texture resembles coarse crumbs.

In a small bowl, whisk together the egg yolks, vanilla, and 1 tablespoon of cream. Add this mixture to the flour mixture and process until a ball begins to form and the dough comes together. Use the remaining tablespoon of cream if necessary.

Remove the dough and divide it into two disks. Wrap each disk in plastic and refrigerate for at least 1 hour before rolling.

TO PARTIALLY OR FULLY PRE-BAKE: Roll one piece of dough out to a 12-inch circle on a lightly floured surface. Place the dough over a 9-inch pie plate and gently press the dough into the dish. Trim the edges with scissors or a paring knife, then refrigerate the dish for 30 minutes, or freeze for 15 minutes.

Preheat the oven to 375°F.

Line the pie dough with foil and then fill with pie weights or dried beans. Bake 20 minutes or until dough looks dry. Carefully remove hot foil and weights. For a partially baked crust, continue baking another 5 minutes, or until light brown. For a fully baked crust continue baking for 10 to 12 minutes, or until deep brown. Place on a wire rack to cool.

Whole Wheat Vegetable Oil Piecrust

This wonderfully flaky crust does not need refrigeration and should be rolled out right away. You can have your filling ready to go and then make the dough, if you wish. You'll want to use floured wax paper to keep it from sticking to the rolling surface and pin. To make just a single crust, use ⅓ cup whole wheat pastry flour, ⅔ cup unbleached white flour, and cut the remaining ingredient amounts in half.

Makes two 9-inch crusts

- 1 cup whole wheat pastry flour
- 1 cup unbleached white flour
- 1 teaspoon salt
- ½ cup vegetable oil
- ¼ cup whole or 2 percent milk, chilled, plus more as needed

Preheat the oven to 375°F.

Combine the flours and salt in a large bowl, then quickly add the oil and milk and stir briskly, adding just a little more milk if the mixture is too dry. Form slightly more than half of the dough into a ball and, on a lightly floured surface, immediately roll it out to a 12-inch circle. Place the dough over a 9-inch pie plate and gently press it into the dish. Prick the dough with a fork. Leave the other half of the dough at room temperature until you are ready to top the pie.

Bake the crust for 15 minutes or until it browns. While it is baking, check the crust frequently (without opening your oven, if possible) to see if bubbles form. Use a fork to prick any bubbles and release air pockets. Place on a wire rack to cool.

Buttermilk Piecrust

This delicious and slightly tangy piecrust is great with both sweet and savory pies.

Makes two 9-inch crusts

- 1 cup whole wheat pastry flour
- 1½ cups unbleached white flour
- 2 tablespoons sugar
- 1 teaspoon salt
- ¼ pound (1 stick) unsalted butter, chilled and diced
- ¼ cup shortening, chilled and diced
- ¼ cup plus 2 tablespoons buttermilk

Place the flours, sugar, and salt in the bowl of a food processor and pulse to blend. Sprinkle the butter over the mixture. Pulse until just incorporated, then add the shortening and pulse until the texture resembles crumbs.

Pour this mixture into a chilled bowl, add ¼ cup of buttermilk, and stir with a spatula until the dough comes together, adding more buttermilk as needed. Divide the dough into two balls, one slightly larger than the other, flatten each piece into a disk, wrap them in plastic, and refrigerate at least 1 hour before rolling.

TO PARTIALLY OR FULLY PRE-BAKE: Roll one piece of dough out to a 12-inch circle on a lightly floured surface. Place the dough over a 9-inch pie plate and gently press the dough into the dish. Trim the edges with scissors or a paring knife, then refrigerate the dish for 30 minutes, or freeze for 15 minutes.

Preheat the oven to 375°F.

Line the pie dough with foil and then fill with pie weights or dried beans. Bake for 20 minutes or until dough looks dry. Carefully remove hot foil and weights. For a partially baked crust continue baking another 5 minutes, or until light brown. For a fully baked crust continue baking for 10 to 12 minutes, or until deep brown. Place on a wire rack to cool.

Sorghum Piecrust

GLUTEN-FREE

This gluten-free piecrust gets a lightness lift from the rice flour, and a rich molasses taste from the sorghum. It's especially good with your favorite nut pie recipe.

Makes one 9-inch crust

- ¾ cup sorghum flour
- ¼ cup rice flour
- ½ teaspoon salt
- 1 teaspoon sugar
- 1 teaspoon xanthan gum
- 5 tablespoons unsalted butter or shortening, chilled and diced
- ¼ cup cold water

Place the flours, salt, sugar, and xanthan gum in the bowl of food processor and pulse to blend. Sprinkle the butter over the mixture. Pulse until just incorporated.

Pour this mixture into a chilled bowl and sprinkle 2 tablespoons of the water over the mixture. Press with the spatula to blend together. Add more water as needed to just bind the dough together (you may not need all of the water).

TO PARTIALLY OR FULLY PRE-BAKE: Since this dough doesn't roll out well, press it into a 9-inch pie plate. Trim the edges with scissors or a paring knife, then refrigerate the dish for 30 minutes, or freeze for 15 minutes.

Preheat the oven to 400°F.

Line the pie dough with foil and then fill with pie weights or dried beans. Bake for 15 minutes or until dough looks dry. Carefully remove hot foil and weights. For a fully baked crust continue baking another 5 minutes, or until light brown.

Cottage Cheese Piecrust

This light and flaky piecrust is rich in flavor and great with fruit pies.

Makes two 9-inch crusts

- 1 cup whole wheat pastry flour
- 1 cup unbleached white flour
- 1½ teaspoons baking powder
- ½ teaspoon salt
- 2 tablespoons unsalted butter, chilled and diced
- ⅔ cup low-fat cottage cheese
- ½ cup sugar
- ¼ cup vegetable oil
- 2 tablespoons milk

Place the flours, baking powder, and salt in the bowl of a food processor and pulse to blend. Sprinkle the butter over the mixture. Pulse until the texture resembles crumbs. Pour this mixture into a chilled bowl.

In a blender, puree the cottage cheese, then add the sugar, oil, and milk. Blend until smooth, stopping once or twice to scrape down the sides of the blender. Add this mixture to the flour mixture and mix with a fork until the dough clumps together. Do not over-mix.

Turn the dough out onto a lightly floured work surface and knead several times. Shape the dough into a ball, and then flatten it into a disk. Wrap the dough in plastic and refrigerate for 45 minutes.

TO PARTIALLY OR FULLY PRE-BAKE: Roll the dough out to a 12-inch circle on a lightly floured surface. Place the dough over a 9-inch pie plate and gently press the dough into the dish. Trim the edges with scissors or a paring knife, then refrigerate the dish for 30 minutes, or freeze for 15 minutes.

Preheat the oven to 375°F.

Line the pie dough with foil and then fill with pie weights or dried beans. Bake for 20 minutes or until dough looks dry. Carefully remove hot foil and weights. For a partially baked crust, continue baking another 5 minutes, or until light brown. For a fully baked crust continue baking for 10 to 12 minutes, or until deep brown. Place the pie plate on a wire rack to cool before filling.

Almond Oat Piecrust

Almonds and oats make a fantastic combination, especially in this crust. If you don't have almond flour on hand, grind a handful of almonds in a coffee grinder or small food processor.

Makes two 9-inch crusts

- ½ cup oat flour
- ¼ cup almond flour
- 1 cup rice flour
- ¼ teaspoon salt
- 1½ tablespoons sugar
- 2 tablespoons vegetable oil, plus 1 teaspoon vegetable, hazelnut, walnut, or other nut oil
- ½ cup plus 3 tablespoons ice water

Combine the dry ingredients in a bowl. Drizzle the oil over the mixture and combine slightly, then add ½ cup of ice water and mix, adding additional water as necessary.

Preheat the oven to 375°F.

Roll the dough out to a 12-inch circle on a lightly floured surface. Place the dough over a 9-inch pie plate and gently press the dough into the dish. Trim the edges with scissors or a paring knife.

Prick the dough with a fork in many places. Bake the crust for 20 minutes or until it looks dry and brown. While it is baking, check the crust frequently (without opening your oven if possible) to see if bubbles form. Use a fork to prick any bubbles and release air pockets. Place on a wire rack to cool.

Egg and Vinegar Whole Wheat Piecrust

This exceptionally flaky crust is our version of a popular Southern piecrust. Because this can be difficult to roll, you may want to use a pastry cloth (a specially designed cloth used in baking) or two pieces of wax paper.

Makes two 9-inch crusts

- 1½ cups unbleached white flour
- 1½ cups whole wheat flour
- 1 teaspoon salt
- 1¼ cups shortening
- 1 egg
- 2 teaspoons distilled white vinegar
- 6 tablespoons ice water

Place the flours and salt in the bowl of a food processor and pulse to mix. Add the shortening and pulse until the texture resembles crumbs. Pour this mixture into a chilled bowl.

In a separate bowl, combine the egg, vinegar, and 4½ tablespoons of the ice water. Add the egg mixture to the flour mixture and mix until dough forms. Add more water as needed to just bind the dough together (you may not need all of the water).

TO PARTIALLY OR FULLY PRE-BAKE: Roll the dough (between two sheets of wax paper if it's too sticky) out to a 12-inch circle. Place the dough over a 9-inch pie plate and gently press the dough into the dish. Trim the edges with scissors or a paring knife, then refrigerate the dish for 30 minutes, or freeze for 15 minutes.

Preheat the oven to 375°F.

Line the pie dough with foil and then fill with pie weights or dried beans. Bake 20 minutes or until dough looks dry. Carefully remove hot foil and weights. For a partially baked crust continue baking another 5 minutes, or until light brown. For a fully baked crust continue baking for 10 to 12 minutes, or until deep brown. Place on a wire rack to cool.

Spelt Piecrust

This is another crust that doesn't need refrigeration. It's ready to be rolled out right after preparing. Because it is sticky and a little more difficult to handle, we recommend this for single crust pies only.

Makes one 9-inch piecrust

- 1 cup plus two tablespoons spelt flour
- ⅛ teaspoon salt
- 1 teaspoon sugar, optional
- 2½ tablespoons unsalted butter, chilled and diced
- 3 tablespoons vegetable oil
- 2 tablespoons cold water

Place the flour, salt, and sugar in the bowl of a food processor and pulse to blend. Add the butter and pulse until the mixture resembles coarse crumbs.

Remove to a chilled bowl and quickly add the vegetable oil and water, mixing well and adding a little more cold water if the dough doesn't come together.

Preheat the oven to 375°F.

Roll the dough out to a 12-inch circle on a slightly floured surface. Place the dough over the 9-inch pie dish and gently press into the dish. Trim the edges.

Prick the dough with a fork in many places. Bake the crust for 15 minutes or until it looks dry. While it is baking, check the crust frequently (without opening your oven if possible) to see if bubbles form. Use a fork to prick any bubbles and release air pockets. For a fully baked crust continue baking for 10 to 12 minutes, or until deep brown. Place on a wire rack to cool before filling.

Sweet or Savory Cornmeal Piecrust

This cornmeal piecrust is great for both sweet and savory fillings, but if you use it for savory ones, use a little less sugar when you make it.

Makes two 9-inch piecrusts

- 1½ cups unbleached white flour
- ¼ cup whole wheat flour
- 1¼ cups yellow cornmeal
- 6 tablespoons sugar
- ½ teaspoon baking soda
- ½ teaspoon salt
- 6 tablespoons unsalted butter, chilled and diced
- 2 tablespoons vegetable shortening, chilled
- 1 egg
- ⅓ cup buttermilk

Place the flours, cornmeal, sugar, baking soda, and salt in the bowl of a food processor and pulse to blend. Sprinkle the butter over the mixture. Pulse until just incorporated, then add the shortening and pulse until the texture resembles crumbs.

Pour this mixture into a chilled bowl, add 4 tablespoons of buttermilk, and mix until the dough begins to clump together. Add more buttermilk as needed to just bind the dough together (you may not need all of the buttermilk). Divide the dough into two balls, one slightly larger than the other, flatten each piece into a disk, wrap in plastic, and refrigerate at least 1 hour.

TO PARTIALLY OR FULLY PRE-BAKE: Roll the larger disk out to a 12-inch circle on a lightly floured surface. Place the dough over a 9-inch pie plate and gently press the dough into the dish. Trim the edges with scissors or a paring knife, then refrigerate the dish for 30 minutes, or freeze for 15 minutes.

Preheat the oven to 375°F.

Line the pie dough with foil and then fill with pie weights or dried beans. Bake 20 minutes or until dough looks dry. Carefully remove hot foil and weights. For a partially baked crust continue baking another 5 minutes, or until light brown. For a fully baked crust continue baking for 10 to 12 minutes, or until deep brown. Place on a wire rack to cool.

Barley Piecrust

This dough has a very bold flavor because of the barley, so keep that in mind when you fill it. Also, it won't roll out easily because of the barley, so we recommend pressing it directly into the pie dish. It should always be at least partially pre-baked before you fill it.

Makes one 9-inch piecrust

- ²/₃ cup barley flour
- ¹/₃ cup whole wheat flour
- ¹/₂ teaspoon salt
- 3 tablespoons vegetable oil
- ¹/₃ cup ice water

Combine the flours, salt, and oil in a large bowl. Add 3 tablespoons of ice water, stirring to form a dough. Use additional ice water if needed.

Preheat the oven to 375°F.

Press the dough into a 9-inch pie plate and prick the dough with a fork in several places. Bake for 8 to 10 minutes, or until it looks dry. While it is baking, check the crust frequently (without opening your oven if possible) to see if bubbles form. Use a fork to prick any bubbles and release air pockets. For a fully baked crust continue baking for 12 to 15 minutes, or until deep brown. Place on a wire rack to cool.

Rice Flour Piecrust

GLUTEN-FREE

This gluten-free pie dough often won't roll out as thin as other piecrusts, so you may want to use a deep-dish pan when making this recipe.

Makes one 9-inch piecrust

- 1 cup rice flour
- 2/3 cup tapioca flour
- 1/2 cup arrowroot or cornstarch
- 1 teaspoon xanthan gum
- 1 teaspoon baking powder
- 1 teaspoon salt
- 2 tablespoons sugar
- 1/2 cup vegetable shortening, chilled and diced
- 4 tablespoons unsalted butter, chilled and diced
- 2 eggs, lightly beaten
- 4 tablespoons ice water

Place the flours, cornstarch, xanthan gum, baking powder, salt, and sugar in the bowl of a food processor and pulse to blend. Sprinkle the butter and shortening over the mixture. Pulse until just incorporated, then add the eggs and pulse until the dough comes together. If it doesn't, mix in a little ice water until it does. Form the dough into a 4-inch disk, wrap in plastic and refrigerate for at least 1 hour.

TO PARTIALLY OR FULLY PRE-BAKE: Roll the dough out to a 12-inch circle on a lightly floured surface. Place the dough over the 9-inch pie plate and gently press into the dish. Trim the edges with scissors or a paring knife, then refrigerate the dish for 30 minutes or freeze for 15 minutes.

Preheat the oven to 400°F.

Line the pie dough with foil and fill with pie weights or dried beans. Bake for 10 minutes or until dough looks dry. Carefully remove the hot foil and weights. For a partially baked crust continue baking another 5 minutes, or until light brown. For a fully baked crust, continue baking for 8 to 10 minutes, or until deep brown. Place on a wire rack to cool.

Amaranth Piecrust

This dough does not need to be refrigerated after making it; just place in a pan, partially or completely pre-bake, and fill. This dough tears easily so use pieces to patch it up. This crust is best for pre-baked pies, but should always be at least partially pre-baked. It will shrink and be a bit smaller than most other crusts.

Makes one 9-inch piecrust

- ¾ cup amaranth flour
- ½ cup arrowroot or cornstarch
- ¼ cup almond flour
- ¼ teaspoon salt
- ½ teaspoon ground cinnamon
- 3 tablespoons vegetable oil
- 4 tablespoons ice water

Amaranth tends to stick, so butter or oil a 9-inch pie plate.

Combine the dry ingredients in a bowl and blend well. In a separate bowl, combine the oil and 3 tablespoons of water and blend with fork, then add this mixture quickly to the flour mixture. Stir just until the dough forms a ball. If the dough looks dry, add a little more water, one teaspoon at a time, until ball hangs together.

TO PARTIALLY OR FULLY PRE-BAKE: Preheat the oven to 400°F. Roll the dough out to a 12-inch circle on a lightly floured surface. Place the dough over the prepared pie plate and gently press into the plate. Trim the edges with scissors or a paring knife.

Prick the dough with a fork in many places. Bake the crust for 5 minutes or until it looks dry. While it is baking, check the crust frequently (without opening your oven if possible) to see if bubbles form. Use a fork to prick any bubbles and release air pockets. For a fully baked crust, continue baking for 10 to 12 minutes, or until deep brown. Place on a wire rack to cool.

Nut Piecrust

This crust is great with the Simple Pear Pie (page 316), among others. If you decide to use soy flour, keep in mind your crust may brown faster, and depending upon your pie or tart, you may need to protect the crust toward the end of baking by covering the crust with a foil or a pie protector.

Makes one 9-inch crust

- ½ cup whole wheat flour or soy flour
- ½ cup unbleached white flour
- 3 tablespoons sugar
- ¼ teaspoon salt
- ⅓ cup (about 1½ ounces) walnuts, hazelnuts, or pecans
- ¼ pound (1 stick) unsalted butter, chilled and cut into ½-inch pieces; or 4 tablespoons unsalted butter plus 4 tablespoons vegetable shortening; or 4 tablespoons vegetable shortening
- 2 egg yolks

Pour the flours, sugar, and salt in the bowl of a food processor and pulse to blend. Add the nuts and process until chopped. Sprinkle the butter over the mixture, and pulse until just incorporated, when the texture resembles crumbs. Add the egg yolks and process just until moist clumps form. Form the dough into a disk, wrap in plastic, and chill for 30 minutes or freeze for 15 minutes.

TO PARTIALLY OR FULLY PRE-BAKE: Roll the dough out to a 12-inch circle on a lightly floured surface. Place the dough over a 9-inch pie plate and gently press into the dish. Trim the edges with scissors or a paring knife, then refrigerate the dish for 30 minutes or freeze for 15 minutes.

Preheat the oven to 375°F. Prick the dough with a fork in many places. Bake the crust for 20 minutes or until it looks dry. While it is baking, check the crust frequently (without opening your oven if possible) to see if bubbles form. Use a fork to prick any bubbles and release air pockets. For a fully baked crust, continue baking for 10 to 12 minutes, or until deep brown. Place on a wire rack to cool.

SAVORY PIES AND TARTS

Mixed Mushroom Tart

This is a quiche-like tart with a mushroom-flavored custard. Substitute freely for any mushroom types you can't find.

Makes one 9-inch tart

- Single crust cornmeal or other pie dough (pages 278-292), rolled out
- 3 tablespoons unsalted butter
- 1 medium onion, minced
- 1 garlic clove, peeled and minced
- 1 cup chanterelle mushrooms, chopped
- 1 cup shiitake mushrooms, sliced, stems discarded
- 1½ cups button or cremini mushrooms, sliced
- ½ cup dried then reconstituted porcini mushrooms, sliced
- Salt and pepper to taste
- ⅓ cup chopped red or yellow bell pepper
- 1 teaspoon fresh thyme, chopped
- 1 tablespoon fresh parsley, chopped
- 4 eggs
- 2 cups heavy cream

Prepare and partially pre-bake the piecrust according to the recipe instructions.

Preheat oven to 375°F.

Melt the butter in a large skillet and sauté the onion for 3 minutes. Add the garlic and sauté another minute, then the mushrooms, salt and pepper, bell peppers, and thyme, and cook for another 3 to 4 minutes or until the mushrooms have released their liquid and it has evaporated. Remove from the heat, stir in the parsley.

In a large bowl, beat the eggs and then whisk in the cream, blending well. Add the mushroom mixture and stir to combine.

Pour into the pie shell and bake for 15 minutes, then reduce the temperature to 300°F. and bake until set, about another 20 minutes. Let stand 10 minutes before serving.

Leek Tart

This tart is a wonderful way to use those beautiful leeks that are so plentiful in the spring. It makes an excellent appetizer.

Makes one 9-inch tart

- Single crust basic or other pie dough (pages 278–292)
- 2 pounds leeks, woody ends removed
- 3 tablespoons unsalted butter
- 3 tablespoons extra-virgin olive oil
- 1 red or yellow bell pepper, chopped
- 2 tablespoons whole wheat flour
- ⅓ cup whole milk ricotta cheese
- 3 eggs
- ½ cup heavy cream
- ¼ teaspoon ground nutmeg
- Salt and pepper

Prepare and partially pre-bake the piecrust according to the recipe instructions.

Preheat the oven to 375°F.

Slice the leeks lengthwise, wash, drain, and coarsely chop. Melt the butter with the extra-virgin olive oil in a large skillet. Sauté the leeks and bell pepper, cover, and cook over low heat, stirring frequently until the leeks are just tender, about 15 minutes. Do not brown. Uncover the pan, sprinkle in the flour, and stir well. Remove from heat.

In a medium bowl, vigorously whip the ricotta cheese (or place in a blender) for 1 or 2 minutes. In a large bowl, beat the eggs and then add the ricotta, cream, nutmeg, salt, and pepper.

Pour into the cooled pie shell and bake for 35 to 40 minutes, until the top is lightly brown. Cool for at least 10 minutes before serving.

Country Pie

Filled with pork and vegetables, this pie is a satisfying supper unto itself. It's even better the next day.

Makes one 9-inch pie

- Double crust basic or other pie dough (pages 278-292)
- 1 tablespoon vegetable oil
- 1 pound ground pork
- 1 medium onion, chopped
- 1 small carrot, chopped
- 1 garlic clove, minced
- Salt and pepper
- 1 teaspoon fresh or ¼ teaspoon dried oregano
- ¼ teaspoon ground allspice
- ½ cup vegetable broth or water
- ⅓ cup dried or fresh breadcrumbs, plus more if necessary

Prepare the piecrust dough and refrigerate until you are ready to roll it out.

On a lightly floured surface, roll out a little more than half of the dough into a 12-inch circle. Place over a 9-inch pie plate, center, and gently tuck the dough into the pan. Trim the edges and place in the refrigerator. Roll out the second portion of dough and place on parchment paper or floured wax paper on a cookie sheet. Refrigerate until ready to use.

Preheat the oven to 400°F.

Heat the oil in a skillet over medium heat and add the pork, breaking up any clumps. Add the onion and cook for another minute or so, then add the remaining ingredients, except the breadcrumbs, and stir. Bring to a boil, stirring, then reduce the heat and simmer uncovered for 15 minutes.

Remove from the heat and stir in the breadcrumbs. Stir and let stand for 5 minutes, or until any excess liquid is absorbed (if liquid remains, add up to 2 more tablespoons of breadcrumbs).

Pour the filling into the prepared piecrust. Cover with the second sheet of dough, press to seal, and slice 2 or 3 vents on top. Bake for 20 minutes or until crust is golden. Serve warm.

Curried Winter Vegetable Pie

A high-quality, fresh curry powder makes all the difference in this recipe.

Makes one 9-inch pie

- Double crust basic or other pie dough (pages 278-292)
- 8 shallots or cipollini onions, peeled
- 2 medium carrots, peeled and thinly sliced
- 1 large parsnip, peeled and thinly sliced
- 1 large turnip, peeled and thinly sliced
- 2 tablespoons unsalted butter
- 2 tablespoons whole wheat flour
- 2 teaspoons curry powder
- 1 tablespoon fresh ginger, peeled and grated
- ¾ cup milk
- ½ cup coconut milk, or substitute whole milk
- 1¼ cups grated cheddar cheese
- Salt and pepper

Prepare the piecrust dough and refrigerate until you are ready to roll it out.

On a lightly floured surface, roll out a little more than half of the dough into a 12-inch circle. Place over a 9-inch pie plate, center, and gently tuck the dough into the pan. Trim the edges and place in the refrigerator. Roll out the second portion of dough and place on parchment paper or floured wax paper on a cookie sheet. Refrigerate until ready to use.

Preheat the oven to 375°F.

Place the vegetables in a medium pot with water to cover and bring to a boil. Cook for 4 minutes over medium heat and drain, reserving the vegetables and 1 ¼ cups of the cooking liquid.

In the same pot, melt the butter, and stir in the flour, curry powder, and ginger. Gradually whisk in the reserved liquid and then the milk and coconut milk until thickened. Remove form heat, stir in the cheese, the vegetable mixture, and salt and pepper to taste.

Pour into the pie shell. Cover with the second sheet of dough, press to seal, and slice 2 or 3 vents on top. Bake for 30 minutes, or until brown. Cool 10 minutes before serving.

Omelet Pie

We call this an "omelet pie" because many of our favorite omelet ingredients are included, wrapped in a delectable crust.

Makes one 9-inch pie

- Single crust buttermilk or other pie dough (pages 278-292)
- ¼ cup grated Cheddar cheese
- ¼ cup grated Gruyere cheese
- 2 tablespoons extra-virgin olive oil
- 2 red or green bell peppers, seeded and cut into 1-inch pieces
- 1 medium onion, peeled and chopped
- ⅓ cup scallions, finely chopped
- 2 garlic cloves, peeled and minced
- 4 medium tomatoes, peeled, seeded, and chopped
- 2 tablespoons fresh basil, chopped, or 2 teaspoons dried
- 1 tablespoon fresh marjoram, chopped, or 1 teaspoon dried
- Pinch of red pepper flakes, or to taste
- Salt and pepper to taste
- 3 eggs
- 3 egg whites

Prepare and partially pre-bake the piecrust according to the recipe instructions. While the crust is still hot, sprinkle the bottom with the cheeses.

Preheat the oven to 350°F.

Heat the oil in a large skillet, then add the peppers and onion and cook over medium heat for 5 minutes until soft. Add the scallions and garlic and cook, stirring, until onions and peppers are translucent, another 3 or 4 minutes. Add the tomatoes, basil, marjoram, red pepper, and salt and pepper. Cook another few minutes, or until almost dry. Remove from heat and cool for 20 minutes.

Beat the eggs and egg whites together and mix into the vegetables. Spread the mixture into the pastry shell and bake for 30 minutes, or until a knife comes out clean. Serve warm or at room temperature.

Vegetable Pie

Ratatouille in a pie. What better way is there to enjoy your vegetables?

Makes one 9-inch pie

- Single crust cornmeal or other pie dough (pages 278-292)
- ⅔ cup grated Parmesan cheese, divided
- 1 ¼ cups plain fresh breadcrumbs
- 4 garlic cloves, peeled and minced, divided
- 1 tablespoon fresh thyme, finely chopped, or 1 teaspoon dried
- 2 tablespoons extra-virgin olive oil
- 1 medium onion, thinly sliced
- 2 medium zucchini, sliced
- 1 small eggplant (under 1 ½ pounds), diced
- 2 bell peppers, any color, diced
- 3 tomatoes, peeled, seeded, and diced
- ⅓ cup fresh basil, chopped
- 1 cup ricotta cheese
- 2 eggs
- Salt and pepper

Prepare and partially pre-bake the piecrust according to the recipe instructions. Spread half the Parmesan cheese on the bottom of the warm pie shell.

Preheat the oven to 375°F.

Combine the remaining Parmesan with the breadcrumbs, half of the garlic, and the thyme and set aside.

Heat the olive oil in a skillet over medium heat and add the onion. Cook for 5 minutes, then add the remaining garlic and stir another minute or two, until fragrant. Add the zucchini, eggplant, and peppers and cook, stirring frequently, for another 8 minutes. Add the tomatoes and basil and stir to combine. Remove from the heat and allow to cool to room temperature.

In a separate bowl, mix the ricotta with the eggs, and salt and pepper until well blended, then stir into the vegetables. Scrape into the piecrust and sprinkle with the breadcrumb mixture.

Bake for 20 minutes, or until set. Serve warm or at room temperature.

Quinoa Pie

This pie can also be made without the piecrust. Lightly grease an 8 x 8-inch pie plate and pour in the mixture. Reduce the baking time by 10 minutes.

Makes one 9-inch pie

- Single crust herbed or other pie dough (pages 278-292)
- 2 tablespoons vegetable oil
- 1 medium onion, finely chopped
- 1 red bell pepper, chopped
- ¾ cup peas, fresh or frozen
- 1 cup cooked quinoa (page 122)
- 1 cup cooked and diced or shredded chicken
- 2½ teaspoons fresh thyme, chopped, or 1 teaspoon dried
- Salt and pepper
- 3 eggs
- 1 cup heavy cream
- ½ cup ricotta cheese

Prepare and partially pre-bake the piecrust according to the recipe instructions. (Follow directions in headnote to make this pie without the crust.)

Preheat the oven to 400°F.

Heat the oil in a skillet over medium heat and add the onion. Sauté for 1 minute, then add the bell pepper and cook until softened, about 5 minutes. Add the peas, quinoa, chicken, thyme, and salt and pepper to the skillet and mix well. Remove from heat.

In a separate bowl, beat the eggs with the cream, then beat in the cheese. Add the quinoa mixture, stirring to mix well, then pour into the prepared pie shell.

Bake for 30 minutes, then reduce the temperature to 325°F. and bake until set, about another 10 minutes. Let stand for 10 minutes before serving.

Asparagus Gruyere Quiche

Asparagus and Gruyere cheese make a wonderfully tangy quiche.

Makes one 9-inch quiche

- Single crust basic or other pie dough (pages 278-292)
- 1³⁄₄ pounds asparagus, woody ends removed, cut into 2-inch pieces
- ¼ cup grated Parmesan cheese
- ⅓ cup grated Gruyere cheese
- ½ cup plain breadcrumbs
- 1 tablespoon fresh thyme, chopped, or 1 teaspoon dried
- 2 eggs, separated
- 1½ cups sour cream
- 2 tablespoons whole wheat flour
- Salt and pepper

Prepare and partially pre-bake the piecrust according to the recipe instructions.

Preheat the oven to 425°F.

In a pot of boiling water, cook the asparagus pieces for 2 minutes, then place in cold water to stop cooking. Drain and set aside.

In a separate bowl, mix the cheeses with the breadcrumbs and thyme and spread across the bottom of the pie shell.

In a small bowl, whisk the egg yolks with the sour cream, flour, and salt and pepper. Beat the egg whites until stiff, then fold into the sour cream mixture.

Place half of the asparagus—choosing the pieces rather than the tips—on top of the breadcrumb mixture in the pie shell. Add half of the egg mixture, then scatter the remaining asparagus over the top before topping with the remaining egg mixture.

Bake for 10 minutes, then reduce the temperature to 325°F. and bake another 35 to 40 minutes, or until set. Allow to cool slightly before serving.

Smoked Salmon and Dill Quiche

This flavorful quiche is a wonderful brunch or dinner item, and quick to make.

Makes one 9-inch quiche

- Single crust basic or other pie dough (pages 278-292)
- 3 eggs
- 1 ½ cups heavy cream
- Salt and pepper
- 3 tablespoons fresh dill, minced
- ¼ pound smoked salmon, chopped

Prepare and partially pre-bake the piecrust according to the recipe instructions.

Preheat the oven to 375°F.

Beat the eggs, cream, and salt and pepper until well blended. Gently stir the dill and salmon into the mixture and pour into cool pie shell.

Bake until filling is set, 15 to 20 minutes. Cool for 10 minutes on a wire rack before serving.

Onion Apple Tart

Onion tarts are delicious when you add all sorts of savory items, such as anchovies and black olives. For a twist, here is one with thinly sliced apples.

Makes one 9-inch tart

- Single crust cornmeal or other pie dough (pages 278-292)
- 2 tablespoons extra-virgin olive oil
- 3 pounds medium onions, thinly sliced
- 1 firm apple, such as Granny Smith or Honeycrisp, peeled and cut into 16 very thin slices
- 1 tablespoon fresh thyme, chopped, or 1 teaspoon dried
- Salt and freshly ground black pepper, to taste

Prepare the piecrust dough and refrigerate until you are ready to roll it out.

On a lightly floured surface, roll out the dough into a 12-inch circle. Place over a 9-inch tart pan with removable bottom or pie dish, center, and gently tuck the dough into the pan. Refrigerate until ready to use.

Preheat the oven to 375°F.

Heat the oil in a large skillet over high heat. Add the onions and cook, stirring until the onions begin to color slightly, about 10 minutes. Reduce heat and continue to cook, stirring occasionally, until the onions begin to brown, about 20 minutes. Remove from the heat, stir in the apple slices, thyme, and salt and pepper.

Remove the piecrust from the refrigerator and prick the bottom with a fork in several places. Place the onion mixture in the shell and bake for 35 to 40 minutes, until crust is golden.

Spinach, Ham, and Mozzarella Pie

This pie is simple to make and especially good with a basic crust with a pinch of fresh thyme added to the flour.

Makes one 9-inch pie

- Double crust basic or other pie dough (pages 278-292)
- 1¼ pounds spinach, stemmed and rinsed
- 3 medium tomatoes, peeled and coarsely chopped
- ½ tablespoon fresh dill, chopped, or ½ teaspoon dried
- 6 ounces cooked ham, diced
- 1 pound mozzarella, grated
- ½ cup crumbled feta
- Salt and pepper

Prepare the piecrust dough and refrigerate until you are ready to roll it out.

On a lightly floured surface, roll out a little more than half of the dough into a 12-inch circle. Place over a 9-inch pie plate, center, and gently tuck the dough into the pan. Trim the edges and place in the refrigerator. Roll out the second portion of dough and place on parchment paper or floured wax paper on a cookie sheet. Refrigerate until ready to use.

Preheat the oven to 400°F.

Add the wet spinach to a saucepan and cook over medium heat until wilted, about 2 minutes or so. Remove to a colander and press any water out.

In a bowl, toss the tomatoes with the dill. Spread the spinach on the bottom of the unbaked piecrust. Layer the tomato mixture over the spinach, then sprinkle with the ham. Combine the two cheeses together and sprinkle over the ham, then sprinkle with salt and pepper.

Cover with the second sheet of dough, press to seal, and cut 2 or 3 vents on top. Bake for 15 minutes, turn the heat down to 300°F. and bake another 25 minutes, or until golden. Cool slightly on a wire rack before serving.

Blue Cheese, Apple, and Walnut Quiche

Modest? Unimposing? Subtle? Not this quiche. Four ounces of blue cheese make a bold statement on your tongue, but pair very well with the sweet apple and savory walnut.

Makes one 9-inch quiche

- Single crust basic or other pie dough (pages 278-292)
- 2 ripe firm apples, peeled, cored, and sliced 1/4-inch thick
- 1 cup (about 4 ounces) blue cheese, crumbled
- 1/2 cup walnuts, toasted and chopped
- Scant cup heavy cream
- 1 egg, lightly beaten
- 1 teaspoon salt
- 1/4 teaspoon pepper

Prepare and partially pre-bake the piecrust according to the recipe instructions.

Preheat the oven to 425°F.

Arrange the apples on the bottom of the crust and sprinkle with the cheese and walnuts. In a separate bowl, beat together the cream, egg, salt, and pepper and then pour over the filling.

Bake until just set, about 30 to 35 minutes. Let cool for 30 minutes before serving.

Spinach and Goat Cheese Quiche

Popeye, renowned promoter of spinach, might have been persuaded to eat his spinach in another form had he tried this little quiche. Spinach and goat cheese are a natural match, made even better in this amazing quiche.

Makes one 9-inch quiche

- Single crust cornmeal or other pie dough (pages 278-292)
- 2 tablespoons extra-virgin olive oil
- ½ cup minced onions
- 1 pound spinach, stemmed, cleaned, and coarsely chopped
- Salt and pepper
- 1 cup heavy cream
- 1 egg
- ½ cup crumbled goat cheese
- ¼ cup grated Asiago, Pecorino Romano, or Parmesan cheese
- 2 tablespoons Kalamata olives, pitted and minced

Prepare and partially pre-bake the piecrust according to the recipe instructions.

Preheat the oven to 350°F.

Heat the oil in a large skillet over medium heat. Add the onions and sauté, stirring frequently, until translucent, about 3 to 4 minutes. Add the spinach and toss until the spinach wilts, about 2 or 3 minutes. Remove from the heat. Season with salt and pepper.

In a separate bowl, beat together the cream and egg. Stir in the cheeses and olives, and season with salt and pepper.

Spread the spinach mixture over the bottom of the piecrust. Slowly add the egg mixture, stirring with a fork to make sure the filling ingredients are evenly spread. Set the tart pan on a baking sheet and bake until a tester inserted in the center comes out clean, about 40 minutes.

Cool at least 15 minutes before slicing. Serve warm or at room temperature.

Chicken and Mushroom Pie

You can cook the chicken for this recipe any way you like—roast a whole chicken and pull the meat off the bone, grill some skinless breasts, even poach in chicken broth. However you make it, it's great in this pie.

Makes one 9-inch pie

- Double crust egg and vinegar or other pie dough (pages 278-292)
- 1 (3½ pound) chicken, cooked, or 3 boneless, skinless chicken breasts, cooked
- 2 tablespoons unsalted butter
- 1 carrot, peeled and finely chopped
- 1 celery stalk, chopped
- 1 medium onion, finely chopped
- ½ pound white mushrooms, sliced
- 1 tablespoon fresh or 1 teaspoon dried rosemary
- 2 teaspoons fresh or ½ teaspoon dried thyme
- Salt and pepper
- ¼ cup white wine, optional
- 2 tablespoons arrowroot or cornstarch
- 1¾ cups good quality chicken broth, divided
- 1 egg white mixed with 2 tablespoons of water for glazing

Prepare the piecrust dough and refrigerate until you are ready to roll it out.

On a lightly floured surface, roll out a little more than half of the dough into a 12-inch circle. Place over a 9-inch pie plate, center, and gently tuck the dough into the pan. Trim the edges and place in the refrigerator. Roll out the second portion of dough and place on parchment paper or floured wax paper on a cookie sheet. Refrigerate until ready to use.

Preheat the oven to 375°F.

Tear the chicken into pieces and set aside.

Melt the butter in a skillet over medium-high heat and add the carrot, celery, and onion. Sauté for 2 minutes and then add the mushrooms, and sauté, stirring constantly, until the mushrooms soften and darken, about 5 to 7 minutes. Stir in the herbs, and salt and pepper to taste. Add the white wine, and cook until almost dry.

Combine the arrowroot or cornstarch with ½ cup of the chicken broth and set aside. Add the remaining broth to the skillet and cook down for 2 to 3 minutes, then stir in the arrowroot or cornstarch and broth mixture. Cook, stirring, for about 5 minutes to thicken.

Remove from heat, stir in the chicken pieces and mix, then pour the mixture into a piecrust. Top with the second sheet of dough, cutting vents to release steam. Crimp edges and brush with egg wash.

Bake for 30 minutes until bubbling and brown.

Empanadas

(MEAT TURNOVERS)

In Argentina, this street food is often deep fried, but here it is baked for a more healthy dish. A true empanada cook would hand-chop the meat very fine, but you may use ground meat, if you prefer.

Makes 10 empanadas

- 3 tablespoons extra-virgin olive oil, divided
- 1⅓ pounds boneless round steak, finely chopped, or ground beef
- 2 medium onions, minced
- 3 tomatoes, peeled, seeded, and cut into small pieces (or canned, drained)
- 1 tablespoon pimento, minced
- 1 teaspoon cumin
- 1½ teaspoons fresh or 1 teaspoon dried oregano
- ¼ teaspoon red pepper flakes
- 12 to 14 large green olives, pitted and cut into 3 or 4 slices
- 2 hard boiled eggs, chopped
- Double crust basic or other pie dough (pages 278-292)
- 1 egg white mixed with 2 tablespoons of water or water for glazing, optional

Heat half the oil in a skillet and cook the meat over medium-high heat until no longer pink. Place the meat in a colander to drain.

Heat the remaining oil in the skillet and add the onion. Cook until soft, about 5 minutes, then return the meat to the skillet along with the tomatoes, pimento, spices, and olives and cook to blend the flavors, about 7 minutes. Remove from heat and stir in the eggs. Allow to cool.

Preheat the oven to 375°F. Line a baking sheet with foil or parchment paper.

Divide the dough into 10 pieces. Roll and then cut 1 piece into about a 6-inch circle, lay on the prepared baking sheet, and spoon about 3 tablespoons of the filling onto half of the circle, leaving a 1-inch border. Brush the edge of the pastry with an egg wash or a little warm water, fold over the empty half, seal the edges and cut 3 or 4 steam vents on top. Repeat with remaining dough and filling.

Bake for 20 to 25 minutes, until browned. Cool for at least 10 minutes before serving. Enjoy warm.

Millet Turnovers

Every society has some filling wrapped in dough—call it a turnover, empanada, pasty, samosa, calzone . . . you get the idea. Here we've mixed millet with some beef and vegetables for a healthy snack. To easily peel tomatoes, drop in boiling water for about 30 seconds, then plunge into cold water (or cold running water). The skins will slip off. Seeds give a slightly bitter taste, so the tomatoes can be seeded.

Makes 10 turnovers

- ½ cup hulled millet
- 2½ cups water
- 1 pound spinach, cleaned and stemmed
- 3 tablespoons extra-virgin olive oil, divided
- ¾ pound ground beef
- 1 onion, minced
- 2 bell peppers, chopped
- 3 garlic cloves, peeled and minced
- ½ teaspoon ground nutmeg
- 3 tomatoes, peeled and chopped (or canned, drained)
- 1 small russet potato, peeled and diced
- ¼ cup beef broth or water
- Salt and pepper
- Double crust basic or other pie dough (pages 278-292)
- 1 egg white mixed with 1 tablespoon water or water for glazing, optional

Bring millet and 2½ cups water to boil in a small saucepan; simmer until just tender, about 15 minutes. Drain and set aside.

Wash the spinach, but do not dry it. Place in a saucepan over medium heat until the spinach wilts, 1 or 2 minutes. Remove from heat, press excess water out, and chop.

Heat half the oil in a skillet and cook the beef over medium high heat until no longer pink. Place in a colander to drain.

Heat the remaining oil in the skillet, add the onion and cook until soft, about 5 minutes. Add the peppers, garlic, nutmeg, tomatoes, potato, broth and salt and pepper to taste. Cook, stirring frequently, until the liquid has evaporated and the potatoes are just beginning to soften, about 5 minutes. Return the meat to the skillet along with the millet and the spinach and mix well. Allow to cool.

Preheat the oven to 375°F. Line a baking sheet with foil or parchment paper.

Divide the dough into 10 pieces. Roll and then cut 1 piece into about a 6-inch circle, lay on prepared baking sheet, and spoon about 3 tablespoons of the filling onto half of the circle, leaving a 1-inch border. Brush the edge of the pastry with egg wash or a little warm water, fold over the empty half, seal the edges and cut 3 or 4 steam vents on top. Repeat with remaining dough.

Bake for 20 to 25 minutes, until browned. Cool for at least 10 minutes before serving. Enjoy warm.

SWEET PIES, TARTS, COBBLERS, AND CRISPS

Pumpkin Maple Syrup Pie

Use Grade B real maple syrup in this recipe for the ultimate maple syrup flavor.

Makes one 9-inch pie

- Single crust buttermilk or other pie dough (pages 278-292)
- 1 cup Grade B maple syrup
- 2 cups canned, solid-pack pumpkin
- 1 teaspoon ground cinnamon
- ½ teaspoon salt
- 1 cup heavy cream
- ⅔ cup milk
- 2 eggs
- 1 egg white mixed with 1 tablespoon water, optional

Prepare and partially pre-bake the piecrust according to the recipe instructions.

Preheat the oven to 375°F.

In a large, heavy saucepan over medium-high heat, slowly bring the maple syrup to a boil and cook until it reaches about 210°F. on a candy thermometer, or until a small amount dropped into a bowl of cold water forms a soft ball, or the syrup begins to solidify. Cool slightly for about 10 minutes.

Place the pumpkin, cinnamon, salt, cream, milk, and eggs in a blender and combine well, or whisk by hand. Add the warm maple syrup and combine well.

Pour the filling into the cooled shell (you will have slightly too much filling). Brush the edges of the shell with egg wash. Bake in the middle of the oven for 1 hour, or until the filling is set but the center still shakes slightly. The filling will continue to set as the pie cools. Transfer the pie to a rack to cool to room temperature, about 2 hours.

Quince Meringue Pie

This is an old-fashioned pie, from when quinces were much more plentiful in markets. Today, quince is making a comeback; we hope this pie will, too.

Makes one 9-inch pie

- Single crust basic or other pie dough (pages 278-292)
- 3 medium quinces
- ⅓ cup apple juice or water
- ½ cup plus ⅓ cup sugar
- 1 teaspoon lemon juice
- ¼ teaspoon ground cinnamon
- Pinch ground cloves
- ¼ teaspoon cardamom
- 2½ tablespoons unsalted butter, melted and cooled
- 3 eggs, separated
- 1 cup milk
- ¼ teaspoon cream of tartar

Prepare the piecrust dough and refrigerate until you are ready to roll it out.

On a lightly floured surface, roll out the dough into a 12-inch circle. Place over a 9-inch pie plate, center, and gently tuck the dough into the pan. Refrigerate until ready to use.

Peel, quarter, and core the quinces and place them in a saucepan with the apple juice and ½ cup of sugar. Bring to a boil, then simmer until the fruit is tender, about 25 minutes.

Preheat the oven to 350°F.

Pour the quince and the juice into the bowl of a food processor and purée. Remove 1 cup plus 2 tablespoons of the purée to another bowl and set aside any extra for another use. Stir in the lemon juice, spices, and butter into the purée in the bowl.

Beat the egg yolks until thickened. Scald the milk in a saucepan, then slowly whisk the milk into the yolks. Slowly whisk this mixture into the quince puree.

Pour into the refrigerated pie shell and bake until set, about 40 minutes.

Meanwhile, beat the egg whites with the cream of tartar until they form soft peaks. Add the remaining ⅓ cup of sugar in a steady stream, beating until the meringue is stiff.

Remove the pie from the oven and spread the meringue over the filling, covering it completely and pulling it up to form decorative peaks. Return the pie to the oven until the meringue is golden, about 15 minutes.

Pear & Apple Pie

This lattice-style fruit pie is a favorite in the Northwest, where we pick our own pears and apples during the fall from among the hundreds of orchards that dot our landscape.

Makes one 9-inch pie

- Double crust cornmeal or other pie dough (pages 278-292)
- 1 pound Granny Smith or other firm apple, peeled, cored, and cut into thin slices
- 1½ pounds firm, ripe pears, peeled, cored, and cut into thin slices
- 2 tablespoons lemon juice
- ½ teaspoon ground cinnamon
- 1½ tablespoons whole wheat flour
- 3½ tablespoons ground cinnamon
- ¼ teaspoon salt

Prepare the piecrust dough and refrigerate until you are ready to roll it out.

On a lightly floured surface, roll out a little more than half of the dough into a 12-inch circle. Place over a 9-inch pie plate, center, and gently tuck the dough into the pan. Trim the edges and place in the refrigerator. Roll out the second portion of dough and place on parchment paper or floured wax paper on a cookie sheet. Refrigerate until ready to use.

Preheat the oven to 375°F.

Place the apples, pears, and lemon juice in a large bowl, and toss. Combine the remaining ingredients in a small bowl, sprinkle over the apple-pear mixture, and toss to coat.

Spoon the apple mixture into the piecrust, smoothing with the back of a wooden spoon. Cut the second half of the dough into strips about ½-inch wide. Lay the strips of dough over the filling in a criss-cross pattern, sealing at the edges with a bit of water.

Bake for 40 minutes, or until crust is brown. Remove from oven and cool on a rack for at least 20 minutes before slicing.

Tarte au Sucre (Sugar Pie)

This is a Canadian tradition, made with maple sugar. Substitute brown sugar if you don't have maple sugar on hand.

Makes one 9-inch pie

- Double crust egg and vinegar or other pie dough (pages 278-292)
- 3 cups maple sugar, or brown sugar, packed
- ¼ cup whole wheat flour
- ⅔ cup heavy cream
- ¾ cup plus 1 tablespoon milk
- 1½ tablespoons light corn syrup
- 4 tablespoons unsalted butter, softened

Prepare the piecrust dough and refrigerate until you are ready to roll it out.

On a lightly floured surface, roll out a little more than half of the dough into a 12-inch circle. Place over a 9-inch pie plate, center, and gently tuck the dough into the pan. Trim the edges and place in the refrigerator. Roll out the second portion of dough and place on parchment paper or floured wax paper on a cookie sheet. Refrigerate until ready to use.

In a medium saucepan, stir together the sugar and the flour. Stir in the cream, the ¾ cup of milk, corn syrup, and butter and bring to a boil over medium-low heat, stirring constantly. Boil, stirring, for 2 minutes, remove from heat, and allow to cool completely, about 90 minutes.

Preheat the oven to 400°F.

Pour the filling into the piecrust. Moisten the edges of the second half of the dough, place it over the pie, and press the top and bottom edges together. Cut 4 or 5 vents on top. Bake for 40 minutes or until crust is nicely browned. Cool on a wire rack for at least 2½ hours to let the filling set.

Oatmeal Pie

If you like oatmeal cookies, you'll love this pie.

Makes one 9-inch pie

- Single crust basic or other pie dough (pages 278-292)
- ²/₃ cup sugar
- 5 tablespoons unsalted butter, softened
- 2 eggs, lightly beaten
- ²/₃ cup dark corn syrup
- ²/₃ cup rolled oats
- 1 tablespoon whole wheat flour
- 1 teaspoon vanilla extract
- ¹/₂ cup raisins, pecans, or walnuts, optional

Prepare the piecrust dough and refrigerate until you are ready to roll it out.

On a lightly floured surface, roll out the dough into a 12-inch circle. Place over a 9-inch pie plate, center, and gently tuck the dough into the pan. Refrigerate until ready to use.

Preheat the oven to 325°F.

In a large bowl, cream together the sugar and butter until the mixture is light and fluffy, about 3 minutes. Beat in the eggs one at a time, then the corn syrup. Beat another 30 seconds to blend well. Stir in the rolled oats, flour, vanilla, and raisins or nuts. Pour into the piecrust.

Bake for 45 to 55 minutes, or until the filling is set. Remove from the oven and cool on a rack.

Fresh Fig Pie

If you can't get enough of luscious fresh figs, simply add more and omit the pear.

Makes one 9-inch pie

- Double crust basic or other pie dough (pages 278-292)

- 8 or 9 fresh ripe figs, peeled and cut into sixths
- 1 large pear, peeled, cored, cut into ¼ inch slices
- ¼ cup brown sugar, packed
- ¼ cup confectioners' sugar
- ¼ teaspoon ground allspice
- 2 tablespoons arrowroot or cornstarch
- ¼ cup apple juice

Prepare the piecrust dough and refrigerate until you are ready to roll it out.

On a lightly floured surface, roll out a little more than half of the dough into a 12-inch circle. Place over a 9-inch pie plate, center, and gently tuck the dough into the pan. Trim the edges and place in the refrigerator. Roll out the second portion of dough and place on parchment paper or floured wax paper on a cookie sheet. Refrigerate until ready to use.

Preheat the oven to 350°F.

Toss the ingredients in a large bowl, and let the mixture sit for 10 minutes.

Scrape the mixture into the piecrust. Cut the second half of the dough into strips. Lay the strips of dough over the filling in a criss-cross pattern, sealing at the edges with a bit of water.

Bake for 35 to 40 minutes, or until the pear is tender and crust is brown. Cool before serving.

Sweet Potato Pie

Plenty of spices in this southern favorite.

Makes one 9-inch pie

- Single crust cornmeal or other pie dough (pages 278-292)
- 1 large sweet potato, baked and peeled
- 1 cup milk
- 1 egg
- 2 egg yolks
- 1 tablespoon brown sugar
- 1/3 cup sugar
- 1 teaspoon ground cinnamon
- 1/4 teaspoon ground allspice
- 1/4 teaspoon ground nutmeg
- 1/8 teaspoon salt
- 2 tablespoons unsalted butter, melted and cooled

Prepare and partially pre-bake the piecrust according to the recipe instructions.

Preheat the oven to 350°F.

Push the sweet potato through a food mill or sieve and set aside.

Whisk the milk, egg, and egg yolks until evenly combined. Add the sweet potato, sugars, spices, salt, and butter, and whisk until smooth. Pour into the cooled pie shell.

Bake until set, about 35 to 40 minutes or until a tester comes out clean.

Remove the pie from the oven and cool on a wire rack. Let the pie rest for at least 15 minutes before slicing. Serve warm or at room temperature.

Simple Pear Pie

Almond cookies are traditionally used in this Italian favorite, but for a twist, ginger or even lemon cookies are great.

Makes one 9-inch pie

- Double crust basic or other pie dough (pages 278-292)
- 7 or 8 pears, peeled, cored, and sliced
- Juice from ½ lemon
- 2 tablespoons brown sugar
- 10 small (2½- to 3-inch), thin almond, ginger, or lemon cookies, crushed
- ½ teaspoon ground cinnamon
- ¼ teaspoon ground allspice

Prepare the piecrust dough and refrigerate until you are ready to roll it out.

On a lightly floured surface, roll out a little more than half of the dough into a 12-inch circle. Place over a 9-inch pie plate, center, and gently tuck the dough into the pan. Trim the edges and place in the refrigerator. Roll out the second portion of dough and place on parchment paper or floured wax paper on a cookie sheet. Refrigerate until ready to use.

Preheat the oven to 375°F.

In a bowl, toss the pear slices in the lemon juice and brown sugar. Add the crushed cookies and spices and stir gently, then place in the pie shell.

Moisten the edges of the second half of the dough, place it over the pie, and press the top and bottom edges together. Cut 2 or 3 vents on top.

Bake for 15 minutes, turn the heat down to 350°F, and then bake until the pie and the fruit are cooked through, another 30 minutes.

Plum and Walnut Pie

Plums and walnuts are a delicious combination in this early fall pie.

Makes one 9-inch pie

- Double crust basic or other pie dough (pages 278-292)
- 1¾ pounds plums, halved, pitted, and chopped
- ¼ cup brown sugar, packed
- ¼ cup sugar
- 1 cup walnuts, toasted and coarsely chopped
- 1 teaspoon ground cinnamon
- ½ teaspoon ground nutmeg
- 3 tablespoons unsalted butter, melted and cooled
- Beaten egg white to glaze
- Sugar and ground cinnamon, mixed

Prepare the piecrust dough and refrigerate until you are ready to roll it out.

On a lightly floured surface, roll out a little more than half of the dough into a 12-inch circle. Place over a 9-inch pie plate, center, and gently tuck the dough into the pan. Trim the edges and place in the refrigerator. Roll out the second portion of dough and place on parchment paper or floured wax paper on a cookie sheet. Refrigerate until ready to use.

Preheat the oven to 375°F.

Combine the plums with the sugars and toss to mix. Add the walnuts, spices, and butter and stir to combine.

Pour into the piecrust and cover with the second sheet of dough, crimp the edges, and cut 2 or 3 vents on top. Brush the top of the crust with egg white and sprinkle with a little sugar/cinnamon mix.

Bake for 55 minutes or until dark brown.

Black Bottom Pie

You can also melt the chocolate for this recipe in a microwave, but stir and check frequently to make sure it doesn't burn.

Makes one 9-inch pie

- Single crust buttermilk or other pie dough (pages 278-292)
- 1½ ounces unsweetened chocolate
- 1 teaspoon brown sugar
- 2 teaspoons unflavored gelatin
- ¼ cup water
- 1¼ cups milk
- 2 eggs, separated
- ⅓ cup plus 2 teaspoons sugar
- 1½ tablespoons arrowroot or cornstarch
- ½ teaspoon salt
- 1 teaspoon vanilla extract
- 2 tablespoons confectioners' sugar
- ½ cup heavy cream

Prepare and completely pre-bake the piecrust according to the recipe instructions.

Place the chocolate in the top of a double boiler. Place water in the bottom half to just touch the bottom of the pan above. Bring the water to a boil and melt the chocolate, stirring with a spatula. Stir in the brown sugar and set aside.

In a small bowl, combine the gelatin and the water.

Bring the milk to a simmer in a saucepan, remove from heat and slowly pour the milk over the egg yolks, whisking constantly. Return the mixture to the saucepan.

Combine the ⅓ cup sugar, arrowroot or cornstarch, and salt and add to the milk mixture. Whisk in the gelatin. Cook this mixture over medium heat, stirring constantly, until the custard thickens and barely reaches a simmer. Do not boil.

Remove the pan from the heat and combine ⅔ cup of the custard with the chocolate. Pour the chocolate mixture into the pie shell. Add the vanilla to the remaining custard and chill for 45 minutes, until cool.

Whip the egg whites until soft peaks form, gradually adding the confectioners' sugar. Fold into the custard and spread over the chocolate in the piecrust.

Whip the cream with the remaining 2 teaspoons sugar until stiff, then spoon over the tart. Refrigerate for 1 hour before serving.

Persimmon Pie

Light and airy, we think this is one of the best ways to use those fall persimmons.

Makes one 9-inch pie

- Single crust basic or other pie dough (pages 278-292)
- 1 tablespoon unflavored gelatin
- ¼ cup water
- 3 large ripe Hachiya persimmons
- 4 eggs, separated
- ⅔ cup sugar
- 1 teaspoon ground cinnamon
- ¾ teaspoon ground nutmeg
- Zest of one lemon
- ¼ teaspoon salt
- 1 cup heavy cream
- ¼ cup confectioners' sugar

Prepare and completely pre-bake the piecrust according to the recipe instructions.

Place a medium bowl in the refrigerator to chill.

In a small bowl, sprinkle the gelatin over the water and let stand for a few minutes. Peel and cut the persimmons into slices. Place the persimmon in a blender and blend until smooth.

Place the egg yolks in a heavy saucepan and stir. Add the sugar along with the cinnamon, nutmeg, zest, and salt, and combine. Whisk in the persimmon puree. Cook over medium-low heat, whisking constantly, until the mixture thickens a little, about 5 to 10 minutes. Do not boil.

Whisking constantly, add the softened gelatin and cook about 1 minute longer. Pour the mixture into a bowl and refrigerate, stirring every 10 minutes or so until it thickens to the consistency of unbeaten egg whites, about 1 hour.

In the chilled bowl, whip the cream until stiff.

In another bowl, beat the egg whites until soft peaks form. Slowly add the confectioners' sugar and continue beating until stiff peaks form. Fold the beaten whites and whipped cream into the persimmon mixture and pile into the piecrust. Chill several hours before serving.

Sour Cherry Pie

Cherries are a popular crop throughout western Oregon, the place Bob's calls home. Sour cherries make this pie especially delectable. We think you'll think so, too.

Makes one 9-inch pie

- Double crust basic or other pie dough (pages 278-292)
- ¾ cup sugar
- ¼ teaspoon ground cinnamon
- 3 tablespoons arrowroot or cornstarch
- 1 tablespoon lemon zest
- 4 cups fresh sour cherries, washed, dried, stems and pits removed
- 1 egg white, beaten for glaze
- 1 teaspoon ground cinnamon and sugar mixed

Prepare the piecrust dough and refrigerate until you are ready to roll it out.

On a lightly floured surface, roll out a little more than half of the dough into a 12-inch circle. Place over a 9-inch pie plate, center, and gently tuck the dough into the pan. Trim the edges and place in the refrigerator. Roll out the second portion of dough and place on parchment paper or floured wax paper on a cookie sheet. Refrigerate until ready to use.

Preheat the oven to 400°F.

Combine the sugar, cinnamon, arrowroot or cornstarch, and lemon zest with the cherries and toss to coat. Pour the cherries into the pie shell, piling them higher in the center. Scrape any liquid left in the bowl over the cherries.

Moisten the edges of the second half of the dough, place it over the pie, and crimp the edges. Brush beaten egg on the crust edges. Sprinkle with cinnamon and sugar and cut a few steam vents in the top of the pie.

Place the pie on a cookie sheet and bake for 20 minutes. Lower the oven temperature to 375°F. Continue baking until the crust is golden brown and the fruit is bubbling, about 35 to 40 minutes more. Transfer the pie to a wire rack and cool.

Fresh Strawberry Pie

For years, children in Oregon have earned their spending money picking strawberries in the Willamette Valley. When school lets out for the summer, the school bus still comes—to take kids to the strawberry fields instead.

Makes one 9-inch pie

- Double crust basic or other pie dough (pages 278-292)
- ½ cup water
- 2 tablespoons plus ½ cup sugar
- 2 tablespoons arrowroot or cornstarch
- 4 cups fresh strawberries, hulled and thickly sliced
- 2 tablespoons fresh lemon juice
- 1½ tablespoons unsalted butter, chilled and diced

Prepare the piecrust dough and refrigerate until you are ready to roll it out.

On a lightly floured surface, roll out a little more than half of the dough into a 12-inch circle. Place over a 9-inch pie plate, center, and gently tuck the dough into the pan. Trim the edges and place in the refrigerator. Roll out the second portion of dough and place on parchment paper or floured wax paper on a cookie sheet. Refrigerate until ready to use.

In a small saucepan, combine the water and the 2 tablespoons sugar over low to medium heat. Dissolve the sugar and bring to a boil. Cook down for about 3 or 4 minutes, remove from heat and let cool for 15 minutes.

Preheat the oven to 400°F.

Combine the ½ cup sugar with the arrowroot or cornstarch. Place the berries in a large bowl, and toss with the arrowroot mixture. Stir in the lemon juice and 2 tablespoons of the sugar syrup and gently stir.

Fill the piecrust with the strawberry mixture. Dot with the pieces of butter. Moisten the edges of the second half of the dough, place it over the fruit, and press the top and bottom edges together. Cut a few steam vents in the top of the pie.

Bake the pie for 20 minutes, the reduce the heat to 375°F. and bake another 40 to 45 minutes, or until the juices bubble. If the crust begins to darken, cover the pie loosely with foil for the final 10 to 15 minutes.

Fresh Fruit Pie

This pie is quick to make and a great opportunity to get those fruits in your diet, and while the recipe below includes suggestions for fruits to include, feel free to use whichever fruit you have on hand.

Makes one 9-inch pie

- Single crust cottage cheese or other pie dough (pages 278-292)
- 4 cups fruit: berries, peaches, nectarines, or pears, cut into 2-inch pieces. (If you're using berries with other fruit, use about 1/3 berries to 2/3 fruit.)
- 1/2 to 3/4 cup sugar (use more if your fruit is tart)
- 4 mint leaves
- 3 tablespoons arrowroot or cornstarch
- 1 cup apple juice or water
- 2 tablespoons lemon juice
- 2 tablespoons unsalted butter

Prepare and partially pre-bake the piecrust according to the recipe instructions.

Coarsely chop or lightly smash 1¼ cups of fruit. Combine the sugar, mint leaves, arrowroot, and apple juice in a large saucepan and whisk until smooth. Stir in the smashed fruit and bring to a slight boil, then simmer over medium to low heat for 3 minutes. Carefully remove the mint leaves. Continue to simmer another 5 minutes or until the mixture has thickened. remove from heat, and then stir in the lemon juice. Stir in the butter and the rest of the fruit.

Let the mixture rest for 45 minutes, remove from pan, and spoon into the cooked piecrust. Chill for at least 2 hours.

Blueberry Peach Pie

Oregon has plenty of "U Pick" farms where you can grab a basket and walk among the berry vines or peach trees and pick your own. It's a great way to get the freshest fruit and spend a weekend afternoon.

Makes one 9-inch pie

- Double crust basic or other pie dough (pages 278-292)
- 3 cups blueberries
- 4 or 5 peaches
- 3 tablespoons lemon juice
- ¾ cup sugar
- ⅛ teaspoon ground nutmeg
- 2 tablespoons arrowroot or cornstarch
- 3 tablespoons unsalted butter

Prepare the piecrust dough and refrigerate until you are ready to roll it out.

On a lightly floured surface, roll out a little more than half of the dough into a 12-inch circle. Place over a 9-inch pie plate, center, and gently tuck the dough into the pan. Trim the edges and place in the refrigerator. Roll out the second portion of dough and place on parchment paper or floured wax paper on a cookie sheet. Refrigerate until ready to use.

Preheat the oven to 425°F.

To peel the peaches, drop them, one at a time, into boiling water for 30 seconds to 1 minute, remove with a slotted spoon to cold running water, and peel when they're cool enough to handle. Cut each peach into 5 or 6 slices.

In a large bowl, combine all ingredients except the butter. Mound the mixture into the chilled piecrust and dot with the butter. Moisten the edges of the second half of the dough, place it over the fruit, and press the top and bottom edges together. Cut a few steam vents in the top of the pie and place on the center rack of the oven.

Bake for 10 minutes, then reduce heat to 350°F. and bake for an additional 35 minutes.

Hazelnut Pie

Don't worry about all of the skins on the nuts. Rub to remove the big pieces, but leaving some on doesn't make any difference.

Makes one 9-inch pie

- Single basic crust or other pie dough (pages 278-292)
- 3 eggs
- ½ cup brown sugar, packed
- ¼ cup molasses
- ¾ cup light corn syrup
- ½ teaspoon salt
- 1 teaspoon vanilla
- ¼ pound (1 stick) unsalted butter, melted and cooled
- 1½ cups hazelnuts, roasted and coarsely chopped

Prepare and partially pre-bake the piecrust according to the recipe instructions.

Preheat the oven to 375°F.

Cream the eggs and sugar until light lemon-yellow in color, about 3 minutes, then beat in the molasses, syrup, salt, and vanilla. Stir in the butter to incorporate, then the hazelnuts.

Pour into the piecrust and bake for 40 to 45 minutes, or until set in center. Cool.

Cinnamon Vanilla Cream Pie

You may use any crust, but we think this goes especially well with the Nut Piecrust on page 292.

Makes one 9-inch pie

- Single basic crust or other pie dough as suggested above (pages 278-292)
- 1 cup sugar
- 3 tablespoons arrowroot or cornstarch
- ¼ teaspoon salt
- 2¼ cups whole milk
- 4 egg yolks
- 1 cinnamon stick
- 3 tablespoons unsalted butter, cut into pieces
- ¾ to 1½ teaspoons vanilla

Prepare and completely pre-bake the piecrust according to the recipe instructions.

Mix the sugar, arrowroot or cornstarch, and salt in a medium heavy saucepan. Whisk in the milk and eggs yolks and place over medium heat. Toss in the cinnamon stick. Cook, whisking constantly, until the mixture comes to a low boil. Whisk until thickened, about 2 more minutes. Remove the cinnamon stick and stir in the butter, a couple of pieces at a time, whisking until incorporated. Stir in the vanilla, using less for a more cinnamon flavored pie, or slightly more if you prefer more of a vanilla pie with a hint of cinnamon. Pour into the piecrust.

Place plastic wrap tightly over the pie and cool for 1 hour, then refrigerate for at least 2 hours before serving.

Apple Cranberry Pie

This pie is great for the holidays, since it combines two of the most traditional flavors Americans love—apples and cranberries. Try it with the cornmeal crust on page 288.

Makes one 9-inch pie

- Double crust basic or other pie dough (pages 278-292)
- 1¼ cups fresh cranberries
- 1 cup plus 2 tablespoons sugar
- 1 teaspoon ground allspice
- ½ teaspoon ground ginger
- 3 pounds Granny Smith or other firm apples, peeled, cored, cut into ½-inch thick slices
- 4 tablespoons whole wheat flour

Prepare the piecrust dough and refrigerate until you are ready to roll it out.

On a lightly floured surface, roll out a little more than half of the dough into a 12-inch circle. Place over a 9-inch pie plate, center, and gently tuck the dough into the pan. Trim the edges and place in the refrigerator. Roll out the second portion of dough and place on parchment paper or floured wax paper on a cookie sheet. Refrigerate until ready to use.

Preheat the oven to 375°F.

In a food processor or by hand, chop the cranberries but do not puree. Remove to a large bowl and combine with sugar and the spices. Add the apples and flour and toss well. Pour into the piecrust.

Moisten the edges of the top crust and place over the fruit, pressing the top and bottom edges together. Cut a few steam vents in the top of the pie.

Place the pie on a baking sheet and bake for 40 minutes. Loosely cover the pie with foil and continue baking for about 35 more minutes or until the juices are thick and bubbling. Transfer pie to rack and cool.

Cherry Pie

What can be said about this classic pie except that it's made all the better with a Bob's Red Mill piecrust?

Makes one 9-inch pie

- Double crust basic or other pie dough (pages 278-292)
- 4 cups Bing cherries
- 2 tablespoons unsalted butter, chilled and diced
- 2 tablespoons lemon juice
- 3 tablespoons arrowroot or cornstarch
- 2 tablespoons cherry brandy, cherry juice, or orange juice
- 3/4 cup sugar, or more as needed
- 1/4 teaspoon ground cinnamon
- 1/4 teaspoon salt
- 1 tablespoon lemon zest

Prepare the piecrust dough and refrigerate until you are ready to roll it out.

On a lightly floured surface, roll out a little more than half of the dough into a 12-inch circle. Place over a 9-inch pie plate, center, and gently tuck the dough into the pan. Trim the edges and place in the refrigerator. Roll out the second portion of dough and place on parchment paper or floured wax paper on a cookie sheet. Refrigerate until ready to use.

Preheat the oven to 450°F.

Pit the cherries over a large bowl to catch any juices. In a medium bowl, mix the lemon juice with the arrowroot or cornstarch, then combine with the brandy, sugar, cinnamon, and salt. Toss with the cherries, their accumulated juices, and the lemon zest, and let the mixture rest for 10 minutes.

Spoon the cherry filling into the chilled piecrust, mounding slightly. Dot with the butter.

Moisten the edges of the second half of the dough, place it over the fruit, and press the top and bottom edges together. Cut a few steam vents in the top of the pie and place on the center rack of the oven.

Bake for 10 minutes, then reduce the heat to 350°F. and bake for 45 minutes more, or until the crust is nicely golden. Let cool on a rack before serving warm or at room temperature.

Dried Apricot Pie

This pie is especially good in the winter, when fresh apricots can't be found, but when they are especially missed.

Makes one 9-inch pie

- Double crust cornmeal or other pie dough (pages 278-292)
- 2 cups dried apricots
- ½ cup sugar
- 1 teaspoon ground cinnamon
- ¼ teaspoon ground allspice
- 1 tablespoon whole wheat flour
- 2 tablespoons lemon juice
- 2 tablespoons unsalted butter, chilled and diced

Prepare the piecrust dough and refrigerate until you are ready to roll it out.

On a lightly floured surface, roll out a little more than half of the dough into a 12-inch circle. Place over a 9-inch pie plate, center, and gently tuck the dough into the pan. Trim the edges and place in the refrigerator. Roll out the second portion of dough and place on parchment paper or floured wax paper on a cookie sheet. Refrigerate until ready to use.

Preheat the oven to 425°F.

Cut the apricots into quarters (scissors work very well), then place them in a saucepan, cover with cold water, and bring to a boil over medium to high heat. Reduce the heat to low and simmer until the apricots absorb most of the water, about 20 minutes. Remove from the heat and stir in the sugar, spices, flour, and lemon juice. Pour into the refrigerated piecrust and dot with butter.

Moisten the edges of the top crust and place over the fruit, pressing the top and bottom edges together. Cut a few steam vents in the top of the pie.

Bake for 10 minutes, then reduce heat to 400°F. and continue baking for 35 minutes. Serve warm or at room temperature.

Pecan Pie

Rich and mouth-watering, this classic recipe makes a very satisfying pie. Serve it warm, topped with your favorite vanilla ice cream for a real treat.

Makes one 9-inch pie

- Single basic crust or other pie dough (pages 278-292)
- ¼ pound (1 stick) unsalted butter, softened
- ¾ cup sugar
- ¼ cup brown sugar, packed
- 3 eggs, lightly beaten
- ½ cup light corn syrup
- ⅓ cup molasses
- ½ teaspoon salt
- 1 teaspoon vanilla extract
- 1 cup pecans, coarsely chopped

Prepare the piecrust dough and refrigerate until you are ready to roll it out.

On a lightly floured surface, roll out the dough into a 12-inch circle. Place over a 9-inch pie plate, center, and gently tuck the dough into the pan. Refrigerate until ready to use.

Preheat the oven to 375°F.

Cream the butter and sugars until light lemon-yellow in color. Add the remaining ingredients and stir well to blend. Pour into the prepared piecrust and bake 40 to 45 minutes. Cool on a wire rack for at least 45 minutes before serving.

Peach Turnovers

Feel free to substitute nectarines or apples in this recipe.

Makes 10 turnovers

- 2¾ cups peaches (about 5 or 6 medium), peeled, pitted, and sliced about ⅜-inch thick
- ⅓ cup plus 1 tablespoon sugar
- ½ teaspoon ground cinnamon
- Pinch of salt
- 1½ teaspoons lemon zest
- 1½ teaspoons lemon juice
- ½ teaspoon vanilla extract
- 2 teaspoons cornstarch
- 2 tablespoons unsalted butter, melted and cooled
- Double crust basic or other pie dough (pages 278-292)
- 1 egg white mixed with 1 tablespoon water, or warm water for glazing
- Sugar or ground cinnamon-sugar mixture for sprinkling

In a large bowl, combine the peaches, sugar, cinnamon, salt, zest, juice, and vanilla, and toss well. Allow to rest for 30 minutes in a colander for excess juices to drain, then toss with the cornstarch and butter.

Divide the dough into 10 pieces. Roll 1 piece and cut it into about a 6-inch circle. Lay the dough circle on top of a piece of plastic wrap and spoon about 3½ tablespoons of the fruit mixture onto half of the circle, leaving a 1-inch border. Brush the edge of the pastry with egg wash or a little warm water, fold over the empty half and seal the edges. Wrap in the plastic and place on a plate in the refrigerator. Repeat with remaining dough and filling. Refrigerate the turnovers for about 1 hour.

Preheat the oven to 400°F. Line a baking sheet with foil or parchment paper.

Unwrap the turnovers and place them on the prepared sheet. Cut 3 or 4 small steam vents though the top of each turnover and sprinkle with sugar or a cinnamon sugar mixture.

Bake for 20 to 30 minutes, until brown and fruit is bubbling. Cool on a wire rack. Serve warm.

VARIATIONS

Apple Turnovers

- 2 Granny Smith or other firm apples, peeled, cored and coarsely grated
- ½ teaspoon ground cinnamon
- 1 tablespoon lemon juice
- ½ cup sugar
- ½ cup applesauce

Place the apples in a bowl and combine with the cinnamon, lemon juice, and sugar. Place in a colander and allow to drain for 30 minutes. Return to a bowl, stir in the applesauce, and continue with the instructions for filling and baking peach turnovers.

Blueberry Turnovers

- 2³/₄ cups blueberries, fresh or frozen
- ⅓ cup plus 1 tablespoon sugar
- 1½ tablespoons cornstarch
- 1 tablespoon lemon juice
- 1 teaspoon lemon zest
- ¼ teaspoon ground cinnamon

Toss all ingredients together in a large bowl. Remove any smashed or damaged blueberries. Allow the mixture to rest for 30 minutes. Continue with the instructions for filling and baking peach turnovers.

Tarts

Simple Chocolate Mint Tart

Fresh mint leaves add just a hint of coolness to this chocolate tart. For a really special treat, stir a little crème de menthe into the filling at the end.

Makes one 9-inch tart

- Single crust cottage cheese or other pie dough (pages 278-292)
- 16 ounces bittersweet chocolate, chopped
- 1 teaspoon brown sugar
- 2 cups heavy cream
- 6 mint leaves
- 3 egg yolks, at room temperature

Prepare and completely pre-bake the piecrust in a tart pan according to the recipe instructions.

Melt the chocolate with the brown sugar in the top of a double boiler set over a medium pot of gently simmering water, stirring constantly. Remove from heat and set aside.

In a medium saucepan, combine the cream with the mint leaves and gently heat until bubbles appear around inside edge of pan, then remove the pan from the heat and let the leaves steep for 10 minutes. Remove mint leaves and discard, reserving the cream.

Place the egg yolks into a medium mixing bowl and whisk until smooth. Slowly whisk about $\frac{1}{3}$ cup of the hot cream into yolks, then stir the egg-cream mixture back into pot of cream. Slowly whisk the egg-cream mixture into the bowl of melted chocolate, whisking until smooth.

Pour the filling into the prepared crust and set aside until cool, about 30 minutes. Refrigerate until the filling is set, about 2 to 3 hours.

Gooseberry Tart

Gooseberries can be on the sour side, so this dessert has a little more sugar.

Makes one 9-inch tart

- Single crust basic or other pie dough (pages 278-292)
- 2 tablespoons gooseberry jam or currant jelly
- 2 tablespoons whole wheat flour
- 3 cups gooseberries, tops and bottoms removed
- 2/3 cup sugar

Prepare the piecrust dough and refrigerate until you are ready to roll it out.

On a lightly floured surface, roll out the dough into a 12-inch circle. Place over a 9-inch tart pan with removable bottom or pie plate, center, and gently tuck the dough into the pan. Refrigerate until ready to use.

Preheat the oven to 375°F.

Brush the bottom of the piecrust with jam.

In a bowl, combine the flour, gooseberries, and sugar and spread into the piecrust. Bake for 10 minutes, then reduce the heat to 350°F. and continue baking until the gooseberries burst and the edges of the crust are golden, about 35 to 40 minutes. Allow the tart to cool at least 45 minutes before serving.

Raspberry Custard Tart

Drizzle a little chocolate syrup on top if you'd like.

Makes one 9-inch tart

- Single crust buttermilk or other pie dough (pages 278-292)
- 1 egg
- 1 egg white
- ½ cup sugar
- ½ teaspoon salt
- 4 tablespoons unsalted butter, melted and cooled
- 1½ teaspoons vanilla extract
- 2 teaspoons lemon juice
- 1 teaspoon lemon zest
- 2 tablespoons whole wheat flour
- 2 tablespoons heavy cream
- 2 cups (10 ounces) fresh raspberries

Prepare and partially pre-bake the piecrust in a tart pan according to the recipe instructions. Cool completely.

Preheat the oven to 375°F.

Whisk the egg and egg white in a medium bowl. Add the sugar and salt and whisk or beat until light, a minute or two. Gradually whisk in the butter until combined. Whisk in the vanilla, lemon juice, and zest. Whisk in the flour and then the cream.

Spread the raspberries in a single layer over the bottom of the tart shell. Pour the filling over the berries, place the tart on a baking sheet, and bake until the filling is set, about 30 minutes. Cool to room temperature before serving, at least 90 minutes.

Lemon Tart

This tart has a wonderful combination of sweet and tart, and is even more delicious when made with a sugar dough.

Makes one 9-inch tart

- Single crust sugar tart or other pie dough (pages 278-292)
- 9 tablespoons unsalted butter
- 1⅓ cups sugar
- 2 eggs
- ½ cup lemon juice
- Zest of 2 lemons

Prepare the piecrust dough and refrigerate until you are ready to roll it out.

On a lightly floured surface, roll out the dough into a 12-inch circle. Place over a 10-inch tart pan with removable bottom or pie plate, center, and gently tuck the dough into the pan. Partially pre-bake according to the recipe instructions. Cool completely.

Preheat the oven to 375°F.

Melt the butter and set aside to cool. Place a cookie sheet covered with foil on the lower rack of the oven to catch drips.

Beat the sugar and eggs together until light, about 4 or 5 minutes. With the beater on low, gradually add the butter and incorporate, then beat in the lemon juice. Stir in the lemon zest, then pour the mixture into the tart shell (you may have a little extra, do not fill to the rim) and bake until set, about 25 minutes. It will be slightly jiggly, but will finish setting as it cools. Allow to cool completely before serving.

Strawberry Chocolate Tart

Fresh strawberries and chocolate are a spectacular combination; use the freshest strawberries you can find for this delectable tart.

Makes one 9-inch tart

- Single crust basic or other pie dough (pages 278-292)
- ½ cup good quality strawberry jam, or 1½ cups roughly pureed strawberries with 1 tablespoon sugar added
- ¾ cup plus 3 tablespoons heavy cream
- 1 cinnamon stick
- 6 ounces bittersweet (not unsweetened) or semisweet chocolate, chopped
- 2 (1-pint) baskets strawberries, hulled and halved

Prepare and completely pre-bake the piecrust in a tart pan according to the recipe instructions. Cool completely.

Spread the jam or puree over the bottom of the cooled piecrust and refrigerate while preparing the chocolate.

Heat the cream with the cinnamon stick in a small, heavy saucepan over medium to low heat until just about to boil. Remove from heat, remove the cinnamon stick, and stir in the chocolate until completely melted. Cool to room temperature stirring occasionally, about 45 minutes (it should still be thin enough to pour).

Gently pour the chocolate filling over the jam, spreading with a spatula to cover, and refrigerate until set, about 2 hours. Arrange strawberries cut side down atop filling. Serve immediately or refrigerate until ready to serve.

Chocolate Hazelnut Tart

Chocolate and hazelnut make this tart amazingly rich, so it's best to use a basic piecrust for this tart.

Makes one 9-inch tart

- Single crust tart or other pie dough (pages 278-292)
- ³/₄ cup brown sugar, packed
- ¼ pound (1 stick) unsalted butter, softened
- 3 eggs
- ³/₄ cup dark corn syrup
- 2 tablespoons molasses
- 2 tablespoons hazelnut liqueur, brandy or apple cider
- 2 teaspoons vanilla extract
- 1²/₃ cups hazelnuts, roasted and chopped
- 5 ounces bittersweet chocolate, chopped
- 3 tablespoons whole wheat flour

Prepare and partially pre-bake the piecrust in a tart pan according to the recipe instructions.

Preheat the oven to 325°F.

In a large bowl, cream the brown sugar and butter until light and fluffy. Add the eggs, one at a time, beating well after each addition. Add the corn syrup, molasses, hazelnut liqueur, and vanilla, and beat until well blended. Stir the hazelnuts, chocolate, and flour into the batter until well blended.

Pour the mixture into the cooled piecrust and bake for 20 minutes or until the crust is a deep golden brown. Cover with aluminum foil very loosely and bake for another 25 to 30 minutes or until the edges of the filling are set but the center still jiggles slightly when shaken. Remove from the oven and cool completely on a wire rack. Cover and refrigerate for at least 2 hours, or overnight, before cutting and serving.

Coffee Coconut Tart

Coconut and chocolate are a popular combination—think macaroons dipped in chocolate. This tart captures the flavor combination wonderfully! For best results when making this tart, first mix one can of coconut cream or milk in a blender until smooth, then measure as called for here. Coconut cream may be found in Asian supermarkets; if you can't find it, substitute full fat coconut milk.

Makes one 9-inch tart

- Single crust basic or other pie dough, with ⅓ cup toasted coconut added with the butter (pages 278-292)
- ¼ cup sugar
- 2 tablespoons arrowroot or cornstarch
- ⅔ cup heavy cream, chilled
- 6 tablespoons coconut cream or coconut milk, measured after stirring the contents of the can very well (see headnote)
- ⅓ cup strong coffee or espresso, at room temperature
- 4 egg yolks
- 1 teaspoon vanilla extract

Topping

- ¾ cup heavy cream, chilled
- ¼ cup coconut cream or milk, measured after stirring the contents of the can very well (see headnote)
- 2 tablespoons confectioners' sugar
- ¼ cup pecans or walnuts, toasted and finely chopped (optional)

Prepare and completely pre-bake the piecrust in a tart pan according to the recipe instructions. Cool completely.

Whisk the sugar and arrowroot or cornstarch in a medium-sized heavy saucepan until well blended. Gradually whisk in ⅔ cup of cream, then the coconut cream, and the coffee. Mix in the egg yolks. Over medium heat, whisk until the mixture thickens and boils, about 7 minutes. Remove from the heat, whisk in the vanilla and cool in the pan for about 20 minutes, stirring occasionally. Spread the filling in the cooled crust and chill until cold, about 2 hours. Remove the tart from the pan and set aside on a plate.

TO MAKE THE TOPPING: beat the heavy cream, coconut cream, and confectioners' sugar until firm peaks form. Spread or pipe over the cold filling. Refrigerate another hour. Sprinkle with nuts.

Blueberry Cream Tart with Mixed Berries

Use whatever fresh fruit appeals to you for this tart, both for the cream filling and the topping. If you're using raspberries or other berries with seeds, strain the puree before putting into the saucepan.

Makes one 9-inch tart

- Single crust sugar tart or other pie dough (pages 278-292)
- 1 egg
- 2 egg yolks
- 2 tablespoons arrowroot or cornstarch
- 2 tablespoons warm water
- 1 (¼ pint) basket fresh blueberries, or frozen unsweetened berries, thawed
- ½ cup sugar
- 4 tablespoons unsalted butter
- 5 tablespoons currant jelly
- 1 (1 pint) strawberries, hulled, stemmed, and halved
- 1 (½ pint) fresh raspberries
- 1 (½ pint) fresh boysenberries
- 1 banana, sliced

Prepare and completely pre-bake the piecrust in a tart pan according to the recipe instructions. Cool completely.

Beat the egg and egg yolks in a small bowl. In a separate small bowl, dissolve the cornstarch in the water and add this mixture to the eggs.

Puree the blueberries and sugar in a blender, then pour into a medium saucepan. Add the butter and bring to simmer over medium to high heat. Slowly drizzle 2 to 3 tablespoons of the hot berry mixture into the egg mixture and whisk to warm up the eggs gradually, then gradually add the remaining berry mixture to the eggs. Return the combination to the saucepan and cook, whisking constantly, until the filling is very thick and just begins to boil, about 3 minutes.

Transfer the filling to the cooled piecrust. Press plastic wrap directly onto the surface of the filling to prevent a skin from forming, and let it sit for 1 hour, then refrigerate for at least 3 hours. Remove the tart from the pan and set aside on a plate.

Melt the currant jelly in a small, heavy saucepan over low heat. Arrange the strawberries, cut side down, on the filling. Fill in with raspberries, boysenberries, and banana slices, and brush melted jelly over the fruit to glaze. Refrigerate until ready to serve.

Apricot Tart

The flavor of apricots goes nicely in a tart, and if you add ¼ teaspoon almond extract to your pastry, it makes your tart soar. If fresh apricots aren't available, use plums or peaches.

Makes one 9-inch tart

- Single crust basic or other pie dough (pages 278-292)
- ½ cup heavy cream
- 1 egg, lightly beaten
- ½ teaspoon almond extract
- ½ teaspoon vanilla extract
- 3 tablespoons honey
- 1 tablespoon whole wheat pastry flour
- About 1½ pounds fresh apricots, pitted and halved (do not peel)
- Confectioners' sugar or ground cinnamon-sugar mix, for sprinkling

Prepare the piecrust dough and refrigerate until you are ready to roll it out.

On a lightly floured surface, roll out the dough into a 12-inch circle. Place over a 9-inch tart pan with removable bottom or pie plate, center, and gently tuck the dough into the pan. Refrigerate until ready to use.

Preheat the oven to 350°F.

In a medium-size bowl, combine the heavy cream, egg, extracts, and honey, and whisk to blend. Whisk in the flour.

Pour the filling over the apricots in a large bowl and stir to combine, then pour this mixture into the piecrust, spreading the apricots around the shell as evenly as possible.

Place the tart pan on a baking sheet and put in the center of the oven. Bake until the filling is firm, about 50 to 55 minutes. Remove from the oven and sprinkle with confectioners' sugar or a cinnamon and sugar mix. Cool before serving.

Peach Crisp with Rye Topping

Rich rye flavor is a natural complement to peaches; both are delicious in this hearty recipe.

Makes 6 to 8 servings

Filling

- 6 or 7 peaches, sliced (about 4 cups)
- 2 tablespoons granulated sugar
- ½ teaspoon ground cinnamon
- 2 tablespoons lemon juice
- 1 tablespoon whole wheat flour

Topping

- ¾ cup rye flour
- ¼ cup whole wheat flour
- ¾ cup brown sugar, packed
- 1 teaspoon ground cinnamon
- ¼ teaspoon ground allspice
- 4 tablespoons unsalted butter, cut into pieces

Preheat the oven to 350°F. Lightly grease a 1½-quart baking dish.

Combine the filling ingredients in a large bowl and let rest for 10 minutes. Pour into the prepared baking dish.

FOR THE TOPPING: combine all of the topping ingredients, except the butter, in a food processor and process until combined. Cut in the butter until the mixture resembles coarse crumbs. Spread over the peaches and bake for 30 minutes or until the topping is brown and peaches bubbly. Serve warm.

Blueberry Rhubarb Crisp

Blueberries are traditional in this recipe, but if you can't find them, feel free to use strawberries.

Makes 6 to 8 servings

Topping

- ¼ cup unbleached white flour
- ¼ cup teff, soy, or barley flour*
- ½ cup brown sugar, packed
- ½ teaspoon ground cinnamon
- ¼ teaspoon ground nutmeg
- 5 tablespoons unsalted butter, chilled and diced

Filling

- ⅓ cup sugar
- ¼ teaspoon ground cinnamon
- 2 tablespoons whole wheat flour
- 2 cups (about ¾ pound) rhubarb, cut into ½-inch pieces
- 2 cups blueberries

Preheat the oven to 375°F. and grease a 2-quart shallow baking dish.

For the topping, combine the flours, brown sugar, cinnamon, and nutmeg in a small bowl. Add the butter and work it into the flour mixture with your fingers until crumbly. Refrigerate while making the filling.

In a small bowl, stir together the sugar, cinnamon, and flour. Add the rhubarb and blueberries, tossing well.

Spread the mixture in the prepared baking dish. Sprinkle topping over the fruit and bake for 35 to 40 minutes, until the topping is brown and the fruit is bubbling. Serve warm.

NOTE: If you use soy flour, the crisp may brown more quickly.

Blueberry Nectarine Crisp

Nectarines go wonderfully with blueberries, but feel free to substitute peaches or even pears in this recipe.

Makes one 13 x 9-inch crisp

Topping

- 1 cup whole wheat flour
- ½ cup unbleached white flour
- ¾ cup brown sugar, packed
- 1 teaspoon *Quatre Epices* (French spice blend) or ¼ teaspoon ground cloves, ½ teaspoon ground allspice, and ½ teaspoon ground cinnamon
- ¼ pound (1 stick) unsalted butter, chilled and diced

Filling

- 2 pounds nectarines (around 6 or 7), halved, pitted, and cut into wedges
- 4 cups blueberries
- 1 tablespoon arrowroot or cornstarch
- ½ cup sugar
- 1 teaspoon vanilla extract
- 1 tablespoon lemon zest

Preheat the oven to 375°F. Grease a 13 x 9 x 2-inch glass baking dish.

To make the topping, combine the flours, brown sugar, and spices in medium bowl and whisk to blend. Add the butter and rub in with your fingertips to make small, moist clumps. Refrigerate while you make the filling.

For the filling, mix the nectarines and blueberries in a large bowl with the cornstarch, sugar, vanilla, and zest, and let it sit for 10 minutes.

Transfer the filling to the prepared baking dish and sprinkle the topping evenly over the fruit. Bake until the nectarines are tender and the topping is crisp and brown, about 40 minutes. Cool for 15 minutes. Serve warm.

Rhubarb-Ginger Crumble

Ginger is not only delicious, but it's good for the stomach and aids digestion—so now you have an excuse for seconds.

Makes one 13 x 9-inch crumble

- 1½ pounds rhubarb stalks, cut into 1-inch pieces
- 1 pear, peeled and cut into thin slices
- 1 tablespoon grated ginger
- 2¼ cups sugar, divided
- 1 cup whole wheat flour
- ¾ cup unbleached white flour
- ¼ teaspoon salt
- 12 tablespoons (1½ stick) unsalted butter, chilled and diced

Preheat the oven to 350°F. Grease a 13 x 9 x 2-inch baking dish.

Put the rhubarb, pear, ginger, and 1¾ cups of the sugar into a medium bowl and gently toss, mixing thoroughly. Transfer to the prepared baking dish.

Combine the flours, salt, and the remaining sugar together in the bowl of a food processor. Scatter the butter into the flour mixture and pulse until it resembles coarse crumbs. Sprinkle the topping evenly over the rhubarb mixture.

Bake until the topping is golden brown and the rhubarb is soft, about 70 minutes. Set aside to cool on a wire rack at least 10 minutes before serving warm, or allow to cool to room temperature.

Apple Walnut Crisp with Oat Topping

Apples, walnuts, and oats make a great and wholesome combination, especially on a cool fall or winter evening.

Makes one 13 x 9-inch crisp

Topping

- ¾ cup whole wheat flour
- ¾ cup unbleached white flour
- 1 cup old-fashioned oats
- 1 cup brown sugar, packed
- 1½ cups walnuts, toasted and chopped
- 1 teaspoon ground cinnamon
- ½ teaspoon salt
- 12 tablespoons (1½ stick) unsalted butter, cut into ½-inch cubes and softened

Filling

- 4½ pounds Granny Smith or other firm apples, peeled, cored, and cut into wedges
- 3 tablespoons lemon juice
- ½ teaspoon ground cinnamon
- ½ cup sugar
- 2 tablespoons whole wheat flour

Preheat the oven to 375°F. Grease a 13 x 9 x 2-inch glass baking dish.

Stir together the flours, oats, brown sugar, walnuts, cinnamon, and salt in a bowl, then blend in the butter with your fingertips until the mixture resembles coarse crumbs. Refrigerate while making the filling.

For the filling, toss the apples with the lemon juice, cinnamon, sugar, and the remaining whole wheat flour in a large bowl. Transfer to the baking dish, spreading evenly.

Crumble the oat topping evenly over the apple mixture and bake until the topping is golden and the apples are tender, about 45 minutes. Cool slightly and serve warm.

Cranberry Apple Crisp with Oatmeal Streusel

Because fresh cranberries are usually only available in the fall, you might want to pick up extra bags and stick them in the freezer for later on in the year. Then you can make this delicious crisp anytime.

Makes one 13 x 9-inch crisp

Topping

- 1 cup brown sugar, packed
- 1 cup old-fashioned oats
- ½ whole wheat flour
- ¼ cup unbleached white flour
- ¼ teaspoon salt
- ¼ pound (1 stick) unsalted butter, chilled and diced

Filling

- 2 (12-ounce) bags cranberries
- 1 cup sugar
- 3 tablespoons apple juice or cider
- 1¼ pounds Granny Smith or other firm apples (about 3 medium), peeled, cored, cut into cubes

Combine the brown sugar, oats, flours, and salt in large bowl and toss to blend. Add the butter and rub in with your fingertips until the mixture resembles crumbs. Refrigerate while preparing the filling.

Preheat the oven to 375°F. Grease a 13 x 9 x 2-inch glass baking dish.

Combine the cranberries, sugar, and apple juice in a large pot. Bring to a boil over medium heat, stirring often for about 2 minutes. Stir in the apples and cook until the cranberries are softened and their juices thicken slightly, about 4 minutes more. Transfer the mixture to the prepared dish and sprinkle on the topping.

Bake until the filling bubbles thickly and the topping is brown, about 35 to 45 minutes. Let cool at least 10 minutes before serving.

Apple Pear Cobbler with Jack Cheese Topping

Great northwest flavors come together in this satisfying cobbler.

Makes one 13 x 9-inch cobbler

Filling

- 3 tablespoons unsalted butter
- 3 pounds pears, peeled, cored, and cut into ½-inch pieces
- 3 pounds Granny Smith or other firm apples, peeled, cored, and cut into wedges
- ¼ cup sugar
- ¼ cup brown sugar, packed
- 2 tablespoons lemon zest
- 2 tablespoons whole wheat flour
- ¼ cup apple juice

Topping

- 1 cup whole wheat flour
- 1 cup unbleached white flour
- 2 tablespoons sugar
- 1 tablespoon baking powder
- ½ teaspoon baking soda
- ½ teaspoon salt
- 10 tablespoons unsalted butter, chilled and diced
- ¾ to 1 cup (packed) shredded Monterey Jack cheese
- ⅔ cup buttermilk

Preheat the oven to 375°F. Grease a 13 x 9 x 2-inch glass baking dish.

Melt the butter in a large, heavy skillet over medium heat. Add the pears and apples and sauté until the fruit is soft, about 7 or 8 minutes. Transfer the fruit to a large bowl and gently mix the sugars, zest, and flour into the fruit. Stir in the apple juice. Spread the filling in the prepared baking dish.

FOR THE TOPPING: in a medium bowl, sift or whisk together the flours, sugar, baking powder, baking soda, and salt. Add the butter and rub in with your fingertips until the mixture resembles coarse crumbs. Stir in the cheese and buttermilk (the dough will be stiff, but if it is unworkable, add a little more buttermilk).

Drop the dough by heaping tablespoonfuls onto the filling. Bake until the filling is bubbling and a tester inserted into the topping comes out clean, about 40 minutes. Serve warm.

Peach Cobbler

Peach cobbler is a truly delicious and traditional American dessert. Use peaches that are ripe, but not too soft, for this recipe. To peel peaches, use a vegetable peeler or drop in boiling water for 15 or 20 seconds, then drop into cold water.

Makes one 8 x 8-inch cobbler

Filling

- 6 to 7 large peaches, peeled, pitted, and cut into 4 or 5 wedges each
- 3 tablespoons sugar
- 1 tablespoon lemon juice
- ¼ teaspoon ground cinnamon
- 1 tablespoon whole wheat flour

Topping

- ¾ cup whole wheat flour
- ⅓ cup unbleached white flour
- ¼ cup sugar
- ½ teaspoon ground cinnamon
- ¼ teaspoon ground allspice
- 1 teaspoon baking powder
- ¼ teaspoon baking soda
- ½ teaspoon salt
- 5 tablespoons unsalted butter, chilled and diced
- ⅓ cup buttermilk

Preheat the oven to 400°F. Grease a 8 x 8-inch glass baking dish.

For the filling: Toss the peaches with the sugar, lemon juice, cinnamon, and flour in a bowl. Spread the mixture in the prepared baking dish and bake for 15 minutes.

For the topping: in a large bowl, sift or whisk together the flours, sugar, cinnamon, baking powder, baking soda, and salt. Blend in the butter with your fingertips or a pastry blender until the mixture resembles coarse crumbs. Stir in the buttermilk until just combined.

Remove the peaches from the oven and drop spoonfuls of topping over them. Don't worry about covering all the peaches, as the topping will spread as it bakes. Bake in the middle of oven until the topping is golden brown, about 25 minutes. Serve warm or at room temperature.

Sweet Potato Cobbler

Oat flour goes very well in the topping for this cobbler.

Makes one 8 x 8-inch cobbler

Filling

- 2 cups cooked, skinned, and diced sweet potatoes
- ½ cup molasses
- ¼ cup brown sugar, packed
- 4 tablespoons unsalted butter, softened
- ½ cup milk
- ½ teaspoon ground allspice
- ½ teaspoon ground cinnamon

Topping

- ½ cup sugar
- 1 tablespoon baking powder
- 1 cup unbleached white flour
- 1½ cups oat, whole wheat, or barley flour, or a combination of the three
- 5 tablespoons unsalted butter, chilled and diced
- 1¼ cups plus 2 tablespoons buttermilk

Preheat the oven to 375°F. Grease an 8 x 8-inch glass baking dish.

Combine the filling ingredients in a large bowl, and blend thoroughly. Pour into the prepared baking dish and bake for 10 minutes while preparing the topping.

To make the topping: combine the sugar, baking powder, and flours in a food processor. Cut in the butter until it resembles coarse crumbs. Remove the contents to a bowl and add the 1¼ cups buttermilk, adding the additional buttermilk if needed, and combine to form a dough.

Remove the cobbler from the oven and spoon the biscuit topping over the top, in heaping tablespoons. Return to the oven and bake for 25 minutes, or until the top is brown. Allow to cool 15 minutes before serving.

Skillet Cherry Cobbler

Traditionally, the French leave the pits in cherries when making Cherry Clafoutis. Here, we suggest you do the same. The nutty flavor of the pits adds a lovely taste to this cherry cobbler. If you don't remove the pits, slice each cherry once to the release juices, and be sure to warn your guests.

Makes one 8-inch round cobbler

Filling

- 4 cups fresh, frozen, or jarred cherries, rinsed, and drained (thawed, if frozen)
- 2 tablespoons arrowroot or cornstarch
- ½ cup sugar
- 2 tablespoons fresh lemon juice
- 1 tablespoon lemon zest
- ¼ teaspoon almond extract

Topping

- ¾ cup whole wheat flour
- ⅓ cup unbleached white flour
- ¼ cup sugar
- ¼ teaspoon ground cinnamon
- 1 teaspoon baking powder
- ¼ teaspoon baking soda
- ½ teaspoon salt
- 5 tablespoons unsalted butter, chilled and diced
- ⅓ cup buttermilk
- Ground cinnamon and sugar mixed for dusting, optional

Preheat the oven to 350°F.

If you are pitting the cherries, do so over a bowl so you can catch any juices. Toss cherries with the cornstarch, sugar, lemon juice, zest, and almond extract.

In a large bowl, sift or whisk together the flours, sugar, cinnamon, baking powder, baking soda, and salt. Blend in the butter with your fingertips or a pastry blender until the mixture resembles coarse crumbs. Stir in the buttermilk until just combined.

Set an 8-inch cast-iron skillet or flameproof baking dish over a medium flame, and add the cherry mixture, bringing it to a boil, stirring until slightly thickened.

Remove from the heat, drop the batter by heaping tablespoons onto the cherry mixture, and sprinkle with the cinnamon-sugar mixture.

Place the skillet in the oven and bake for 25 minutes, or until the top is golden. Serve warm or at room temperature.

Cookies

The earliest incarnation of what we now know as the cookie is thought to date back to the seventh century when Persian cooks—among the first in the world to cultivate sugar—made a sort of flatbread/cake with sugar. However, we suspect most cookie lovers hold the time period around 1937 in the highest esteem, since that is when Ruth Wakefield, owner of the Toll House Restaurant in Whitman, Massachusetts, invented the chocolate chip cookie. Her original recipe came about as many great ideas do—she was out of baker's chocolate so she substituted a bar of semisweet chocolate, which she chopped into chunks. She thought the chocolate would spread throughout the batter—instead it remained in chunks, to her customers' delight.

We've taken that famous Tollhouse idea and a number of other classic and not-so-classic recipes, added ingredients and ideas from the Bob's Red Mill family and friends, and now have some 75 cookie recipes using a variety of whole grains. The recipes in this section range from gluten-free cookies made with rice and other whole grain flours to whole wheat Tollhouse, yet another adaptation of Ruth's classic 1937 invention.

Whole grains make great cookies but may produce a slightly lower volume compared to cookie recipes with unbleached white flour. To adapt a family favorite, start with half whole wheat or whole wheat pastry flour, add a pinch more liquid, and keep an eye on the baking time, which may be a little shorter. You'll likely end up with a lot of delicious experiments until you get your whole grain favorite just the way you want it.

Unless otherwise specified in the recipe, always bake your cookies in the center rack of your oven. If you're baking two sheets at a time, bake one on a rack on the second rung from the bottom, and the other on the top rung. If you're baking in a convection oven, drop the temperature by 25 degrees, and the time by about 10 percent. If you are baking in a conventional oven, you may want to turn the cookies—reverse the baking sheet front to back—about halfway through the cooking time. That's because the front of a conventional oven will be cooler than the back and turning the baking sheet helps prevent uneven cooking.

Substitutions, talked about in the front of the book, are welcome in cookie baking. You may use margarine or shortening in place of butter with the understanding that some recipes that rely heavily on a butter taste— for example, butter cookies and shortbread—will suffer in quality. Applesauce is another substitution for fat and liquid that generally works well in many cookie recipes.

Many of these recipes call for creaming the butter or shortening, sometimes with the sugar. Creaming is simply beating the ingredient(s) until they are well aerated and have a light lemony color and fluffy texture. Unsalted butter is always best for creaming and for flavor, but if you use margarine, use the stick type rather than the softer tub margarine that contains more oil, and won't cream as well. We don't recommend using applesauce as a substitute for those recipes in which creaming is important to the final product.

You can make other easy substitutions in drop cookie recipes. If you want more chocolate in a recipe, substitute a tablespoon of cocoa or carob powder for the same amount of flour. For a mocha flavor, substitute coffee extract for vanilla. Chopped dried fruit also works well in place of chocolate chips.

When a recipe calls for a high proportion of fat, you may want to use a food processor to mix the ingredients. Begin the process as you would a pastry—mix the dry ingredients by pulsing, then cut in the cold fat until it resembles pebbles. Drizzle in the liquid—beaten egg, milk, water, etc.—and pulse just a few times until it just comes together. Don't allow the dough to form a ball in the food processor; instead, remove it and form it into a ball with your hands.

A few more tips:

- Dough with a high fat content should be chilled to firm it up.
- Keep in mind that the times given for baking cookies are the minimum, since over-baking cookies for even a minute or two may result in dry or even burned cookies. Don't expect the cookies to necessarily be ready at the lowest time stated, but check for doneness at that time.
- Unless otherwise instructed, eggs and other ingredients should be at room temperature. If you are storing your whole grain flour in the refrigerator, take it out at least 15 minutes before starting so it is room temperature, as well. If you are in a hurry, remember that broken eggs come to room temperature faster than those left in the shell.
- Always preheat the oven before baking and never put more than 2 baking sheets in the oven at once, since this may cause the temperature to drop too low.
- Rolled cookies should always be chilled before cutting and baking, usually for 1 hour. If chilled longer than 1 hour, you might need to let the dough sit out for 5 to 10 minutes before cutting. If you are in a hurry, you can place the dough in the freezer for 20 minutes for faster chilling.
- Cutting rolled cookies too thick—more than $\frac{1}{3}$ inch—may result in soggy centers. Conversely, cookies cut too thin will be fragile and bake more quickly, so keep an eye on them if your preference is a thinner cookie.
- If the dough is too sticky, roll it out between two sheets of parchment paper or wax paper. A simple trick to keep wax paper from sliding is to put a little water on the counter.
- There are a few recipes in this chapter that call for a pastry bag. Pastry bags, which used to be made of cotton canvas, are now made of nylon, which makes for easier clean up. They are handy, not just for piping uncooked cookie dough, but also for decorating cookies with icing. If you don't have a pastry bag, snipping the corner off of a small plastic zip-top bag makes a good substitute.
- When making bar cookies, use non-stick pans with a dull finish rather than a shiny one to give your cookies a crispier texture. An ovenproof glass dish generally works well as a substitute, but does take a little longer to heat up and retains heat longer after being removed from the oven.
- For easier cutting, you may wish to score bar cookies baked in pans, such as shortbread, before placing

them in the oven. Also, lining the pan you are using for bars with parchment paper makes it much easier to remove the bars from the pan. If you use wax paper, you will need to add vegetable oil to the paper to prevent sticking.

- A wire rack allows air to circulate around the cookies, keeping moisture from being trapped against a baking sheet or plate. Moisture can make cookies soggy. Some cookies need to stay on the baking sheet for a few minutes before being transferred to a wire rack, or they may need to stay there and cool completely. Place that sheet or dish on a wire rack if possible.

Problem Solving

If your dough won't hold its shape, it may have too much liquid or fat, or might not have been chilled long enough. Try chilling the dough or kneading in a little more flour. Dough with too much fat is also the reason for cookies that spread too much in the oven. Conversely, if your dough is dry or won't hold together there is not enough liquid or fat. Simple kneading may bring the dough together, or knead in a little milk or soft butter. When cookies come out dry and crumbly, too little liquid, a too hot oven, or too long a baking time are generally the culprits.

Cookies that are not evenly cooked may have been made of uneven sizes, placed too near the edge of the baking sheet, or the front of the oven was too cool and the baking sheet needed to be turned around halfway through the baking time.

If your cookies are stuck to the baking sheet, the problem may have been too little grease, or they might have been greased with salted butter. Cookies that crumble easily probably contain a high fat quotient, so make sure you allowed them to cool for a few minutes on the sheet to firm up before transferring them to a wire rack.

If the end result is cookies that are burned at the base, but not on top, you may be baking the cookies at too low a temperature, in a place too low in the oven, or on baking sheets that are too dark.

Cinnamon Wafers

A thin wafer that is thick with cinnamon flavor.

Makes approximately 6 or 7 dozen wafers

- 1 cup unbleached white flour
- ½ cup whole wheat pastry flour
- ¼ cup barley flour, or substitute same amount whole wheat pastry flour
- 2½ teaspoons ground cinnamon
- ½ pound (2 sticks) unsalted butter, softened
- 1 cup sugar
- 1 egg, separated
- 3 tablespoons turbinado sugar

In a large bowl, sift or whisk together the flours and cinnamon.

Cream the butter with the sugar until light lemon-yellow in color, about 4 minutes. Beat in the egg yolk until well combined, scraping down the sides of the bowl as needed.

Whisk the flour mixture into the butter mixture until just combined. Cover the bowl with plastic wrap and refrigerate for at least 1 hour.

Preheat the oven to 350°F. Lightly oil 2 baking sheets or line them with parchment paper.

Beat the egg white with 2 teaspoons cold water and set aside.

Roll the dough into balls slightly less than 1-inch around, then flatten on the prepared sheets into 2½-inch circles. Brush with the egg wash and sprinkle with a little turbinado sugar.

Bake for 10 minutes, or until the edges turn brown. Let the cookies rest on the pan for a few minutes before cooling on a wire rack.

Oatmeal-Raisin Refrigerator Cookies

These cookies have a great old-fashioned oat flavor. We've made these using fructose, a pure form of natural sugar made from corn syrup. It tastes twice as sweet as sugar so you can use half as much, and cut calories.

Makes approximately 32 cookies

- ½ pound (2 sticks) unsalted butter, softened
- ¾ cup fructose, or 1¼ cup sugar
- 2 teaspoons vanilla extract
- 2 eggs, lightly beaten
- ¾ cup unbleached white flour
- ¾ cup whole wheat flour
- ¼ teaspoon ground nutmeg
- 1 teaspoon baking soda
- 1½ cups old-fashioned rolled oats
- ½ cup golden raisins
- 1 cup walnuts, chopped

In a large bowl, cream the butter with the fructose and vanilla until light and fluffy. Beat in the eggs one at a time until well incorporated.

In another bowl, whisk together the flours, nutmeg, and baking soda. Gradually beat the flour mixture, about ½ cup at a time, into the butter mixture. Stir in the oats, raisins, and walnuts.

Divide the dough in half and roll to form two logs about 10-inches each. Wrap each log in plastic wrap or wax paper and refrigerate for at least 6 hours or overnight.

Preheat the oven to 350°F. Lightly oil a baking sheet or line it with parchment paper.

Slice the dough logs into ½-inch thick slices and place them on the prepared cookie sheet.

Bake approximately 15 to 20 minutes, or until lightly brown. Cool for 5 minutes before removing from the cookie sheet and cooling on a wire rack.

Double Chocolate (or Double Carob) Cookies

These cookies hit the spot whenever you're in the mood for chocolate. Turbinado sugar gives them a nice crunch.

Makes approximately 3 dozen cookies

- 12 tablespoons (1½ stick) unsalted butter, softened
- 1 cup turbinado, or ¾ cup plus 1 tablespoon brown sugar, packed
- 2 eggs
- 1 teaspoon vanilla extract
- 1½ cups whole wheat pastry flour
- ½ cup soy flour
- ½ cup cocoa powder or toasted carob powder
- ½ teaspoon baking soda
- ½ teaspoon baking powder
- ½ teaspoon salt
- 6 ounces chocolate or carob chips
- ½ cup walnuts, chopped

Preheat the oven to 350°F. Lightly oil 2 baking sheets or line them with parchment paper.

In a large bowl, cream the butter with the brown sugar, eggs, and vanilla, scraping down the side of the bowl a few times.

In another bowl, whisk or sift together the flours, cocoa powder, baking soda, baking powder, and salt, then add to the butter mixture and stir. Stir in the chocolate chips and walnuts.

Drop the dough by teaspoonfuls about 1½ inches apart onto the prepared cookie sheets and bake about 8 minutes, or until done.

Quinoa Brownies

GLUTEN-FREE

Even though these brownies have far less fat than traditional brownies, they still taste chocolaty, rich, and amazing.

Makes approximately 20 brownies

- Scant ½ cup vegetable oil
- 4½ ounces semi-sweet chocolate, chopped
- 2 eggs, at room temperature
- 1 teaspoon vanilla extract
- ¾ cup quinoa flour
- 3 tablespoons rice flour
- 1 teaspoon baking powder
- ½ cup sugar

Preheat the oven to 400°F. Lightly oil an 8 x 8-inch baking pan or dish.

Stir the oil with the chocolate in the top of a double boiler set over simmering water, until the chocolate is melted and the mixture is smooth. Remove from heat.

Beat the eggs and add to the chocolate, whisking vigorously. Beat in the vanilla and let the mixture cool until it's warm.

Combine the flours, baking powder, and sugar, then beat into the chocolate mixture to form a dough.

Spread the dough into the prepared pan and bake for 10 to 15 minutes. Allow to cool then cut into squares.

Cherry Yogurt Cookies

These cookies are wonderfully delicate and full of cherry zing. Add chocolate chips for an even better alternative—cherry chocolate chip cookies.

Makes approximately 2 dozen cookies

1½ cups whole wheat flour

½ cup unbleached white flour

2 teaspoons baking powder

1¼ teaspoons ground cinnamon

1½ cups brown sugar, packed

1¼ cups rolled oats

1 cup dried cherries, chopped (or other dried fruit)

1½ tablespoons slivered almonds

2 cups plus 1 tablespoon plain yogurt

¼ cup vegetable oil

Preheat the oven to 350°F. Lightly oil 2 baking sheets or line them with parchment paper.

In a large bowl, sift the flours together with the baking powder and cinnamon. Whisk in the sugar and oats, then stir in the cherries and almonds.

Beat the yogurt with the oil, then stir add to flour mixture to make a dough.

Roll into small balls and place on the prepared baking sheet. Flatten and bake for 17 to 20 minutes, or until firm and brown. Transfer to a wire rack to cool.

Bran Nut Drops

These little cookies are packed with vitamins—and they taste great.

Makes approximately 3 dozen cookies

- 1 egg
- 3 tablespoons orange juice
- ¼ cup vegetable shortening or unsalted butter, cut into pieces
- ¼ cup honey
- ½ cup plain yogurt
- 2 teaspoons vanilla extract
- 1½ tablespoons orange zest
- ¼ cup wheat germ
- 1¼ cups whole wheat pastry flour
- ¼ cup wheat bran
- ½ teaspoon baking soda
- ½ cup walnuts, chopped

Preheat the oven to 350°F. Lightly oil 2 baking sheets or line them with parchment paper.

In a large bowl, beat together the egg with the orange juice, shortening, honey, yogurt, and vanilla. Stir in the zest.

In a medium bowl, whisk together the wheat germ, flour, bran, and baking soda. Add to the egg mixture just until combined. Stir in the walnuts.

Drop teaspoon-sized pieces of the dough onto the prepared cookie sheet and flatten slightly. Bake for 15 to 18 minutes, or until browned.

Amy's Dairy Free Delights

Amy Loy of Portland created these delicious egg- and dairy-free cookies for her kids. Store these in an airtight container and they will stay soft.

Makes approximately 3 dozen cookies

- 1 cup dairy-free margarine or vegetable shortening
- 1 cup sugar
- 1 cup brown sugar
- 1 teaspoon vanilla extract
- 3 tablespoons vegetable oil
- 3 tablespoons water
- 2 teaspoons plus 1 teaspoon baking powder
- 1 cup whole wheat flour
- 1½ cups unbleached white flour
- 1 teaspoon baking soda
- ⅛ teaspoon salt
- 2 cups quick cooking oats, or rolled oats for a chewier cookie
- 1 cup chocolate or carob chips

Preheat the oven to 350°F. Lightly oil a baking sheet or cover with parchment paper.

In a large bowl, cream together the margarine with the sugars until light in color, about 4 minutes. In a separate bowl, combine the vanilla with the vegetable oil, water and the 2 teaspoons of baking powder and stir until frothy, then add to the margarine mixture.

In a large bowl, sift or whisk together the flours, baking soda, remaining baking powder and salt, and then stir into the margarine mixture to form a batter. Stir in the oats and chocolate chips.

Spoon heaping tablespoons of batter onto the prepared sheet. Bake for 9 minutes, or until lightly browned. Cool on baking sheet to firm up, then remove to a wire rack to cool completely.

The Whole Wheat Tollhouse Cookie

Here is our version of Ruth Wakefield's classic from 1937, made a bit more nutritious.

Makes 4 to 5 dozen cookies

- 1 cup whole wheat pastry flour
- ½ teaspoon baking soda
- ½ teaspoon salt
- 10 tablespoons unsalted butter, softened
- 1 cup brown sugar, packed
- 1 egg, lightly beaten
- 1½ teaspoons vanilla extract
- ½ cup old-fashioned rolled oats
- 1 cup chocolate chips
- ½ cup walnuts, chopped

Preheat the oven to 350°F. Lightly oil a baking sheet or cover with parchment paper.

In a large bowl, sift or whisk together the flour, baking soda, and salt. Cream the butter with the brown sugar until light in color, about 4 minutes. Beat in the egg until well incorporated. Stir in the vanilla.

Add the flour mixture to the butter mixture and blend well. Stir in the oats, chocolate chips, and nuts.

Drop by teaspoonfuls onto the prepared cookie sheet. Bake for 10 minutes, or until brown. Cool on a wire rack.

Spring Cookies

These colorful cookies are an Italian Easter tradition, but you don't need to wait until spring to enjoy them.

Makes 24 cookies

Dough

- 3½ cups unbleached white flour
- 2 cups whole wheat pastry flour
- 2 teaspoons baking powder
- ½ teaspoon salt
- 6 eggs
- 1 cup sugar
- 12 tablespoons (1½ stick) unsalted butter, melted and cooled
- 2 tablespoons vanilla extract

Icing

- 4 cups confectioners' sugar
- 3 tablespoons water
- 1½ tablespoons lemon juice
- Nonpareils, for sprinkling

Preheat the oven to 350°F. Lightly oil 2 baking sheets or cover with parchment paper.

In a medium bowl, sift or whisk together the flours, baking powder, and salt. In a large bowl, cream together the eggs with the sugar until light lemon-yellow in color. Add the butter in a steady stream, whisking to incorporate. Whisk in the vanilla extract.

Fold the flour mixture into the wet ingredients until just incorporated.

Turn the dough out onto a floured surface and knead just until the dough comes together. Divide into 24 pieces. Make a roughly 6-inch rope out of each piece, then pinch the ends together to form a circle.

Place the circles on the prepared baking sheets and bake for about 20 minutes, or until puffy and golden brown.

For the icing, combine all ingredients in a saucepan over low heat and whisk until well blended and just warm. Add more water or sugar to achieve the consistency of syrup. Dip the cookies in the icing and sprinkle with nonpareils.

Bob's Protein Bars

Expensive store-made protein bars are no match for these delicious homemade ones.

Makes approximately 2 dozen bars

- ½ cup quinoa flour
- 2 tablespoons unbleached white flour
- 1¼ cups soy protein powder
- ¾ cup oat bran
- 2¼ cups rolled oats
- 1 teaspoon ground cinnamon
- ¼ teaspoon ground allspice
- 1 teaspoon salt
- ¾ cup brown sugar, packed
- ¼ cup peanut butter
- 1½ tablespoons vegetable oil
- 2 cups plain yogurt
- 2½ teaspoons vanilla extract
- ½ cup pecans, chopped
- ½ cup semisweet chocolate chips
- ½ cup sunflower seeds, optional

Preheat the oven to 350°F. Lightly oil a 13 x 9-inch baking pan or dish. Lightly oil a baking sheet or cover with parchment paper.

In a large bowl, whisk or sift together the flours, protein powder, oat bran, rolled oats, cinnamon, allspice, salt, and brown sugar.

In a large microwave-safe bowl, whisk the peanut butter together with the oil. Microwave for a few seconds until soft, but not heated. Combine with the yogurt and vanilla, then add to the dry ingredients along with the pecans, chocolate chips, and sunflower seeds. Mix the dough thoroughly (it will be thick).

Pat the dough into the prepared pan and bake for 18 minutes, until lightly browned and a tester comes out clean. Remove from the oven and cut into bars. Place the bars on the baking sheet and return to the oven for 15 minutes or until brown around the edges. Place the bars on a wire rack to cool. Store in an airtight container for 3 or 4 days, or freeze for up to a month.

Bob's Energy Boosters

These easy-to-make bars make for a quick pick me up.

Makes approximately 10 bars

- ³/₄ cup brown sugar, packed
- 3 tablespoons maple syrup
- 12 tablespoons (1½ stick) unsalted butter, softened
- 2 cups rolled oats
- ½ cup hazelnuts, chopped
- ⅓ cup dried apricots, chopped

Preheat the oven to 325°F. Lightly oil an 8 x 8-inch baking dish.

In a medium saucepan, combine the brown sugar, syrup, and butter. Stir over low heat until the butter melts and the mixture is well blended. Remove from heat and stir in the oats, hazelnuts, and apricots and combine well.

Spread the batter in the prepared pan, score the bars, and bake for 25 minutes or until golden brown. Cut through the scored lines, then cool to room temperature before removing from pan.

Chocolate Mint Teff Cookies

GLUTEN-FREE

Like a chocolate mint in a cookie. Teff makes for superbly crisp cookies. It also makes for a very crumbly cookie, so let them cool completely if you want to keep them in one piece.

Makes about 18 cookies

- ¼ pound (1 stick) unsalted butter, softened
- ½ cup honey
- ½ teaspoon vanilla extract
- ¼ teaspoon mint extract, peppermint schnapps, or simple syrup made with a few fresh mint leaves (see below)
- 1 cup teff flour
- 1 teaspoon baking powder
- ¼ cup cocoa powder
- ⅛ teaspoon salt
- ¾ cup chocolate chips, or chopped hazelnuts or walnuts

Preheat the oven to 350°F. Lightly oil 2 baking sheets or cover with parchment paper.

In a medium bowl, cream together the butter and honey until smooth, then stir in the vanilla and mint extracts.

Whisk together the flour, baking powder, cocoa powder, and salt, then stir in the chocolate chips or walnuts. Combine the flour mixture with the butter mixture until blended.

Drop the dough by rounded tablespoons onto the prepared cookie sheet, about 2 inches apart. Bake until the cookies are golden brown, about 15 minutes. Cool completely before moving to a plate.

SIMPLE SYRUP

To make simple syrup, combine 1 cup sugar with ⅔ cup water and ¼ teaspoon cream of tartar in a saucepan. Stir with a wooden spoon over low heat until most of the sugar is dissolved and the mixture is hot, but not simmering. Stop stirring, brush down the insides of the pan with a wet pastry brush, and then bring the mixture to a low simmer. Cover and simmer very gently for 2 minutes. Uncover, remove from the heat, and allow to cool. Store in a covered jar in the refrigerator for up to 6 months.

Whole Wheat Vanilla Wafers

These delicious wafers are full of vanilla flavor.

Makes approximately 4 dozen wafers

- ¾ cup whole wheat pastry flour
- ¾ cup unbleached white flour
- 1 teaspoon baking powder
- ¼ teaspoon salt
- ¼ pound (1 stick) unsalted butter, softened
- ⅔ cup sugar
- 2 eggs
- 3½ teaspoons vanilla extract

Preheat the oven to 400°F. Lightly oil 2 baking sheets or cover with parchment paper.

In a medium bowl, whisk together the flours, baking powder, and salt.

Cream the butter with the sugar until light lemon-yellow in color, about 2 minutes. Beat in the eggs one at a time, scraping down the sides of the bowl after each addition. Stir in the vanilla. Stir in the flour mixture to make a dough.

Drop scant tablespoons of dough on the prepared sheets, flatten slightly, and bake about 10 minutes or until golden. Cool on a wire rack.

Apricot Bars

If you like apricot, you'll love these bars, which are basically apricot butter glazing a cookie. Yum.

Makes 3 dozen bars

Topping

- 2 cups dried apricots
- 1½ cups water
- 1¼ cups sugar

Base

- 1 cup unbleached white flour
- 1 cup whole wheat flour
- ½ cup confectioners' sugar
- ½ pound (2 sticks) unsalted butter, softened

Preheat the oven to 350°F. Oil a 13 x 9-inch baking dish.

In a saucepan, combine the apricots, water, and sugar and bring to a boil. Cover and simmer until the fruit is soft enough to mash, about 20 minutes. Puree in a blender or food processor.

In a large bowl, sift or whisk together the flours with the confectioners' sugar.

In a medium bowl, cream the butter until light, about 2 minutes. Beat the flour mixture into the butter about ½ cup at a time. Press the mixture into the prepared dish, then top with the apricot mixture.

Bake for about 20 to 25 minutes, or until golden brown. Cool to room temperature and cut into bars.

Cranberry Orange Oatmeal Cookies

These filling cookies combine the tangy-tart flavors of cranberry and orange with the wonderful flavor and texture of oatmeal.

Makes 4 to 5 dozen cookies

- 1 cup whole wheat flour
- 1 cup unbleached white flour
- 2 teaspoons baking powder
- ½ teaspoon baking soda
- 1 teaspoon salt
- 2 cups quick cooking rolled oats
- ½ pound (2 sticks) unsalted butter, softened
- 1½ cups sugar
- 2 eggs
- 1 teaspoon vanilla extract
- 1 cup cranberries, chopped
- ¾ cup raisins
- 1 tablespoon orange zest

Preheat the oven to 350°F. Lightly oil a baking sheet or cover with parchment paper.

In a large bowl, whisk together the flours, baking powder, baking soda, salt, and oats.

In another large bowl, cream together the butter and sugar until light lemon-yellow, about 4 minutes. Beat in the eggs one at a time, scraping down the sides of the bowl as needed. Stir in the vanilla. Add the flour mixture to the butter mixture and stir until mixed well. Fold in the cranberries, raisins, and zest.

Drop by teaspoonfuls onto the prepared baking sheet. Bake for 10 to 12 minutes, or until the edges are browned. Cool on a wire rack.

Old-Fashioned Molasses Cookies

Versions of molasses cookies, very popular in the south, have been around a long time. They were very popular during World War II when sugar was rationed. Here is our healthier version that tastes just as great as the originals.

Makes approximately 40 cookies

- 12 tablespoons (1½ stick) unsalted butter, softened
- ⅓ cup sugar
- 1½ cups unbleached white flour
- 1½ cups whole wheat pastry flour
- 1½ teaspoons baking soda
- 1 teaspoon salt
- 1 teaspoon ground cinnamon
- ½ teaspoon ground ginger
- ¼ teaspoon ground cloves
- ½ teaspoon ground allspice
- ⅔ cup molasses

Preheat the oven to 350°F. Lightly oil a baking sheet or cover with parchment paper.

In a large bowl, cream together the butter with the sugar until light lemon-yellow, about 3 or 4 minutes.

In a medium bowl, sift together the flours with the baking soda, salt, and spices. Beat half of the flour mixture into the butter and sugar, then beat in half the molasses, scraping down the sides of the bowl as needed. Repeat with remaining flour and molasses.

Divide the dough into three parts, wrap each in plastic wrap, and refrigerate for at least 1 hour, or overnight.

Remove one piece of dough from the refrigerator and let soften for 5 minutes. Roll out to a 10-inch square and then cut with a cookie cutter into 3-inch cookies. Press scraps together and chill, and repeat with remaining dough and scraps.

Bake for 10 minutes or until golden. Cool on wire racks.

Apple Cookies

These cookies are a little like a piece of apple pie, but much quicker to make.

Makes approximately 2 dozen cookies

- 10 tablespoons unsalted butter, softened
- 3/4 cup sugar
- 2 egg yolks
- 1 cup whole wheat flour
- 1 cup unbleached white flour
- 2 teaspoons baking powder
- 1/2 teaspoon ground cinnamon
- 1/4 teaspoon ground allspice
- 1/8 teaspoon ground cardamom
- 1/2 cup dried apple, chopped

Preheat the oven to 375°F. Lightly oil a baking sheet or cover with parchment paper.

In a large bowl, cream the butter with the sugar until light, about 4 minutes. Beat in the egg yolks.

In another large bowl, sift or whisk together the flours, baking powder, and spices, then add to the butter mixture along with the apple pieces.

On a lightly floured surface, roll the dough to about 1/4-inch thickness. Cut your cookies into whatever shape you'd like, and place them on the prepared baking sheet. Bake for about 10 to 15 minutes, or until lightly browned. Cool on a wire rack.

Little Maple Pecan Wafers

These are airy little cookies, thin and brittle, with a strong pecan-maple flavor.

Makes approximately 4 dozen wafers

- ¼ pound (1 stick) unsalted butter, softened
- 1 cup pure maple syrup
- ¾ cup sifted whole wheat pastry flour
- ⅓ cup sifted unbleached white flour
- ½ teaspoon salt
- ½ teaspoon baking powder
- ¼ teaspoon baking soda
- ½ cup pecans, finely chopped

Preheat the oven to 350°F. Lightly oil 2 cookie sheets or line them with parchment paper.

In a saucepan set over low heat, melt the butter and then stir in the maple syrup until blended. Remove from heat.

In a large bowl, sift or whisk together the flours with the salt, baking powder, and baking soda. Stir into the butter mixture along with the pecans, just to blend. Let stand for a minute or two to thicken slightly.

Spoon teaspoonfuls of the batter onto the prepared pans and bake for 10 to 12 minutes, until browned. Allow to cool on the baking sheet, or transfer to a wire rack after 15 minutes.

Whole Wheat Oatmeal Cookies

Chewy and delicious, just what you'd expect from a perennial favorite. Add your choice of raisins, carob chips, chocolate chips, or chopped walnuts to the dough. Just add ½ to ¾ cup of your addition to the batter along with the oats.

Makes approximately 3 dozen cookies

- ½ pound (2 sticks) unsalted butter, softened
- 1 cup brown sugar, packed
- 2 eggs
- 2 cups sifted whole wheat flour
- 1 teaspoon salt
- 1 teaspoon baking soda
- ½ teaspoon ground allspice
- 1 teaspoon ground cinnamon
- 1 teaspoon ground nutmeg
- ½ cup plus 2 tablespoons milk
- 2 cups quick-cooking rolled oats

Preheat the oven to 350°F. Lightly oil a baking sheet.

In a large bowl, cream together the butter and brown sugar, then beat in the eggs one at a time, scraping down the sides of the bowl as needed.

In another bowl sift the flour, salt, baking soda, and spices. Add half the flour mixture to the butter mixture, then half the milk, whisking to incorporate. Repeat with the rest of the flour and milk. Gently fold in the oats.

Drop the dough by rounded tablespoons onto the prepared cookie sheet, about 2 inches apart. Bake until the cookies are golden brown, but the centers are still soft, about 10 minutes. Transfer to a wire rack to cool.

Double-Wheat Cookies

These whole grain cookies are so buttery, rich, and yummy, you'll want to make them again and again.

Makes approximately 36 cookies

- ½ pound (2 sticks) unsalted butter, softened
- ½ cup brown sugar, packed
- ¼ cup wheat germ, toasted, plus more for topping
- 1¾ cups whole wheat flour
- 1 teaspoon baking powder

Preheat the oven to 350°F. Lightly oil 2 cookie sheets.

In a large bowl, cream together the butter, brown sugar, and the wheat germ until light and fluffy.

In a separate bowl, sift or whisk together the flour with the baking powder, then stir into the butter mixture to form a batter.

Form the dough into 1-inch balls. Roll each ball in the remaining wheat germ. Place on the prepared cookie sheets and flatten with the tines of a fork.

Bake for 10 to 12 minutes until brown. Remove from the cookie sheet to cool on wire rack.

5-Grain Daybreak Cookies

A wonderful way to start your day, these cookies are full of healthful benefits.

Makes approximately 24 cookies

- 2¼ cups unbleached white flour
- 1½ teaspoons baking soda
- 1½ teaspoons salt
- 1½ cups unsalted butter, softened
- 2¼ cups brown sugar, packed
- 1½ teaspoons vanilla extract
- ¾ cup water
- 3 eggs
- 3 cups 5-Grain rolled cereal
- 1 cup coconut flakes
- 1 cup cranberries, fresh or dried
- 1 cup pecan halves, coarsely chopped
- 1 cup golden raisins

Preheat the oven to 375°F. Lightly oil 2 cookie sheets.

In a medium bowl, sift or whisk together the flour, baking soda, and salt.

In a large bowl, cream the butter, brown sugar, vanilla, and water. In a separate bowl, beat the eggs, then add them to the butter mixture. Stir the flour mixture into the butter mixture, then add remaining ingredients and mix well.

Divide the dough into approximately 24 balls and press down with the tines of a fork. Bake for 10 to 12 minutes, or until the cookies are soft in the center and the edges are lightly brown.

Whole Wheat Brownies

These brownies are just as rich and chocolaty as the original recipe.

Makes approximately 24 brownies

- ²/₃ cup whole wheat flour
- ¹/₃ cup unbleached white pastry flour
- 1 teaspoon baking powder
- ¹/₄ pound (1 stick) unsalted butter, softened, plus 1 tablespoon, melted
- ²/₃ cup honey
- 2 eggs, lightly beaten
- 1 teaspoon vanilla extract
- ¹/₂ cup carob powder, toasted, or cocoa powder
- 3 tablespoons milk
- 1 cup walnuts, chopped
- ¹/₂ cup carob or chocolate chips
- ¹/₂ cup golden raisins

Preheat the oven to 350°F. Lightly grease a 9 x 9-inch baking pan.

In a medium bowl, sift or whisk together the flours and baking powder.

In a large bowl, cream together the ¹/₄ pound of butter with the honey until smooth, then add the eggs one at a time, scraping down the sides of the bowl after each addition. Beat in the vanilla and blend well.

In a small bowl, combine the carob powder with the melted butter and the milk. Pour into the honey mixture, blending well. Whisk in the flour mixture until smooth. Stir in the walnuts, carob chips and raisins.

Pour the batter into the prepared baking pan. Bake for 25 minutes or until a tester comes out clean. Let cool for at least 20 minutes before cutting into bars.

Walnut Wedding Cookies

The popular Mexican Wedding Cookies are made with walnuts here, and, of course, whole grains.

Makes approximately 30 cookies

- ½ pound (2 sticks) unsalted butter, softened
- 1½ cups confectioners' sugar, divided
- 1 teaspoon vanilla extract
- 1¾ cups unbleached white flour
- 1 cup whole wheat pastry flour
- 2 cups walnuts, toasted and finely chopped

Preheat the oven to 375°F. Lightly oil 2 cookie sheets.

In a large bowl, cream the butter until light, about 4 minutes. Beat in 1 cup of the sugar along with the vanilla and beat another minute or so.

In a medium bowl, sift or whisk together the flours then add to the butter mixture ⅓ cup at a time, beating well after each addition, until a dough forms. Add the walnuts with the last of the flour.

Form the dough into small balls, about 1 inch in size. Roll in the remaining confectioners' sugar. Place on the prepared sheets and bake for 10 to 15 minutes, or until they start to brown. Cool on the baking sheets for 15 minutes then transfer to a wire rack.

Barley Brownies

Barley makes for surprisingly light brownies.

Makes approximately 16 brownies

- 2 eggs, slightly beaten
- 6 tablespoons carob powder or cocoa powder
- 1 cup brown sugar, packed
- ½ cup vegetable oil
- 1 teaspoon vanilla extract
- ¾ cup barley flour
- ½ teaspoon baking powder
- ¾ teaspoon salt
- ¾ cup walnuts or pecans, chopped

Preheat the oven to 350°F. Lightly oil an 8 x 8-inch baking dish.

In a large bowl, cream together the eggs with the carob, sugar, oil and vanilla.

In a medium bowl, sift or whisk together the barley flour, baking powder, and salt. Gradually add the flour mixture to the egg mixture, mixing well. Stir in the walnuts, incorporating them well.

Pour the batter into the prepared pan. Bake for 30 to 35 minutes, or until a tester comes out clean.

Maple Date Kamut Cookies

The nuttiness of Kamut pairs beautifully with the well-known taste of maple, and the dates add a nice texture, making these cookies a delightful whole grain treat.

Makes 24 cookies

- 2½ cups quick cooking rolled oats
- ¾ cup kamut flour
- ½ teaspoon salt
- ½ teaspoon baking powder
- ½ cup maple syrup
- 2 eggs
- 1 teaspoon vanilla extract
- ¼ cup fresh or dried dates, chopped

Preheat the oven to 350°F. Lightly oil a baking sheet or line it with parchment paper.

In a large bowl, whisk together the oats, flour, salt, and baking powder.

In another bowl, beat together the syrup with the eggs and vanilla, then stir in the dates. Add to the dry ingredients and blend well.

Drop the batter by teaspoons onto the prepared sheet and bake for 10 minutes, or until a tester comes out clean.

Caramelized Apple Bars

Caramelized apples are delicious and easy to make, and even better in these bars. For an added treat, make extra, store in an airtight container, and warm in the morning to add to pancakes.

Makes about 18 bars

Caramelized Apples

- 2 tablespoons unsalted butter
- 5 apples, peeled, cored and sliced about ¼-inch thick
- ¼ cup brown sugar, packed
- 1 tablespoon sugar

Cookies

- ½ pound (2 sticks) unsalted butter, softened
- 1 cup unbleached white flour
- 1¼ cups whole wheat flour
- ½ cup confectioners' sugar

Topping

- ¾ cup brown sugar, packed
- ½ cup unbleached white flour
- ¼ cup whole wheat flour
- ¼ pound (1 stick) unsalted butter, softened
- 2 teaspoons ground cinnamon
- 1 cup pecans, coarsely chopped (or walnuts)

Preheat the oven to 350°F. Oil a 13 x 9-inch baking dish.

To prepare the apples: in a large skillet set over medium heat, melt the butter and add the apples. Toss with the sugars and cook, stirring frequently, until the apples turn brown, about 15 minutes. Remove from the heat and set aside.

To make the cookies: cream the butter until light, about 2 minutes. In a separate bowl, whisk together the flours with the confectioners' sugar, then beat the flour mixture into the butter. Press the dough into the bottom of the prepared pan. Bake for about 20 to 25 minutes, until just barely brown. Top with the apples, spreading them across the cookies.

For the topping, combine the sugar, flours, butter, and cinnamon in a bowl and mix with a fork until the mixture resembles coarse crumbs. Stir in the pecans. Sprinkle the topping over the apples and bake another 15 minutes, or until the topping is brown.

Cool in the pan on a wire rack, then cut into bars.

Orange Chocolate Chip Barley Cookies

Orange and chocolate are a classic flavor combination that goes great in this yummy little cookie.

Makes about 36 cookies

- ½ cup barley flour
- ½ cup unbleached white flour
- ½ teaspoon baking soda
- ½ teaspoon salt
- ¼ pound (1 stick) unsalted butter, softened
- ½ cup sugar
- 4 ounces cream cheese, softened
- 1 egg, lightly beaten
- 2 teaspoons orange zest
- 1 cup chocolate chips

Preheat the oven to 350°F. Lightly oil a baking sheet or line it with parchment paper.

In a large bowl, sift or whisk together the flours, baking soda, and salt.

In a medium bowl, cream together the butter, sugar, and cream cheese until smooth. Beat in the egg, then stir in the zest. Add the flour mixture and mix well. Fold in the chocolate chips.

Drop by teaspoonfuls onto the prepared baking sheet. Bake for 10 to 12 minutes, or until browned. Transfer to a wire rack to cool.

Buckwheat Cookies

These cookies are a great high fiber snack. Buckwheat groats, which are used here, are the seed, stripped of its hull. When roasted, they have a significantly stronger taste and are called kasha. Be sure to use unroasted groats in this recipe.

Makes approximately 4 dozen cookies

- 1 egg
- ⅓ cup vegetable oil
- ¼ cup sugar
- 1 cup applesauce
- 1⅓ cups whole wheat pastry flour
- ¼ cup wheat germ
- 1 teaspoon baking soda
- ½ teaspoon baking powder
- ¼ teaspoon salt
- ½ teaspoon ground allspice
- ½ teaspoon ground ginger
- 1 teaspoon ground cinnamon
- ⅓ cup uncooked buckwheat groats
- ½ cup rolled oats

Preheat the oven to 350°F. Lightly oil 2 baking sheets or line them with parchment paper.

In a large bowl, cream together the egg with the oil and sugar for 2 minutes. Beat in the applesauce.

In a medium bowl, whisk together the flour, wheat germ, baking soda, baking powder, salt, and spices. Add the flour mixture to the egg mixture and stir until just blended. Stir in the buckwheat groats and rolled oats.

Drop the batter by teaspoonfuls on the prepared cookie sheets and bake for 10 to 12 minutes, or until lightly browned.

Pumpkin Cookies

GLUTEN-FREE

Like a piece of pumpkin pie.

Makes approximately 3 dozen cookies

- 2 cups millet flour
- ½ cup amaranth flour
- 3 teaspoons baking powder
- 2 teaspoons ground cinnamon
- 1 teaspoon salt
- ½ teaspoon ground nutmeg
- ¼ teaspoon ground ginger
- 1 cup golden raisins
- 1 cup pecans, chopped
- ½ cup vegetable oil
- 1½ cups honey
- ¾ cup sugar
- 2 eggs, lightly beaten
- 1 tablespoon molasses
- ½ teaspoon vanilla extract
- 1½ cups cooked, mashed pumpkin or unsweetened canned pumpkin

Preheat the oven to 400°F. Lightly oil a baking sheet or line it with parchment paper

In a mixing bowl, whisk together the flours, baking powder, cinnamon, salt, nutmeg, ginger, raisins, and pecans until combined well.

In a large bowl, beat together the oil with the honey, sugar, eggs, molasses, and vanilla, then add the pumpkin and blend well. Stir in the flour mixture to make a thick batter.

Spoon by teaspoonfuls onto the prepared baking sheet. Bake for 12 minutes or until done.

Wheat Germ Blondies

These chewy treats are even chewier with whole wheat goodness.

Makes approximately 4 dozen bars

- 1 cup whole wheat flour
- 1 cup unbleached white flour
- ½ cup wheat germ
- 1 teaspoon baking soda
- ½ teaspoon salt
- ½ pound (2 sticks) unsalted butter, divided
- ½ cup brown sugar, packed
- ¾ cup sugar
- 2 eggs
- 2 teaspoons vanilla extract
- 1 cup walnuts, chopped
- ⅓ cup chocolate or carob chips

Preheat the oven to 375°F. Grease a 15 x 10-inch jelly roll pan.

In a large bowl, whisk together the flours, wheat germ, baking soda, and salt.

In a small saucepan set over low heat, melt half of the butter, then stir in the brown sugar and mix well.

In a medium bowl, cream together the remaining butter with the sugar until light lemon-yellow, about 4 minutes. Add the eggs one at a time, scraping down the sides of the bowl as needed. Whisk in the melted butter, then beat for one minute until thick, scraping down the sides of the bowl as needed. Stir in the vanilla.

Whisk the flour mixture into the butter mixture, stirring to just blend, then fold in ⅔ cup of the walnuts and the chocolate chips. Scrape the batter into the prepared dish and top with the remaining nuts.

Bake for 25 minutes, or until a tester comes out clean. Take care not to overbake. Cool in the pan on a rack then cut into bars.

Carrot Almond Bars

Carrots and almonds taste great together, and because they're so good for you, you can feel less guilty about enjoying these nutritious and lip-smacking bars.

Makes approximately 18 bars

Cookies

- ⅓ cup turbinado sugar
- 1 cup whole wheat flour
- ¼ cup unbleached white flour
- ¼ teaspoon salt
- ½ teaspoon baking powder
- 6 tablespoons unsalted butter, chilled and diced
- ½ teaspoon vanilla extract
- 2 teaspoon water

Filling

- 6 tablespoons unsalted butter, softened
- ½ cup sugar
- 1 tablespoon vegetable oil
- 2 eggs
- ½ teaspoon almond extract
- 1½ cups almond meal
- 1 medium carrot, grated
- 2 to 3 tablespoons flaked or grated coconut
- 2 to 3 tablespoons chopped nuts

Preheat the oven to 375°F. Lightly oil an 11 x 7-inch baking dish.

Combine the sugar, flours, salt, and baking powder in a food processor or large bowl. Cut in the butter by pulsing, or with two knives, until the mixture resembles coarse crumbs. Stir in the vanilla and water to make a dough, adding a little more water if needed.

Turn the dough out onto a lightly floured surface and roll it out to fit the baking dish, or simply press the dough into the prepared pan.

For the filling, cream the butter with the sugar until light lemon-yellow, about 4 minutes. Beat in the vegetable oil and the eggs one at a time, scraping down the sides of the bowl as needed, then add the almond extract. Stir in the almond meal and carrot.

Spread the filling over the cookie base and bake for about 25 minutes, until golden brown. Cool in the pan. Sprinkle with coconut and chopped nuts.

Whole Wheat Pear Cookies

These cookies make it easy to enjoy the benefits and flavors of whole wheat and pear. Each bite has juicy little pieces of pear.

Makes about 3 dozen cookies

- 2 cups whole wheat flour
- 2 teaspoons baking powder
- ½ teaspoon salt
- ½ teaspoon ground nutmeg
- ¼ teaspoon ground ginger
- ¼ teaspoon ground cloves
- ¼ pound (1 stick) unsalted butter, softened
- 1 cup brown sugar, packed
- 1 egg
- ¼ cup milk
- ³/₄ cup minced pear (about 1 large or 2 medium)

Preheat the oven to 350°F. Lightly oil a baking sheet or line it with parchment paper.

In a large bowl, sift or whisk together the flour, baking powder, salt, and spices.

In a medium bowl, cream the butter with the sugar until light lemon-yellow, about 4 minutes. Beat in the egg until well incorporated. Stir in the milk, then add this mixture to the flour mixture. Fold in the pear.

Drop by teaspoonfuls onto the prepared cookie sheet. Bake 15 to 18 minutes, or until crisp and light brown in color. Cool on a wire rack.

Whole Wheat Honey Cookies

Honey and brown sugar give these whole wheat cookies a rich flavor.

Makes approximately 4 dozen cookies

- 2 cups unbleached white flour
- 1 cup whole wheat pastry flour
- 1/2 cup barley flour, or substitute same amount unbleached white flour
- 2 1/2 teaspoons baking soda
- 1/4 teaspoon salt
- 1/2 pound (2 sticks) unsalted butter, softened
- 1 cup brown sugar, packed
- 2 eggs
- 7 tablespoons honey
- 2 tablespoons milk

Preheat the oven to 350°F. Lightly oil 2 baking sheets or line them with parchment paper.

Whisk together the flours, baking soda, and salt.

Cream the butter with the brown sugar until light, about 4 minutes. Add the eggs one at a time, scraping down the sides of the bowl as needed, and incorporate well. Beat in the honey and the milk, then stir in the flour mixture.

Wrap the dough in plastic wrap and refrigerate at least 1 hour, or until firm.

Shape the dough into 1-inch balls, place on the prepared baking sheet, and press just slightly to flatten a little. Bake for 12 to 15 minutes, or until golden. Transfer to a wire rack to cool.

Whole Wheat Sugar Cookies

These wheaty sugar cookies are perfect for making into holiday shapes.

Makes approximately 4 dozen cookies

- 2 cups whole wheat flour
- 2 teaspoons baking powder
- ½ teaspoon salt
- 1 cup sugar
- ¼ pound (1 stick) unsalted butter, softened
- 1 egg
- 1 teaspoon vanilla extract
- 2 tablespoons milk
- Sugar for sprinkling

Preheat the oven to 375°F. Lightly oil 2 baking sheets or line them with parchment paper.

In a medium bowl, sift or whisk together the flour with the baking powder and salt.

In another bowl, cream the sugar with the butter until light lemon-yellow, about 4 minutes. Beat in the egg until incorporated. Stir in the vanilla and milk, then add the flour mixture ½ cup at a time and mix until blended.

Wrap the dough in plastic wrap and refrigerate for at least 1 hour, or until firm.

On a lightly floured surface, roll the dough out until thin, about ⅛ inch. Cut into desired shapes, sprinkle with sugar, and place on the prepared baking sheets. Bake for 8 to 10 minutes, until browned. Transfer to wire rack to cool.

Sugar Cookies, Take One

GLUTEN-FREE

Handle these cookies carefully: the rice flour makes for a delicate cookie that tastes great but breaks easily.

Makes approximately 2 dozen small cookies

- 1 cup white or brown rice flour
- ½ cup tapioca flour
- ½ teaspoon cream of tartar
- 1 teaspoon baking soda
- 2 teaspoons xanthan gum
- ⅛ teaspoon salt
- ¼ pound (1 stick) unsalted butter, chilled and diced
- 1 egg, cold
- ½ cup sugar
- ½ teaspoon vanilla extract
- Confectioners' sugar, for rolling

Preheat the oven to 350°F. Lightly oil a baking sheet.

In a food processor, combine the flours, cream of tartar, baking soda, xanthan gum, and salt, and pulse to blend. Cut in the butter until the mixture resembles coarse crumbs.

Beat the egg with the sugar and vanilla. Add to the flour mixture and pulse until the dough pulls away from the sides. Press the dough into a ball, wrap it with plastic wrap, and refrigerate for at least 1 hour.

On a surface dusted with confectioners' sugar, roll the dough to ¼-inch thick. Cut into desired shapes, place on the prepared baking sheet, and bake for about 10 to 12 minutes, until browned. Cool on a wire rack.

Sugar Cookies, Take Two

GLUTEN-FREE

These sweet treats are easy to make, and especially yummy dusted with a little turbinado or confectioners' sugar while they are still warm.

Makes about 4 dozen cookies

- ½ pound (2 sticks) unsalted butter, softened
- 1 cup sugar
- 1 cup powdered sugar
- 1 cup vegetable oil
- 2 eggs
- 1 teaspoon vanilla extract
- 1½ cups cornstarch
- 1½ cups tapioca flour
- 1 cup garbanzo and fava flour
- ¼ cup rice flour
- ¼ cup sorghum flour
- 1 teaspoon cream of tartar
- 1 teaspoon baking soda
- 1 teaspoon xanthan gum

Preheat the oven to 350°F. Lightly oil 2 baking sheets or line them with parchment paper.

In a large bowl, cream the butter and sugars until light, about 3 minutes, then gradually add the oil and beat in the eggs, one at a time, scraping down the sides of the bowl after each addition. Add the vanilla and mix until combined.

In another bowl, sift together the cornstarch, flours, cream of tartar, baking soda, and xanthan gum, then gradually add the flour mixture to the butter mixture.

Drop the dough by teaspoonfuls onto the prepared baking sheets. Bake for 9 minutes, or until lightly browned. Cool on a wire rack.

Granola Cookies

These cookies give you another great way to enjoy your granola. Be sure to use a granola that is chock-full of fruits and nuts for these cookies.

Makes approximately 28 cookies

- ¼ pound (1 stick) unsalted butter
- 2 tablespoons honey
- 1 tablespoon light corn syrup
- Scant ½ cup turbinado sugar
- 1½ cups granola
- ¾ cup whole wheat flour
- 1 teaspoon baking powder
- ¼ teaspoon salt
- 1 teaspoon ground cinnamon

Preheat the oven to 325°F. Lightly oil a baking sheet or line it with parchment paper.

In a medium saucepan set over low heat, combine the butter, honey, corn syrup, and sugar until the butter melts and the ingredients are blended. Remove from the heat and stir in the granola, flour, baking powder, salt, and cinnamon.

Place heaping tablespoonfuls of the mixture on the prepared baking sheet and bake for 15 minutes, or until just brown on the edges. Cool on a wire rack.

Bran-Jack Cheese Cookies

Bran and Monterrey Jack cheese might seem like an unusual combination, but they really pair well in this spectacular energy booster.

Makes approximately 5 dozen cookies

- 1 cup unbleached white flour
- ³/₄ cup whole wheat pastry flour
- 1 teaspoon baking powder
- ½ teaspoon baking soda
- ½ teaspoon salt
- 12 tablespoons (1½ stick) unsalted butter, softened
- 1 cup brown sugar, packed
- 1 egg
- 1 teaspoon vanilla extract
- 1½ cups bran
- ½ cup grated Monterey Jack cheese
- ½ cup walnuts, chopped

Preheat the oven to 350°F. Lightly oil 2 baking sheets or line them with parchment paper.

In a medium bowl, sift or whisk together the flours, baking powder, baking soda, and salt.

In another bowl, cream together the butter with the sugar until light, about 4 minutes. Beat in the egg, then stir in the vanilla and the flour mixture. Fold in the bran, cheese, and walnuts. (The dough will be slightly crumbly.)

Shape the dough into 1-inch balls and place on the prepared baking sheet. Bake for 15 to 17 minutes, or until light brown. Transfer to a wire rack to cool.

Ginger Snaps

Who doesn't love a ginger snap? For an extra ginger kick, stir a teaspoon of fresh minced ginger into the wet ingredients.

Makes approximately 2 dozen cookies

- 1 cup whole wheat flour
- 1 cup unbleached white flour
- 1 teaspoon baking soda
- ¼ teaspoon baking powder
- ¼ teaspoon salt
- 1 teaspoon ground cinnamon
- 1¼ teaspoons ground ginger
- ¼ teaspoon ground cloves
- 12 tablespoons (1½ stick) unsalted butter, softened
- 1 cup sugar
- 1 egg
- ¼ cup molasses
- 1 teaspoon lemon juice
- Sugar, for rolling

Preheat the oven to 350°F. Lightly oil 2 baking sheets or line them with parchment paper.

In a large bowl, sift or whisk together the flours, baking soda, baking powder, salt, and spices.

Cream together the butter and sugar until light lemon-yellow, about 4 minutes. Add the egg and incorporate well. Stir in the molasses and lemon juice, then add the flour mixture and mix well.

Shape the dough into 1-inch balls and roll in sugar. Place on the prepared baking sheet and press to flatten just slightly. Bake for 10 to 14 minutes, or until brown. Cool on a wire rack.

Sorghum Crisps

These cookies are traditionally made with lard, which gives them a terrific flakiness. Here we've substituted vegetable shortening, but feel free to make them the traditional way.

Makes approximately 4 dozen cookies

- 1 cup sorghum flour
- 2 cups unbleached white flour
- 1½ teaspoons baking soda
- 1 teaspoon salt
- 1 cup vegetable shortening
- Scant 1 cup brown sugar
- 1 egg
- 4 teaspoons apple cider vinegar
- ½ cup sorghum or light molasses

In a large bowl, sift or whisk together the flours, baking soda, and salt.

In another large bowl, cream together the shortening and brown sugar until light brown, about 3 or 4 minutes. Beat in the egg and the vinegar to incorporate well, then beat in the sorghum. Stir in the flour mixture until well blended. If the dough is too soft, add up to ¼ cup more white flour.

Divide the dough into 2 pieces. On a piece of wax paper, roll the first piece to about 3/8-inch thickness. Place the paper and dough on a baking sheet. Repeat with the second piece of dough.

Refrigerate the dough on the sheet for 2 hours or freeze the sheet for 1 hour.

Preheat the oven to 375°F. Lightly oil 2 baking sheets or line them with parchment paper.

Cut the dough into the desired shapes, about 2 to 3 inches in size. Place on the baking sheet about 2 inches apart. Roll scraps for more cookies.

Bake for 5 to 10 minutes, or until just turning brown. Transfer to a wire rack and cool. The cookies will keep in an airtight container for up to 2 weeks.

Banana Cream Cookies

Banana cream pie in a cookie. Yum.

Makes approximately 2 dozen cookies

- 2 eggs
- 1⅓ cups brown sugar, packed
- 1 teaspoon vanilla extract
- ½ cup heavy cream
- 7 tablespoons vegetable oil
- 1½ cups whole wheat pastry flour
- 2 cups unbleached white flour
- 2 teaspoons baking powder
- 2 medium bananas, peeled, halved lengthwise, and sliced ¼-inch thick
- Confectioners' sugar for dredging

Beat the eggs with the brown sugar until light, about 4 minutes. Beat in the vanilla. Stir in the cream and oil.

Whisk together the flours with the baking powder, then stir into the egg mixture. Cover the bowl with plastic wrap and chill for 1 hour.

Preheat the oven to 350°F. Lightly oil 2 baking sheets or line them with parchment paper.

Remove the dough from the refrigerator and stir in the banana. Drop tablespoons of cookie dough onto the prepared sheets and bake for 15 to 18 minutes, or until lightly brown and crispy. Dredge in the confectioners' sugar and cool on a wire rack.

Maple Syrup Cookies

Maple syrup sugar makes a rich replacement for sugar in this cookie, but if you don't have it on hand substitute more brown sugar.

Makes approximately 3 dozen cookies

- 1¼ cups whole wheat flour
- ½ cup unbleached white flour
- 1¼ teaspoons baking powder
- ⅓ teaspoon salt
- ¼ pound (1 stick) unsalted butter, softened
- ¼ cup brown sugar, packed
- ⅓ cup maple syrup sugar
- 1 egg
- ½ teaspoon vanilla extract
- 3 tablespoons maple syrup

Preheat the oven to 350°F. Lightly oil 2 baking sheets or line them with parchment paper.

In a large bowl, sift or whisk together the flours, baking powder, and salt.

In another bowl, cream together the butter with the sugar until light, about 4 minutes. Beat in the egg until incorporated. Stir in the vanilla and maple syrup, then add the flour mixture gradually, incorporating well after each addition.

Wrap the dough and refrigerate overnight, or for at least 3 hours.

Divide the dough into 2 pieces and roll out each piece to about ¼-inch thick between sheets of wax paper (anchor the paper to the counter by placing a little water down first). Cut into 2-inch cookies or desired shapes.

Bake for 8 to 10 minutes or until brown. Cool on a wire rack.

Molasses Soy Flour Cookies

Soy flour gives these cookies a delicate texture, making them a bit more crumbly than the usual cookie.

Makes approximately 4 dozen cookies

- 12 tablespoons (1 ½ stick) unsalted butter, softened
- ¾ cup sugar
- 1 egg
- ½ cup molasses
- 1½ cups whole wheat pastry flour
- 1 cup soy flour
- 2 teaspoon baking soda
- ½ teaspoon salt
- ½ teaspoon ground cloves
- 1 teaspoon ground cinnamon
- ½ teaspoon ground ginger
- ½ teaspoon ground nutmeg
- ½ teaspoon ground allspice
- ½ teaspoon ground cardamom
- ½ cup raisins
- Sugar for dusting, optional

Preheat the oven to 350°F. Lightly oil 2 baking sheets or line them with parchment paper.

In a large bowl, cream the butter with the sugar, egg, and molasses, scraping down the sides of the bowl as needed.

In another bowl, mix the remaining ingredients, except for the raisins and dusting sugar. Add the flour mixture to the butter mixture and stir to combine. Stir in the raisins.

Roll tablespoons of dough into balls and dip the tops in the sugar. Place the balls sugar-side-up on the prepared cookie sheets, at least 2 inches apart. Bake for 8 to 10 minutes, or until golden brown. Cool on a wire rack.

Triticale Peanut Butter Cookies

The wheat rye blend of triticale makes for a deliciously different peanut butter cookie.

Makes approximately 4 dozen cookies

- ¼ pound (1 stick) unsalted butter, softened, or ½ cup vegetable shortening
- ½ cup sugar
- ½ cup brown sugar, packed
- 1 egg, beaten
- ½ teaspoon vanilla extract
- ½ cup peanut butter
- 1½ cups triticale flour
- 1 teaspoon baking soda
- ¼ teaspoon salt

Preheat the oven to 350°F. Lightly oil a baking sheet or line it with parchment paper.

In a large bowl, cream together the butter and sugars, then beat in the egg. Add the vanilla and peanut butter and beat well, scraping down the sides of the bowl as needed.

In another bowl, sift or whisk together the flour, baking soda, and salt, and add to the butter mixture, blending well.

Shape the dough into 1 inch balls and place on the prepared cookie sheet. Flatten with the prongs of a fork. Bake for about 10 minutes or until done. Cool on a wire rack.

Whole Wheat Peanut Butter Cookies

Another variation on the peanut butter cookie—a little lighter in texture than the triticale cookies, but still dense and rich.

Makes approximately 20 cookies

- 1 cup whole wheat pastry flour, sifted
- ¼ cup soy flour
- 1½ teaspoons baking powder
- ½ teaspoon baking soda
- ½ teaspoon salt
- ¼ pound (1 stick) unsalted butter, softened
- 1 cup brown sugar, packed
- 1 egg
- ½ cup peanut butter
- 1 teaspoon vanilla extract

In a medium bowl, sift the whole wheat flour with the soy flour, baking powder, baking soda, and salt.

In a large bowl, cream the butter with the sugar, then beat in the egg, peanut butter, and vanilla, scraping down the sides of the bowl as needed. Add the flour mixture to the butter mixture and stir to combine.

Wrap the dough in plastic wrap and chill for at least 1 hour.

Preheat the oven to 375°F. Lightly oil a baking sheet or line it with parchment paper.

Pinch teaspoonfuls of dough out and roll between your palms. Place on the prepared baking sheet, about 2 to 3 inches apart, and flatten.

Bake for 10 minutes or until lightly golden. Allow to cool for 3 or 4 minutes before removing to a wire rack. Repeat with remaining dough.

Teff Chocolate Cookies

This North African grain presents a new spin on a traditional favorite. We know you'll love these.

Makes approximately 18 cookies

- ¾ cup white rice flour
- ¼ cup barley flour
- 1½ tablespoons cocoa or toasted carob powder
- ¼ cup uncooked whole grain teff
- ¼ cup molasses
- ½ cup water or milk
- ¼ teaspoon almond extract

Preheat the oven to 350°F. Lightly oil a baking sheet or line it with parchment paper.

In a large bowl, combine the flours, cocoa powder, and teff. Whisk together the molasses, water, and almond extract and then stir into the dry ingredients.

Drop teaspoonfuls of dough onto the prepared baking sheet and bake for 8 to 10 minutes. Allow to cool on baking sheet for 4 to 5 minutes before transferring to a cooling rack.

Flaxsnax Cookies

These healthy snacks provide an energy pickup along with great taste.

Makes approximately 30 cookies

- 2 cups unbleached white flour
- 1½ cups whole wheat flour
- 1½ cups cornmeal
- ½ cup flaxseed
- 1½ teaspoons salt
- ½ cup brown sugar
- 6 teaspoons baking powder
- ½ cup vegetable shortening, chilled and diced
- 1½ cups water

Preheat the oven to 300°F. Lightly oil a baking sheet or line it with parchment paper.

Combine the flours, cornmeal, flaxseed, sugar, baking powder, and salt in a food processor. Cut in the shortening with pulses until combined.

Remove the mixture to a bowl and stir in the water to form a dough.

Turn the dough out onto a lightly floured surface and roll out to a thin (¼ inch) sheet. Cut into desired size and shape.

Bake until lightly brown, about 30 minutes.

Low-Fat Brownies

Yogurt makes a nice replacement for butter in this brownie recipe.

Makes approximately 16 brownies

- 2 cups whole wheat flour
- 1½ cups unbleached white flour
- 1 teaspoon baking powder
- ¼ teaspoon salt
- 3 tablespoons cocoa powder or toasted carob powder
- 1¼ cups sugar
- 2 eggs
- ⅔ cup plain yogurt
- 1 teaspoon vanilla extract
- 1 cup milk
- ⅔ cup water
- 2 teaspoons vegetable oil

Preheat the oven to 375°F. Oil an 8 x 8-inch baking dish.

In a medium bowl, sift or whisk together the flours, baking powder, salt, cocoa powder, and sugar.

In a separate bowl, beat the eggs with the yogurt, vanilla, milk, water, and oil, then beat this mixture into the flour mixture. Spread into the prepared pan.

Bake for about 25 minutes, until firm. Cool in the pan before cutting.

Whole Wheat Sesame Seed Cookies

These delicious little snacks will keep for almost a week in an airtight container.

**Makes about 8 dozen small or
6 dozen medium cookies**

- 2½ cups whole wheat pastry flour
- ½ teaspoon baking powder
- ¼ teaspoon salt
- ½ pound (2 sticks) unsalted butter, softened
- 2 egg yolks
- ½ cup plus 1 tablespoon sugar or fructose
- ¼ cup milk
- ½ teaspoon vanilla extract
- ¼ cup sesame seeds

Preheat the oven to 400°F. Lightly oil a baking sheet or line it with parchment paper.

In a large bowl, sift or whisk together the flour, baking powder, and salt in a large bowl, then cut in the butter.

In a separate bowl, cream the egg yolks and the sugar. Stir in the milk and vanilla to blend well, then add this mixture to the flour mixture to make a dough.

Turn the dough out onto a lightly floured surface and roll very thin. Sprinkle with the sesame seeds, pressing the seeds into the dough. Cut into desired shapes and place on the prepared baking sheet.

Bake for 8 minutes or until browned. Cool on a wire rack.

Cornmeal Butter Cookies

Cornmeal makes for a crisp butter cookie.

Makes approximately 22 cookies

- 10 tablespoons unsalted butter, softened
- ½ cup sugar
- 1 teaspoon vanilla extract
- 2 egg yolks
- 1¼ cups whole wheat pastry flour
- ½ cup yellow cornmeal

Preheat the oven to 325°F. Lightly oil a baking sheet or line it with parchment paper.

In a large bowl, cream the butter with the sugar until light lemon-yellow, about 3 minutes, then beat in the vanilla and egg yolks until well blended, another minute or two.

In a separate bowl, whisk together the flour and cornmeal and then stir into the butter mixture.

Place the dough in a pastry bag and pipe onto the prepared pan to a length about 2 to 3 inches long. The cookies spread so leave about 1½ inches between each cookie.

Bake for 15 minutes or until they are firm and golden. Cool on a wire rack.

Whole Wheat Rugelach

These traditional Jewish treats are made even better with whole wheat.

Makes approximately 5 dozen rugelach

- 1 cup whole wheat flour
- 1 cup unbleached white flour
- ½ teaspoon salt
- ½ pound (2 sticks) unsalted butter, softened
- 8 ounces cream cheese, softened
- 1½ cups pecans
- 1 cup raspberry or blueberry jam
- ⅓ cup sugar
- ½ teaspoon ground cinnamon
- Milk, for glaze

Sift or whisk the flours and salt in a large bowl.

Cream together the butter and cream cheese until well blended, about 2 minutes. Beat in the flour mixture until just mixed. Wrap the dough in plastic wrap and refrigerate for 30 minutes, or until firm.

Divide the dough into 4 equal pieces. Wrap the dough again and refrigerate for 1 hour, or overnight.

Combine the pecans and jam in a food processor and pulse until you have a coarse paste.

Preheat the oven to 375°F. Lightly oil a baking sheet or line it with parchment paper.

Combine the sugar and cinnamon in a small bowl. Roll each piece of dough into a 9- or 10-inch round. Spread equal parts of the filling on each round, sprinkle with 1 tablespoon of the cinnamon-sugar, then cut each round into 16 wedges. Roll the wedges up starting with the wide end, and bend into the shape of a crescent.

Place the crescents on the prepared baking sheet, brush each wedge with a little milk, and sprinkle with some of the remaining cinnamon sugar.

Bake until the cookies are golden about 25 to 30 minutes. Transfer to a wire rack to cool.

Butterscotch Bars

The richness of butterscotch is reigned in with the wonderful whole wheat flavor. If you'd like, replace the pecans with white chocolate or carob chips.

Makes approximately 18 bars

- 1½ cups whole wheat pastry flour
- 1½ teaspoons baking soda
- ½ teaspoon salt
- ¼ pound (1 stick) unsalted butter, softened
- 1¾ cups brown sugar, packed
- 1¼ teaspoons vanilla extract
- 2 eggs
- ⅔ cup pecans, chopped

Preheat the oven to 350°F. Lightly oil a 13 x 9-inch baking dish.

In a large bowl, sift or whisk together the flour, baking soda and salt.

In another bowl, cream the butter with the sugar until light lemon-yellow, about 4 minutes. Beat in the vanilla and then the eggs, one at a time until blended, stopping to scrape down the bowl once or twice. Stir in the flour mixture until just blended. Stir in the pecans.

Spread the batter into the prepared pan and bake until the top is golden, about 30 minutes. (Bars will be gooey inside.) Cool for 30 minutes in the pan before cutting into bars.

Lemon Bars

Another alternative take on a classically luscious dessert.

Makes approximately 2 dozen bars

- 1 cup unbleached white flour
- 1¼ cups whole wheat pastry flour
- ½ cup confectioners' sugar
- ½ pound (2 sticks) unsalted butter, softened
- 4 eggs, room temperature
- 2 cups sugar
- ⅔ cup lemon juice
- 1 teaspoon baking powder
- Zest of two lemons
- Confectioners' sugar for dusting, optional

Preheat the oven to 350°F. Oil a 13 x 9-inch baking dish.

Set aside 2 tablespoons of the unbleached white flour and 2 tablespoons of the whole wheat pastry flour. Whisk together the remaining flour with the confectioners' sugar.

Cream the butter until light, about 2 minutes. Beat the flour and confectioners' sugar mixture into the butter about ½ cup at a time. Press the mixture into the prepared dish and bake until golden, about 15 to 20 minutes.

Whisk together the eggs with the remaining flour, sugar, lemon juice, and baking powder just to blend well, but not until frothy. Stir in the zest. Pour the mixture over the crust and return to the oven until set and just browned, about 25 minutes.

Cool in the pan on a wire rack, then cut into bars. Dust with confectioners' sugar.

Snickerdoodles

The flavors of cinnamon, butter, and sugar really stand out in this cookie made with whole grain goodness.

Makes approximately 2 dozen cookies

- 2 cups whole wheat pastry flour
- 1 cup unbleached white flour
- ½ cup oat flour
- 1½ teaspoons baking soda
- ¼ teaspoon salt
- ¼ pound (1 stick) unsalted butter, softened
- ½ cup sugar
- 1 teaspoon vanilla extract
- 2 eggs
- 1⅓ cups milk
- ¼ teaspoon ground cinnamon mixed with 2 tablespoons sugar

Sift together the flours, baking soda, and salt.

Cream the butter with the sugar until light, about 2 minutes. Beat the eggs, one at a time, into the vanilla. Scrape down the sides of the bowl as needed, then beat in the milk. Fold in the flour mixture just to blend. Cover the bowl with plastic wrap and chill for 20 minutes.

Preheat the oven to 375°F. Lightly oil a baking sheet or line it with parchment paper.

Roll tablespoons of the dough into balls, then roll each ball in the cinnamon/sugar mixture. Place the balls on the prepared baking sheet and flatten slightly.

Bake for 10 minutes or until golden. Cool on a wire rack.

Shortbread

Rice flour gives shortbread a wonderful tenderness. Substitute cornstarch if you don't have rice flour on hand.

Makes approximately 18 cookies

- ¼ cup white or brown rice flour
- ¾ cup whole wheat pastry flour
- 1 cup unbleached white flour
- 1 cup cornstarch
- 1 teaspoon salt
- ¾ pound (3 sticks) unsalted butter, softened
- 1¼ cups confectioners' sugar

Preheat the oven to 350°F. Lightly oil a baking sheet or line it with parchment paper.

In a large bowl, sift together the flours, cornstarch, and salt.

Cream the butter with the sugar until light, about 4 minutes, scraping down the sides of the bowl as needed. Stir in the flour mixture until just blended.

On a lightly floured surface, or between two sheets of wax or parchment paper, roll out the dough to ¼-inch thickness, sprinkling with flour as needed to prevent sticking. Cut the dough into 2½-inch squares and place the squares on the prepared baking sheet an inch apart.

Bake until the edges of the shortbread are lightly golden, about 20 minutes. Cool on a wire rack.

Apricot Pinwheel Cookies

Apricot lovers, look out. These pinwheels are addictive.

Makes about 4 dozen cookies

- ½ pound (2 sticks) unsalted butter, softened
- 8 ounces cream cheese, softened
- 1½ cups whole wheat pastry flour
- ½ cup unbleached white flour
- ½ teaspoon salt
- ¾ cup apricot preserves
- 1 cup pecans, minced

Cream the butter together with the cream cheese until well blended, about a minute. Stir in the flours and salt until a dough forms. Wrap in plastic and refrigerate for at least 4 hours or overnight.

Stir the preserves with the pecans until well combined.

Turn the dough out onto a lightly floured surface and roll out to a 14 x 12-inch rectangle. Spread the apricot mixture over the dough, leaving a ¼-inch border. Beginning with one of the longer sides, roll the dough like a jellyroll. Seal the seam, cut the log in half, wrap each half in plastic, and refrigerate for 45 minutes.

Preheat the oven to 350°F. Lightly oil a baking sheet or line it with parchment paper.

Unwrap the dough and cut each log into slices about ½ inch thick. Place the slices on the prepared baking sheet and bake for 14 minutes, or until golden. Cool on a wire rack.

Lemon Cookies

Cookies don't get much more lemony than these.

Makes about 3 dozen cookies

- 1½ cups whole wheat pastry flour
- ¼ cup cornmeal
- ½ teaspoon baking powder
- ¼ teaspoon salt
- ¾ cup sugar
- 2 teaspoons lemon zest
- 12 tablespoons (1½ stick) unsalted butter, chilled and diced
- 2 tablespoons lemon juice
- 1 egg yolk
- ½ teaspoon vanilla extract

In a food processor, combine the flour, cornmeal, baking powder, salt, and sugar to blend. Pulse in the zest, then cut in the butter until the mixture resembles coarse crumbs.

Whisk together the lemon juice, egg yolk, and vanilla and then pour it into the flour mixture with the motor running, just until a dough forms.

Turn the dough out onto a lightly floured surface and knead just until the dough comes together. Shape into a 9- or 10-inch log, wrap in plastic, and chill for at least 2 hours.

Preheat the oven to 375°F. Lightly oil a baking sheet or line it with parchment paper.

Remove the dough from the plastic wrap and slice into rounds about ¼ inch thick. Place on the prepared baking sheet and bake until slightly browned, about 12 to 14 minutes. Cool on a wire rack.

Biscotti

We've adapted this classic Italian treat to include whole grains, which make them even better than the norm. Enjoy them with a cup of espresso for dessert, or as a snack.

Makes approximately 4 to 5 dozen biscotti

- 2 cups whole wheat flour
- 1 cup unbleached white flour
- 2½ teaspoons baking powder
- ½ teaspoon salt
- 4 eggs
- 1 cup sugar
- ¼ pound (1 stick) unsalted butter, melted and cooled
- 2½ teaspoons vanilla extract
- ¾ teaspoon almond extract
- 2 teaspoons orange zest
- ⅔ cup almonds, finely chopped

In a large bowl, sift or whisk together the flours, baking powder, and salt.

In another bowl, cream the eggs together with the sugar until light lemon-yellow, then beat in the butter until well blended. Add the vanilla, almond extract, zest, and almonds, and mix well. Stir in the flour mixture until a dough forms. Cover the bowl and refrigerate for 1 hour.

Preheat the oven to 350°F. Lightly oil a baking sheet or line it with parchment paper.

Turn the dough out onto a lightly floured surface, and shape it into two 12-inch long logs. Place on the prepared baking sheet and bake for 18 minutes, or until just beginning to brown.

Remove the logs from oven and leave them on the sheet to rest for 10 minutes. Cut each log into ½-inch thick slices, return the slices to the baking sheet, and bake for 10 to 12 minutes. Turn the slices over and bake for another 2 to 3 minutes, or until golden brown. Cool on a wire rack.

Cornmeal Rosemary Biscotti

These are tasty twists on traditional biscotti, with delicious fresh rosemary. They're great with soups.

Makes about 4 dozen biscotti

- 1¼ cups unbleached white flour
- ¾ cup cornmeal
- 2 tablespoons rosemary sprigs, chopped
- 2 teaspoons baking powder
- ¼ pound (1 stick) unsalted butter, softened
- ¾ cup sugar
- 2 eggs

In a large bowl, whisk together the flour, cornmeal, rosemary, and baking powder.

In a separate bowl, cream together the butter with the sugar until light, about 4 minutes. Add the eggs one at a time, scraping down the bowl after each addition, until well combined. With your electric mixer on low speed, beat in the flour mixture until just combined. Cover the bowl and refrigerate for 1 hour.

Preheat the oven to 350°F. Lightly oil a baking sheet or line it with parchment paper.

Turn the dough out onto a lightly floured surface, and shape it into two 12-inch long logs. Place on the baking sheet and bake for 18 minutes, or until just beginning to brown.

Remove the logs from oven and leave them on the sheet to rest for 10 minutes. Cut each log into ½-inch thick slices, return the slices to the baking sheet, and bake for 10 to 12 minutes. Turn the slices over and bake for another 2 to 3 minutes, or until golden brown. Cool on a wire rack.

Whole Wheat Jam Cookies

Any flavor jam will work perfectly here, or use several different types to create a colorful plate of cookies.

Makes approximately 2 to 3 dozen cookies

- 1½ cups whole wheat pastry flour
- ½ cup unbleached white flour
- 1 tablespoon sugar
- 4 teaspoons baking powder
- ½ teaspoon salt
- 5 tablespoons vegetable shortening, chilled
- ¾ cup plus 2 tablespoons milk

Preheat the oven to 300°F. Lightly oil a baking sheet or line it with parchment paper.

In a large bowl, sift or whisk together the flours, sugar, baking powder, and salt. Cut the shortening into the flour mixture using two knives, or your fingers. Stir in the milk.

Turn the dough out onto a lightly floured surface and knead the dough until it just comes together, 4 or 5 times. Roll the dough into a thin (¼-inch flat) square and use a cookie cutter or knife to cut into 2-inch square cookies. Press your thumb in the center of each cookie to make an indentation and place a scant teaspoon of jam in the center. Bring the corners to the center and pinch them together, making a little envelope to hold the jam.

Place the cookies on the prepared baking sheet and bake for 15 to 18 minutes, or until golden brown. Transfer to a wire rack to cool.

Applesauce Cookies

These chewy cookies will be a favorite among the kids.

Makes about 3 dozen cookies

- ¼ pound (1 stick) unsalted butter, softened
- ½ cup brown sugar, packed
- ½ cup sugar
- 1 egg
- 1 cup applesauce
- 1 cup unbleached white flour
- ¾ cup whole wheat flour
- ¼ cup wheat germ
- 1 teaspoon baking soda
- ½ teaspoon salt
- 1 teaspoon ground cinnamon
- ½ teaspoon ground nutmeg
- ½ teaspoon ground cloves
- 1 cup golden raisins

Preheat the oven to 375°F. Lightly oil 2 baking sheets or line them with parchment paper.

In a large bowl, cream the butter with the sugars and beat until light lemon-yellow, about 3 or 4 minutes. Beat in the egg and the applesauce.

In a medium bowl, sift or whisk together the flours, wheat germ, baking soda, salt, and spices until well combined, then add to the butter mixture, whisking until smooth. Stir in the raisins.

Arrange tablespoonfuls of dough on the prepared baking sheets and bake for about 5 to 7 minutes, until browned. Cool on a wire rack.

Pecan Squares

Redolent of luscious pecans, these squares smell wonderful coming out of the oven.

Makes 50 to 60 squares

Crust

- 1½ cups whole wheat pastry flour
- 1½ cups unbleached white flour
- 1½ teaspoons baking powder
- ½ teaspoon salt
- 11 tablespoons unsalted butter, softened
- 6 tablespoons vegetable shortening
- ⅔ cup sugar
- 2 eggs
- ½ teaspoon vanilla extract

Topping

- ¼ pound (1 stick) unsalted butter
- 1 cup brown sugar
- ⅔ cup sugar
- ½ cup honey
- ¼ cup heavy cream
- 3½ cups pecans, chopped

Grease a 15 x 10-inch or 17 x 9-inch baking sheet or pan.

In a large bowl, sift or whisk together the flours, baking powder, and salt. In another bowl, cream the butter with the shortening for 2 minutes, then add the sugar and cream another 4 minutes or until light. Beat in the eggs one at a time, scraping down the bowl as needed, then add the vanilla.

With your electric mixer on low speed, beat the flour mixture into the butter mixture until just combined. Press the dough into the prepared baking pan. Refrigerate for 2 hours or freeze for 30 minutes.

Preheat the oven to 375°F.

Prick the crust with the tines of a fork all over and bake until just browned, about 30 minutes.

For the topping, combine the butter, sugars and honey in a saucepan over medium heat and simmer, stirring constantly. Stir until the sugars melt and the mixture darkens and begins to foam, about 5 minutes. Remove from the heat and carefully stir in the cream (it will splatter) and the pecans.

Spread the filling over the crust. Bake about 15 minutes, or until bubbly. Cool the pan on a wire rack before cutting into squares.

Pecan Wafers

These wafers are thin, crisp, and full of pecan goodness.

Makes about 60 wafers

- 4 tablespoons unsalted butter
- ¾ cup sugar
- 1 egg, well beaten
- 2 tablespoons milk
- 1 teaspoon vanilla extract
- 1 cup whole wheat pastry flour
- ⅓ cup unbleached white flour
- 1 teaspoon baking powder
- ½ teaspoon salt
- ¼ cup pecans, chopped

Preheat the oven to 325°F. Lightly oil 2 baking sheets.

In a large bowl, cream the butter with the sugar until well blended. Add the egg, milk, and vanilla, and beat another minute or so, until well incorporated.

In a large bowl, sift or whisk together the flours, baking powder, and salt, then beat this mixture into the butter mixture.

Turn the dough out onto a lightly floured baking sheet and roll to ¼ inch or thinner, then sprinkle with the pecans and press them into the dough. Score the dough into small cookies in any shape you'd like.

Place the dough on the baking sheets and bake for about 12 minutes or until light brown. Remove from the oven and, when cool enough to handle, cut into cookies.

Persimmon Cookies

GLUTEN-FREE

These cookies make it easy to enjoy the great taste of persimmon.

Makes approximately 2 dozen cookies

- 1½ cups sugar
- ¼ pound (1 stick) unsalted butter, softened
- 2 eggs
- 1 cup Hachiya persimmon pulp
- 2 cups sorghum flour
- 1 teaspoon xanthan gum
- 2 teaspoons baking powder
- 1 teaspoon baking soda
- ½ teaspoon ground allspice
- ⅔ cup walnuts, chopped

Preheat the oven to 350°F. Lightly oil 2 baking sheets or line them with parchment paper.

In a large bowl, cream the sugar and butter until light lemon-yellow, about 4 minutes. Add the eggs one at a time and beat until incorporated, scraping down the sides of the bowl as needed. Beat in the persimmon pulp.

In a separate bowl, sift or whisk together the flour, xanthan gum, baking powder, baking soda, and allspice, then add this mixture to the butter mixture. Stir in the walnuts.

Drop tablespoonfuls of dough onto the prepared baking sheets and bake for about 5 to 7 minutes, until browned. Cool on a wire rack.

Honey Lemon Cookies

GLUTEN-FREE

Sprinkle these cookies with a few poppy seeds if you like. They have a mild, yet sweet, lemony flavor.

Makes 30 cookies

- ½ cup garbanzo and fava flour
- 1¼ cups white or brown rice flour
- 1 teaspoon baking powder
- ¾ teaspoon xanthan gum
- ½ teaspoon salt
- ¼ pound (1 stick) unsalted butter, softened
- Scant ½ cup sugar
- 1 egg
- 1 teaspoon lemon extract
- Zest of two lemons
- ⅓ cup honey
- ¼ cup plain yogurt
- 1 cup confectioners sugar
- 2 tablespoons lemon juice

Preheat the oven to 350°F. Lightly oil 2 baking sheets or line them with parchment paper.

In a medium bowl, sift together the flours, baking powder, xanthan gum, and salt.

In a large bowl, cream the butter with the sugar until light, about 3 minutes. Add the egg and beat until incorporated, scraping down the sides of the bowl. Stir in the lemon extract and half of the lemon zest, then add the honey. Add half of the flour mixture, fold in the yogurt, then add the remaining flour mixture.

Drop the dough by teaspoonfuls onto the prepared baking sheets and bake about 12 minutes, or until golden.

While the cookies bake, whisk together the remaining zest with the confectioners' sugar and lemon juice, mixing well. When the cookies are baked, brush them with the lemon-sugar glaze, then transfer them to a wire rack to cool completely.

Cornmeal Biscotti

GLUTEN-FREE

Cornmeal makes a wonderfully crunchy biscotti.

Makes approximately 2 dozen biscotti

- ½ cup hazelnut meal
- 1 cup cornmeal
- 1 cup cornstarch
- ½ teaspoon baking soda
- ¼ teaspoon ground allspice
- ¼ cup hazelnuts, chopped
- 1 egg
- ¾ cup sugar
- 2 tablespoons honey
- 2 tablespoons molasses
- 2 tablespoons butter, melted and cooled

Preheat the oven to 350°F. Lightly oil a 13 x 9-inch baking pan or dish and line 2 baking sheets with parchment paper.

In a medium bowl, combine the hazelnut meal, cornmeal, cornstarch, baking soda, allspice, and hazelnuts.

In a large bowl, cream the egg and sugar, then beat in the honey, molasses, and butter. Add the flour mixture and mix until well incorporated.

Press the dough into the prepared pan and bake for 30 minutes. Cool in the pan on a wire rack, then cut into 3 x ½-inch strips. Place the strips on a baking sheet and bake an additional 15 minutes, or until golden brown.

Tea Cookies

GLUTEN-FREE

Choose your favorite tea leaves for this recipe. If you enjoy a particularly strong tea, you may want to use just 1 tablespoon.

Makes about 24 cookies

- 1 cup white or brown rice flour
- ⅓ cup tapioca flour
- ⅓ cup potato starch
- 1½ tablespoons cornstarch
- 1½ teaspoons xanthan gum
- 9 tablespoons unsalted butter, softened
- ½ cup brown sugar, packed
- 1½ tablespoons Earl Grey or other tea leaves
- 1 egg, lightly beaten
- 2 tablespoons turbinado sugar

Preheat the oven to 375°F. Lightly oil 2 baking sheets or line them with parchment paper.

In a medium bowl, sift together the flours, potato starch, cornstarch, and xanthan gum.

In a large bowl, cream the butter with the sugar until light, about 3 minutes, then stir in the tea leaves. Add the egg and beat until incorporated, scraping down the sides of the bowl, then fold in the flour mixture.

Drop the dough by teaspoonfuls approximately 1 inch apart onto the prepared baking sheets, sprinkle with sugar, and bake about 10 minutes, or until done. Transfer to a wire rack to cool.

Rosemary Citrus Tuiles

GLUTEN-FREE

Tuiles are traditionally thin and curved. This take on the original presents a wonderful marriage of rosemary and citrus. Refreshing and delicious.

Makes approximately 2 dozen tuiles

- ¼ cup rice flour
- 1 tablespoon garbanzo and fava flour
- 1 tablespoon cornstarch
- ½ teaspoon xanthan gum
- 2 egg whites
- ½ cup superfine sugar
- 2 teaspoons lemon zest
- 2 teaspoons orange zest
- 2 teaspoons fresh rosemary, minced
- 4 tablespoons unsalted butter, melted and cooled

Preheat the oven to 375°F. Lightly oil 2 baking sheets or line them with parchment paper.

In a medium bowl, sift together the flours, cornstarch, and xanthan gum.

In a large bowl, beat the egg whites until stiff, then gradually beat in the sugar. Stir in the zests, the rosemary, and the flour mixture, then fold in the butter.

For each cookie, drop 2 tablespoons of batter onto the prepared sheet, then spread the batter to make a very thin cookie. Bake for 5 minutes, or until golden brown. Using a spatula, transfer the cookie to a wire rack to cool, or lay the still-warm cookies over a rolling pin for a traditional tuile shape.

Lemon Bars

GLUTEN-FREE

Traditional lemon bars taste great even if they don't have any gluten.

Makes about 30 bars

- 1⅓ cups white or brown rice flour
- ⅓ cup tapioca flour
- ⅓ cup potato starch
- 2 teaspoons xanthan gum
- 2 tablespoons cornstarch, divided
- ½ pound (2 sticks) unsalted butter, softened
- 4 eggs
- 2 cups sugar
- ⅔ cup lemon juice
- 1 teaspoon baking powder
- Zest of two lemons
- Confectioners' sugar, for dusting

Preheat the oven to 350°F. Oil a 13 x 9-inch baking dish.

In a large bowl, sift or whisk together the flours, potato starch, xanthan gum, and 1 tablespoon of cornstarch.

In a separate large bowl, cream the butter until light, about 2 minutes. Beat the flour mixture into the butter, then press the dough into the bottom of the prepared pan.

Bake for about 20 to 25 minutes, until brown.

In a large bowl, whisk together the eggs with the remaining cornstarch, sugar, lemon juice, and baking powder just to blend, but not until frothy. Stir in the zest.

Pour the mixture over the crust and return to the oven until set and just browned, about 25 minutes.

Cool in the pan on a wire rack, then cut into bars. Dust with confectioners' sugar.

Apple Cookies

GLUTEN-FREE

Use a firm apple in this recipe—Granny Smith is perfect—for perfectly apple-icious cookies.

Makes about 2 dozen cookies

- ¼ pound (1 stick) unsalted butter, softened
- 1¼ cups brown sugar
- 1 egg
- ½ teaspoon salt
- ½ teaspoon ground cloves
- 1 cup garbanzo and fava flour
- 1 cup rice flour
- 1¼ teaspoons baking soda
- ¾ teaspoon xanthan gum
- 1 medium apple, peeled, cored, minced or grated
- ⅓ cup milk

Preheat the oven to 375°F. Lightly oil a baking sheet or line it with parchment paper.

In a large bowl, cream the butter and brown sugar until light, about 3 minutes, then beat in the egg, scraping down the sides of the bowl. Add the salt and the cloves and mix until combined.

In another bowl, whisk together the flours, baking soda, and xanthan gum. Beat half of the flour mixture into the butter mixture, then add the apple and the milk. Add the remaining flour and mix well.

Drop the dough by teaspoonfuls onto the prepared baking sheet. Bake for 12 minutes, or until lightly browned. Cool on a wire rack.

Cakes

Cakes are one of the most satisfying creations for a home baker. They are relatively easy to make, they look wonderful when finished, and they always bring delight to a table of guests, especially when the cake is part of a celebration. Whole grain flours work well in cakes, giving both traditional and contemporary cakes a nice flavor. Whole grain flours make for a more dense cake, but they taste great and are a healthy alternative to those made with all-purpose flour.

The chemistry of baking, especially baking cakes, leaves some cooks a bit wary. After all, you can't taste your creation as you prepare it and make whatever corrections are necessary, so baking winds up being a bit more like chemistry than cooking. So in baking, a little attention to detail goes a long way.

The first thing to consider when baking a cake is the pan. Professional tinned steel or medium-weight aluminum pans with dull surfaces are best. Glass and dark metal pans tend to absorb and hold more heat, which will give your cake a crust you may not want. Reduce the heat slightly if you're using one of these pans. If you need to substitute a type of pan because you don't have the pan called for in a recipe, consider that a cake baked in a larger pan will spread more and require less cooking time, while one in a smaller pan will likely require more baking time. See the pan chart on page 427 to find which pan is nearest the size called for in the recipe.

We recommend that you lightly grease or line your cake pans, although it isn't absolutely necessary. We prefer the use of parchment paper, especially for layer cakes, so that your cake may be easily lifted from the pan without damage. Parchment, unlike wax paper, does not need to be greased and allows for easy clean-up. If slippage is a problem, lightly grease the pan before putting in the parchment paper.

For layer cakes that will be frosted on the top only, not the sides, you may choose to grease the pan so that the sides are more tender, or grease and then lightly dust the pan with flour to give the sides a bit of a crust. (To flour a pan, first grease it, then sprinkle it with a little flour. Shake the pan to spread the flour, then turn it over and tap to knock out excess flour). Use either unbleached white flour or whole wheat flour if you decide to grease and flour.

For greasing your pan, shortening or vegetable oil are best (try using a small plastic sandwich bag to cover your hand to spread the shortening or oil). Of course, you can always spray your pan with nonstick baking spray. Margarine and butter do not work as well, especially if salted.

Decorative molds, bundt pans, and the like need to be greased to make sure the cake releases easily and holds the desired shape. This is also when the nonstick baking sprays come in handy.

Don't overfill a pan. When baking a layer cake, the pan should be no more than two-thirds full, although others may filled a little more.

Preparing and Using Ingredients

While it's important with any type of baking, starting off with room temperature ingredients is especially important for whole grain cakes. Many cake recipes are emulsions and can break down or curdle if your eggs, milk, or other ingredients are too cold. If your batter breaks down, your cake will be heavy. Whole grain cakes are already a little heavier or denser than those made with cake or unbleached white flour, so it's essential to do everything you can to keep your cakes light.

Ideally, butter should be at 68 to 70 degrees. If you're baking on a hot day, make sure your butter hasn't partially melted while sitting out.

Cold eggs can ruin chocolate recipes because they don't blend well. Cold eggs also don't expand in volume as well as warm eggs. If you are in a hurry, break your eggs into a bowl (or bowls, if the recipe calls for adding them one at a time) and carefully microwave them on low for just a few seconds to warm them up. Or place unbroken eggs in a bowl of warm water for 5 to 10 minutes. Separating eggs is a little easier when they're cold, so you may want to separate the eggs then let them warm while you gather other ingredients.

The microwave is also useful for cold milk, but be careful not to heat it. Butter is a bit more tricky because it may melt on the inside while you're keeping a close eye on the outside. Cut it into pieces and microwave it for just a very few seconds.

When measuring, be sure to follow the recipe instructions. A cup of sifted flour is about 20 percent less than flour that is simply scooped. A lot of things cause variations in cake recipes—altitude differences, variable oven temperatures, even baking pans that are different sizes. With that in mind, carefully measure your ingredients and make notes so you can make adjustments for your kitchen temperature and equipment, or replicate a recipe when it comes out perfectly.

Never use tableware for measuring teaspoons and tablespoons—use measuring spoons. A glass measuring cup is best for measuring liquids since you can see through the glass for a more exact measurement.

Most of these cake recipes call for using an electric mixer to cream ingredients. Creaming helps increase the volume and improve the texture of a cake, so while it's an important step when making any cake, it is especially so with whole grain cakes. If you are using a professional stand mixer rather than the standard hand-held two-beater mixer, you can reduce the time you beat the ingredients by about a third. If you're whisking by hand, you will need to beat vigorously and probably a third longer, or more. Food processors will not replace beating, nor will blenders, so don't use them.

If you overbeat butter, it may separate. If this happens, refrigerate it for a few minutes, then stir to bring it back together.

After you've added your dry ingredients to the wet, the recipe may call for folding in egg whites or other final items. The goal of folding is to incorporate the ingredient without losing the increased volume you've just worked so hard to attain by creaming. To fold something in, first add it, then use a spatula to bring the bottom of the batter up over the top. Repeat that stroke to gently incorporate the new ingredients into the batter.

As with many aspects of whole grain cakes, folding in ingredients without deflating the batter is important for a lighter cake. For most cakes, stirring the batter as little as possible also helps keep the final product light.

Baking, Testing, Storing

If you are using a convection oven, follow the general rule mentioned in other parts of this book and reduce the temperature by 25 degrees, and the cooking time slightly. Bake in the middle of the oven unless otherwise instructed, and push the pan away from the door, which is the coolest part of the oven.

A toothpick or wooden skewer works best for testing for doneness. Be sure to poke it into the center of the cake. When it comes out clean, the cake is done. A few cakes have gooey centers so your toothpick may have some of that gooey center attached. A wooden skewer will help you recognize whether batter is coming out, or just filling.

As mentioned earlier, oven temperatures vary. For that reason, all of the recipes here have what we consider to be a minimum baking time. If you have a slightly hot oven, you should be okay, but check before the time indicated to make sure. If your oven is accurate or slightly cold, don't be surprised to find the cake is not quite done by the time listed here. We want to help you avoid over baking, which makes for dry cake.

If you want to store a whole or part of a cake, remember that richer cakes freeze better so most cakes can be frozen for up to 4 months. Low fat and spice cakes may start to suffer in as little as 5 weeks.

To freeze cakes, make sure they are wrapped tightly with as little air as possible. Leave the cake wrapped when thawing, and thaw at room temperature, not in a microwave.

We hope you enjoy these whole grain cakes.

Pan Dimensions and Volumes

PAN DIMENSIONS (inches)	PAN VOLUME (cups)	PAN DIMENSIONS (centimeters)
Round		
6 x 2	3¾ cups	15.2 x 5.1
8 x 1½	4 cups	20.3 x 3.8
8 x 2	6 cups	20.3 x 5.1
9 x 1½	6 cups	22.9 x 3.8
9 x 2	8 cups	22.9 x 5.1
10 x 2	11 cups	25.4 x 5.1
Springform		
6 x 3	4 cups	15.2 x 7.6
7 x 2½	5½ cups	17.8 x 6.4
8 x 3	10 cups	20.3 x 7.6
9 x 3	11 cups	22.9 x 7.6
10 x 2½	12 cups	25.4 x 6.4
Pie		
8 x 1¼	3 cups	20.3 x 3.2
8 x 1½	4 cups	20.3 x 3.8
9 x 1¼	4 cups	22.9 x 3.2
9 x 1½	5 cups	22.9 x 3.8
9½ x 2	7 cups	24.1 x 5.1
10 x 1½	6½ cups	25.4 x 3.8
Bundt		
7½ x 3	6 cups	19.1 x 7.6
9 x 3	9 cups	22.9 x 7.6
10 x 3½	12 cups	25.4 x 8.9
Tube		
7½ x 3	6 cups	19.1 x 7.6
9 x 3	12 cups	22.9 x 7.6
10 x 4	16 cups	25.4 x 10.2

Square		
8 x 8 x 1½	6 cups	20.3 x 20.3 x 3.8
8 x 8 x 2	8 cups	20.3 x 20.3 x 5.1
9 x 9 x 1½	8 cups	22.9 x 22.9 x 3.8
9 x 9 x 2	10 cups	22.9 x 22.9 x 5.1
10 x 10 x 2	12 cups	25.4 x 25.4 x 5.1
Rectangular		
11 x 7 x 2	6 cups	27.9 x 17.8 x 5.1
13 x 9 x 2	12 cups	33 x 22.9 x 5.1
13 x 9 x 3	14 cups	33 x 22.9 x 7.6
Jelly Roll		
10½ x 15½ x 1	10 cups	26.7 x 39.4 x 2.5
12½ x 17½ x 1	12 cups	31.8 x 44.5 x 2.5
Loaf		
2¼ x 4 x 1¼	⅔ cup	5.7 x 10.2 x 3.2
8 x 4 x 2½	4 cups	20.3 x 10.2 x 6.4
8½ x 4½ x 2½	6 cups	21.6 x 11.4 x 6.4
9 x 5 x 3	8 cups	22.9 x 12.7 x 7.6
Muffin		
1¾ x ¾	⅛ cup	4.4 x 1.9
2¾ x 1⅛	¼ cup	7 x 2.9
2¾ x 1½	½ cup	7 x 3.8
3 x 1¼	⅝ cup	7.6 x 3.2
Heart-Shaped		
8 x 2½	8 cups	20.3 x 6.4

Buttermilk Layer Cake

Buttermilk batter makes for a very fluffy cake.

Makes two 9-inch layers

- 2½ cups sifted whole wheat pastry flour
- 2 teaspoons baking powder
- ½ teaspoon baking soda
- ¼ teaspoon salt
- 13 tablespoons unsalted butter, softened
- 1¼ cups sugar
- 3 eggs, separated
- 1 teaspoon vanilla extract
- 1 cup plus 1 tablespoon buttermilk

Make sure all of your ingredients are at room temperature. Preheat the oven to 350°F. Grease or line two 9-inch round cake pans with parchment paper.

In a large bowl, sift or whisk together the flour, baking powder, baking soda, and salt. Cream the butter with the sugar until light, about 4 minutes, scraping down the sides of the bowl as necessary. Beat in the egg yolks and vanilla.

Beat the egg whites until stiff and set aside. Add a third of the flour mixture to the butter mixture, just to blend, then add half the buttermilk. Repeat with another third of flour, the rest of the buttermilk, and then the rest of the flour. Gently fold in the egg whites.

Pour the batter into the prepared pans and bake until the cakes are puffy and a tester comes out clean, about 20 minutes. Cool the pans on a wire rack for 10 minutes, then remove the cakes from the pans and allow them to cool directly on the rack.

Eat as is or frost as desired using frostings on pages 481 to 483.

7-Layer Chocolate Caramel Torte

In 1885, Jozsef Dobos created his famous Dobos Torte, a 6- or 7-layer Hungarian torte that was highly cherished. He kept his recipe a serect for quite some time, forcing rival bakers to try, in vain, to duplicate the recipe. Finally, in 1906, Dobos shared his secrets. The recipe is so good, it has remained in circulation since then. Our version, using whole wheat flours, is surely as rich and delicious as the original.

Makes one 9-inch torte

- ½ cup whole wheat pastry flour
- ½ cup unbleached white flour
- 1 tablespoon cornstarch
- ¼ teaspoon salt
- 6 eggs, separated
- 1½ cups confectioners' sugar
- 1 teaspoon vanilla extract
- 4½ cups Chocolate Buttercream Frosting (page 483)
- 1 cup Caramel Glaze (page 480)
- ½ cup hazelnuts, toasted and chopped

Make sure all of your ingredients are at room temperature. Preheat the oven to 375°F. Grease or line two 9-inch cake pans with parchment paper.

In a large bowl, sift the flours, cornstarch, and salt.

Beat the egg yolks with ¾ cup of the confectioners' sugar and vanilla until light in color and thick, about 4 minutes. Beat the egg whites until frothy, then gradually add the remaining confectioners' sugar and beat until stiff. Fold the egg whites into the yolk mixture, then fold in the flour mixture.

Spoon ⅔ cup of the batter into each pan and bake until brown, about 6 minutes. Cool in the pans for a few minutes, then turn onto the racks to cool. Cool the pans and clean them, then repeat until all of the batter is used.

Set one layer of cake on a dish and spread the top with some buttercream filling. Set another layer on top of the first one and top with filling. Repeat with all but one layer. Use the remaining buttercream to cover the sides of the cake. Press chopped hazelnuts into the sides of the cake.

Place the reserved layer of cake on a plate. Make the caramel glaze according to the directions (page 480), then spread the glaze over the cake layer and let it set for about 30 seconds. Cut the layer into 10 or 12 equal-sized portions, let cool and set completely. Reassemble the wedges on the top of the cake, and use them as a guide to slice the cake.

Chocolate Ricotta and Almond Cake

Sweet Italian ricotta filling and chocolate frosting match up just right with this almond cake. There must be something for you to celebrate with this cake!

Makes one 9-inch layer cake

- 1 cup almond flour
- 2/3 cup whole wheat pastry flour
- 1/2 cup cocoa powder
- 2 teaspoons baking powder
- 1/4 teaspoon salt
- 8 eggs, separated
- 1 1/3 cups sugar
- 1 1/2 teaspoons vanilla
- 2/3 cup milk
- Ricotta Filling (page 482)
- Chocolate Buttercream Frosting or Chocolate Glaze (pages 483 and 479)

Make sure all of your ingredients are at room temperature. Preheat the oven to 375°F. Grease or line two 9-inch cake pans with parchment paper.

Sift the flours with the cocoa, baking powder, and salt.

Cream the egg yolks with the sugar and vanilla until light in color and thick, about 4 minutes, scraping down the sides of the bowl as necessary. Turn the mixer to low, add half of the flour mixture and incorporate, then half the milk and blend until smooth. Repeat with the remaining flour and milk.

Beat the egg whites until stiff, stir about one-third of them into the batter, then gently fold in the remaining egg whites. Pour the batter into the prepared pans and bake for 20 minutes, or until a tester comes out clean. Cool in the pans for 15 minutes then turn onto wire racks and cool completely.

Split the cakes horizontally and place one layer on a plate. Spread some filling on the top, stack with another layer, and repeat for two more layers. Frost.

Tangerine Cake

Tangerines add a wonderful sweet tanginess to this cake that is great for any day.

Makes one 8-inch layer cake

- 2 tangerines, or substitute 1 orange
- 3 eggs
- 2 egg whites
- Scant 1 cup sugar
- ⅓ cup cornstarch
- ½ cup unbleached flour
- ½ cup whole wheat flour
- ½ teaspoon baking powder
- Tangerine Glaze or Buttercream Frosting (pages 479 or 483)

Make sure all of your ingredients are at room temperature. Zest the tangerines and reserve the zest. Peel and seed the tangerines, then place the flesh in a food processor or blender and puree. Combine with the zest and set aside.

Preheat the oven to 350°F. Grease two 8-inch round baking pans or line with parchment paper.

Beat the eggs and egg whites until foamy, then slowly add the sugar and continue to beat until thick, about 6 minutes. Whisk together the cornstarch with the flours and baking powder, then stir into the egg mixture. Gently fold in the tangerine mixture.

Spread the batter in the prepared pans and bake for about 40 minutes, or until a tester comes out clean. Let the cakes rest in the pans for 5 minutes, then cool them completely on a wire rack before frosting.

Millet Cake

The additional millet flour makes for a magnificently flavorful cake.

Makes one 8 x 4-inch cake

- 1 cup brown sugar
- 1¼ cups water
- ¾ cup raisins
- 4 tablespoons unsalted butter
- 1 teaspoon ground cinnamon
- ¼ teaspoon ground cloves
- ¼ teaspoon ground ginger
- ¾ cup whole wheat pastry flour
- ¼ cup millet flour
- ½ cup unbleached white flour
- ½ teaspoons salt
- 1 teaspoon baking powder
- ½ teaspoon baking soda
- ½ cup walnuts or pecans, optional

Make sure all of your ingredients are at room temperature. Preheat the oven to 350°F. Grease or line an 8 x 4-inch baking pan with parchment paper.

In a saucepan, bring the brown sugar, water, raisins, butter, and spices to a boil and simmer gently for 4 or 5 minutes. Remove from the heat and let the mixture rest until cool enough to touch.

Sift the flours, salt, baking powder, and baking soda, into the sugar mixture, beating until smooth. Stir in the walnuts.

Spread the batter into the prepared pan and bake for 25 minutes or until a tester comes out clean. Let the cake cool in the pan for 10 to 15 minutes then remove to a wire rack to cool completely. Eat as is or frost as desired using frostings on pages 481 to 483.

Candied Lemon Cake

The addition of candied lemon to this lemon cake makes a sweet and sour cake that any lemon lover is sure to crave.

Makes one 8 x 8-inch cake

- 1½ cups water
- 1 cup sugar
- 4 lemons, sliced very thinly
- ¼ cup wheat germ
- 1 cup unbleached white flour
- 1¼ cups whole wheat flour
- 2½ teaspoons baking powder
- ½ teaspoon baking soda
- 2 tablespoons lemon zest
- ½ teaspoon salt
- ¼ pound (1 stick) unsalted butter, softened
- 1 cup brown sugar, packed
- 2 eggs
- 1 cup plus 2 tablespoons buttermilk

Make sure all of your ingredients are at room temperature. Preheat the oven to 325°F. Lightly grease an 8 x 8-inch baking pan or dish or line it with parchment paper.

To make the candied lemon: Heat the water and sugar in a skillet until the sugar has dissolved. Bring to a boil, stirring, until the syrup begins to thicken, about 5 minutes.

Add the lemon slices and simmer for about 3 or 4 minutes. Use tongs to turn the slices and continue for another 3 or 4 minutes, or until the lemon is tender. Place the slices on a plate or large baking dish to cool. When they are cool enough to handle, chop the lemon coarsely into ½-inch or so sized pieces. Reserve the syrup.

Whisk together the wheat germ, flours, baking powder, baking soda, zest, and salt.

In a large bowl, cream the butter with the brown sugar until well blended, about 2 minutes. Add the eggs, one at a time, scraping down the sides of the bowl as needed.

Add one-third of the flour mixture to the butter mixture, beating slowly until just blended. Beat in half the buttermilk. Repeat with another third of the flour and half the buttermilk, then beat in the remaining flour. Fold in the candied lemon. Scrape the batter into the prepared pan and bake for 40 minutes, or until a tester comes out clean. Cool completely in the pan set on a wire rack. Drizzle with the lemon syrup.

Orange Cream Gateau

This cake presents the orange in a lovely and delicate delight.

Makes one 9-inch layer cake

- 1½ cups whole wheat pastry flour
- ½ teaspoon cornstarch
- ½ teaspoon baking powder
- 3 eggs, separated
- ⅓ cup sugar
- 1 cup Orange Buttercream Filling (page 483)
- Confectioners' sugar for dusting, optional

Make sure all of your ingredients are at room temperature. Preheat the oven to 350°F. and grease two 9-inch cake pans or line them with parchment paper.

In a large bowl, sift together the flour, cornstarch, and baking powder.

Cream the egg yolks with the sugar until light in color and thick, about 4 minutes, scraping down the sides of the bowl as necessary. In a separate bowl, beat the egg whites until stiff.

Gently fold the flour mixture into the yolk mixture, then fold in the egg whites. Spoon into the prepared pans and bake for 20 minutes, or until a tester comes out clean. Cool the cakes in the pans on a wire rack for 10 minutes, then remove them from the pan and cool completely on the rack.

Place one layer of cake on a plate and top with the orange filling. Place the second cake on top and sprinkle with confectioners' sugar.

Sugarless Banana Spice Cake

Applesauce and banana are the sweeteners for this cake, not sugar. Fruit is good for you, so go ahead and have two pieces.

Makes one 9 x 9-inch cake

- ½ cup milk
- ¼ cup vegetable oil
- 2 eggs, separated
- ¾ cup plus 2 tablespoons applesauce
- 1½ cups whole wheat flour
- 2 tablespoons rice flour
- ¼ cup wheat germ
- ½ teaspoon ground nutmeg
- ½ teaspoon ground allspice
- 1½ teaspoons ground cinnamon
- 2 teaspoons baking powder
- 1 teaspoon baking soda
- ½ teaspoon salt
- 1 cup mashed banana

Make sure all of your ingredients are at room temperature. Preheat the oven to 350°F. and grease a 9-inch square pan or line it with parchment paper.

In a large bowl, beat together the milk, oil, egg yolks, and applesauce.

Whisk together the flours, wheat germ, spices, baking powder, baking soda, and salt. Whisk in the milk mixture and bananas to form a batter.

Beat the egg whites until stiff peaks form, then fold into the batter.

Scrape the batter into the prepared pan and bake for 45 minutes, or until a tester comes out clean. Cool in the pan on a wire rack. Eat as is or frost as desired using frostings on pages 481 to 483.

Hazelnut Torte

This sophisticated cake is the perfect ending for a fancy dinner or any dinner at all.

Makes one 9-inch torte

- 2½ cups of hazelnuts
- ⅓ cup whole wheat flour
- ½ teaspoon baking powder
- Pinch salt
- ½ pound (2 sticks) unsalted butter
- ¾ cup sugar
- 1½ teaspoons vanilla extract
- 5 eggs, separated
- ¾ cup confectioners' sugar
- Chocolate Buttercream Frosting (page 483)

Make sure all of your ingredients are at room temperature. Preheat the oven to 350°F. and grease a 9-inch springform pan.

Place 2¼ cups of the hazelnuts in a small food processor or coffee grinder and process until finely ground. Pour the ground hazelnuts into a bowl and combine with the flour, baking powder, and salt.

In a large bowl, cream the butter with the sugar and the vanilla until light in color and thick, about 4 minutes. Beat in the egg yolks one at a time, scraping down the sides of the bowl as needed.

In a separate bowl, beat the egg whites until frothy then gradually add the confectioners' sugar and beat until stiff. Fold the egg whites into the yolk mixture, then fold in the flour mixture.

Scrape the batter into the prepared pan and bake for 45 minutes, or until a tester comes out clean. Cool in the pan for 15 minutes, then remove the sides of the pan and cool completely.

Place the cake on a plate and frost. Chop the remaining ¼ cup of hazelnuts and sprinkle over the cake.

Coconut Layer Cake

This cake is a coconut lover's delight, with coconut in every bite.

Makes one 9-inch layer cake

- 1½ cups unbleached white flour
- 1 cup whole wheat flour
- 1 tablespoon baking powder
- ½ teaspoon salt
- ½ pound (2 sticks) unsalted butter, softened
- 1¾ cups sugar
- 1 teaspoon vanilla extract
- **4 eggs**
- ⅓ cup milk
- ⅔ cup coconut milk, well shaken
- ½ cup hazelnuts, chopped
- Coconut Buttercream Filling (page 483)
- 1 cup heavy cream
- ⅓ cup confectioners' sugar
- ⅓ cup shredded coconut

Make sure all of your ingredients are at room temperature. Preheat the oven to 350°F. and grease two 9-inch cake pans or line them with parchment paper.

In a medium bowl, sift or whisk together the flours, baking powder, and salt.

Cream the butter with the sugar until light, about 4 minutes. Beat in the vanilla. Add the eggs one at a time, scraping down the sides of the bowl as needed.

Combine the milk and coconut milk in a small bowl.

Add half of the flour mixture to the butter mixture, beating gently to blend. Add half of the milk mixture and stir to just incorporate. Repeat with remaining flour and milk. Stir in the hazelnuts.

Scrape the batter into the prepared pans and bake for 25 minutes, or until a tester comes out clean. Cool the cakes in the pans for 10 minutes then remove them from the pans to cool completely on a wire rack.

Place one cake on a plate and top with Coconut Buttercream. Place the second cake on top.

Beat the heavy cream in a cold bowl and gradually add the confectioners' sugar, until stiff. Fold in the coconut then spread on top of the cake.

Upside Down Pear & Pumpkin Cornmeal Cake

Pear and pumpkin make a great pair in this spectacular cake.

Makes one 8 x 8-inch cake

- ³/₄ cup unbleached white flour
- ¹/₂ cup whole wheat pastry flour
- ¹/₂ teaspoon ground ginger
- ¹/₂ teaspoon ground cinnamon
- ¹/₄ teaspoon ground nutmeg
- 1 teaspoon baking powder
- ¹/₄ teaspoon baking soda
- ¹/₄ teaspoon salt
- ¹/₂ pound (2 sticks) unsalted butter, softened
- ¹/₂ cup plus ²/₃ cup brown sugar, packed
- ¹/₂ cup sugar
- 2 eggs
- ¹/₂ cup pumpkin puree
- ¹/₂ cup cornmeal
- 2 ripe pears, peeled, seeded and diced
- ¹/₃ cup milk

Make sure all of your ingredients are at room temperature. Preheat the oven to 350°F. Lightly grease an 8 x 8-inch baking pan or dish.

Sift together the flours, spices, baking powder, baking soda, and salt.

Cream half of the butter, then add ¹/₂ cup of the brown sugar along with the sugar. Add the eggs one at a time, incorporating well and scraping down the sides of the bowl. Beat in the pumpkin and cornmeal just to blend.

In a small saucepan set over medium to low heat, heat the remaining half of the butter with the remaining ²/₃ cup of the brown sugar. Warm until the sugar dissolves, then stir in the pear.

Whisk one-third of the flour mixture into the butter mixture, then add half of the milk. Repeat with one-third of the flour, the remaining milk, and the remaining flour, blending after each addition.

Spread the pear mixture across the bottom of the prepared pan. Spread the batter on top and bake for 30 minutes, or until a tester comes out clean. Cool in the pan for 10 minutes, then invert onto a plate. Serve warm or at room temperature.

Vanilla Cake with Quinoa

Replacing some wheat flour with quinoa flour makes for a very moist cake. Enjoy it with the frosting of your choice, perhaps the Rum Buttercream (page 483).

Makes two 9-inch layers

- 1¼ cups unbleached white flour
- 1¼ cups whole wheat flour
- ½ cup quinoa flour
- 1 tablespoon baking powder
- ½ teaspoon salt
- ½ pound (2 sticks) unsalted butter, softened
- 1½ cups sugar
- 4 eggs
- ½ cup honey
- 1¼ teaspoons vanilla extract
- 1 cup milk

Make sure all of your ingredients are at room temperature. Preheat the oven to 350°F. Grease or line two 9-inch round cake pans with parchment paper.

Whisk together the flours, baking powder, and salt.

Cream the butter with the sugar until light, about 4 minutes. Add the eggs one at a time and beat until incorporated, scraping down the sides of the bowl 3 or 4 times. Beat in the honey and the vanilla. Turn the beater to low and add one-third of the flour mixture and beat just until incorporated. Add half of the milk and blend, then another third of the flour. Beat to incorporate, add the remaining milk and blend, then finish with the rest of the flour.

Spread the batter in the prepared pans and bake for 30 minutes, or until a tester comes out clean. Cool to room temperature in the pans on a wire rack. Eat as is or frost as desired using frostings on pages 481 to 483.

Apple Bundt Cake

Applesauce not only flavors this cake, but it makes it tremendously moist as well.

Makes one bundt cake

- 1 cup whole wheat pastry flour
- 1 cup unbleached white flour
- 1½ cups sugar
- ½ teaspoon ground cinnamon
- ½ teaspoon ground allspice
- 1½ teaspoons baking powder
- ½ teaspoon baking soda
- ½ teaspoon salt
- 2 tablespoons milk
- 6 tablespoons vegetable oil
- ½ cup applesauce
- 3 eggs
- 2 apples, peeled, cored, and chopped

Make sure all of your ingredients are at room temperature. Preheat the oven to 350°F. and grease a bundt pan.

Sift the flours, sugar, cinnamon, allspice, baking powder, baking soda, and salt into a large bowl. Whisk together the milk, oil, applesauce, and eggs and stir into the flour until just combined.

Fold in the apples, then pour the batter into the prepared pan and smooth. Bake about 1 hour, or until a tester comes out clean. Cool in the pan for 15 minutes, then invert onto a wire rack to cool completely.

Basic Birthday Cake

This is just a great, plain cake recipe. Dress it up with your choice of frostings.

Makes one 9-inch layer cake

- 1 cup sifted whole grain flour
- 1 cup sifted unbleached white flour
- 2½ teaspoons baking powder
- Pinch of salt
- ½ pound (2 sticks) unsalted butter, softened
- 1²/₃ cups sugar
- 4 eggs
- ²/₃ cup whole milk
- 2 teaspoons vanilla
- Chocolate Buttercream Frosting (page 483)

Make sure all of your ingredients are at room temperature. Preheat the oven to 350°F. Line two 9-inch round cake pans with parchment paper.

Sift together the flours, baking powder, and salt.

Cream the butter for a minute, then add the sugar and mix until pale, about 3 minutes. Beat in the eggs one at a time, scraping down the sides of the bowl after each addition. In a small bowl, combine the milk and the vanilla.

Whisk one-third of the flour mixture into the butter mixture, then add half the milk mixture. Repeat with another third of the flour and half of the milk, whisking well. Then add the last portion of the flour.

Pour the batter into the prepared pans and bake until the cakes are puffy and a tester comes out clean, about 20 minutes. Cool on a wire rack.

Place one layer of cake on a plate and spread about one-third of the frosting over the cake, then layer the second cake on top and spread the remaining frosting over the cake. Refrigerate for 20 minutes to set.

Devil's Food Cake

Devil's Food Cake is so rich it's considered "sinful" (diet-wise, that is), or inspired by the devil. Here's a whole grain version that is not so rich that the devil inspired it, but an angel might feel a little guilty enjoying it all the same.

Makes one 9-inch layer cake

- 1 cup whole wheat flour
- ³/₄ cup unbleached white flour
- 1 teaspoon baking powder
- Pinch salt
- ¹/₂ cup cocoa powder
- ¹/₂ cup hot water
- 12 tablespoons (1¹/₂ stick) unsalted butter, softened, or shortening
- 1¹/₃ cups sugar
- 3 eggs
- ¹/₂ cup buttermilk
- 1 teaspoon vanilla
- Chocolate Buttercream Frosting (page 483)

Make sure all of your ingredients are at room temperature. Preheat the oven to 350°F. Line two 9-inch round cake pans with parchment paper.

In a large bowl, sift together the flours, baking powder, and salt. In a separate bowl, combine the cocoa powder with the hot water.

Cream the butter for a minute, then add the sugar and mix until pale, about 3 minutes. Beat in the eggs one at a time, scraping down the sides of the bowl after each addition.

Stir the buttermilk into the cocoa mixture. Add the vanilla and stir to blend.

Whisk into the butter mixture one-third of the flour mixture, then half the buttermilk mixture. Repeat with another third of the flour and the other half of the buttermilk combination, whisking well. Whisk in the last portion of the flour.

Pour the batter into the prepared pans and bake until the cakes are puffy and a tester comes out clean, about 20 minutes. Cool on a wire rack.

Place one layer of cake on a plate and spread about one-third of the frosting over the cake, then layer the second cake on top and spread the remaining frosting over the cake. Refrigerate for 25 minutes to set.

Ginger Apple Hazelnut Upside-Down Cake

Here's a contemporary take on the traditional pineapple upside-down cake. Ginger adds a nice sweet bite to this cake, which is especially nice topped with whipped cream.

Makes one 8 x 8-inch cake

- **4 tablespoons** unsalted butter, melted and cooled
- **⅓ cup** brown sugar
- **2 tablespoons** crystallized ginger, finely chopped
- **2 medium** apples, peeled and thinly sliced
- **1 tablespoon** lemon juice
- **1¼ cups** whole wheat flour
- **½ teaspoon** baking powder
- **¼ teaspoon** salt
- **2 eggs**
- **⅓ cup** sugar
- **1 teaspoon** vanilla
- **¼ cup** hazelnuts, finely chopped
- **Whipped cream**, optional, for topping

Make sure all of your ingredients are at room temperature. Preheat the oven to 375°F.

Combine the butter, brown sugar, and ginger in a small bowl, then pour into the bottom of an 8 x 8-inch baking dish. Toss the apple slices with the lemon juice and then lay across the top of the butter mixture.

Sift together the flour, baking powder, and salt. Cream the eggs with the sugar and vanilla until light, about 4 minutes.

Fold the flour mixture into the egg mixture and stir in the hazelnuts. Pour the batter over the apple slices and bake for 20 minutes or until a tester comes out clean. Allow to cool in the pan placed on a rack, for 15 minutes. Run a knife around the edge of the pan and invert the cake onto a serving plate. Top with whipped cream and enjoy!

Carrot Cake

Ginger and carrot make this carrot cake spicy and very flavorful.

Makes one 13 x 9-inch cake

- ²/₃ cup whole wheat flour
- ²/₃ cup unbleached white flour
- ³/₄ cup sugar
- 2 tablespoons brown sugar
- 1½ teaspoons baking soda
- 1 teaspoon baking powder
- 1 teaspoon ground cinnamon
- ¼ teaspoon ground nutmeg
- ½ teaspoon ground allspice
- ½ teaspoon salt
- ½ cup vegetable oil
- 3 tablespoons unsalted butter, softened
- 3 eggs, room temperature
- 1½ cups grated carrots
- ¼ cup crystallized ginger, minced, optional

Make sure all of your ingredients are at room temperature. Preheat the oven to 350°F. Grease a 13 x 9-inch pan or baking dish, or line it with parchment paper.

Sift the flours, sugars, baking soda, baking powder, spices, and salt.

Lightly beat together the oil and butter, then beat in the eggs. Whisk this mixture into the flour mixture to blend. Stir in the carrots and ginger.

Spread the batter in the prepared pan. Bake for 25 minutes, or until a tester comes out clean. Let cool in the pan for 15 minutes, invert onto a rack and cool to room temperature.

Eat as is or frost as desired using frostings on pages 481 to 483.

Ginger Cake

Third in a trio of ginger-inspired cake recipes, this one is made with fresh rather than crystallized ginger for a more piquant taste. Pick a frosting like cream cheese and honey, or vanilla buttercream (page 483).

Makes one 8 x 8-inch cake

- ³/₄ cup whole wheat flour
- ³/₄ cup unbleached white flour
- 1 teaspoon baking soda
- ¹/₂ teaspoon ground allspice
- ¹/₂ teaspoon salt
- ¹/₂ cup brown sugar, packed
- ¹/₃ cup molasses
- 3 tablespoons honey
- 1 egg
- ¹/₄ cup grated fresh ginger
- 6 tablespoons unsalted butter, melted and cooled
- ¹/₂ cup apple juice or water
- 2 tablespoons vegetable oil

Make sure all of your ingredients are at room temperature. Preheat the oven to 350°F. Grease an 8 x 8-inch pan or baking dish, or line it with parchment paper.

In a large bowl, whisk together the flours, baking soda, allspice, and salt.

In another bowl, beat briefly the brown sugar, molasses, honey, and egg. Stir in the ginger, butter, apple juice, and oil.

Whisk the flour mixture into the wet mixture until smooth. Pour the batter into the prepared dish and bake for 25 minutes, or until a tester comes out clean. Cool to room temperature on a wire rack. Eat as is or frost as desired using frostings on pages 481 to 483.

Quick Chocolate Sheet Cake

A good basic chocolate cake recipe, but not plain by any means.

Makes one 13 x 9-inch cake

- 1 cup unbleached white flour
- ⅔ cup whole wheat flour
- ⅓ cup oat flour
- 1½ teaspoons baking soda
- ½ teaspoon salt
- 1¾ cups sugar
- 4 ounces unsweetened chocolate, coarsely chopped
- ¼ pound (1 stick) unsalted butter, softened
- 1 cup hot water
- ½ cup sour cream or plain yogurt
- 2 eggs, lightly beaten

Make sure all of your ingredients are at room temperature. Preheat the oven to 350°F. Grease a 13 x 9-inch baking pan, or line it with parchment paper.

In a large bowl, whisk the flours, baking soda, salt, and sugar.

In the top of a double boiler placed over boiling water, melt the chocolate with the butter, then stir in the water until smooth and remove from the heat. Whisk the flour mixture into the chocolate mixture, then beat in the sour cream and eggs.

Pour the batter into the prepared pan and bake 35 minutes, or until a tester comes out clean. Cool on a wire rack. Eat as is or frost as desired using frostings on pages 481 to 483.

Almond Butter Cake

This cake is rich, rich, rich. Serve small slices, unfrosted or frosted. Did we mention that it's rich?

Makes two 9-inch layers

- 1 cup unbleached white flour
- ¾ cup whole wheat flour
- ¼ cup almond flour
- 2 teaspoons baking powder
- ¼ teaspoon salt
- ½ pound (2 sticks) unsalted butter, softened
- 1⅓ cups sugar
- 1 teaspoon almond extract
- 3 eggs
- Scant 1 cup milk

Make sure all of your ingredients are at room temperature. Preheat the oven to 350°F. Line two 9-inch round cake pans with parchment paper.

In a large bowl, sift together the flours, baking powder, and salt.

Cream the butter with the sugar until light, about 4 minutes. Beat in the almond extract and then the eggs, one at a time, scraping down the sides of the bowl after each addition. Slowly beat in half the flour mixture, then half of the milk. Repeat with remaining flour and milk.

Scrape the batter into the prepared pans and bake for 30 minutes, or until a tester comes out clean. Cool on a wire rack in the pan for 10 minutes, then remove to the rack to cool completely. Eat as is or frost as desired using frostings on pages 481 to 483.

Pumpkin Bundt Cake

This is a really fun cake to make for a Halloween party. If you have a pan in the shape of a pumpkin, it's even more fun. Try it with Rum or Vanilla Buttercream Frosting (page 483).

Makes one bundt cake

- ½ cup whole wheat flour
- ½ cup unbleached white flour
- ½ teaspoon baking soda
- 1 teaspoon ground cinnamon
- ½ teaspoon ground ginger
- ¼ teaspoon ground nutmeg
- Pinch of ground cloves
- 2 eggs
- 1 cup sugar
- ½ cup vegetable oil
- 2 tablespoons unsalted butter, softened
- 1 cup fresh or canned pumpkin puree
- Rum or Vanilla Buttercream Frosting (page 483)

Make sure all of your ingredients are at room temperature. Preheat the oven to 350°F. Grease a 10-cup Bundt pan.

In a large bowl, sift together the flours, baking soda, and spices.

Cream the eggs with the sugar, oil, and butter, about 5 minutes, scraping down the sides of the bowl as necessary. Add the flour mixture until well combined, then stir in the pumpkin.

Scrape the batter into the prepared pan and bake for 35 minutes, or until a tester comes out clean. Cool on a wire rack then frost.

Chocolate Oatmeal Cake

Rich oat flavor is paired with just a hint of chocolate flavor for a delightfully down-home cake.

Makes one 13 x 9-inch cake

- ½ cup unbleached white flour
- ½ cup whole wheat flour
- 1 teaspoon baking soda
- ¼ cup cocoa powder
- ½ teaspoon salt
- 5 tablespoons unsalted butter, softened
- 1¼ cups sugar
- 2 eggs, beaten
- 1 teaspoon vanilla
- 1 cup buttermilk
- 2 cups rolled oats

Make sure all of your ingredients are at room temperature. Preheat the oven to 350°F. Grease a 13 x 9-inch pan or baking dish, or line it with parchment paper.

In a large bowl, sift together the flours, baking soda, cocoa, and salt.

Cream the butter with the sugar until light, about 4 minutes, then beat in the eggs one at a time until incorporated, scraping down the sides of the bowl as necessary. Add the vanilla. Whisk half of the flour mixture into the butter mixture and blend, then whisk in half the buttermilk. Repeat with remaining flour and buttermilk. Stir in the oats.

Spread the batter in the prepared pan. Bake for 30 minutes, or until a tester comes out clean. Let cool in the pan on a rack. Frost with your choice of frostings. Eat as is or frost as desired using frostings on pages 481 to 483.

Lemon Pound Cake

For plain pound cake, just hold the lemon zest. Be sure not to over-mix this batter or the cake will become heavy.

Makes one 8 x 4-inch loaf

- ²/₃ cup unbleached white flour
- ½ cup whole wheat flour
- 1½ teaspoons baking powder
- ¼ teaspoon salt
- 2 eggs
- ¾ cup sugar
- 2 teaspoons vanilla
- 2 teaspoons lemon zest
- 5 tablespoons unsalted butter, melted and cooled
- ½ cup sour cream

Make sure all of your ingredients are at room temperature. Preheat the oven to 400°F. and grease an 8 x 4-inch loaf pan or line it with parchment paper.

In a large bowl, sift the flours, baking powder, and salt.

Combine well (but do not beat) the eggs with the sugar, vanilla, and zest in a large bowl. Gently add the flour mixture to blend and then stir in the butter and sour cream.

Pour the batter into the prepared pan and bake for 15 to 20 minutes, or until a crust forms on the top. Make a 1-inch cut down the center of the cake, reduce the heat to 350°F. and continue to bake until a tester comes out clean, about 30 minutes longer. Allow to cool for 10 minutes in the pan then remove from the pan and cool on a wire rack. Serve warm or at room temperature.

Apple Pie Barley Pound Cake

Barley flour is not often used in cakes—with it's bold flavor can take over a recipe. We think we've incorporated just the right amount in this recipe and combined it with applesauce and warm spices associated with apple pie, not cake. Drizzle with puréed berries or berry syrup.

Makes one 10-inch round cake

- 1½ cups unbleached white flour
- 1¼ cups whole wheat flour
- ¾ cup barley flour
- 2½ teaspoons baking soda
- 1 teaspoon ground ginger
- 1 teaspoon ground cinnamon
- ½ teaspoon ground nutmeg
- ¼ teaspoon ground mace
- ½ teaspoon salt
- ¼ pound (1 stick) unsalted butter, softened
- 2 cups brown sugar, packed
- 2 eggs
- Scant 1 cup applesauce
- Mixed berry purée, for topping

Make sure all of your ingredients are at room temperature. Preheat the oven to 375°F. and grease a 10-inch tube pan.

In a large bowl, whisk together the flours, baking soda, spices, and salt.

Cream the butter with the sugar until well blended, about 2 or 3 minutes. Beat in the eggs one at a time, scraping down the bowl as needed.

On low speed beat in one-third of the flour, followed by half of the applesauce. Repeat with one-third of the flour, the remaining applesauce, and the remaining flour mixture, beating until smooth.

Scrape the batter into the prepared pan and bake for 1 hour, 15 minutes, or until a tester comes out clean. Let the cake rest in the pan for 10 minutes, then remove from the pan, place on a rack and cool completely. Drizzle with mixed berry purée or berry syrup.

Kamut® Cake

Kamut grain adds a light nuttiness to this cake that we think you'll love.

Makes one 8 x 8-inch cake

- 2 cups Kamut grain flour
- ½ cup barley flour
- 2 tablespoons baking powder
- ¼ teaspoon salt
- ½ cup vegetable oil
- ½ cup honey
- 1 cup orange juice
- ½ cup water
- ½ cup walnuts or peanuts

Make sure all of your ingredients are at room temperature. Preheat the oven to 325°F. and grease an 8 x 8-inch loaf pan or line it with parchment paper.

In a large bowl, combine the flours with the baking powder and salt.

Beat the oil, honey, orange juice, and water together until well blended, then add to the flour mixture to make a smooth batter. Stir in the nuts.

Spread the batter in the prepared pan and bake for 25 minutes, or until a tester comes out clean. Allow to cool for 10 minutes then remove it from the pan and cool completely on a wire rack. Eat as is or frost as desired using frostings on pages 481 to 483.

Spelt Spice Cake

Spice cakes often tend to be dense, and this one, made with spelt, is dense and hearty.

Makes one 8 x 8-inch cake

- ¾ cup spelt flour
- 1½ teaspoons baking powder
- 1 teaspoon ground cinnamon
- ½ teaspoon ground allspice
- ¼ teaspoon ground nutmeg
- ¼ teaspoon salt
- 5 tablespoons unsalted butter, softened
- ⅓ cup brown sugar, packed
- 2 eggs
- ⅓ cup plain yogurt
- Rum Buttercream or Cream Cheese and Honey Frosting (page 483 or 481)

Make sure all of your ingredients are at room temperature. Preheat the oven to 350°F. Grease an 8 x 8-inch pan or baking dish, or line it with parchment paper.

In a large bowl, whisk together the flour, baking powder, spices, and salt.

Cream the butter with the brown sugar until light, about 4 minutes, then beat in the eggs one at a time, scraping down the sides of the bowl as necessary. Whisk in the yogurt, then add the flour mixture to blend.

Pour the batter into the prepared pan and bake for 30 minutes, or until a tester comes out clean. Cool in the pan for 10 minutes, then cool completely on a wire rack. Frost.

Cinnamon Applesauce Cake

Cinnamon and applesauce are a great combination, making this cake truly impressive.

Makes one 8 x 8-inch cake

- ³/₄ cup unbleached white flour
- ³/₄ cup whole wheat flour
- ¹/₄ teaspoon salt
- 1¹/₂ teaspoons ground cinnamon
- Pinch of ground cloves
- 2 teaspoons baking powder
- ¹/₄ pound (1 stick) unsalted butter, softened
- ³/₄ cup brown sugar, packed
- ¹/₂ cup sugar
- 2 eggs
- ³/₄ cup plus 1 tablespoon applesauce
- ¹/₂ cup pecans, chopped

Make sure all of your ingredients are at room temperature. Preheat the oven to 350°F. Grease an 8 x 8-inch pan or baking dish, or line it with parchment paper.

In a large bowl, sift together the flours, salt, cinnamon, cloves, and baking powder.

Cream the butter with the sugars until light, about 4 minutes. Beat in the eggs one at a time until incorporated, scraping down the sides of the bowl as necessary. Beat half of the flour mixture into the butter mixture on low speed, then add half of the applesauce. Repeat with remaining flour mixture and applesauce. Fold in the pecans.

Pour the batter into the prepared pan and bake for 30 minutes. Cover with foil and bake another 15 minutes, or until a tester comes out clean. Cool in the pan on a wire rack. Eat as is or frost as desired using frostings on pages 481 to 483.

Yogurt Cake with Blueberry Sauce

Yogurt for tang, oat flour for texture. We picked blueberries for this sauce, but feel free to substitute with peaches, nectarines, or even another berry.

Makes one 9-inch round cake

- 1 pound blueberries, fresh or frozen
- 1 teaspoon lemon juice
- ¼ cup sugar
- 1 cup unbleached white flour
- ¾ cup whole wheat flour
- ¼ cup oat flour, or substitute with same amount whole wheat flour
- ¼ teaspoon salt
- 2 teaspoons baking powder
- 2 eggs
- 1 cup sugar
- 1 cup plain yogurt, at room temperature
- ½ teaspoon vanilla
- 5 tablespoons unsalted butter, melted and cooled

Make sure all of your ingredients are at room temperature. Preheat the oven to 350°F. Grease a 9-inch round pan, or line it with parchment paper.

Heat the berries, lemon juice, and sugar in a saucepan over medium-low heat until berries burst and thicken slightly. Remove from the heat, place in a blender and puree. Set aside.

In a large bowl, sift together the flours, salt, and baking powder.

Cream the eggs with the sugar until light, about 2 minutes, scraping down the sides of the bowl when necessary. Whisk in the yogurt until combined, then whisk in the vanilla and butter and combine well. Whisk the flour mixture into the wet ingredients to make a smooth batter.

Pour the batter into the prepared pan and bake for 30 minutes or until a tester comes out clean. Cool in the pan on a wire rack.

Mixed Grains Cocoa Cake

Healthy cake? You betcha, but delicious too. If there is such a thing as too healthy when it comes to dessert, you can always add a little frosting.

Makes one 9 x 9-inch cake

- 1 cup unbleached white flour
- 1 cup sugar
- ½ teaspoon salt
- ¼ pound (1 stick) unsalted butter, chilled and diced
- ¼ cup rolled wheat flakes
- ¼ cup rolled oats
- ¼ cup rolled triticale flakes
- ⅓ cup cocoa powder
- 2 teaspoons baking powder
- ¼ teaspoon baking soda
- 1 cup milk
- 1½ teaspoons vanilla

Make sure all of your ingredients are at room temperature. Preheat the oven to 350°F. and lightly grease a 9-inch square baking pan.

Combine the flour, sugar, and salt in the bowl of a food processor or a large bowl. Pulse to cut in the butter, or use two knives, until mixture resembles coarse crumbs. Remove to a bowl and stir in the wheat, oats, and triticale. Reserve ¼ cup of this mixture.

Whisk together the cocoa, baking powder, and baking soda and then stir into the flour mixture.

Combine the milk and vanilla, then stir into the flour mixture until well blended. Turn the mixture into the prepared pan and sprinkle the reserved crumbs over top.

Bake for 35 to 40 minutes or until the topping is golden brown and a tester comes out clean. Cool for 20 minutes in the pan on a wire rack. Serve warm or at room temperature.

Buttermilk Apple Cake

The sourness of buttermilk wonderfully contrasts with the tartness of the apples and the hearty whole wheat flour in this recipe.

Makes one 9 x 9-inch cake

- 1 cup unbleached white flour
- ¾ cup whole wheat flour
- ¼ cup barley flour, substitute same amount whole wheat flour
- 2½ teaspoons baking powder
- ½ teaspoon ground cinnamon
- Pinch of salt
- ¼ pound (1 stick) unsalted butter, softened
- ¾ cup sugar
- 1 teaspoon vanilla
- 1 egg
- 1 cup plus 1 tablespoon buttermilk
- 1 medium-sized firm apple, peeled, cored, and grated
- Apricot Glaze (page 479)

Make sure all of your ingredients are at room temperature. Preheat the oven to 350°F. and grease a 9-inch square baking pan or dish, or line it with parchment paper.

Whisk together the flours, baking powder, cinnamon, and salt.

Cream the butter with the sugar until light, about 4 minutes. Beat in the vanilla and then the egg, scraping down the sides of the bowl as needed.

Add one-third of the flour mixture to the butter mixture, beating slowly until just blended. Beat in half the buttermilk. Repeat with another third of the flour and half the buttermilk, then beat in the remaining flour. Fold in the apples.

Scrape the batter into the prepared pan and bake for 55 minutes, or until a tester comes out clean. Cool on a wire rack. Serve warm or at room temperature and glaze just before serving.

Hood River Valley Apple Bake

The Hood River Valley, on the north side of Oregon's beautiful Mount Hood, is famous for its apples. We think this apple bake is just as good as the great name the valley has earned.

Makes one 9-inch round cake

- ¼ pound (1 stick) unsalted butter, softened
- ½ cup sugar
- ½ teaspoon vanilla
- 2 eggs
- 1½ cups whole wheat flour
- ½ teaspoon ground cinnamon
- 2 teaspoons cornstarch
- 2 teaspoons baking powder
- ½ teaspoon salt
- 6 tablespoons milk
- 3 tablespoons lemon juice
- 4 firm apples, such as Granny Smith, peeled, cored, and halved
- 2 tablespoons turbinado sugar, optional

Make sure all of your ingredients are at room temperature. Preheat the oven to 350°F. and grease a 9-inch springform pan or line it with parchment paper.

Cream the butter with the sugar until light, about 4 minutes. Beat in the vanilla. Add the eggs one at a time, scraping down the sides of the bowl as needed.

Whisk together the flour, cinnamon, cornstarch, baking powder, and salt. Beat half of the flour mixture into the butter mixture, then add half of the milk. Repeat with remaining flour and milk.

Scrape the batter into the prepared dish, and drizzle with half of the lemon juice. Arrange the apples in the batter, cut side down and then drizzle the apples with the remaining lemon juice. Sprinkle with the turbinado sugar.

Bake for 40 minutes or until the apples are tender and a tester comes out clean. Allow to cool in the pan on a wire rack, serve warm.

Gooey Fudge Cake

The name, "Gooey Fudge Cake" pretty much sums this up. Serve with a little ice cream or whipped cream, if you like.

Makes one 13 x 9-inch cake

- 1 cup whole wheat pastry flour
- ¾ cup unbleached white flour
- 2 teaspoons baking powder
- ½ teaspoon salt
- 1 cup sugar
- 1 cup cocoa powder, divided
- 1 cup milk
- 7 tablespoons unsalted butter, melted and cooled
- 2 teaspoons vanilla
- ⅓ cup honey
- 1 cup pecans or hazelnuts, chopped
- 1¾ cup brown sugar, packed
- 2 cups boiling water

Make sure all of your ingredients are at room temperature. Preheat the oven to 350°F. and grease a 13 x 9-inch baking pan or dish, or line it with parchment paper.

Whisk together the flours, baking powder, salt, sugar, and half of the cocoa. In another bowl, combine the milk with the butter and vanilla.

On low speed, gradually beat the milk mixture and the honey into the flour mixture. Stir in the nuts. Scrape the batter into the prepared pan.

Combine the remaining cocoa with the brown sugar and sprinkle it over the batter. Drizzle the water on top.

Bake for 40 minutes, or until a tester comes out without bits of flour. Allow the cake to cool in the pan on a wire rack. Serve warm or at room temperature.

Chocolate Yogurt Cake

Cookbooks with cake recipes are certain to have more than one recipe for that favorite of favorites — chocolate cake. Here, yogurt jumps in to give tang and lift to a whole wheat cake.

Makes two 9-inch layers

- ½ cup water
- ½ cup cocoa powder
- 2½ teaspoons baking soda
- 1 cup whole wheat flour
- 1 cup unbleached white flour
- ½ cup cornstarch
- ½ teaspoon salt
- 12 tablespoons (1½ stick) unsalted butter, softened
- 1¾ cups sugar
- 2 teaspoons vanilla
- 2 eggs
- 1 cup plain yogurt or sour cream

Make sure all of your ingredients are at room temperature. Preheat the oven to 350°F. and grease two 9-inch cake pans or line them with parchment paper.

Combine the water, cocoa, and baking soda in a saucepan over low heat and heat until completely combined. Allow to cool.

In a large bowl, whisk together the flours, cornstarch, and salt.

Cream the butter with the sugar until light, about 4 minutes. Beat in the vanilla. Add the eggs one at a time, scraping down the sides of the bowl as needed. Whisk half of the flour mixture into the butter mixture. Add half of the yogurt along with the cocoa mixture. Whisk in the remaining flour, followed by the rest of the yogurt.

Scrape the batter into the prepared pans and bake for 45 minutes, or until a tester comes out clean. Cool in the pans for 10 minutes, then cool completely on a wire rack.

Whole Wheat Rosemary Cake

You may think rosemary an odd choice for a cake, but after you taste this wonderful adaptation from Mario Batali, author of the Babbo Cookbook, *you will think it odd no longer. This cooks in a very slow oven.*

Makes one 10-inch cake

- 1 cup whole wheat pastry flour
- ½ cup unbleached white flour
- 1 tablespoon baking powder
- ½ teaspoon salt
- 4 eggs
- ⅔ cup sugar
- ⅔ cup extra virgin olive oil
- 2½ tablespoons fresh rosemary, chopped

Make sure all of your ingredients are at room temperature. Preheat the oven to 350°F. Grease a 10-inch baking pan, or line it with parchment paper.

In a large bowl, whisk together the flours, baking powder, and salt.

Beat the eggs for about 30 seconds, then beat in the sugar until foamy, 3 or 4 minutes. With the beater running, drizzle in the olive oil. Whisk in the flour mixture and rosemary.

Scrape the batter into the prepared pan and bake for 45 minutes, or until a tester comes out clean. Cool in the pan for 10 minutes, then cool completely on a wire rack.

Spice Cake

Whole wheat and millet flour give this spice cake a bit more earthiness. If you don't have the millet just add more whole wheat.

Makes one 9-inch round cake

- 1 cup whole wheat flour
- ¾ cup unbleached white flour
- ¼ cup millet flour
- 2½ teaspoons baking powder
- 1 teaspoon ground allspice
- 1 teaspoon ground cinnamon
- ½ teaspoon ground nutmeg
- ½ teaspoon salt
- 1 teaspoon vanilla
- ¾ cup plus 1 tablespoon milk
- 12 tablespoons (1½ stick) unsalted butter, softened
- 1 cup brown sugar, packed
- ½ cup sugar
- 2 eggs
- ⅓ cup honey

Make sure all of your ingredients are at room temperature. Preheat the oven to 350°F. Grease a 9-inch round pan, or line it with parchment paper.

Sift together the flours, baking powder, spices, and salt. Combine the vanilla and the milk.

Cream the butter with the sugars until light, about 4 minutes. Beat in the eggs one at a time until incorporated, then beat in the honey, scraping down the sides of the bowl as necessary. Whisk half of the flour mixture into the butter then add half of the milk. Repeat with remaining ingredients to make a smooth batter.

Pour the batter into the prepared pan and bake for 35 minutes or until a tester comes out clean. Cool in the pan on a wire rack. Eat as is or frost as desired using frostings on pages 481 to 483.

Blue Cornmeal Pear Cake

The intensity of blue cornmeal pairs very well with sweet pear flavors in this purplish-blue delight. For a lighter flavor, not to mention lighter color, feel free to switch to yellow cornmeal.

Makes one 9-inch round cake

- 1 pear, peeled, cored, and sliced thin
- 3 tablespoons lemon juice
- 1½ cups blue cornmeal
- 1¼ cups unbleached white flour
- ¼ cup whole wheat flour
- 2 teaspoons baking powder
- ½ pound (2 sticks) unsalted butter
- ¾ cup sugar
- ⅔ cup oil
- ½ cup pear or apple juice
- 2 tablespoons turbinado sugar, optional

Make sure all of your ingredients are at room temperature. Preheat the oven to 350°F. and grease a 9-inch springform pan.

Toss the pear slices with one tablespoon of the lemon juice. Whisk together the cornmeal, flours, and baking powder.

Cream the butter with the sugar until light, about 4 minutes. Add the flour mixture to blend, then the oil. Beat in the apple juice.

Scrape the batter into the prepared pan. Arrange the pear slices on top of the batter and drizzle with the remaining lemon juice. Sprinkle with the turbinado sugar. Bake for 40 minutes, or until a tester comes out clean. cool in the pan on a wire rack for 10 minutes, then remove the pan sides and cool completely.

Persimmon Cake

If you haven't tasted persimmons, this cake is a great place to start.

Makes one 13 x 9-inch cake

- 5 to 6 Hachiya persimmons
- 1½ cups sugar
- ½ cup brown sugar
- 2 eggs, beaten
- 1½ cups buttermilk
- 1 cup whole wheat flour
- ½ cup unbleached white flour
- 1 teaspoon baking soda
- 1 teaspoons baking powder
- ¼ teaspoon ground allspice
- ½ teaspoon ground cinnamon
- Pinch of salt
- ⅓ cup heavy cream
- 3 tablespoons unsalted butter, melted and cooled

Make sure all of your ingredients are at room temperature. Preheat the oven to 350°F. Grease a 13 x 9-inch baking dish.

Halve the persimmons and scoop out enough pulp to make 2 cups. Combine the pulp with the sugars, then beat in the eggs and the buttermilk.

Sift together the flours, baking soda, baking powder, spices, and salt. Add the flour mixture to the pulp mixture ½ cup at a time, stirring to combine. Stir in the cream and the butter.

Pour the batter into the dish and bake until dark brown and a toothpick comes out clean, about 55 minutes. Cool in the pan on a wire rack.

Marble Cake

Chocolate and vanilla make a wonderful combination in this beautifully marbled cake.

Makes one 10-inch round cake

- 4 eggs, separated
- 1 cup confectioners' sugar
- 12 tablespoons (1½ stick) unsalted butter
- 1 cup sifted whole wheat pastry flour
- 1 cup sifted unbleached white flour
- 1½ tablespoons baking powder
- ²⁄₃ cup plus 1 tablespoon warm milk
- ¹⁄₃ cup raisins
- 2 teaspoons cocoa powder

Make sure all of your ingredients are at room temperature. Preheat the oven to 300°F. and grease a 10-inch springform tube pan.

Cream together the egg yolks, confectioners' sugar, and butter in a medium bowl, until light, about 4 minutes, scraping down the sides of the bowl as necessary. In a separate bowl, sift together the flours and baking powder.

Whisk half the flour mixture, along with ¹⁄₃ cup of the milk, into the yolk mixture and incorporate until combined. Repeat with remaining flour mixture and another ¹⁄₃ cup of the milk. Combine well.

Beat the egg whites in a non-reactive bowl until stiff peaks form. Fold the egg whites into the batter, then stir in the raisins.

Reserve ¹⁄₃ cup of the batter, then pour the remainder into the prepared pan. Stir the cocoa powder and the remaining tablespoon of milk into the reserved ¹⁄₃ cup of batter, then spoon the batter into the pan. Swirl a small spatula through batters to create a marble effect.

Bake for 45 minutes or until a tester comes out clean. Cool in the pan for 15 minutes, then cool on a wire rack.

Orange-Raisin Cake

With equal parts pastry and unbleached white flour, this cake has a great texture. The orange and raisin give it great taste!

Makes one 9 x 5-inch loaf

- 1 orange
- ¾ cup unbleached white flour
- ¾ cup whole wheat pastry flour
- ½ teaspoon baking soda
- 1 teaspoon baking powder
- ⅓ cup unsalted butter, chilled and diced
- ⅔ cup sugar
- ¾ cup raisins
- ½ cup milk

Make sure all of your ingredients are at room temperature. Preheat the oven to 350°F. and grease a 9 x 5-inch loaf pan, or line it with parchment paper.

Zest and juice the orange.

Combine the flours, baking soda, and baking powder in the bowl of a food processor or large bowl. Cut the butter into the flour mixture by pulsing, or with two knives, until the mixture resembles coarse crumbs. Stir in the sugar, raisins, and the orange zest.

Combine the orange juice with the milk and stir into the flour mixture to make a smooth batter. Scrape the batter into the prepared pan and bake for 55 to 70 minutes, or until a tester comes out clean. Cool completely in the pan on a wire rack.

Whole Wheat Cupcakes

Everyone likes cupcakes, don't they? No slicing and highly portable, these have a nice spicy flavor with allspice and mace.

Makes 12 cupcakes

- ³/₄ cup whole wheat pastry flour
- ½ cup unbleached white flour
- 2 teaspoons baking powder
- ⅛ teaspoon mace
- ¼ teaspoon salt
- ¼ teaspoon ground allspice
- 12 tablespoons (1½ stick) unsalted butter
- 1 cup sugar
- 2 eggs
- ½ cup plus 1 tablespoon milk

Make sure all of your ingredients are at room temperature. Preheat the oven to 350°F. Grease a muffin tin or line with paper muffin tin liners.

Whisk together the flours, baking powder, and spices.

Cream the butter with the sugar until light, about 4 minutes. Beat in the eggs one at a time until incorporated, scraping down the sides of the bowl as needed. Beat in the flour mixture until just combined, then the milk.

Spoon the batter into the prepared tin and bake for 15 minutes, or until a tester comes out clean. Remove from the pan and cool on a wire rack.

All-Purpose Cake Recipe

GLUTEN-FREE

This recipe was adapted from one by Carol Fenster, author of several books on gluten-free cooking. It's versatile and tasty.

Makes one 9 x 5-inch loaf, 12 cupcakes, an 8-inch round layer cake, or an 11 x 17-inch sheet cake

- 6 tablespoons unsalted butter
- 1 cup sugar
- 2 eggs
- 1 tablespoon lemon zest
- 1 cup rice flour
- 2 tablespoons tapioca flour
- 6 tablespoons potato starch
- 1 teaspoon xanthan gum
- ¼ teaspoon baking powder
- ¼ teaspoon baking soda
- ½ teaspoon salt
- ¾ cup buttermilk
- 1 teaspoon vanilla

Make sure all of your ingredients are at room temperature. Preheat the oven to 350°F. and grease a 9 x 5-inch loaf pan.

Cream the butter with the sugar until light in color, about 4 minutes. Beat in the eggs one at a time, scraping down the sides of the bowl as needed. Stir in the lemon zest.

Whisk together the flours, potato starch, xanthan gum, baking powder, baking soda, and salt. In a small bowl, combine the buttermilk and vanilla. On low speed, beat half of the dry ingredients into the butter mixture, then beat in half the buttermilk. Repeat with remaining flour and buttermilk.

Scrape the batter into the prepared pan and bake for 50 minutes, or until a tester comes out clean. Cool the cake in the pan for 5 minutes then remove and cool on a wire rack.

FOR CUPCAKES: Grease a muffin tin or line with paper muffin cups. Bake for 20 minutes, or until a tester comes out clean. Cool on a wire rack

FOR A LAYER CAKE: Grease two 8-inch round pans or line them with parchment paper. Bake for 25 minutes or until a tester comes out clean. Cool on a wire rack.

FOR A SHEET CAKE: Grease a 17 x 11-inch pan or line it with parchment paper. Bake for 25 minutes, or until a tester comes out clean. Cool in the pan on a wire rack.

Mocha-Oatmeal Cupcakes

Coffee lovers will gobble up these deliciously coffee-flavored cupcakes. The rolled oats add more texture than flavor.

Makes 12 cupcakes

- ½ cup hot water
- ½ cup quick cooking rolled oats
- ⅔ cup (one 5.5-ounce can) chocolate syrup
- 4 tablespoons unsalted butter, softened
- 1 teaspoon coffee crystals
- 1 teaspoon vanilla
- ⅔ cup unbleached white flour
- ⅓ cup sugar
- ½ teaspoon baking soda
- ½ teaspoon salt
- 2 eggs
- ⅓ cup pecans, chopped
- Quick Coffee Frosting (page 481)

Make sure all of your ingredients are at room temperature. Preheat the oven to 375°F. Grease a muffin pan or line with paper baking cups.

Pour the hot water over the oats, then add the chocolate syrup, butter, coffee crystals, and vanilla. Stir well and let the mixture stand for 10 minutes.

Whisk together the flour, sugar, baking soda, and salt. Beat in the eggs and the oatmeal mixture on low speed of an electric mixer until well combined. Stir in the pecans.

Spoon into the prepared muffin tin and bake for 20 minutes or until a tester comes out clean. Cool on wire rack. Frost with the Quick Coffee Frosting.

Mango Sour Cream Cupcakes

GLUTEN-FREE

Mangos are among the most widely cultivated tropical fruit, and here they match perfectly with sour cream.

Makes 12 cupcakes

- ½ cup garbanzo fava bean flour
- 1 cup rice flour
- ¾ teaspoon xanthan gum
- Pinch salt
- ¾ teaspoon ground cinnamon
- ½ teaspoon ground ginger
- ¼ teaspoon ground allspice
- 6 tablespoons unsalted butter, softened
- ½ cup sugar
- 1 teaspoon vanilla
- 1 egg yolk
- ¾ cup mashed mango (from 2 large mangoes)
- ¼ cup honey

Make sure all of your ingredients are at room temperature. Preheat the oven to 350°F. and grease a 12-cup muffin tin or line with paper muffin tin liners.

In a medium bowl, sift together the flours, xanthan gum, salt, cinnamon, ginger, and allspice.

In a large bowl, cream the butter with the sugar until light, about 3 minutes. Add the vanilla and the egg yolk and beat until incorporated, scraping down the sides of the bowl once or twice. Stir in the mango and the honey, then add the flour mixture and stir until well blended.

Spoon the batter into the prepared muffin tin and bake for 25 minutes, or until a tester comes out clean. Remove the cupcakes from the pan and cool on a wire rack.

Peach Upside-Down Cake

GLUTEN-FREE

Here's another whole grain version of those popular upside down cakes, only with peaches.

Makes one 8 x 10-inch cake

- ¼ pound (1 stick) unsalted butter
- 1 cup light brown sugar, firmly packed
- 1 teaspoon ground cinnamon
- ½ cup garbanzo fava bean flour
- ¼ cup sorghum flour
- ½ cup cornstarch
- 1 teaspoon xanthan gum
- 1 teaspoon baking powder
- ½ teaspoon salt
- ½ cup molasses
- 1 egg
- ⅓ cup plus 2 tablespoons milk
- 1½ teaspoons vanilla
- 3 medium peaches, peeled, pitted, and sliced

Make sure all of your ingredients are at room temperature. Preheat the oven to 350°F.

In a heavy oven-proof skillet, melt half of the butter. Turn off the heat and sprinkle ¾ cup of the brown sugar over the butter, stirring to blend. Sprinkle ½ teaspoon of the cinnamon over this mixture.

In a medium bowl, combine the flours, cornstarch, xanthan gum, baking powder, salt and the remaining cinnamon.

In a large bowl, cream the remaining butter with the remaining brown sugar, then add the molasses and the egg. Combine the milk with the vanilla. Add one-third of the flour mixture to the egg mixture, then add one-third of the milk mixture. Repeat until remaining flour and milk mixtures are incorporated.

Arrange the peaches on the bottom of the skillet. Spoon the batter over the top and bake for 40 minutes, or until a tester comes out clean. Allow the cake to cool in the skillet for 10 minutes, then invert onto a cake plate. Serve warm or at room temperature.

Banana Cake

This recipe comes from Christina Zugar, one of the winners of our "Every Meal of the Day" recipe contest, which was hosted by Cooking Light Magazine.

Makes one 8 x 8-inch cake

Cake

- 1 cup whole wheat pastry flour
- ½ cup soy flour
- ½ cup flaxseed meal
- 2 teaspoons baking soda
- 1 teaspoon baking powder
- ¼ teaspoon salt
- ½ cup soy milk
- ⅓ cup honey
- 1 egg, beaten
- 1 teaspoon vanilla
- 3 medium bananas, mashed

Topping

- ⅓ cup brown sugar, packed
- 3 tablespoons unsalted butter
- ½ cup walnuts, chopped

Make sure all of your ingredients are at room temperature. Preheat the oven to 350°F. Lightly grease an 8 x 8-inch baking pan or line it with parchment paper.

In a large bowl, whisk together the flours, flaxseed meal, baking soda, baking powder, and salt.

In a medium bowl, mix together the soy milk, honey, egg, vanilla, and bananas. Combine the milk mixture with the flour mixture until combined. Spread the batter in the prepared pan. Combine the topping ingredients and mix until crumbly, then sprinkle evenly over the batter.

Bake for 30 to 35 minutes, or until a tester comes out clean. Cool in the pan on a wire rack.

474 Bob's Red Mill Baking Book

Apricot Gateau

GLUTEN-FREE

With rice flour as its base, this gateau is very light. The apricot and almond flavors blend beautifully, as well.

Makes one 10-inch layer cake

Cake

- ⅔ cup rice flour
- 3 tablespoons tapioca flour
- 3 tablespoons potato starch
- 1 tablespoon cornstarch
- ¾ teaspoon xanthan gum
- 1½ teaspoons baking powder
- ¼ teaspoon salt
- ½ pound (2 sticks) unsalted butter, softened
- 1¼ cups sugar
- 1 teaspoon vanilla
- 4 eggs

Filling

- 1½ cups dried apricots, finely chopped
- 1½ cups water
- 3 tablespoons apricot preserves
- 1½ cups mascarpone or cream cheese
- 3 tablespoons almond liqueur or ¾ teaspoon almond extract
- ⅓ cup heavy cream
- Slivered almonds

Make sure all of your ingredients are at room temperature. Preheat the oven to 400°F. and grease a 10-inch springform pan or line it with parchment paper.

In a large bowl, sift together the flours, potato starch, cornstarch, xanthan gum, baking powder, and salt.

In a medium bowl, cream the butter with the sugar until light, about 3 minutes, then add the vanilla. Add the eggs one at a time, scraping down the sides of the bowl as needed. Add this mixture to the flour mixture, stirring until well incorporated. Scrape the batter into the prepared pan and bake for 30 minutes, or until a tester comes out clean. Cool in the pan for 5 minutes, then remove to a wire rack and let cool completely.

For the filling, combine the apricots and water in a saucepan and cook, stirring occasionally, until the apricots are very soft and most of the liquid is absorbed, about 15 minutes. Stir in the preserves and cool completely.

Beat the mascarpone with the liqueur, then beat in the cream until thick, about 2 minutes.

Split the cake horizontally and place one half on a cake plate. Spread half of the mascarpone mixture over the cake, then top with half of the apricot compote. Place the other half of the cake on top and spread with the remaining mascarpone mixture and then the compote. Sprinkle with the slivered almonds. Refrigerate at least 3 hours before serving.

Oatmeal Cake

GLUTEN-FREE

Here's a cake that's good for breakfast or any time of day!

Makes one 13 x 9-inch cake

- 1¼ cups boiling water
- 1 cup instant oats
- 1 teaspoon baking soda
- 4 tablespoons unsalted butter, softened
- 1 cup sugar
- 1 cup brown sugar
- 2 eggs
- ⅔ cup garbanzo fava bean flour
- ⅔ cup rice flour
- ½ teaspoon ground cinnamon

Make sure all of your ingredients are at room temperature. Preheat the oven to 350°F. Grease a 13 x 9-inch pan, or line it with parchment paper.

Pour the boiling water over the oats and stir. Add the baking soda and allow to stand for 20 minutes.

In a large bowl, cream the butter and sugars until light, about 3 minutes, then beat in the eggs one at a time, scraping down the sides of the bowl. Add the flours and cinnamon and blend well.

Fold the oat mixture into the batter to combine. Pour the batter into the prepared pan and bake for 35 minutes, or until a tester comes out clean. Cool in the pan on a wire rack.

Yogurt Cake

GLUTEN-FREE

Choose any frosting for this easy and great tasting cake.

Makes two 8-inch layers

- 1 cup rice flour
- ³/₄ cup garbanzo fava bean flour
- 1 teaspoon baking powder
- ³/₄ teaspoon baking soda
- ³/₄ teaspoon xanthan gum
- ¼ pound (1 stick) unsalted butter, softened
- 1³/₄ cups sugar
- 3 eggs
- ³/₄ cup plain yogurt
- Frosting of your choice (pages 481-183)

Make sure all of your ingredients are at room temperature. Preheat the oven to 325°F. Grease two 8-inch round baking pans.

In a medium bowl, sift together the flours, baking powder, baking soda, and xanthan gum.

In a large bowl, cream the butter and sugar until light, about 3 to 4 minutes, then beat in the eggs, one at a time, scraping down the sides of the bowl after each addition. Add half of the flour mixture to the butter mixture, then half of the yogurt, combining well. Repeat with the remaining flour mixture and yogurt.

Spread the batter into the prepared pans and bake for 40 minutes, or until a tester comes out clean. Allow to cool in the pans for 15 minutes, then place on a wire rack to cool completely. Frost and enjoy.

Almond Polenta Cake

GLUTEN-FREE

This cornmeal cake is good with or without frosting. For a treat, serve it warm with ice cream on the side.

Makes one 9-inch round cake

- ³/₄ cup extra-virgin olive oil
- 1¹/₂ cups sugar
- 1¹/₄ cups cornmeal
- ³/₄ cup almond meal
- 3 eggs
- 1 teaspoon almond extract
- 1 cup milk
- ¹/₂ cup garbanzo fava bean flour
- ¹/₂ cup rice flour
- 1¹/₂ teaspoons baking powder
- ³/₄ teaspoon baking soda
- 1 teaspoon salt

Make sure all of your ingredients are at room temperature. Preheat the oven to 325°F. Grease a 9-inch round pan.

In a large bowl, beat together the oil, sugar, cornmeal, and almond meal, then add the eggs one at a time, scraping down the sides of the bowl as necessary. Beat an additional minute.

Combine the almond extract with the milk.

Combine the flours, baking powder, baking soda, and salt in a separate bowl.

Add half of the milk mixture to the egg mixture, then half the flour. Repeat with remaining milk and flour mixtures. Pour the batter into the prepared pan and bake for 1 hour, or until a tester comes out clean. Cool in the pan on a wire rack.

Gingerbread Cake

GLUTEN-FREE

The lack of gluten in this cake doesn't affect its delightfully gingery flavor.

Makes one 13 x 9-inch cake

- ³/₄ cup shortening
- ¹/₃ pound unsalted butter, softened
- 1¹/₂ cups sugar
- 3 eggs
- 1¹/₂ cups garbanzo fava bean flour
- 1¹/₂ cups rice flour
- 1¹/₂ teaspoons baking soda
- 1 teaspoon baking powder
- 1 teaspoon xanthan gum
- ³/₄ teaspoon ground cinnamon
- 2 teaspoons ground ginger
- ¹/₂ cup honey
- 1 cup molasses
- 1¹/₂ cups boiling water

Make sure all of your ingredients are at room temperature. Preheat the oven to 350°F. Grease a 13 x 9-inch pan, or line it with parchment paper.

In a large bowl, cream the shortening and butter, then gradually add the sugar and the eggs, one at a time, until incorporated, scraping down the sides of the bowl as necessary.

Sift together the flours, baking soda, baking powder, xanthan gum, cinnamon, and ginger.

Add the flour mixture, honey, molasses, and water to the shortening mixture and combine well. Pour the dough into the prepared pan and bake for 30 minutes, or until a tester comes out clean. Cool in the pan on a wire rack.

GLAZES

Tangerine/Orange Glaze

Makes about ²/₃ cup

- ½ cup tangerine or orange juice
- 2 tablespoons lemon juice
- 6 tablespoons sugar

Whisk the ingredients together in a saucepan over low heat until the sugar is dissolved.

Chocolate Glaze

Makes about 1½ cups

- 8 ounces semisweet or bittersweet chocolate
- ⅓ cup sugar
- 1 cup heavy cream
- 1 tablespoon unsalted butter, optional

In the top of a double boiler set over boiling water, melt the chocolate, then stir in the sugar until well combined. Remove from heat. In a small saucepan, warm the cream (don't boil it), then stir it into the chocolate. Add the butter and combine until melted.

Apricot Glaze

Makes about ²/₃ cup

- ²/₃ cup apricot preserves
- 2 teaspoons lemon juice

Melt the ingredients in a saucepan. Spread the glaze while it's still warm.

Caramel Glaze or Frosting

Makes about 1 cup

- 2 cups brown sugar, packed
- 1 cup heavy cream
- 2½ tablespoons unsalted butter
- 1 teaspoon vanilla

Combine the sugar and cream in a saucepan and cook over medium heat, stirring, until it just begins to simmer. Cover and allow to simmer for 2 minutes or until the sugar is dissolved. Uncover and use a moistened pastry brush to wash the sugar crystals from the sides of the pan. Continue to cook, uncovered, until the syrup reaches 238°F. on a candy thermometer. Remove from the heat and carefully add the butter, but do not stir. Allow the mixture to cool until it reaches 110°F., about 50 minutes. Add the vanilla and transfer to a mixing bowl. Beat until the mixture is cooled, thick, and spreadable. If the frosting is too thick, thin it with a little more cream. If you are not using the frosting immediately, cover it with a sheet of plastic wrap to prevent a film from forming on the top.

FROSTINGS

Cream Cheese & Honey Frosting

Makes about 2 cups

- 4 tablespoons unsalted butter, softened
- 1 pound full fat cream cheese, chilled
- 1 teaspoon vanilla
- ¼ cup honey
- ⅔ cup confectioners' sugar, or to taste

Beat the butter with the cream cheese and vanilla until just smooth. Beat in the honey and sift in half of the sugar, adding more as necessary to achieve the desired consistency and sweetness.

Quick Coffee Frosting

Makes about 1 cup

- 2½ cups confectioners' sugar, plus more if necessary
- 5 tablespoons unsalted butter, softened
- 5 tablespoons brewed coffee, plus more as needed
- 1 teaspoon vanilla

Sift the sugar into a bowl then beat in the butter until combined. Beat in the coffee and vanilla. You may need to add more coffee or sugar for desired consistency or flavor.

Quick Maple Frosting

Makes about 1 cup

- 2 cups confectioners' sugar, plus more as necessary
- 1½ tablespoons unsalted butter
- ¼ teaspoon vanilla
- 3 tablespoons milk, plus more as necessary
- ⅓ cup pure maple syrup

Sift the sugar into a bowl then beat in the butter until combined. Beat in the vanilla and milk, then gradually add the syrup. You may need to add more milk or sugar for desired consistency or flavor.

Ricotta Filling

Makes about 2 cups

- 1 cup heavy cream
- 15 ounces ricotta cheese
- ½ cup confectioners' sugar

In a chilled bowl and using chilled beaters, beat the cream until stiff. Whisk together the ricotta and the sugar, then fold in the cream.

Buttercream Frosting or Filling

Makes about 1½ cups

- 2 egg yolks
- ¼ cup confectioners' sugar
- ½ cup milk, scalded
- 2 teaspoons vanilla
- ½ pound (2 sticks) butter, softened

Set a bowl large enough to hold a saucepan on the counter and fill with cold water and a few ice cubes.

In a separate bowl, vigorously whisk the yolks with the sugar until smooth. Using a spoon, slowly pour a little hot milk over the yolk mixture and blend. Slowly stir in the rest of the milk, then scrape the mixture into a saucepan and heat, stirring constantly, until just starting to thicken, about 4 minutes (do not boil).

Remove the saucepan from the heat and whisk in the vanilla. Continue to whisk while placing the pan in the bowl of ice water (don't allow any water to get into the pan). Stir until the mixture is cool, then remove from the ice water and begin adding the butter just a teaspoon or so at a time to incorporate (if it separates, beat with an electric mixer to bring back together).

Cover with plastic wrap and refrigerate until needed.

VARIATIONS

Rum Buttercream

Beat up to 2 tablespoons rum into the finished buttercream.

Chocolate Buttercream

Melt 1½ tablespoons unsweetened chocolate and allow to cool. Beat into the finished buttercream.

Lemon or Orange Buttercream

Add 2½ teaspoons zest with the vanilla.

Coconut Buttercream

Leave out the vanilla. Replace half of the milk with coconut milk and stir in ⅓ cup shredded coconut.

Index